European Banks and the Rise of International Finance

T0358982

The banking and financial sector has expanded dramatically in the last 40 years, and the consequences of this accelerated growth have been felt by people around the world.

European Banks and the Rise of International Finance examines the historical origins of the financialised world we live in by analysing the transformations in world finance which occurred in the decade from the first oil crisis of 1973 until the debt crisis of 1982. This a crucial and formative decade for understanding the modern financial landscape, but it is still mostly unexplored in economic and financial history. The availability of new archival evidence has allowed for the re-examination of issues such as the progressive privatisation of international financial flows to less developed countries, especially in Latin America and South-East Asia, and its impact on the expansion of the European banking sector, and for the development of an invaluable financial and political history.

This book is well suited to those interested in monetary economics and economic history, as well as those studying international political economy, banking history and financial history.

Carlo Edoardo Altamura is a postdoctoral fellow at the Paul Bairoch Institute of Economic History at the University of Geneva, Switzerland, a visiting college research associate at Wolfson College, Cambridge, UK, and a visiting scholar at the Faculty of History of the University of Cambridge, UK. His interests lie in post-war banking and financial history in the West and in the developing regions.

Routledge Explorations in Economic History
Edited by Lars Magnusson
Uppsala University, Sweden

European Banks and the Rise of International Finance

The post-Bretton Woods era

Carlo Edoardo Altamura

Routledge
Taylor & Francis Group

LONDON AND NEW YORK

First published 2017 by Routledge

2 Park Square, Milton Park, Abingdon, Oxfordshire OX14 4RN

52 Vanderbilt Avenue, New York, NY 10017

Routledge is an imprint of the Taylor & Francis Group, an informa business

First issued in paperback 2019

British Library Cataloguing in Publication Data
A catalogue record for this book is available from the British Library

Library of Congress Cataloging in Publication Data
Names: Altamura, Carlo Edoardo, author.
Title: European banks and the rise of international finance : the post-Bretton Woods era / Carlo Edoardo Altamura.
Description: 1 Edition. | New York : Routledge, 2016. | Includes bibliographical references.
Identifiers: LCCN 2016012305| ISBN 9781138191563 (hardback) | ISBN 9781315640426 (ebook)
Subjects: LCSH: Banks and banking—Europe—History—20th century. | Petroleum industry and trade—History—20th century. | Capital movements—Developing countries—History. | Investments, Foreign—Developing countries—History. | International finance.
Classification: LCC HG2974 .A48 2016 | DDC 332/.04209409045—dc23
LC record available at http://lccn.loc.gov/2016012305

ISBN: 978-1-138-19156-3 (hbk)
ISBN: 978-0-367-87694-4 (pbk)

Typeset in Times New Roman
by Swales & Willis Ltd, Exeter, Devon, UK

I don't see anything evil in a desire to make money. But money is only a means to some end. If a man wants it for a personal purpose – to invest in his industry, to create, to study, to travel, to enjoy luxury – he's completely moral. But the men who place money first go much beyond that. Personal luxury is a limited endeavor. What they want is ostentation: to show, to stun, to entertain, to impress others. They're second-handers.

(Ayn Rand, *The Fountainhead*, 1943)

Contents

Figures

Tables

Preface

Many readers would agree that the banking and the financial sectors are increasingly shaping, for better or for worse, the world we live in. Personally, this conviction first struck me when, after finishing a Bachelor's degree in finance in 2007, I started working in the banking sector as an intern in Milan, first, and then in an American bank in Geneva. It was the time of the most severe economic and financial crisis since the Great Depression and I still remember my colleagues frantically talking to (justifiably) hysterical clients who had just lost millions. At that time financial scandals, crashes, failures and bailouts were the daily routine.

As the crisis grew worse, I became more and more interested in understanding the origins of the chaos reigning in the banking and financial sector at that time for, even though my historical knowledge was still limited, I knew that it had not always been like that. This is why I decided to quit finance and enter academia.

Financial markets and institutions play a crucial role in our economies by helping companies to obtain risk capital from investors, thus creating jobs and prosperity for the society as a whole. Besides, the international financial system, by channelling savings to productive uses and investments has the potential to play an important role in delivering sustainable economic growth for the poorest regions of the world. Even academics, far from benevolent towards the financial sector, have argued that 'over the long sweep of history, financial innovation has been important in promoting growth'.[1] In similar fashion, John Eatwell and Lance Taylor pointed out:

> A liquid, highly innovative financial system is necessary for the growth of modern economies. It is not only the lubricant that smooths the frictions of exchange from the neighbourhood shop to global money markets, it is also, when mixed with entrepreneurship, skills, and innovation, the fuel in the engine of economic growth.[2]

However, in the late 2000s and early 2010s we saw the 'dark side' of the modern financial world. Unwise and speculative decisions damaged entire economies, destroying 'the very engine it oils and fuels'.[3] As financial misbehaviour was revealed to the general public through inquiry reports and newspapers, mass protests mushroomed throughout the world, from Madrid to New York, from London to Cape Town. This state of affairs was far from inevitable. In fact, as noted by Maurice Obstfeld and Alan Taylor about the Asian financial turmoil of 1997–98, but still valid for recent economic turbulences:

> Such turns of events would have been *inconceivable . . . during the 1950s and 1960s*. During those years, most countries' domestic financial systems labored under extensive government restraint and were cut off from international influences by official firewalls. Yet, despite those restrictions, which were a legacy of the Great Depression and World War Two, international financial crises occurred from time to time. Between 1945 and 1970, however, their effects tended to be *localized*, with *little discernible impact* on Wall Street, let alone Main Street [emphasis added].[4]

This convergence of economic destinies or, as Milan Kundera would say, this 'unity of mankind',[5] is a peculiar, albeit not exclusive, feature of the late twentieth and early twenty-first centuries. After the Great Depression, markets were mainly domestic and financial products almost riskless. Banks specialised in certain activities and/or areas. Financial conglomerates or 'financial supermarkets' did not exist.

Historical research can help us trace the origins of the modern economic world characterised by the increasing importance of financial markets and institutions in our everyday lives and the increased frequency and scope of economic turbulences. Some would call it 'financialisation', meaning 'the increasing role of financial motives, financial markets, financial actors and financial institutions in the operation of the domestic and international economies';[6] others the 'financial globalisation' or financial revolution; and yet others 'the triumph of financial capital'[7] or 'financial capitalism'.[8]

Even though all these definitions and the many others we have not mentioned yet are somewhat acceptable, we prefer, and we will employ throughout our research, the term 'rise' of international banking and finance.

The term rise has been chosen because it indicates both that we went through a previous phase of banking and financial expansion (even though remarkably different from the present one) and that there has been a hiatus in this process. Ultimately, finance was able to born again out of its ashes to become one of the most emblematic industries of the last few decades.

The primary concern of this book is to explain precisely how international finance rose from the ashes of the Bretton Woods regime and to analyse the impact of the re-opening of international capital markets on the major commercial banks in France and the United Kingdom.

Notes

1 Joseph E. Stiglitz, 'Financial Innovation: Against the Notion That Financial Innovation Boosts Economic Growth', *The Economist*, February–March 2010, reported in Luigi Zingales, 'Presidential Address: Does Finance Benefit Society?', *The Journal of Finance*, Vol. LXX, No. 4, August 2015, 1340.

2 John Eatwell and Lance Taylor, *Global Finance at Risk. The Case for International Regulation*, Polity Press, Cambridge, UK, 2000, 208.

3 Ibid.

4 Maurice Obstfeld and Alan M. Taylor, *Global Capital Markets. Integration, Crisis, and Growth*, Cambridge University Press, New York, 2004, 15.

5 Milan Kundera, *L'Art du Roman*, Gallimard, Paris, 1986.

6 Gerald A. Epstein, 'Introduction: Financialization and the World Economy', in Gerald A. Epstein (ed.), *Financialization and the World Economy*, Edward Elgar, Cheltenham, UK and Northampton, MA, 2005. The book provides a good survey of the literature on financialisation. See also Greta R. Krippner, *Capitalizing on Crisis. The Political Origins of the Rise of Finance*, Harvard University Press, Cambridge, MA and London, 2011. For a different interpretation of financialisation, see William Lazonick and Mary O'Sullivan, 'Maximizing Shareholder Value: A New Ideology for Corporate Governance', *Economy and Society*, Vol. 29, No. 1, February 2000, 13–35.

7 Paul M. Sweezy, 'The Triumph of Financial Capital', *Monthly Review*, Volume 46, Issue 02, June 1994; Aaron Major, 'The Fall and Rise of Financial Capital', *Review of International Political Economy*, 15: 5, December 2008, 800–825.

8 Michel Aglietta and Antoine Ribérioux, *Dérives du capitalisme financier*, Albin Michel, Paris, 2004.

Acknowledgements

Even though a famous novelist stated that 'we live as we dream . . . alone', a doctoral thesis and a book are collective efforts, which would simply be impossible without the support and contribution of many people.

First of all, I would like to thank my PhD supervisors, Youssef Cassis and Mats Larsson, for accepting me as a doctoral candidate, believing in my project and supporting me throughout four years of research. I benefited greatly from their historical knowledge, expertise and guidance.

The many talks I have had with Professor Cassis since I met him as a graduate student have helped me to understand how a good historian is supposed to work, which questions they are supposed to ask and the best way to try to find the answers. I have always felt his trust in me, even during the most challenging times, and for that I will always be grateful to him.

Professor Larsson was able to make an Italian feel at home in Sweden from the very first time we discussed my project in a warm August in the Uppland region. Our discussions had a crucial impact in shaping my thesis and suggesting new research paths.

The thesis would not have been the same without an autumn spent at the Economic History Department of the University of Uppsala, a winter at the Business History Unit of the London School of Economics and Political Science, LSE, and a spring at the Department of History and Civilization of the European University Institute. I thank all the people who made this sabbatical year possible and extremely enriching, in particular Mary O'Sullivan for allowing me to go, Terry Gourvish for arranging my stay at the LSE and José Maria Ortiz-Villajos for his advice and suggestions.

My thesis and the present book benefited greatly from the commentaries and suggestions of members of my thesis committee. I wish to thank Richard Roberts for being my opponent and the members of my committee: Harold James, Mary O'Sullivan, Jan Ottosson, Catherine Schenk and Eva Wallerstedt. I also thank David Gilbert for his precious help with the proofreading of the manuscript.

My research received help from several scholars who were kind enough to advise me and share their knowledge at various stages of my research. I wish to thank, in particular, Carlos Marichal, who shared with me his immense knowledge on Latin American financial history, Kazuhiko Yago for pointing out the role of international organisations such as the Organisation for Economic Co-operation and Development, Olivier Feiertag, who suggested looking at the role of central banks, and Giuliano Garavini for his insights on the Organization of the Petroleum Exporting Countries.

I thank all my colleagues at the Paul Bairoch Institute of Economic History of the University of Geneva. The debates, the laughs, the coffees and beers we had made the process of writing much more pleasant than might have been the case.

The historian is always indebted to the archives and the archivists, and this work could not have been possible without them. I wish to thank all the people I met and worked with at the archives of the *Banca Commerciale Italiana* in Milan, at the *Association pour l'Histoire de Paribas*, at *Société Générale*, at *Crédit Lyonnais*, at the *Banque de France*, at the Organisation for Economic Co-operation and Development in Paris, at Barclays in Manchester, at HSBC, at Lloyds Bank, at the Bank of England in London, at the International Monetary Fund in Washington, DC and at the Bank for International Settlements in Basel.

I was fortunate enough to present preliminary versions of chapters at several conferences and seminars in Europe and overseas, including at several conferences of the International Economic History Association, of the European Business History Association, at the Doctoral Colloquium of the Business History Conference in Philadelphia, at the European University Institute, at the *Banque de France*, at the University of Cambridge, at the London School of Economics and Political Science and at the University of Padua. I thank all those who were kind and patient enough to attend these meetings.

Of course, I am extremely indebted to all the people at Routledge who followed this project.

I wish to thank especially Emily Kindleysides who was the first to believe in this book, Laura Johnson for her patience and support in the editing phase and Lars Magnusson.

Throughout my doctoral years, I received funding for research from various institutions. I thank particularly the Jan Wallanders and Tom Hedelius Foundation for its generous support during my doctoral studies, the *Mission Histoire* of *Société Générale*, and the Swiss Academy of Humanities and Social Sciences. I thank warmly the *Société Académique de Genève* for financing my postdoctoral studies.

I wish to thank my family, my parents and grandparents for teaching me the love of history, my sister, my friends for supporting me during these long years and listening patiently to my, sometimes arcane, disquisitions. Last but not least, I wish to thank my love for giving me the serenity I needed to finish my research and the strength to pursue my academic projects. Some beloved members of my family were not able to see this book published and it is to them that this work is dedicated.

Abbreviations

ABA	American Bankers Association
ABECOR	Associated Banks of Europe Corporation
BBI	Barclays Bank International
BCEN	Banque Commerciale pour l'Europe du Nord
BCI/COMIT	Banca Commerciale Italiana
BEC	Banque Européenne de Crédit
BHA	Banco Hispano Americano
BIS	Bank for International Settlements
BNP	Banque Nationale de Paris
BOLAM	Bank of London and Montreal
BOLSA	Bank of London and South America
C-20	Committee of Twenty
CCC	Competition and Credit Control
CL	Crédit Lyonnais
COFACE	Compagnie Française d'Assurance pour le Commerce Extérieur
COMECON	Council for Mutual Economic Assistance
DCAIC	Département Central pour les Affaires Internationales et la Coopération
DCE	Département pour le Commerce Extérieur
DGSE	Diréction Générale des Services Etrangers
DOFI	Département pour les Opérations Financières Internationales
EAC	European Advisory Committee
EBIC	European Banks International Company
ECGD	Export Credits Guarantee Department
EEC	European Economic Community
ELSTA	End Loans to Southern Africa
EMS	European Monetary System
FRAB	Banque Franco-Arabe d'Investissements Internationaux
G-10	Group of Ten
IBF	International Banking Facility
IC	Interim Committee
IET	Interest Equalization Tax
IMF	International Monetary Fund

LBI	Lloyds Bank International
LDC	Less Developed Countries
LIBOR	London Interbank Offered Rate
MAIBL	Midland and International Banks
MBID	Midland Bank International Department
NIC	Newly Industrialized Countries
NODC	Non-Oil Developing Countries
OECD	Organisation for Economic Co-operation and Development
OPEC	Organization of the Petroleum Exporting Countries
SFE	Société Fianciére Européenne
SG	Société Générale
UBAF	Union de Banques Arabes et Françaises
UIC	Ufficio Italiano Cambi
VFCR	Voluntary Foreign Credit Restraint program
WP3	Working Party 3 (of the OECD)

Archives

Introduction

'Post fata resurgo'
At the origins of modern finance

Haec tamen ex aliis generis primordia ducunt, una est, quae reparet seque ipsa
reseminet, ales: Assyrii phoenica vocant; non fruge neque herbis, sed turis lacrimis
et suco vivit amomi.

haec ubi quinque suae conplevit saecula vitae, ilicis in ramis tremulaeque
cacumine palmae unguibus et puro nidum sibi construit ore.

quo simul ac casias et nardi lenis aristas quassaque cum fulva substravit cinnama
murra, se super inponit finitque in odoribus aevum.

(Ovid, *'Metamorphoses', XV, 391–400, 8 AD*)[1]

In a most famous passage at the beginning of the second chapter of the *Economic Consequences of the Peace* the British economist, John Maynard Keynes, thus described the period preceding the First World War:

> What an extraordinary episode in the economic progress of man that age was which came to an end in August, 1914! . . . The inhabitant of London could order by telephone, sipping his morning tea in bed, the various products of the whole earth, in such quantity as he might see fit, and reasonably expect their early delivery upon his doorstep; he could at the same moment and by the same means adventure his wealth in the natural resources and new enterprises of any quarter of the world, and share, without exertion or even trouble, in their prospective fruits and advantages; or he could decide to couple the security of his fortunes with the good faith of the townspeople of any substantial municipality in any continent that fancy or information might recommend.

The period between the 1870s and 1914 vividly illustrated by Keynes is usually known as the 'First Globalisation'. For the banking and financial sector it was a period of expansion dominated by the City of London, which doubled its working population from 170,000 in 1871 to 364,000 in 1911,[2] and its merchant banks, specialising in issuing loans on behalf of domestic and foreign entities and in financing international trade. British overseas and merchant banks dominated the world, the former mainly through branches and trade financing, and the latter through innovative products and underwriting activities.[3]

British and European banks were investing abroad on a large scale and for a large variety of clients. Flows of capital, goods and people were facilitated by a revolution in communications, epitomised by the transatlantic electronic telegraph, and transportation, notably the construction of the Suez and Panama canals as well as the appearance of steamships. A common monetary system, the Gold Standard, reassured investors that, at least on paper, peripheral countries would follow the same rules as core countries. Moreover, liberalism was the official religion adopted by the hegemonic power of that time, Great Britain.

Despite the similarities between the two periods of globalisation and the sophistication of pre-1914 economies, several crucial differences must be emphasised to nuance what would resemble an excessively simplistic U-pattern scenario. First, as economic historian, Michael Bordo, and others have pointed out, gross capital flows are much greater today than in the past. Second, the nature of investments is radically different. During the First Globalisation, capital flew into tangible assets such as railroads in Argentina, mines in Southern Africa or public utilities in Australia. Nowadays, capital flows into Auto-callable Barrier Reverse Convertible products or Floored Floaters, which are much less tangible assets indeed. Third, investments in the past were made through the bond market, while now equity plays an equally important role. Finally, portfolio and direct investments are equally important in overseas investments, while in the pre-1914 world very few direct investments were made.[4]

The First Globalisation came to an end with the outbreak of the First World War, the Great Depression and the Second World War.

The instability that followed suit during the inter-war year has already received much attention because of its lasting legacy for the international financial sector.[5] From the Great Depression onwards, the financial and banking sector went through a long period of retreat inside local boundaries and territories.

Banking is by definition a risky business, but after the Great Depression it was moderated and rendered harmless, partly by regulators and partly by the bankers themselves, still conditioned by the experience of the Great Depression. The Bretton Woods' order with all its checks and balances 'was designed to avert the threat posed by volatile capital flows of the sort that were disruptive in both interwar decades'.[6]

The reason for this attitude is apparently straightforward. In the 1930s and early 1940s, the majority of the political elites in Western Europe and Northern America believed that an unregulated banking sector and financial markets had plunged the world into the worst economic crisis in history. In part because of this, some countries – notably Germany – had become barbaric regimes. When the war was over, the efforts in most of Europe and the United States were focused not in freeing the markets but in limiting them, fearing destabilising consequences both politically and economically.

All across Europe, a wave of reforms and regulations fettered the banking and financial sector. As economic historians, Harold James and Barry Eichengreen, have pointed out:

When, in response to policy inconsistencies between countries, capital markets malfunctioned in the 1930s, controls were slapped on their operation. *Financial markets were suppressed, and banks became the agents of governments' industrial policies.* The role of policy became to *supersede rather than to support the markets.* Mostly policy was formulated solely with regard to a national context. After 1945, when internationalism revived, policy at the international level largely meant *coordinating the financial restrictions imposed by governments* and in addition supplying the international financial services that immobilized markets could not [emphasis added].[7]

The economic order developed in Bretton Woods by the two most famous negotiators, Harry Dexter White and John Maynard Keynes, marked a clear break with the *laissez-faire* ideology in banking and finance that had dominated the political scene in the late nineteenth and early twentieth centuries.[8] It was a product of an increasingly critical ideology towards free markets and internationalist liberalism by political elites in Great Britain and the United States. Arthur I. Bloomfield, an influential banker of the Federal Reserve of New York, synthesised the spirit of the time thus:

> It is now a highly respectable doctrine, in academic and banking circles alike, that a *substantial measure of direct* control over private capital movements, especially of the so-called 'hot money' varieties, will be desirable for most countries not only in the years immediately ahead but also in the long run as well. This widely accepted point of view has been officially crystallized in the Bretton Woods Fund Agreement [emphasis added].[9]

As a result – taking as an ex-post example the famous Mundell-Fleming's 'Triangle of Incompatibility' – we could say that the Western powers decided to sacrifice capital mobility to preserve an autonomous monetary policy and fixed exchange rates. This ideological *volte face* regarding both the economic liberalism of the late eighteenth and early nineteenth centuries and the economic nationalism of the 1930s has been most notably studied by international political economists such as John G. Ruggie and Eric Helleiner. Ruggie provided a crucial contribution to the study of the new regime of money and trade designed in New Hampshire by developing the concept of 'embedded liberalism'[10] as a new international regime intended as a set of 'principles, norms, rules, and decision-making procedures'.[11] Ruggie summarised the embedded liberalist compromise thus:

> *Unlike the economic nationalism* of the thirties, it would be multilateral in character; *unlike the liberalism* of the gold standard and free trade, its multilateralism would be predicated upon domestic interventionism [emphasis added].[12]

Helleiner built on the work of Ruggie and other 'revisionist' scholars, who questioned the widely held view that the United States used its power to establish an open, liberal international economic order to present the state as the crucial entity accounting for the repression, first, and then the globalisation of finance.

Helleiner made an important point remarking that 'although market operators were instrumental in its creation and growth, the Euromarket was heavily *dependent on State support* from the outset [emphasis added]'.[13] His intuition forced us to look beyond market actors to understand the rise of international finance and to include in our analysis non-market actors such as regulators and international organisations. In his view, the underlying driver of growing financial globalisation is largely attributed to 'a new liberal approach in American foreign economic policy with regard to international capital movements',[14] thereby implying that the United States could impose its will on other states similarly to Ethan Kapstein's reference to the role of 'US power'.[15] In this volume, we will try to provide new archival-driven understandings of the rise of finance by insisting on the importance of 'states' and other official institutions. We will show how other European actors were crucial in the international debate on the Euromarket, arguing that there was much more contention about their future than existing accounts would suggest. We will also look at the fact that the Euromarket ultimately remaining unregulated was influenced to an important extent by the oil shock of 1973.

The Bretton Woods regime had important consequences for international finance. International (private) capital movements were severely restricted in the immediate after-war period. Foreign exchange convertibility in Europe was restricted until 1958, while commercial banks had very limited overseas representations and in some major European countries, such as France and Italy, were under strict political control, i.e. nationalised.[16]

The limitations imposed on short-term capital flows reflected the particular wish of the post-war political leaders in the Western world to insulate domestic policies from external disequilibria transmitted by speculative capital flows.

The mechanism seemed to work quite effectively until the situation started to change slowly and then at a faster pace by the late 1950s when large pools of US dollars started to accumulate outside the United States, the so-called Eurodollars. This phenomenon was the result of several overlapping factors: for example, increasing investments and a strengthening balance of payments in Europe, Soviet fears of expropriation of their assets detained in the United States, increased activity of US-based multinational companies in Europe and American regulation of interest rates.

These elements – plus the restrictions on the external use of sterling by the Bank of England in 1957 and the fundamental return to current account convertibility by the major European countries in December 1958 – allowed foreign banks in London in particular to accept deposits in dollars offering higher rates to depositors than in the US. This money was then lent at lower rates as it was not constrained by Regulation Q, which since the Great Depression had prohibited banks from paying interest on demand deposits and imposed interest rate ceilings on time and savings deposits and capital adequacy requirements on these deposits. Once the Eurodollar business was born, it represented one of the many, but retrospectively maybe the most important financial innovations that would characterise the second half of the twentieth century; ultimately, 'the new upsurge of international banking coincided with the Eurocurrency system'.[17]

Despite being unanimously considered the progenitor of modern finance, historical literature on the Euromarket is relatively scarce and its study still represents a major gap in the current historiography.

Contemporary economists produced an important wave of studies in the 1970s and 1980s. These studies can be broadly divided into the more technical studies, analysing the functioning of the Euromarket, and a series of narrative studies on the political consequences of the market.[18]

Unfortunately, most of this literature lacks a critical assessment of the Eurodollar revolution and limits itself to a technical account of what happened, providing few insights into the inner workings of the market. Financial historians have not yet dwelt on this topic given the limitations on access to the archives.[19]

From their beginnings as short-term and interbank instruments, Eurodollar borrowings started to lengthen, becoming long-term instruments, what became known as Eurobonds. Financial historian, Richard Roberts, explains the passage from the interbank phase to the long-term one as follows:

> The early 1960s saw an extension of the maximum length of Eurodollar borrowings. At the beginning of the decade the normal maximum period was 12 months, with occasional extensions up to two years by special negotiation. By 1964, the maximum period had lengthened to three years, and attempts were being made to extend it to five.[20]

The origins of the third component of the Euromarkets – the syndicated Euroloans – are not clear.[21] Legend has it that the first fully-fledged syndicated Euroloan was a US$80 million loan to the Iranian Bank Markazi in 1969.

Certainly medium-term Euroloans were a natural development of the short-term Eurodollar and the long-term Eurobond markets. Euroloans were more flexible than Eurobonds (i.e. they carried floating interest rates tied to the London Interbank Offered Rate, or LIBOR, and were modified each semester) and their amount could be larger as well.

The variable rate was a very welcome innovation in a period of sustained inflation but, as we will shall see, it tied once and for all the decisions made in the Western world to the destinies of the less developed countries' (LDC) populations. Moreover, it marked a clear break with the practices of the First Globalisation of finance, because at that time the risk of a fall in the value of foreign bonds or a change in the prevailing interest rates were taken by bondholders. In contrast, international syndicated banking loans exposed entire financial systems to the risk inherent in international lending. A default on a bank loan endangered millions of small savers and, if these deposits were not insured by national governments, the default might force taxpayers to bail out reckless banks.

Together this 'magical trio' – of Eurodollars, Eurobonds and Euroloans – contributed to spark a revolution in the banking and financial sector of which the 1960s represented just the beginning.

Until the late 1960s, the amounts exchanged in the Euromarket were quite small and limited to prime borrowers. It was still an 'elitist' phenomenon in the sense that only governmental and para-governmental institutions had access to them: instead LDCs were excluded and relied mainly on official grants coming from multilateral institutions, such as the World Bank. The real changes happened in the 1970s, when 'the relatively arid years of the 1950s and 1960s turned into a *virtual torrent of finance* [emphasis added]'.[22]

It was the influx of huge quantities of dollars accumulated by oil-producing countries, known as 'petrodollars', that fuelled the engine of international financial growth and crucially accelerated the rise of international finance in Europe through three key channels.

First, the crisis of 1973 put a definitive end to existing proposals for regulating the Euromarket through coordinated capital controls as the recycling need shifted the priorities on the international agenda and the interests of the financial and international communities were realigned after the break with Bretton Woods. Second, the recycling challenge provided huge funds, which the banking sector was able to invest in international operations. Finally, the crisis of 1973 gave rise to powerful incentives to expand overseas given the grim economic outlook in the Western world, pushing European banks to enter new countries, to develop new products and to create new alliances. Starting in 1973–74, as historian, Jeremy Adelman, remarked:

> With the collapse of [the] Bretton Woods system, financial deregulation, and the emergence of the Eurodollar market in the wake of the OPEC oil price hikes of the early 1970s, *banks emerged as major controllers of world liquidity*. In fact a small group of very large banks with extensive overseas operations formed the nucleus of the resulting wave of international borrowing and lending [emphasis added].[23]

The late 1960s and early 1970s were turbulent times. The post-war miracle was fading away, the economy was slowing down almost everywhere, unemployment was starting to rise, social unrest was spreading in all the major cities of the West, the post-war economic order of Bretton Woods was crumbling and less developed but oil-rich countries were determined to take full advantage of their black wealth.

While the real economy in the Western world in the 1970s entered a phase of decline, or a 'post-industrial' phase, as some authors have called it,[24] the banking sector did not. On the contrary, it experienced a second wave of expansion, after the first one at the end of the nineteenth century, which some scholars, as anticipated, have called financialisation.

In this sense, the 1970s must be seen as a *paradoxical decade* of crisis in the industrial economy and expansion of the banking and financial sector. Once we acknowledge that, we should ask ourselves whether there is a link between the economic turbulences of the 1970s and the rise of the banking and financial sector.[25]

Hopefully this book will provide part of the answer by providing new archival-driven understandings of the origins of financial globalisation. What is sure is that a new breed of cosmopolite bankers, open to the world and to new opportunities, began to emerge in the early 1970s. Maybe without knowing it, they were the heralds of a new phase of turbulent capitalist development.

Unanswered questions

The exceptional growth of international capital markets and, consequently, of the banking business, is a central but relatively recent phenomenon. Thus, the primary aim of this book is to explain how international finance rose from the ashes of the Bretton Woods regime and to analyse the impact of the reopening of international capital markets on commercial banks in France and the United Kingdom. In order to frame such a complex topic, we were forced to be selective and decided to focus more precisely on three 'jagged edges' or unanswered questions overlooked by the existing literature, namely:

1   Why was the Euromarket kept unregulated even though several proposals were on the table of international organisations such as the Bank for International Settlements (BIS)?
2   Why were the recycling mechanisms privatised and ultimately delegated to commercial banks in Europe, the United States and Japan?
3   What impact did this privatisation have on the international expansion of European, specifically French and British, commercial banks?

The creation of the Eurodollar market represented a crucial moment for the rise of international finance in the West, yet its course was not the steady one that the existing literature largely assumes. On the contrary, it followed a twisted and bumpy road. In particular, the fact that this market was facing a serious risk of being regulated, starting in 1969, has been largely overlooked. Current literature on the Euromarket seems to forget that the existence of an almost completely unregulated market in a very regulated monetary system such as Bretton Woods, was an extremely unorthodox affair. Regulation of this market would have critically reduced its attractiveness to potential lenders and borrowers, and official initiatives to recycle petrodollars would have stood a better chance against private markets. Had regulation been implemented as some countries wished, the whole process of financial deregulation implemented in the late 1970s and early 1980s would have lost much of its appeal. Thus, the first jagged edge we wish to address is why the Eurodollar market was not regulated in the early 1970s even though several proposals were on the table, notably at the BIS in Basel. The fact that the Euromarket remained unregulated, or the decision not to decide on its fate, represented a major step in the process of financial liberalisation. This is a topic too important both for the historian and for the current debate to be left aside.

A second and related jagged edge is represented by the dynamics underlying the delegation of power to commercial banks. The fact that the task of re-equilibrating world payments imbalances after the first oil crisis was ultimately delegated to market actors, was far from given. As the earlier quote from

James and Eichengreen illustrates, the banking sector had been relegated since the 1940s to a second-lead role in international financial matters. Thanks to their expertise and good command of the Eurodollar market, and the unwillingness of governments to find common solutions to the recycling problem, Western commercial banks gradually regained the centre stage of world finance. We wish to analyse more precisely how European commercial banks became one of the main actors in the recycling of petrodollars by lending directly, and not through the bond market, to governments in LDCs for the first time in history. Even if existing literature has described the broad lines of the recycling mechanism, we still do not know the internal dynamics that pushed commercial banks to the forefront of recycling. Authors who have recently tried to study the petrodollar recycling either have failed to include a European perspective in their work,[26] thus forgetting the important contribution of European commercial banks in the recycling circuit, or have treated the phenomenon only superficially.[27] More crucially, no author has focused on the interactions between international organisations and commercial banks and the impact of such cooperation from a historical point of view. We wish to illustrate how such interactions are crucial to understanding why the task of recycling was ultimately delegated to commercial banks.

Did commercial banks take centre stage? Did international organisations play a role in the privatisation of financial flows? How did commercial banks and international organisations interact? Trying to provide an answer to these and other questions is an important step in understanding the world dynamics at play in the process of financial globalisation.

Finally, the two previous jagged edges raise a third crucial issue that deserves to be addressed. Given the limited number of historical studies on the period investigated, we do not know exactly what impact the reopening of finance and the recycling of petrodollars had on the European banking sector.[28] Up until the early 1970s, international banking consisted of mostly a series of bilateral agreements between banks in different countries, and the types of transaction were mainly related to commerce. International competition was still muted, while financial institutions were geographically and functionally segmented. By the early 1970s, the picture started to change and European banks began to expand overseas, implementing new strategies and developing new financial products for new international customers, gradually becoming global institutions. Most continental banks had to radically reshape their structure, creating new vehicles to penetrate new markets and attract new customers. A few banks succeeded in becoming global banks, while others took serious blows and entered into terminal decline. Nonetheless, several key details are missing in the current picture. How did banks react to the rapidly changing environment? How were their strategies affected by the internationalisation of finance? Did internationalisation prove to be a profitable bet?

Historian, Alan Taylor, has argued that 'in the sphere of economic history the 1970s may yet emerge as one of the most important turning points of the modern era'.[29] By properly addressing these questions outlined above, we hope to shed light not only on a turbulent period of recent economic history but also help further the debate on the reopening of finance since the 1970s.

We will show how the face of European banking had not radically changed by the mid-to-late 1960s, and we will analyse how European banks flourished in the 1970s thanks to their international activities against a background of economic stagnation. It will be argued in this work that in the 1970s the financial sector regained, little by little, its independence, becoming free from the restrictive post-war regime, decoupling in part from their domestic markets and exploring new territories overseas. At the centre of our story lies the crisis of 1973–74 and the subsequent recycling of petrodollars as critical junctures in recent economic history. After the oil crisis, banks became, again, a central part of the world economy, because governments now needed them to sustain struggling industrial corporations. As French economist, Joel Métais, pointed out:

> [i]f one observes very carefully the chronology of the process of multina-
> tionalization of major banks, it is disturbing to see how the intensification of
> efforts to develop international activities coincides with a slowdown – if not
> stagnation – of the economic activity and, consequently, of banking activity
> in their domestic environment.[30]

In this sense, we will argue that the same causes that plunged the world into a deep-seated recession, e.g. energy crises, economic stagnation and fiscal crises, triggered the rise of the European banking and financial sector from the ashes of Bretton Woods. Banks were flooded with money to invest in overseas expansion and gradually became central actors in the economic system by becoming the crucial cog between surplus countries, notably in the Gulf region, and deficit countries in the developing world.

Outline of the book

In order to answer the three main questions of our research, we relied on a wide range of primary and secondary sources. The primary sources can be divided into three main groups: commercial banks, central banks and international organisations.

The analysis of the present book is concentrated on commercial banks in France and the United Kingdom. These two countries had the two largest colonial empires until the first half of the twentieth century and, consequently, had, at least in theory, a banking structure more able to cope with internationalising forces. Besides, as a consequence of their imperial status, France and Great Britain had the largest and most developed banking institutions in the world before the Great War. As Youssef Cassis pointed out, by 1913 *Crédit Lyonnais* was the biggest bank in the world while *Société Générale* and the *Comptoir d'Escompte de Paris* figured in the top ten. Four British banks figured amongst the ten largest banks in the world: Midland Bank, Lloyds Bank, Westminster Bank and National Provincial Bank.[31]

Seventy years later, these two countries continued to have the largest banking institutions in Europe (and the world): by 1982, according to *The Banker* Top 500, there were five French banks in the top ten spots, three British, two

American and just one German bank, *Deutsche Bank*. The commercial banks in our work (Barclays Bank, Midland Bank, Lloyds Bank, *Société Générale* and *Credit Lyonnais*) have been chosen because of their importance in the international scene during both periods of financial expansion. We will analyse two of the three nationalised banks in France and three of the British 'Big Four' clearing banks. These banks ranked amongst the largest in the world and amongst the most active on international markets. Besides, focusing on European banks allows us to use recently disclosed archival evidence that would simply be not available for American banks.

The empirical studies are extremely interesting as case studies because they had different backgrounds as international banks and because their more recent history has not yet been thoroughly analysed by financial historians.[32]

Historically, Barclays had one of the largest overseas networks; *Crédit Lyonnais* had a vast network in the French colonies; Lloyds and *Société Générale* had a more limited presence; and Midland did not have an overseas network, preferring correspondent banking instead. Additionally, some banks, like Midland, were members of banking clubs from the earliest point in the early 1960s, others joined later, like the French banks and Barclays, and yet others preferred to enter the international arena by themselves, like Lloyds. We chose to limit our case study to five institutions, because this number allowed us to perform a thorough analysis of the archives in a manageable time frame, while allowing us to gather a vantage point large enough to generalise our findings. Adding more banks, although tempting and probably worthwhile in the future, would not have significantly altered our results nor modified the conclusions of our work. Being a comparative study, but still manageable in size, our research has the advantages of international political economy narratives, providing an overview of the gradual globalisation of European finance, while allowing us to provide the same kind of details of archival-driven studies.

It is worth pointing out that, even though American and German banks are not included in this book, we will rely throughout our work on published material on Citibank and *Deutsche Bank* to provide the reader with a more detailed picture of international banking.

The central banks in our sample will provide us with a 'bridge' to link the international organisations and the commercial banks in our study, allowing us to illustrate how information and decisions were transmitted and processed.

The international organisations analysed represent the most important forums or, in Susan Strange's words, 'our international guardians' in charge of governing international finance. The International Monetary Fund (IMF) dealt with the stability of the international monetary system, the Organisation for Economic Co-operation and Development (OECD) dealt with general economic and financial issue, notably through its Working Party 3 (WP3) which served as an important informal forum between the delegates of the richest countries, while the BIS dealt with the more technical aspects of international finance by providing a secretive forum to central bankers.[33] Being the institutions at the centre of what would now be called 'global governance', these institutions will help us to understand their attitudes towards financial innovations, such as the Euromarket, and important issues, such as the recycling of petrodollars.

Besides primary sources, we relied on the existing literature and newspapers. Several newspapers and magazines have been of great use to better understand the 'mood of the time', most notably the *Financial Times*, *The Economist* and *The Banker*.

The book is divided into five chapters. Even chapters will focus on the macro-economic context, while odd chapters will look at the dynamics prevailing at the industry level by analysing the empirical studies of the book. After this Introduction, we are going to analyse the world of Bretton Woods in Chapters 1 and 2. The financially conservative world of Bretton Woods had a direct impact on the business strategies of European banks. Banks in several countries came under strict governmental control and became tools to finance post-war reconstruction. Their international activities were severely limited, and most banks relied on their traditional links to correspondent banks, while a few limited their presence to colonies and dominions by dedicating themselves to trade finance or retail banking for expatriates. Even though the world started to gradually become less financially 'repressed' thanks to the birth of the Eurodollar market, the European banking sector did not experience any major revolution, being critically limited by three elements: lack of support by national and international organisations, lack of funds to invest in international ventures and, finally, lack of incentives to move abroad. European commercial banks had only limited representations abroad and even the largest one on the continent, Barclays, remained a 'colonial' bank instead of a global one. Most of its profits were made on the African continent, and some authors have qualified its international activities as 'African banking'. The other continental banks were in no better shape, as we shall see, and their products and structures were very similar to those of the early twentieth century.

As described in Chapter 3, the world of Bretton Woods came to an end under the weight of the Euromarket, increased capital mobility and the oil crisis. The crisis of 1973 radically changed the course of recent financial history by providing huge funds to invest and incentives to commercial banks and by aligning the interest of official organisations to those of the bankers. Because of the impossibility of finding alternative channels, the task of recycling petrodollars was ultimately delegated to banks in the Western world. Funds accumulated by oil-exporting countries were partially deposited with banks in London and, from there, huge loans were made to LDCs. The process proved to be a boon for the banking and financial sector, putting a definitive end to the 'embedded liberalist' era. For others it was a hindrance, most notably for the poorest classes in LDCs.

Chapter 4 looks at the changes in the structure of European banks and the fundamental impact of the recycling of oil funds through the Euromarket on the structures and strategies of British and French banks. By the early 1970s, the shape of European banking started to change with the imperative to grow bigger becoming more and more urgent. The reshaping process accelerated incredibly after the turbulences of the early 1970s and, most notably amongst them, after the oil crisis of 1973, when banks became the central mechanism for smoothing global imbalances. Because of the need to recycle huge surpluses, the regulation of the Euromarket was put aside, and European banks could unleash their potential and explore new grounds. Unsurprisingly, along with new opportunities came new challenges and risks. After a decade of euphoria, thanks to the second recycling phase after the oil crisis of 1979, the risks materialised in the early 1980s. This phase will be analysed in Chapter 5. Commercial banks, with the benign support of international and national organisations, had continued their lending spree. Poland became the first major debtor to default on its debts in 1981 and, after a brief *intermezzo*, the global economic situation went from bad to worse in August 1982 when Mexico declared its inability to repay its loans. The Mexican default triggered a regionalisation syndrome and, in the ensuing years, more than 50 countries from Latin America to South East Asia to Africa had to reschedule their debt. Especially for Latin American countries, the 1980s represented a 'lost decade', and for most countries the economic situation would not improve until the following decade.

The final chapter will conclude our research by summarising our findings, answering the main research questions and illustrating some paths for future research.

Notes

1 'Now these I named derive their origin from other living forms. There is one bird which reproduces and renews itself: the Assyrians gave this bird his name – the Phoenix. He does not live either on grain or herbs, but only on small drops of frankincense and juices of amomum. When this bird completes a full five centuries of life straightway with talons and with shining beak he builds a nest among palm branches, where they join to form the palm tree's waving top. As soon as he has strewn in this new nest the cassia bark and ears of sweet spikenard, and some bruised cinnamon with yellow myrrh, he lies down on it and refuses life among those dreamful odors'.
2 Youssef Cassis, *Capitals of Capital. The Rise and Fall of International Financial Centres 1780–2009*, Cambridge University Press, Cambridge, UK and New York, 2010, 83.
3 See, for example: Geoffrey Jones, *British Multinational Banking 1830–1990*, Clarendon Press, Oxford, UK, 1993; Mira Wilkins, 'Banks over Borders: Some Evidence from Their Pre-1914 History', in G. Jones (ed.) *Banks as Multinationals*, Routledge, London and New York, 1990; Stefano Battilossi, 'Financial Innovation and the Golden Ages of International Banking: 1890–1931 and 1958–1981', *Financial History Review*, 2000, 141–175; Stanley Chapman, *The Rise of Merchant Banking*, Routledge, London and New York, 1984.
4 Michael D. Bordo, Barry Eichengreen and Jongwoo Kim, 'Was There Really an Earlier Period of International Financial Integration Comparable to Today?', National Bureau of Economic Research, Working Paper 6738, September 1998.
5 On interwar instability see, for example: Charles H. Feinstein, Peter Temin and Gianni Toniolo, *The World Economy between the World Wars*, Oxford University Press, Oxford, UK and New York, 2008. On the Great Depression the literature is vast; see for example: Milton Friedman and Anna Jacobson Schwartz, *A Monetary History of the United States, 1867–1960*, Princeton University Press, Princeton, NJ, 1963; John Kenneth Galbraith, *The Great Crash of 1929*, Mariner Books, Boston, MA and New York, 1954; Charles P. Kindleberger, *The World in Depression 1929–1939*, University of California Press, Berkeley, CA and London, 1973; Michael D. Bordo, Claudia

Goldin and Eugene N. White (eds), *The Defining Moment. The Great Depression and the American Economy in the Twentieth Century*, The University of Chicago Press, Chicago, IL and London, 1998; Ben S. Bernanke, *Essays on the Great Depression*, Princeton University Press, Princeton, NJ, 2000.

6 Barry Eichengreen, *Globalizing Capital. A History of the International Monetary System*, Princeton University Press, Princeton, NJ and Oxford, UK, 2008, 92.

7 Barry Eichengreen and Harold James, 'Monetary and Financial Reform in Two Eras of Globalization', in Michael D. Bordo, Alan M. Taylor and Jeffrey G. Williamson, *Globalization in Historical Perspective*, The University of Chicago Press, Chicago, IL and London, 2003, 516.

8 For an alternative account on the balance of power between the banking/financial community and State, see, for example: Marcello de Cecco, 'International Financial Markets and US Domestic Policy Since 1945', *International Affairs*, Vol. 52, No. 3 (July 1976), 381–399.

9 Arthur I. Bloomfield, 'Postwar Control of International Capital Movements', *The American Economic Review*, Vol. 36, No. 2, Papers and Proceedings of the Fifty-eighth Annual Meeting of the American Economic Association (May 1946), 687.

10 See, for example: Eric Helleiner, *States and the Reemergence of Global Finance*, Cornell University Press, Ithaca, NY and London, 1994; Rawi Abdelal, *Capital Rules. The Construction of Global Finance*, Harvard University Press, Cambridge, MA and London, 2007; John Gerard Ruggie, 'International Regimes, Transactions, and Change: Embedded Liberalism in the Post-War Economic Order', *International Organization*, Volume 36, Issue 2, Spring 1982, 379–415. The term 'embeddedness' is borrowed from Karl Polanyi's book *The Great Transformation*, Beacon Press, Boston, MA, 2001 (foreword by Joseph Stiglitz, introduction by Fred Block). For a brief but clear analysis of the concept of embeddedness in Polanyi's work, see the introduction to the book written by Fred Block.

11 Stephen D. Krasner (ed.), *International Regimes*, Cornell University Press, Ithaca, NY, 1983, 2. See also, Douglas J. Forsyth and Ton Notermans (eds), *Regime Changes: Macroeconomic Policy and Financial Regulation in Europe from the 1930s to the 1990s*, Berghahn Books, Providence, RI and Oxford, UK, 1997.

12 John Gerard Ruggie, 'International Regimes, Transactions, and Change: Embedded Liberalism in the Postwar Economic Order', *International Organization*, Volume 36, Issue 2, Spring 1982, 393.

13 Eric Helleiner, *States and the Reemergence of Global Finance*, Cornell University Press, Ithaca, NY and London, 82.

14 Idem, 111.

15 Ethan B. Kapstein, *Governing the Global Economy. International Finance and the State*, Harvard University Press, Cambridge, MA and London, 1994, 62.

16 For an historical analysis of international capital mobility, see Michael D. Bordo, Barry Eichengreen and Jongwoo Kim, 'Was there really an earlier period of international financial integration comparable to today?', NBER, Working Paper 6738, September 1998, 1–68. An overview of capital flows during the first globalisation is provided in Albert Fishlow, 'Lessons from the Past: Capital Markets during the 19th Century and the Interwar Period', *International Organization*, Vol. 39, No. 3 (Summer 1985), 383–439.

17 Stefano Battilossi, 'Financial Innovation and the Golden Ages of International Banking: 1890–1931 and 1958–81', *Financial History Review*, Vol. 7, 2000, 159.

18 The first lineage of studies includes: Paul Einzig, *The Euro-Dollar System. Practice and Theory of International Interest Rates*, Macmillan, London, 1967; E. Wayne Clendenning, *The Euro-Dollar Market*, Clarendon Press, Oxford, UK, 1970; Geoffrey Bell, *The Euro-Dollar Market and The International Financial System*, Macmillan, London and Basingstoke, UK, 1974; Brian Scott Quinn, *The New Euromarkets*, Macmillan, London and Basingstoke, UK, 1975; Gunter Dufey and Ian H. Giddy, *The*

International Money Market, Prentice-Hall, Upper Saddle River, NJ, 1978; Robert B. Johnston, *The Economics of the Euro-Market. History, Theory and Policy*, Macmillan, London and Basingstoke, UK, 1983; Daniel R. Kane, *The Eurodollar Market and the Years of Crisis*, Croom Helm, London, 1983. The second wave of studies includes, for example: Anthony Sampson, *The Money Lenders. Bankers in a Dangerous World*, Viking Press, New York, 1981; Michael Moffitt, *The World's Money. International Banking from Bretton Woods to the Brink of Insolvency*, Simon and Schuster, New York, 1983; Howard M. Wachtel, *The Money Mandarins. The Making of a Supranational Economic Order*, Pantheon Books, New York, 1986; Philip A. Wellons, *Passing the Buck. Banks, Governments, and Third World Debt*, Harvard Business School Press, Boston, MA, 1987.

19 Notable exceptions include: Catherine R. Schenk, 'The Origins of the Eurodollar Market in London: 1955–1963', *Explorations in Economic History*, Vol. 35, 1998, 221–238 and Stefano Battilossi, 'Financial Innovation and the Golden Ages of International Banking: 1890–1931 and 1958–81', *Financial History Review* 7 (2000), 141–175.

20 Richard Roberts (with C. Arnander), *Take Your Partners. Orion. The Consortium Banks and the Transformation of the Euromarkets*, Palgrave, Basingstoke, UK and New York, 2001, 7.

21 For an overview of the Euroloans, see, for example: Claude Dufloux and Laurent Margulici, *Les Euro-crédits, pourquoi? Aspects Techniques Micro et Macro-économiques*, La Révue Banque Editeur, Paris, 1984.

22 Robert Devlin, *Debt and Crisis in Latin America. The Supply Side of the Story*, Princeton University Press, Princeton, NJ, 1989, 20.

23 Jeremy Adelman, 'International Finance and Political Legitimacy. A Latin American View of the Global Shock', in Niall Ferguson, Charles S. Maier, Erez Manela and Daniel J. Sargent (eds), *The Shock of the Global. The 1970s in Perspective*, Harvard University Press, Cambridge, MA and London, 2010, 118.

24 Daniel Bell, *The Coming of the Post-Industrial Society*, Basic Books, New York, 1973.

25 The topic of the dominance of financial activities over productive ones has been notably addressed by Marxist theorists such as Robert Brenner, Harry Magdoff, Paul Sweezy and Giovanni Arrighi to name but a few. Arrighi, who built on the work of French historian, Ferdinand Braudel, saw the emergence of a phase of financial expansion as an historical recurrence since the time of the Italian city-states. Capitalist development proceeded through a phase of material expansion in which profits were accumulated through trade and commerce, and a phase of financial expansion, in which profits were accumulated through financial and speculative channels. See Harry Magdoff and Paul M. Sweezy, *Stagnation and the Financial Explosion*, Monthly Review Press, New York, 1987; Giovanni Arrighi, *The Long Twentieth Century. Money, Power, and the Origins of Our Times*, Verso Press, London and New York, 1994; Robert Brenner, *The Economics of Global Turbulence*, Verso Press, London and New York, 2006.

26 David E. Spiro, *The Hidden Hand of American Hegemony. Petrodollar Recycling and International Markets*, Cornell University Press, Ithaca, NY, 1999; Duccio Basosi, *Finanza e Petrolio. Gli Stati Uniti, l'oro nero e l'economia politica internazionale*, Studio LT2 Edizioni, Venice, Italy, 2012.

27 William R. Clarke *Petrodollar Warfare. Oil, Irak and the Future of the Dollar*, New Society Publishers, Gabriola Island, Canada, 2005.

28 The most useful examples of multinational banking literature are still the early works of Geoffrey Jones, notably his edited book, *Banks as Multinationals* from 1990 and the seminal *British Multinational Banking, 1830–1990* published in 1993.

29 Alan M. Taylor, 'The Global 1970s and the Echo of the Great Depression', in Niall Ferguson, Charles S. Maier, Erez Manela and Daniel J. Sargent (eds), *The Shock of the Global. The 1970s in Perspective*, Harvard University Press, Cambridge, MA, and London, 2010, 97.

30 Joel Métais, 'Le processus de multinationalisation des grandes banques commerciales', *Révue* économique, Volume 30, No. 3, 1979, 487–517: 'Si l'on observe de manière très attentive la chronologie du processus de multinationalisation des grandes banques, il est troublant de constater à quel point l'intensification des efforts pour développer les activités internationales coïncide avec un ralentissement – sinon une stagnation – de l'activité économique et donc de celle des banques, dans le pays d'origine'.

31 Youssef Cassis, *Capitals of Capital. The Rise and Fall of International Financial Centres 1780–2009*, Cambridge University Press, Cambridge, UK and New York, 2010, 92. On the French banking and financial sector in the nineteenth century, see also: Pierre-Cyrille Hautcoeur (eds), *Le Marché Financier Français au XIXe Siècle* (Vol. 1), Publications de la Sorbonne, Paris, 2007.

32 Existing histories on British and French banks, mostly on the period preceding the 1970s, include for example (the list is not exhaustive): R. S. Sayers, *Lloyds Bank in the History and Banking in England*, Oxford University Press, Oxford, UK, 1957; the monumental work of Jean Bouvier, *Le Crédit Lyonnais de 1863 à 1882. Les années de formation d'une grande banque de depôt*, SEVPEN, Paris, 1961; Sir Julian Crossley and John Blandford, *The DCO Story*, Barclays Bank International Limited, London, 1975; R. S. Winton, *Lloyds Bank*, Oxford University Press, Oxford, UK, 1982; Hubert Bonin, *Suez: Du Canal à la Finance (1858–1987)*, Economica, Paris, 1987; Eric Bussière, *Paribas, l'Europe et le Monde. 1872–1992*, Fond Mercator, Anvers, 1992; Margareth Ackrill and Leslie Hannah, *Barclays. The Business of Banking 1690–1996*, Cambridge University Press, Cambridge, UK, 2001; Bernard Desjardins, Michel Lescure, Roger Nougaret, Alain Plessis and André Straus (eds), *Le Crédit Lyonnais 1863–1986*, Droz, Geneva, 2003; Hubert Bonin, *Histoire de la Société Générale (I) 1864–1890*, Droz, Geneva, 2006; Richard Roberts and David Kynaston, *The Lion Wakes. A Modern History of HSBC*, Profile Books, London, 2015.

33 For an overview of the different forums see, for example: Jean-Marc Sore, 'L'évolution des institutions financières internationales: Entre redéploiement et fragilité, une restructuration systémique en chantier', *Annuaire Française de Droit International*, Vol. 52, 2006, 481–504. On the BIS, see Kazuhiko Yago, *The Financial History of the Bank for International Settlements*, Routledge, London and New York, 2013.

1 Halcyon days

If you invest your tuppence wisely in the bank, safe and sound, soon that tuppence, safely invested in the bank, will compound! And you'll achieve that sense of conquest, as your affluence expands! In the hands of the directors, who invest as propriety demands!

(Dick Van Dyke as Director of the Bank, Mr Dawes Sr., in 'Mary Poppins', 1964)

A new world order

The regime designed at the Bretton Woods Conference influenced international finance through the restriction of international capital flows and the marginalisation of the banking and financial sector in favour of the industrial one. This comprehensively critical attitude towards finance and financiers, towards banks and bankers, was reflected in the structure and strategies of banks in Europe.

In the immediate post-war years, international capital flows took the form of direct investment (FDI) by multinational firms. This form of capital 'was an instrument of marginal financial importance, for it was neither mediated by banks nor traded on markets'.[1] Thus the role of banking institutions was crucially dwarfed.

The system of checks and balances built at the Bretton Woods Conference was designed to insulate domestic policies from external interference and facilitate the process of post-war reconstruction. As Rawi Abdelal summarised:

> Capital was to be controlled, and with an important purpose: governments were supposed to be *autonomous from market forces*, free to pursue expansionary monetary and fiscal policies without endangering their exchange-rate commitments or suffering the outflow of capital in search of a higher rate of interest or a lower rate of inflation. Because almost every country would be committed to fixed exchange rates, *the regulation of international finance was the only way to provide some measure of autonomy for domestic policymakers* [emphasis added].[2]

Despite the 'mythology' surrounding Bretton Woods (the 'conference setting, the creative minds, and the visionary task'[3]), the regime proved to be short-lived.

The first cracks in the financially restrictive order devised in New Hampshire had already started to appear in the mid-to-late 1950s when dollar deposits held in Europe were not reinvested in the US but on the Continent, becoming Eurodollars (or continental dollars) – in the words of Howard M. Wachtel 'the first truly supranational form of money'.[4] The origins of this market are clouded in mystery and many explanations have been put forward to justify its existence. We can safely posit that the existence of the Eurodollar market depended on mutual advantages to the final borrowers, to the financial intermediaries and to the final owners.

The phenomenon in itself was not revolutionary. Until the First World War, it had been customary to hold foreign currencies outside their country of origin. What was new was the scale of the phenomenon. As reported in the BIS Annual Report of 1964:

> Since the mid-1950s, and especially since Europe's return to external convertibility at the end of 1958, the foreign currency business of banks in Europe and elsewhere has undergone a very considerable expansion. Such business is not in itself new. But banks have been taking deposits and making loans in currencies other than their local currency *on a much larger scale than before*; and in the process there has also emerged an efficient interbank market in US dollar and other foreign currency deposits, helping to channel short-term funds internationally from lenders to borrowers [emphasis added].[5]

The US market represented the preferred investment market. Consequently, foreign governments, companies and international institutions relied on the US to get the financing they needed, '[bonds] issued in New York by certain European countries were, to a large extent, subscribed by residents of those countries'.[6] It was estimated that around 75 per cent of the bonds issued in New York were subscribed from outside the United States. This practice was interrupted in 1963 when the US market was effectively closed to foreign borrowers as a result of the introduction of a series of restrictive measures on foreign financing, starting with the Interest Equalization Tax (IET) in July, which was designed to reduce the appeal of foreign bonds and equities to American investors by raising their cost (only Canadian and LDCs securities were exempted). The rates of the excise tax ranged from a low of 1.05 per cent of the value of the security for a debt obligation with a term to maturity of between 1 and 1¼ years, to 15 per cent on debt obligations with a term to maturity greater than 28½ years. The tax on foreign stocks was 15 per cent.[7]

Following the implementation of the IET, the total number of issues subject to the IET fell from US$569 million in 1963 to US$26 million in 1964.[8] In this context it did not take much for a new market to develop in Europe, particularly in London, where monetary authorities and bankers were looking to reposition the City as the truly international capital market it had once been.

London welcomed the Eurodollar market as a way to compensate for the declining role of sterling as an international settlement currency and the relative decline of Britain's economic fortunes compared to its continental partners who were experiencing a so-called 'Golden Age'. In October 1962, the Governor of the Bank of England, Rowland Baring, remarked that 'the City once again might well provide an international capital market'. Sir George Bolton of the Bank of London and South America (BOLSA), the most active bank in the early years of the Eurodollar market, said very clearly during a seminar at King's College, Cambridge, that the greatest fear amongst British financiers after the Second World War was that 'the failure of the sterling to survive as an international currency . . . would reduce London to a backwater'.[9]

Luckily for him and the City of London, his fears proved to be unfounded. Between 1963 and 1969, the number of banks and other institutions operating in the foreign currency business in the UK increased from 132 to 193. As reported by the Bank of England, between the end of 1963 and the end of 1965 UK banks' gross foreign currency liabilities to overseas residents 'increased by over 25 per cent per annum'. From the end of 1965 to the end of 1968, they increased by 50 per cent per year.[10]

The Eurodollar market gradually modified the corporate strategies of all the major European banks. However, before the revival of the late 1960s and, in particular, the early 1970s, European banking went through a long phase of retreat inside local boundaries. Almost all major commercial banks severed the ties they had created during the first phase of financial globalisation and once again became domestic banks with a limited array of low risk products. This state of affairs came to be epitomised by the legendary '3–6–3 rule': bankers were borrowing at 3 per cent, lending at 6 and were on the golf course by 3 p.m. Maybe this anecdote should be considered more as a legend than a trustworthy representation of banking practices of the immediate post-war years, but, as we know, legends more often than not contain some elements of truth. As financial historian, Youssef Cassis, has argued: 'Taken in isolation, the 1950s were not a particularly propitious time for European banks'.[11]

All across Europe a wave of reforms and regulations fettered the banking and financial sector. In France, the four major banks were nationalised in 1945: the reconstruction was firmly in the hands of the government as was the credit mechanism, as the *Banque de France* was nationalised too. In Britain, the Bank of England was nationalised in 1946, while the Big Five (Barclays Bank, Lloyds Bank, Midland Bank, National Provincial Bank and Westminster Bank), despite remaining *de jure* independent, were *de facto* largely influenced by the imperatives of the Treasury. As Cassis noted: 'They received precise instructions from the Treasury concerning not only their liquidity but also their lending priorities, especially as far as manufacturing investment and the support of exports were concerned'.[12]

As we hinted above, the implication of such policies, attitudes and ideas was that banking practices in Europe in the post-war period were relegated to domestic borders and to what would now be considered conservative practices aimed at making the banking sector a tool in the hands of European reconstruction.[13] Referring to the French banking sector, Joel Métais pointed out that 'after the Second World War foreign expansion retained a low profile until the turn of the 1970s'.[14]

We are now going to analyse the world of Bretton Woods, its ideological foundations and its impact on the European banking and financial sector. Then we will describe the early years of the Euromarket by looking at its origins, its mechanisms and its impact on the world financial system. Finally, we will study banking strategies under the Bretton Woods regime in order to have a comprehensive view of the banking world in Europe before the turbulent events of the 1970s.

The world of Bretton Woods

The Bretton Woods regime lasted only 30 years if we take 1944 and 1973 as the reference years, but only half that time if we start counting from the return to external convertibility of European currencies in 1958. Nevertheless, the Bretton Woods regime had a remarkable impact on recent economic history and continues to exert a strong fascination on the general public and academics alike. Thus, in order to understand the rise of international finance in the *longue durée*, it is worth starting our analysis in the peaceful village at the foot of Mount Washington.[15]

Post-war planning and the control of finance

The war was still underway when plans started to be elaborated by the American and British Treasuries to devise a new economic regime upon which to build the post-war order.[16] John Maynard Keynes of Britain and Harry Dexter White of the US were the most prominent actors of the negotiations, aiming at 'devising the specific means by which the objective [post-war financial collaboration] could be achieved'.[17]

White had a very adverse reputation, 'aggressive, irascible, and with a remorseless drive for power',[18] but despite this he had a remarkable career at the US Treasury. After arriving in Washington in 1930, he started working on the American Stabilization Fund and the Tripartite Stabilization Agreement along with other economists gathered around the Secretary of the Treasury, Henry Morgenthau. He continued to work on important projects such as the failed attempt to create an Inter-American Bank and, by the end of 1941, he had already written an outline of what later would be known as the 'White Plan'. This bold and idealistic plan marked a departure from the existing practices of political isolation and financial orthodoxy. At the centre of White's project lay the Fund and the Bank as the main agencies for the conduct of international finance. The Stabilization Fund would have total resources of at least US$5 billion coming from the contributions of member countries in gold, local currencies and government securities. The aim of the Fund was to help its members in the event of temporary balance of payments difficulties. As a counterpart to this source of financing, member countries would have to 'surrender the right to vary their exchange rates; abolish all forms of exchange control; and submit to Fund supervision over domestic economic policies'.[19] The Bank would have a capital stock of US$10 billion available for the reconstruction, relief and economic recovery of its members; the institution was designed to 'eliminate world-wide fluctuations of a financial origin and reduce the likelihood, intensity, and duration of world-wide depressions; to stabilize the prices of essential raw materials; and more generally to raise the productivity and living standards of its members'.[20]

John Maynard Keynes is one of the most remarkable personalities of the twentieth century and, unlike his American counterpart, has been more widely studied throughout the century.[21] The centrepiece of Keynes' proposal for post-war reconstruction was a Clearing Union. The mission of the Clearing Union was to make available to its members facilities related to their pre-war share of world trade. Surpluses and deficits in the respective balance of payments would be reflected in the credits and debits on the books of the Clearing Union, expressed in a new international unit of account named *Bancor*. With these vast reserves of liquidity at their disposal, members would be able to eliminate all exchange restrictions on current account, maintain stability in their exchange rates and pursue policies of domestic expansion without fear of the consequences on their foreign balance.

It is clear that the preoccupation of Keynes and the British Treasury was to devise a new world order where countercyclical and demand-stimulating policies could be implemented in order to avoid the mistakes of the 1930s. In Keynes' view, the greatest threat to the post-war era came from deflation and not inflation. Consequently, measures to avoid and fight inflation were not thoroughly elaborated and this would have critical implications once the post-war economic miracle came to an end.

Despite similar ideals, there were major differences between the two plans, mirroring the different state of the US and UK in world affairs. Both plans were published in April 1943 and incurred countless criticisms on both sides of the Atlantic. In Britain, a return to the Gold Standard was particularly feared, for the White Plan involved the fixing of exchange rates in terms of gold and the return of a deflationary environment by limiting domestic expansion. In the US, the Keynes Plan looked like the ideal recipe towards reckless experimentation and inflation and the American Bankers Association (ABA) dismissed it as 'impractical and inflationary'.[22]

Interestingly, both plans managed to particularly upset the conservative financial community, especially in New York, which wanted to go back to the classic Gold Standard and sound monetary practices. For example, in September 1943, the *New York Times* reported the alternative plan proposed by Guaranty Trust. The bank's programme called for 'an international gold standard, with free coinage of gold, free markets and private ownership of gold, and currencies freely convertible into gold, both for domestic use and for shipment abroad'.[23]

Despite early criticism by the financial community, a series of, mostly, bilateral meetings in order to find an acceptable compromise followed the publication of the two plans. The final compromise was made official in the 'Joint statement by experts on the establishment of an international monetary fund' published in April 1944, which would later become the IMF Articles of Agreement.

The Bretton Woods Conference started in July 1944 and 44 countries finally signed the treaty on 22 July. However, the agreement was still subject to ratification by home governments. This process ultimately proved to be almost as difficult as the previous phase, and it would take one year for the agreement to be ratified by the US (July 1945) and a few months more for the UK (December 1945).

The ratification process was slowed by many factors. The UK continued to fear a return to a US-dominated Gold Standard; for example, Robert Boothby, MP, Chairman of the Monetary Parliamentary Policy Committee, demanded the Parliament reject the Bretton Woods monetary plan considering it 'unconstitutional' and calling it a 'racket'. Along the same lines, Sir Charles Morgan-Webb, lately Chief Secretary of the Burma Government, said 'that if Britain went back to the gold standard while the United States had 90 per cent of the gold of the world, Britain would become a vassal of the United States'.[24] Many of those critics were envisaging the creation of a sterling area to pursue autonomous economic policies.[25] The ratification by the British was also slowed by the fact that it was associated with finding acceptable terms for the stabilisation loan; as the *New York Times* wrote in November 1945: 'The British will not ratify the Bretton Woods accord unless an acceptable financial agreement is reached with Washington, it was learned on authority today. This had been rumored unofficially, but there can be no question of it now'.[26]

Wall Street bankers continued to oppose the agreement. They had been absent from the Bretton Woods Conference as the participants were mostly experts from the Treasury and professional economists. This state of affairs was a continuation of President Roosevelt's decision to exclude the Wall Street community from financial policy-making.[27] Most bankers favoured a return to the Gold Standard, fearing that the existence of the Fund would weaken the discipline of debtor countries and that the ultimate effect on the world economy would be inflationary. Fred Block has pointed out that the financial community 'feared that extensive national or international governmental intervention would eliminate the role that private international bankers had historically played'.[28]

In February 1945, the ABA prepared a counter-plan involving notably the elimination of the Fund and the incorporation of its functions in the World Bank. The plan was very badly received by the Treasury. Henry Morgenthau declared that if the ABA proposals were followed, they would 'kill the whole Bretton Woods Monetary Agreement' and advised the bankers to see 'just a little further than their own immediate business'.[29]

Finally, criticisms came from the more conservative State Department officials, particularly its secretary, Cordell Hull ('a firm adherent of Wilsonian internationalism'),[30] Dean Acheson and William Clayton. The Treasury and State Departments had conflicting views on several subjects, notably the role of the Soviet Union, Germany and Britain in the world economy. The State Department saw in the Soviet Union a great threat to American commercial interests in Eastern Europe, while the Treasury Department thought that the best way to deal with the Soviet Union was to strengthen bilateral trade. As for Germany, the State Department saw in it a valuable ally against Soviet ambitions and felt its industrial revival was to be welcomed and facilitated. By contrast, Morgenthau's entrenched antipathy towards the Nazi ideology pushed him to devise a punitive plan in order to pastoralise the country once and for all. With regard to Britain, the views were less divergent; both departments wanted to gain leverage on the declining empire but, if the State Department goal was to open the empire to American trade, the goal of the Treasury was to 'assure British compliance with their own plans for organizing the international monetary system'.[31]

Despite the criticism on both sides of the ocean, the first 24 countries had finally ratified the Bretton Woods agreement by the end of 1945; others would follow in subsequent months, and an official ceremony was held at the State Department in Washington DC on 27 December.

The regime of Bretton Woods represents a hallmark in recent economic history, because it marked a break with the liberal tradition of the first globalisation and officialised the beginning of a new international regime founded on capital controls. As Eric Helleiner noted:

> The restrictive financial provisions in the Bretton Woods Agreement partly reflected the prominence of an embedded liberal framework of thought, which gave priority to the defence of the policy autonomy of the new interventionist welfare state from international financial pressures.[32]

The acceptance and will to implement such principles was the result of an ideological shift, started in the early 1930s, not only away from liberalism, which had dominated the latter part of the nineteenth century and the first years of the twentieth, but also from the protectionism implemented in the 1930s. After the disappointing experiences with *laissez-faire* liberalism and beggar-thy-neighbour policies, the new foundations were to be, as previously anticipated, embedded liberalist.

The debate before and after Bretton Woods was harsh, but, in the end, the agreement was a success. The agreement was possible because, despite the differences, the majority of the actors involved formed a 'community of experts'. Using the words of G. John Ikenberry, this community shared 'a set of technical and normative views about the world economy and . . . were given remarkable discretion in developing policy proposals and negotiating on behalf of their governments'.[33]

This community held common views on the most critical issues of post-war reconstruction, notably: the desirability of currency stability and the convertibility of currencies; the need for a stabilisation fund in order to provide short-term assistance to governments and allow them to pursue expansionary policies; and the need to reconcile the movement of capital and trade with policies promoting stable and full employment. In order to pursue these goals, capital controls on flows of speculative, 'hot money' were crucial. Both plans 'shared a skepticism of private international financial flows, and both plans relied on capital controls to maintain government's autonomy'.[34]

Keynes and White insisted on the undesirability of speculative, short-term capital flows, not on capital flows *tout court*. Productive and equilibrating capital flows were to be encouraged and promoted by the new order. These flows were long-term flows that facilitated trade and foreign direct investments. The urgent need to avoid the mistakes of the inter-war years, by aiding 'the maintenance of exchange stability, macro-economic stability, and orderly, generally non-discriminatory trading relations among nations',[35] was the biggest concern of the British and American experts.

In the US, this community was made up of so-called 'New Dealers', a group of young economists gathered around Henry Morgenthau in the mid-1930s to work on exchange rate stabilisation plans. Amongst them there was, as anticipated, Harry D. White, who had been chosen because of his unorthodox views on economic subjects made clear already in his doctoral thesis on French international payments in the pre-war period.[36] As Ikenberry pointed out, in the late 1930s a new wave of economists 'mostly from Harvard University and embracing Keynesian ideas, had begun to find places in the U.S. Government'.[37] People like Marriner Stoddard Eccles, Chairman of the Federal Reserve under Roosevelt and later Truman, and Lauchlin Bernard Currie, economic adviser to Roosevelt, played a crucial role in recruiting a new generation of economists. The 'enrolment' of Keynesian-minded economists was pursued at several levels of the administration, and, when discussion on the post-war economic order began, 'the experts surrounding White shared his basic views concerning the need for far-reaching and innovative economic proposals'.[38] The new economists also gathered outside the administration, in planning and discussion groups such as the Economics and Financial Group (part of the War and Peace Studies Project of the Council on Foreign Relations) led by Alvin Hansen and Jacob Viner.

In the UK, besides the towering figure of Keynes, the 'new thinking' was embodied by academic economists such as James Meade and Lionel Robbins, civil servants like Richard Hopkins and ministers like Richard Law. As in the US, much of the war and post-war planning took place at the Treasury rather than at the Bank of England, much more influenced by the City bankers.[39] The British Treasury's ideological tendencies had started to shift towards Keynesian economics in 1939; the shift had been accelerated by wartime planning involving the suspension of sterling convertibility for the first time since the Napoleonic wars. As Scott Newton noted: 'It all meant an unprecedented level of state intervention in the City's activities and their subordination to the demands of the national economy'.[40]

In a famous speech at the House of Lords in May 1944, Keynes said: 'Not merely as a feature of the transition, but as a permanent arrangement, the plan accords to every member government the explicit right to control all capital movements. *What used to be a heresy is now endorsed as orthodox* [emphasis added]'.

The agreement was not simply an agreement on monetary technicalities; it was a *feuille de route* on who would be in charge of monetary and financial affairs. As Armand Van Dormael summarised: 'Would the power centre of international finance rest with the private banks *or* with the governments?'[41] By the second half of the 1940s, the answer was clear: banks would be instruments in the hands of national legislators. Bankers and financiers were the sore losers of the post-war compromise, and the structures and scopes of commercial banks would reflect their new role as 'servants' of Western reconstruction.

The Bretton Woods regime had a crucial impact not only on Europe and the United States but also on the developing world, because the character of capital flows to LDCs became *institutional* and *multilateral* as the largest part of their development finance was borrowed from official institutions, at fixed interest rates, on very favourable terms, on a long-term basis and repayable in local currency.[42]

Consequently, as economist, Poul Høst-Madsen, stated in 1963:

> [t]he total increase in the indebtedness of the underdeveloped countries on account of official lending during 1947–61 appears to be of the order of US$10 billion, but *the resulting increase in their debt-service burden is much less than would have been associated with an equal amount of borrowing on commercial terms* [emphasis added].[43]

As we shall see, this situation would be radically modified during the recycling process of the 1970s. As pointed out by Jeffry Frieden in 1981:

> In the 1960s, in fact, foreign direct investment accounted for some 30 percent of the total flow of external financial resources to Latin America, while bank loans and bonds provided only 10 percent. In the 1970s, banks and bond-holders were responsible for 57 percent of this flow-up from an annual average of US$ 214 million in the 1960s to US$ 6.5 billion in the 1970s – while the multinationals' share dropped to about 20 percent.[44]

Capital flows, mostly in the form of loans or grants, came from individual governments and from international organisations such as the World Bank, as the institution turned its attention from post-war reconstruction to development finance, and, starting from the 1960s, the Inter-American Development Bank, export credit organisations such as the ECGD (Export Credits Guarantee Department) of Britain, Hermes of West Germany, COFACE (*Compagnie Française d'Assurance pour le Commerce Extérieur*) of France[45] and the Export-Import Bank[46] of the United States. As Madsen pointed out, 'a characteristic of the post-war period is that official grants and capital have played a much larger role in international transactions than ever before in peacetime'.[47]

A new dawn, a new day? The early years of the Eurodollar market

Unfortunately for those wishing to control finance, the full implementation of the Bretton Woods agreement coincided with the appearance of the Eurodollar market.

The emergence of Eurodollars was the result of several concomitant factors, for example, increasing investments and a strengthening balance of payments in Europe, Soviet fears of expropriation of their assets detained in the US, the increased activity of US-based multinational companies in Europe and American regulation of interest rates.[48]

These elements, as well as the 7 per cent bank rate and restrictions on the external use of sterling by the Bank of England in 1957 and the fundamental return to current account convertibility of European currencies in December 1958, allowed foreign banks, particularly in London, to accept deposits in dollars offering higher rates to depositors than in the US and lending this money at lower rates, not being constrained by domestic regulations and capital adequacy requirements on these deposits. The Eurodollar business was born and it represented one of the many, but retrospectively maybe the most important, of the financial innovations that would characterise the second half of the twentieth century. Some authors have even argued that the Eurodollar revolution was 'the most significant monetary creation since the appearance of banknotes during the seventeenth century'.[49] This assumption is justified by the fact that this money was effectively unregulated, as no one had the authority to impose curbs or controls; to quote Jeffry Frieden: 'Who was going to supervise dollar deposits in a German bank's branches on British soil? The answer came quickly enough: nobody'.[50]

Eurodollars were an external currency market. In the simplest terms, this meant that they were deposits denominated in a currency other than the currency of the country in which the banks were located.[51] Banks known as 'Eurobanks', generally located in London, produced these deposits. Other important centres would come to include Luxembourg, Zurich and, later, Singapore and Panama City. Given the fact that these banks were located outside US jurisdiction, they benefited from an incredible degree of freedom compared to domestic banks in the late Bretton Woods era.

The dollar had the lion's share of this offshore business, but it was not the only currency held by foreigners. Other currencies included Deutschmarks (DM) held outside West Germany, known as 'Eurodeutschmarks', Swiss francs and sterling. All the currencies held outside their home countries were known as 'Eurocurrencies'. In its earliest years (the late 1950s and early 1960s), the Eurocurrency market was mainly an interbank market where Eurobanks lent themselves foreign currencies for very short maturities, often overnight. As time went by, the terms of Eurodollar borrowings gradually lengthened and new products started to appear, notably long-term 'Eurobonds', i.e. bonds in an international currency other than that of the borrower, issued outside the borrower's home country and introduced to the market by an international underwriting syndicate of banks. There was one major factor working against the Eurobond market in the 1960s: interest rates. From the late 1950s, interest rates were rising across the Western world, from a low point of 0.63 per cent on Federal funds in May 1958 (since the world was on a *de facto* dollar standard, this was the most important rate that influenced all the others) to a high point of 9.15 per cent on September 1969.[52] This was partly the result of the leadership of William McChesney Martin, the fiscally conservative Chairman of the Federal Reserve from 1951 to 1970.[53] As Aaron Major pointed out, Martin's conservative ideas on monetary policy were backed by US President Dwight D. Eisenhower's fiscal policies.[54] In the following years, more volatile interest rates represented a major inconvenience for bondholders, and the market started working on some possible solutions.

Thus the end of the 1960s saw the appearance of new financial innovations such as floating rate notes (FRN), i.e. Eurobonds with a variable coupon, and medium-term bank loans, between three to ten years, issued by an international syndicate in Eurocurrencies at floating interest rates, generally tied to LIBOR (the London Interbank Offered Rate), which came to be known as 'Euroloans'. Together, short-term Eurocurrencies, medium-term Euroloans and long-term Eurobonds formed the backbone of the Euromarket.

Being an under-the-counter market, the origins of the Eurodollar market are not fully clear. Since the first Eurodollar transaction was not publicised, we must rely on archival evidence and on existing literature to assess the origins of this offshore market.

Most accounts seem to agree on the fact that the 'fathers' of the modern financial system were, ironically, not greedy bankers in Western Europe or the United States but communists from the Soviet Union, and that the 'birthplace' was not London, but Paris.

In 1921 a small bank was bought by Russian exiles to serve their fellow citizens in Paris; the name of the bank was *Banque Commerciale pour l'Europe du Nord* (BCEN).[55] The small bank failed in 1925 but was bought by the Soviet Central Bank, the *Gosbank*. After the war, BCEN quickly became the largest foreign bank in France, handling commercial and financial transactions between Soviet-dominated countries; its cable address was EUROBANK.

Holding foreign currencies was not an entirely new phenomenon. During the inter-war years, in particular, sterling and US dollars were held and exchanged in Vienna and Berlin, although these deposits disappeared after the crisis of 1931. Nonetheless, the scale and scope of the Eurodollar market were not comparable to its inter-war years' siblings. As economist Paul Einzig wrote, the amounts exchanged before the Great Depression were 'limited and one-sided markets of essentially local significance'.[56] Thus, the main difference between previous foreign currency activities and the Eurodollar market was the size of the latter. Only the Eurodollar market created 'a truly international money market, and has developed a structure of international interest rates that is entirely without precedent'.[57]

After the outbreak of the Korean War, the Chinese government deposited US$5 million with BCEN. Given the size of the amount, the bank redeposited these dollars with other French banks and these dollars started to circulate in France and Europe. In the meantime, another Soviet-owned bank, the Moscow Narodny Bank appeared, this time in London, doing a similar business. The first borrowers in this market were the central governments and commercial banks of Italy, UK, Belgium and the Netherlands.

The communist origin of the Eurodollar market seems to be confirmed by a document redacted by economists Alan R. Holmes and Fred H. Klopstock of the New York Federal Reserve Bank dating from August 1960, found in the archives of the *Banque de France*.

In June 1960, Klopstock and Holmes paid a three-week visit to the main European financial centres to 'obtain a first-hand picture of activities in the so-called Continental dollar market'.[58] During their trip, they visited Zurich, Basel, Rome, Milan, Frankfurt, Düsseldorf, Amsterdam, London and Paris. Even though they had contacts with central bankers, their main objective was to 'make contact with leading commercial bankers so as to obtain information from the men who actually operate large dollar accounts in commercial banks in New York and other United States financial centers'.[59]

They felt obliged to study the Eurodollar market because the appearance of a broad, active and well-established market for dollar deposits in Europe represented 'one of the most significant institutional changes of recent years in the international financial mechanism'. In their report, the two economists confirm that 'the original impetus arose from the desire of Iron Curtain central and foreign-trade banks, notably the Gosbank, to employ dollar accruals profitably outside the confines of the United States'. The report gives us some new information by saying that:

> [i]nquiries were made by these banks [in France] in the mid-fifties among potential borrowers, notably Italian banks, whether these would be interested in taking on dollar balances for limited periods at attractive interest rates, i.e. at rates somewhat lower than these banks would have to pay for dollar accommodations in the United States.

When Italian banks agreed to cover their dollar needs with those offerings, German and Dutch banks followed suit, so that in a short time the market was in full bloom, with the *Banque Commerciale pour l'Europe du Nord* as its hub.

Most economists and historians agree that despite the role of BCEN and Narodny Bank, a proper market would have arisen 'if it had not been for a number of favourable structural and economic factors'.[60] Amongst the most important factors we must mention were the limits on the use of sterling balances to finance international trade between non-sterling area countries and the return to external currency convertibility for several European currencies. Despite the interest in assessing the origins of the Eurodollars, it must be pointed out that the development and persistence of the market would not have been possible without regulatory asymmetries, voluntarily overlooked by national governments, as Richard Roberts has noted: 'An array of market distortions meant that banks operating in offshore dollars enjoyed both competitive advantages and higher profits'.[61]

In fact, Eurodollar transactions were not constrained either by capital controls imposed in the US after the end of the Korean War to counter the gradual balance of payment deterioration, such as the IET, the Voluntary Foreign Credit Restraint Program (VFCR) and the Foreign Direct Investment Program, or by monetary regulations imposed since the Great Depression such as Regulation Q.[62]

As anticipated, the IET, which was presented in July 1963 and signed into law in September 1964, was an excise tax on purchases of foreign securities by US citizens. Exemptions included direct investments, investments in developing countries, investments in Canadian bonds and, last but not least, loans made by foreign branches of US banks to foreign residents. Given these large exemptions, large outflows in the form of direct investments and short-term bank financing provoked a large deficit at the end of 1964. Consequently, the VFCR and FDI programmes were introduced and the scope of the IET extended to long-term loans to foreigners.

The VFCR programme requested banks and non-banks to impose ceilings on foreign lending giving priority to export credits. Its guidelines would be made more stringent in 1968.

The voluntary FDI programme became mandatory, starting from January 1968 when President Johnson issued the extraordinary executive order No. 11,387 prohibiting certain people subject to US jurisdiction from engaging in any transaction involving direct or indirect transfer of capital to or within any foreign country or to any national thereof outside the United States. The programme required US non-financial corporations to refrain from direct investments. Essentially, we can discern three important moments in US capital controls: 1963, 1965 and 1968.

Regulation Q was a product of legislation enacted by the Roosevelt administration after the tumultuous years of banking crises in the early 1930s, notably the Banking Acts of 1933 and 1935. It imposed a ceiling interest rate of 3 per cent on all time and savings deposits,[63] the objective being to push banks to invest in their communities instead of fuelling speculation and to preserve bank profits by limiting 'cut throat' competition.

Not being constrained by regulations and limitations, banks operating in the Eurodollar market were able to pay higher rates to depositors at very short maturities and to lend at lower interest rates than domestic banks. It comes as no surprise, then, that the Eurodollar business became a privileged tool at the disposal of a new generation of bankers born in the 1920s and 1930s, to open a wide breach in the restrictive order built in Bretton Woods. The report of the American economists, Klopstock and Holmes, concluded:

> It had thus become quite apparent that borrowing of foreign exchange deposits, notably dollars, has brought about profound changes in international banking and the relative position of banking centers. Furthermore, it has affected significantly banking practices and operations in European countries. It has given a considerable fillip to foreign exchange markets, set into motion an impressive volume of international capital movements and in particular inter-area movements of dollar balances. All this lends support to the . . . contention . . . that the emergence of this market is an event of great significance for the international financial mechanism and that its evolution deserves our close and continuous study.[64]

By the very first months of the 1960s it was already clear that the Eurodollar market would represent a great innovation for the banking and financial profession and that it had the potential to ignite a new phase of expansion for the banking and financial industry.

Development and evolution of the Eurodollar market

It must be clear from the beginning that the Eurodollar market was an *intended* breach in the restrictive post-war order. Western governments played a crucial role in supporting the Eurodollar market by setting a double regulatory standard, as the BIS noted in its 1964 Annual Report: 'The development of Euro-currency activity has been dependent upon banks having a *considerable measure of freedom* to do business in foreign currencies [emphasis added]'.[65]

The US strictly regulated domestic banks but deliberately spared foreign branches, the result being a 'migration' of banks to Europe and an increased role of the dollar as an international currency. A similar benevolent attitude was common in European countries.

In the UK, foreign currency business, developed in particular by overseas banks, was not constrained by the limitations of 1957. In Switzerland, deposits in foreign currencies remained outside the 'gentleman's agreement' of August 1960, which forbade payments on Swiss deposits held by foreigners. In the Netherlands, limits on domestic lending in 1961 and 1963–64 encouraged banks to maintain liquidity abroad. In Italy, the absence of regulation on the Eurodollar market allowed banks to escape the cartelised domestic market; moreover, demand for Eurodollars was profoundly affected by measures taken by the *Ufficio Italiano Cambi* (UIC) of the Bank of Italy. For example, in November 1959 the UIC offered Italian banks the opportunity to acquire dollars from official reserves on a swap basis at no cost, for it was willing to buy back the dollars at the spot rate. Since at that time the market rate for Eurodollars was approximately 4.25 per cent, while interest on Italian lire reserves at the Bank of Italy yielded only 3.25 per cent, Italian banks had a good opportunity to make a profit. The dollars received by the UIC were used essentially to reduce dollar liabilities abroad, to finance additional dollar requirements or offered in the Eurodollar market. The UIC 'killed several birds with one stone': it reduced the dollar liabilities of the Italian banking system and interest payments to foreign banks, while at the same time lowering the effective cost of dollar borrowing and reducing the excess liquidity of the Italian banks. It is worth pointing out that, along with the relative absence of regulations on foreign currency operations compared with the regulations hampering banks' domestic currency operations, the growth of the Eurodollar market was explained by the ability of Eurobanks to compete effectively, for they were able to operate on thinner margins and were not bound by interest rate conventions and cartel arrangements, and by the willingness of the world to use dollars on a large scale.

Tracing the expansion of the Eurodollar market is a trickier affair than might be imagined. Until the early 1960s, when the BIS started to collect data from reporting countries, there were no comprehensive and credible statistics for the Eurodollar market. Fortunately, things started to change in October 1962 when the first 'Meeting of Experts on the Euro-Currency Market' was convened at the BIS. The most important result was the decision to start pooling domestic statistics on the Eurocurrency market. Finally, at the second Meeting of Experts it was noted: 'For the first time a comprehensive indication of the volume and distribution of funds in the Euro-currency market is becoming available'.[66] Nonetheless, the statistics were far from satisfactory. The *Banque de France* remarked that the debate of November 1963 was extremely 'disappointing' for there were no 'common definitions and terminology', the 'goals to achieve' were unclear and 'the heterogeneity of the statistical data gathered' complicated the task.[67]

The first statistics of the BIS on the Eurodollar market are summarised in Table 1.1. From the table we can see that Italy, Switzerland, the UK, Canada and Japan were the largest sources of Eurodollar deposits. The first year of systematic analysis of the Eurocurrency market is 1963 and during that year the gross (i.e. including interbank deposits) dollar liabilities of 10 reporting countries amounted to US$10.475 billion. The BIS tried to obtain an approximation of the net amount by excluding interbank deposits within Europe and arrived at a net dollar amount of US$4 billion.

The growth of the Eurocurrency market in the second half of the 1960s is summarised in Table 1.2.

As regards the sources of Eurodollars, the experts concluded that most of them were coming from US business concerns, located in the US and abroad, while the role of central banks was diminishing after the important contributions of the first few years. In fact, until 1963, central banks contributed to the growth of the market directly and indirectly: directly because, according to the 1964 BIS Report, central banks had deposited between US$200 million and US$300 million of their reserves with banks outside the US; indirectly, because during 1961 and 1962 the *Bundesbank* enabled German banks to hold dollars, offering them favourable terms for swap transactions. At the beginning of 1962, the amounts involved reached US$1 billion.

The same happened in Italy, where the UIC had accounted for much of the dollar swaps and deposits with commercial banks since 1959. By late 1963, the *Bundesbank*'s swap commitments had fallen to zero as the balance of payments situation improved, while in Italy foreign liabilities with the central bank had declined to US$300 million because, after 1962, commercial banks were again allowed to be net borrowers abroad. The BIS accounted for around US$300 million in deposits. Non-banks gradually became the most important source of

Table 1.1 Dollar liabilities and assets of the banks vis-à-vis non-residents (US$m), end of March 1963.

Countries	Excluding vis-à-vis US			Including vis-à-vis US		
	Liabilities	Assets	Net	Liabilities	Assets	Net
France	560	480	−80	620	620	0
Germany	195	410	+215	270	540	+270
Italy	1,120	640	−480	1,195	970	−225
Netherlands	155	130	−25	190	320	+130
Switzerland	835	865	+30	955	1,245	+290
Sweden	25	45	+20	30	70	+40
United Kingdom	2,585	1,465	−1,120	2,880	2,665	−225
Belgium	160	290	+130	235	420	+185
Canada	850	750	−100	2,350	2,750	+400
Japan	300	300	0	1,750	1,650	−100
Total	6,785	5,375	−1,410	10,475	11,240	+765

Source: BEA, 6A123/1, Confidential 'Report of Meeting of Experts on the Euro-Currency Market at the BIS', 9–11 November 1963.

Table 1.2 Net size of Eurodollar market (US$BN), 1964–69.

1964	1965	1966	June 1967	Dec. 1967	June 1968	Dec. 1968	June 1969	Dec. 1969
9.0	11.5	14.5	15.0	17.5	22.5	25.0	33.5	37.5

Source: BEA, 6A123/7, Confidential Paper 'Joint Supervision of the Euro-Currency Market', 10 December 1970.

Eurodollar funds according to the BIS. Corporations located in the US and overseas branches of US companies started to place increasing amounts of dollars in Europe by the early 1960s, becoming the most important source of Eurodollars.

As for the uses of Eurodollars, the greatest part was used to settle foreign trade and to finance foreign borrowings, especially in Italy, UK, Japan and Belgium. According to the BIS, 'the United Kingdom has been a net borrower of Euro-currencies since the early stages of the market's development';[68] in Japan 'Euro-currencies made up a part of the substantial foreign borrowing by Japanese banks in 1961 and have continued to be a source of credit, particularly for the financing of Japanese foreign trade';[69] in the case of Italy, 'the banks' net indebtedness to non-residents rose between November 1962 and September 1963 by about $1 milliard';[70] and in Belgium, 'the Treasury during 1960–61 and again in 1963 financed part of the budget deficit by running a floating debt in foreign exchange, which at the end of 1963 totalled over US$200 million'.[71]

The first Eurobond was issued in 1963. It was a 15-year, US$15 million issue on behalf of *Autostrade*, the Italian national highway authority, to finance the construction of the final part of the 'Autostrada del Sole' connecting Milan to Naples. The mastermind of the operation, finalised on 1 July, was Sir Siegmund Warburg, who pioneered the concept of a 'US dollar bond issued in London and other European financial centres, brought out by a European syndicate of banks, and sold mainly to European investors'.[72] Co-managers of the issue included *Deutsche Bank, Banque de Bruxelles* and *Rotterdamsche Bank*.[73]

The issue was good news for American officials. As we have previously mentioned, before the development of the Eurobond market, New York functioned as the privileged capital market for European customers, with increasingly negative consequences for the balance of payments of that country. In the immediate post-war period, when there was still a profound 'dollar gap' in Europe, New York became the most important place to raise long-term financing for foreign borrowers. The management of such issues was in the hands of a handful of American investment banks with old ties to the European markets. As Robert Genillard summarised:

At the time it was generally not appreciated that while New York was the clearing place for such operations and the dollar the currency in which the issues were expressed, the securities were bought largely by non-residents of the United States, in spite of the fact that they were offered at rates substantially higher than those available on internal American issues. This remark must be qualified with the statement that, while the bulk of these securities was indeed sold outside of the United States, the preference of American investors varied widely among different borrowers. Some issues of European governments were sold to the extent of 90% to non-residents, while some other issues, such as those of Australia, found a much larger acceptance among resident investors in the United States.[74]

When the dollar gap transformed into a 'dollar glut' and measures such as the IET were introduced, European bankers like Warburg, supported by the Bank of England, saw an opportunity to revive international capital markets and to regild the City's name.

The measures implemented to improve the American balance of payments would ultimately prove a failure given the beginning of hostilities in Vietnam, and the most visible result was to curtail the New York market and accelerate the growth of the Eurobond and Eurocurrency market.

The Eurocurrency and Eurodollar market continued their growth in the following years. At the end of March 1965, according to the BIS, the total foreign dollar liabilities of the nine reporting banking systems amounted to US$11.6 billion and their total foreign dollar assets to US$11.4 billion. As for the Eurocurrency market, between September 1963 and March 1965 the reporting banks' total liabilities to non-residents in all reported currencies rose by US$2.4 to US$14.6 billion. The whole of this increase was in their dollar liabilities.

Late 1965 and 1966 was another important period for the Eurocurrency market, which experienced its most important annual growth. The main expansionary factor was the tightening of credit conditions to fight inflationary pressures in the US, leading to the so-called 'credit crunch of 1966'. The credit crunch pushed American banks to dramatically increase their borrowings on the Eurodollar market through their European branches, especially in London. Consequently, the net size of the Eurodollar market increased from US$9.0 billion in 1964 to US$11.5 billion in 1965 to US$14.5 billion in 1966. That same year, the BIS deposited US$275 million in the Eurodollar market.

The expansion continued unabated in 1967, when the BIS estimated the net size of the Eurodollar market at around US$17.5 billion, up from US$14.5 billion the previous year. The source of this growth did not come from the demand side but from the supply side. In 1967 the slack economic conditions, especially in Europe, increased deposits in the Eurodollar market; compared to the previous year, American borrowers played a minor role, attracting just one-quarter of the new funds in the market. Official monetary authorities took a greater role in the market. During the Six Day War, the BIS activated its swap line with the Federal Reserve and invested the proceeds in the Eurodollar market. By the end of the year, the *Bundesbank* offered dollar swap facilities to commercial banks at preferential rates. Several European central banks cooperated with the Federal Reserve to stabilise the dollar in the forward market in June after the large withdrawals following the Six Day War and again after the 'gold crisis' of November–December 1967.

At the Meeting of Experts of July 1967, delegates discussed for the first time the 'problems posed by the rapid growth of the market'.[75] The general consensus in favour of the Eurocurrency market is clear from the archival evidence. The British delegate, R. A. O. Bridge, Assistant to the Governor, remarked that:

> Although the central banks should keep a close eye on the Euro-currency market *its growth should, if anything, be encouraged.* It performs a useful international function, has proved to be a natural market with a sensitive price mechanism and has survived the shocks to which it has so far been exposed. Last but not least, it makes a significant contribution to the financing of international trade [emphasis added].[76]

Most delegates seemed to agree with the British vision. The Belgian delegate, for example, remarked that 'its growth should be carefully watched but *not counteracted* [emphasis added]'.[77] The *Bundesbank* representative said that '*nothing should be done* to limit the development of the Euro-currency market [emphasis added]'.[78] The Swiss pointed out that 'after some initial hesitation, the Swiss National Bank has now taken a more positive attitude towards the market'.[79]

In the following chapters, we will see how attitudes, especially in Germany, would radically change after the monetary turbulences of the late 1960s. For the time being, the only dissenting view came from the Dutch representative, who argued that 'for smaller countries, such as the Netherlands, the existence of an international monetary market that is very large relative to the domestic sector necessitated the continuance of exchange control regulations since the money flows would otherwise render monetary policy ineffective'.[80]

The growth of the market accelerated further in 1968 following a new wave of tightening policies in the early months of that year, such as the now mandatory FDI programme, and mid-year tight credit conditions led to a heavy demand for Eurodollars by US banks. On the supply side, the gold crisis of March and the turbulences of May 1968 in France, which led to the selling of French francs into dollars, as well as the lax monetary conditions throughout Europe led to deposits in the market. The net size of the Eurodollar market grew from US$17.5 billion to US$25 billion while the net Eurocurrency market rose from US$21 billion to US$30 billion. London continued to account for about two-thirds of the total size of the market: the market in London increased by 60 per cent in one year to US$17 billion.[81]

In 1969 the Eurocurrency market continued to show remarkable growth. On a net basis, the Eurocurrency market grew from US$30 billion to US$45 billion while the Eurodollar market grew from US$25 billion to US$37.5 billion. Three factors accounted for this expansion. First, another tightening of credit conditions in the US, with the Federal Reserve discount rate reaching 6 per cent in April 1969, pushed American banks to use their London branches to borrow Eurodollars. By the end of 1969, American banks had become the single most important actors in the London market; since 1963 the number of London branches of US banks increased from 9 to 24, accounting for around 50 per cent of the Eurodollar market in the City.[82] The most important names in the business were the First National City Bank, Manufacturers Hanover, Chase Manhattan, Bank of America and Bankers Trust. A second influence was the substantial borrowing by French and Italian banks. A third important factor was the demand for dollars for conversion into DM in the wake of a possible revaluation of the currency. This final element is crucial and not only for its contribution to the growth of the Eurodollar market. Even more importantly, it sparked a debate lasting several years on the unregulated nature of this market. The ultimate outcome of this debate would have profound implications for the state of international finance.

Talking about regulation

Since its birth in the late 1950s, the unregulated Euromarket had largely remained under the radar of monetary authorities until the late 1960s. This neglect was justified by the fact that 'at the time [in the early 1960s], central banks felt satisfied that the eurodollar threatened neither macro nor banking stability and only required closer monitoring'.[83]

In a departmental memorandum of the IMF Research Department prepared in 1969 by the economist, Fred Hirsch, (famous for defining the 'positional good' concept[84]) the difficulty in grasping the scope of the Eurodollar phenomenon is clearly evident: 'The Euro-dollar market is not exactly a newcomer to the international financial scene – It has burgeoned for a decade or more – *but its role within the national and international credit mechanisms is only beginning to be understood* [emphasis added]'.[85] In Basel, in 1971, BIS General Manager, Réné Larre, noted in respect of the question of central banks' policy with regard to the commercial banks in the Eurocurrency market that '*The Committee had avoided this problem area until the end of 1971* [emphasis added]'.[86]

In reality, things had started to change from 1969. During that year, German monetary authorities recognised that restraining measures would be needed for domestic purposes because 'foreign and domestic demand for West German goods was rising rapidly, labor shortages were developing despite a large inflow of foreign workers, order backlogs were growing alarmingly long, and prices were beginning to rise'.[87] According to the *Bundesbank*, throughout the first three quarters of 1969 the inflow of new orders from abroad increased by 18 per cent.[88] At first:

> [f]iscal policy was used to restrain the domestic economy as the government was able to achieve a cash surplus in its domestic budget; but fiscal policy could not do the entire job, and monetary policy was needed to reinforce the restraint[89] . . . [and therefore] . . . The Deutsche Bundesbank tried to increase monetary stringency by a series of moves like increasing the reserve ratios of the banks and raising the central bank interest rate. As monetary tightness began to be felt, however, West Germans became less willing to lend to foreigners and *private foreign money was attracted into Germany*. As long as foreign funds were available, the liquidity of German firms could not be effectively squeezed by the Bundesbank [emphasis added].[90]

Speculation on a revaluation of the DM acquired momentum at the end of the first quarter of 1969, when a speech by West Germany's Finance Minister, Franz Josef Strauss, about a possible revaluation of the DM to cool off the German economy set off a rush of funds into DMs. Between 1 and 9 May, an estimated US$4 billion flowed into West Germany through the Eurodollar market.[91] Unfortunately, for speculators, Strauss announced on 9 May that the DM would not be revalued, but only US$1.5 billion left West Germany.

The *Bundesbank* continued to implement a restrictive monetary policy by twice raising the banks' minimum reserve ratios, first in June by about 15 per cent, and then again in August by a further 10 per cent. Further, the central bank's interest rate was increased in April, June and September from 3 per cent to 6 per cent. The effort of the *Bundesbank* continued to be nullified in greater part by the inflows coming from abroad. After a short break, the speculation on the DM continued as the general election on 28 September 28. Ultimately, the *Bundesbank* realised that 'restrictive measures without alteration of the exchange rate . . . largely cancelled each other out'.[92]

The official foreign currency exchanges were closed on the last two business days before the elections, and the *Bundesbank* decided to stop intervening on the foreign exchange market. The DM was allowed to float briefly between 30 September and 24 October before being repegged upward, after consultation with the IMF and the Monetary Committee of the European Economic Community, on 24 October by 9.3 per cent at DM 3.66 per US dollar instead of the former DM 4.00, the most important revaluation since the creation of the Bretton Woods system. The choice of a high revaluation rate was justified by the need to look convincing and by the need to check internal economic activity and domestic price increases, at the same time as most capital controls included in the Foreign Trade and Payments Law (*Aussenwirtschaftsgesetz*) of 1961 were repealed in favour of indirect monetary measures focusing on the operations of the banking system.

The speculation on the DM came as a great shock to the *Bundesbank*, as for the first time since the Great Depression it showed how the Eurodollar market could facilitate speculative flows by providing investors with a more sophisticated and quicker mechanism to reflect confidence flows. Consequently, starting from 1969, the attitude of the *Bundesbank* became gradually but decisively critical of the Eurocurrency market, and German monetary authorities became the most active opponents of these funds that were free to roam from one country to another, impacting negatively on their domestic (anti-inflationary) monetary and credit policies.[93]

A particularly critical issue for the *Bundesbank*, and especially its board member and future president, Otmar Emminger, was the fact that 'German companies and, to a lesser extent, German banks, can borrow or take deposits much more easily than they could have done otherwise if there had not been off-shore banking in London in dollars'.[94] Ultimately, capital mobility was making it more difficult for regulatory authorities to pursue domestic goals and the 'eurocurrency market flows seemed to work against German monetary policy'.[95]

German pressures succeeded in putting the Euromarket, especially its pace of growth, its contribution to world inflation and the risk of default, at the centre of the international agenda. As Gianni Toniolo remarked 'from the early 1970s onward, concerns about the eurocurrency market became widespread in the press as well as in international policy forums'.[96] Nonetheless, the existing literature has not focused enough on the risk of regulation pending on the Euromarket or has treated this crucial topic only superficially. Helleiner mentions the debate around the control of the Euromarket, but attributes its dismissal simply to opposition 'by the US representatives to any type of cooperative controls'.[97] As we will show in Chapter 3, this view is only partially acceptable and it must be nuanced with new archival evidence.

The Swiss and the Dutch authorities experienced, on a smaller scale, the same problems and followed the Germans in their 'battle' for more regulation on speculative international capital flows. Intriguingly, the United States appeared, at this time, to be more in line with the conservative continental faction than with the Bank of England. In a speech in Basel, William McChesney Martin, remarked that:

> [a]t the present there is little, if any, multilateral supervision of these markets [the Eurocurrency markets]. One needs raise no doubt about the soundness of the claims that are created and exchanged in these markets to suggest that a case can be made for giving to an international institution some responsibility for *supervising these markets* [emphasis added].[98]

At the Meeting of Experts of 1969, Emminger 'actively pressed his concern at the current situation, mainly on the grounds that this market, now such a major factor in the world monetary system, should be outside the control of the central banks'.[99]

The control of the Eurodollar market was at the centre of France's preoccupations too. In September 1969, during the weekly meeting of the *Conseil Général* of the *Banque de France*, the Governor was asked by the future BIS General Manager, Réné Larre, 'whether some possible measures exist to prohibit banks stocking up with the euro-dollar market'.[100]

The Eurocurrency market grew, albeit at a slower pace, in 1970. Its net size reached US\$57 billion and the Eurodollar component grew from US\$37.5 billion to US\$46 billion. The supply and demand patterns were radically different compared to 1969.

The share of the dollar in the market decreased, while other currencies increased from around 15 per cent to 30 per cent. Furthermore, the supply came mostly from banks, as opposed to the previous year when non-banks played a larger role. On the demand side, European banks replaced American banks as the largest borrowers, given the tight credit conditions and monetary restrictions in Europe (notably in Germany and the UK) and easing monetary conditions in the US since early 1970. By the end of the year, Emminger launched a first formal offensive against the unregulated Eurocurrency market through a document entitled 'Joint Supervision of the Euro-Currency Market'. In this paper he argued that the market was a source of inflation; it increased the shift of funds from one market to another; and it could delay 'corrective actions by the authorities' thus covering up balance of payments imbalances. The market could have 'amplifying effects on interest rate developments' and provided 'a large pool of liquid resources that may feed speculative excesses; it increased the role of the dollar'.[101] The paper finally called for some sort of '*multilateral supervision* of the market [emphasis added]'.

In part, as a consequence of such positions, in February 1971, during a meeting on the Eurocurrency market held at the Netherlands Bank (called the 'Zijlstra Group' from the name of the Governor of the Netherlands Bank, Jelle Zijlstra), the idea of a Standing Committee on the Euromarkets under the chairmanship of Réné Larre to replace the annual 'Meeting of Experts' on the Euromarket was contemplated. The necessity of regulatory measures was crucial for the *Bundesbank* to 'ward off undesirable money flows'.[102] As Chairman of the Working Party 3 of the OECD from 1969 to 1977, Emminger pushed forward the discussion about possible regulations within the organisation. Thus, around the same time that the Working Party agreed to 'undertake a study of the problems arising from the volatility of short-term capital and the operation of the euro-currency markets', it was noted that 'events leading up to the recent exchange-rate moves have given a vivid illustration of the dimension of the problem and of its urgency'.[103]

The Bank of England read between the lines of Emminger's (labelled the 'most violent critic'[104] of the Euromarket) paper and acknowledged that behind the 'euphemistic BIS term'[105] of joint supervision, the real goal was to impose controls. Nonetheless, the Bank of England decided not to impede the creation of the committee despite a clear malaise. Richard Hallett, adviser to the Governors, remarked in a letter to Jeremy Morse:

> I accept that *we should not resist the proposal for an international committee* . . . to study the Euro-currency markets . . . But we must accept from the outset that *it is unlikely that any action can be taken without diminishing the role of London* . . . London has taken some severe knocks in recent years – the impact of devaluation on sterling as a trading currency and of the Washington agreement on the gold market, and the restrictions placed on the activities of the silver market . . . *The loss of the Euro-dollar market to London would be another serious blow* [emphasis added].[106]

Following the meeting convened by Zijlstra in Amsterdam in February, a proposal for the creation of a 'Standing Committee on the Euro-currency Market' was sent and accepted by the Group of Ten (G-10) Governors in April 1971.[107]

During the February meeting, Zijlstra circulated a paper where the first lines read: 'There is a *growing urge to regulate the Euro-dollar market*, and more generally the Euro-currency market, *one way or another* [emphasis added]'.[108] As we can see from the article of *The Times* in Figure 1.1, the decision to create a

---

Should the Eurodollar market be controlled?

The Eurodollar market has enormously increased the amount of funds shifting from financial centre to financial centre in times of monetary uncertainty. What sort of regulations could be imposed and what would their effect be?
Geoffrey Bell reports

Figure 1.1 Control of the Eurodollar market.

Source: *The Times*, 22 June 1971.

study group on the Eurodollar market become one of the most important topics of discussion in financial circles. The article said, 'the question at issue is whether or not to regulate the Eurodollar market. Following last month's crisis [when Germany left the Bretton Woods system] in the international exchange markets, there has been a wide-spread clamour for controls on Eurodollar transactions'.[109] The battle against the Eurocurrency market was just beginning.

The Eurodollar market was a crucial development in post-war finance and, undoubtedly, represented a fatal breach in the armour against speculative capital flows forged at the Bretton Woods Conference. According to the BIS, its expansion was 'without precedent in international monetary history'.[110] The Euromarket represented a significant vehicle for the international expansion of bank credit; it increased the international pool of liquid funds and facilitated their rapid shift from one market to another; it delayed corrective actions by monetary authorities and it provided a large pool of funds available for speculative excesses.

By the end of the 1960s, the market was in full bloom but, starting with Germany, a certain unease about these unregulated funds became manifest. Another point that it is worth repeating is that the Eurocurrency market first and the Euromarket later were not 'stateless'. As Eric Helleiner rightly said:

> Two states, in particular, Britain and the United States, strongly supported the market in its early years. Britain provided a physical location for the market, permitting it to operate in London free of regulation. U.S. support was equally important because American banks and corporations were a dominant presence in the market in the 1960s.[111]

The UK played a crucial role indeed, creating all the conditions for the renaissance of the City. The US played a more nuanced role for, compared to the British, their contribution to international finance was more indirect as they restricted the domestic market and invited borrowers to use external markets in Europe. Until the late 1960s and particularly during the turbulences of 1969, most Western governments were generally benevolent towards the Eurocurrency market. Subsequently, Germany became the first major country to have a negative attitude towards the market, lobbying for increased controls.

Were then the 1960s the crucial years for the internationalisation of banking and finance in Europe?

The answer is no. Despite the importance of the decade for the history of international finance and the remarkable pace of growth of the Eurocurrency market, it remained a strictly American and European affair. The amounts exchanged on the market were still small compared to domestic banking and, as we will see in the next section, the banking practices were not much different from those of the early post-war period.

International banking strategies under Bretton Woods

The restrictive order devised at Bretton Woods had profound implications on banking practices and strategies in the post-war era. As business historian Geoffrey Jones has pointed out: 'Regulatory controls on capital flows and currency convertibility had reduced the importance of international banking, and minimized the scope for innovation'.[112]

After the war, European banks became instruments of governmental policies as European banks moved from 'commercial to government lending'.[113] In Germany, the big three commercial banks (*Deutsche Bank*, *Dresdner Bank* and *Commerzbank*) were split into a number of regional banks, in accordance with the American banking system of that time. For example, *Deutsche Bank* was succeeded by ten regional banks. Given the impracticality of having such small banks dispersed around the country, the German banking community, through a series of mergers, managed to reduce the number of splinter banks and to reunify the three commercial banks during 1957 and 1958. In France, the *Banque de France* and the four biggest commercial banks (*Crédit Lyonnais*, *Société Générale*, *Comptoir National d'Escompte de Paris* and *Banque Nationale pour le Commerce et l'Industrie*) were nationalised between 1945 and 1946. As the reconstruction was firmly in the hands of the Treasury, commercial banks focused essentially on supporting Treasury issues and collecting short-term deposits. The activities of the nationalised banks were supervised by the National Credit Council, which also had the role of putting into operation the credit policy determined by the government; the Minister of Finance acted as President of the Council, while the Governor of the *Banque de France* acted as Vice-President. In the UK, the Bank of England was nationalised and the largest commercial banks, albeit remaining autonomous, were under stringent official control, receiving instructions, for example, on lending priorities through the so-called 'letters of guidance'. Midland emerged after the war as the largest of the clearing banks, with 2,121 branches and £1,444 million in deposits by the end of 1953,[114] but did not have any branches or interests in subsidiary companies abroad.

In the United States, the 1950s were tremendous years as domestic business activity increased thanks to the wartime demand for military equipment and consumer spending. International business was not very appealing while domestic corporate lending soared.

In France and the UK, just a few commercial banks and overseas banks were active on international markets, mainly as providers of retail services in the colonial territories or intermediaries in trade finance operations, essentially the same kind of business that they had done since the late nineteenth century. Unfortunately, the colonial territories were mostly located in some of the less dynamic areas of economic activity, especially the African continent.

International presence was extremely limited for other continental players as well. *Deutsche Bank*, for example, had representative offices only in Turkey, Argentina, Mexico, Venezuela, Brazil and Chile. These offices served mainly as antennas for advising customers on foreign trade and how to handle payment business.[115] The most international of the Italian commercial banks, *Banca Commerciale Italiana* (also known as COMIT), had to close several overseas branches after the Second World War and its activities in Central and Eastern Europe were shut down because of nationalisation and peace treaties.[116]

Overall, the 1950s were years of conservatism in international banking. The organisational structures, the products, the clients and the areas were the same as 50 years before. International banking played only a minor role in the strategies of the major British and French banks. As Youssef Cassis argued, by the end of the 1950s, 'only three banks worldwide could be considered as multinational banks'.[117]

Amongst the three banks that Youssef Cassis considered multinational in the post-war years, he mentioned Barclays Bank in first place, with 1,000 branches overseas in 1955, followed by the First National City Bank with 76 foreign branches in 1959 and *Crédit Lyonnais* with 200 foreign branches in 1962. We will start by analysing Barclays' international operations to assess its multinational character before comparing its international activities up to the late 1960s with those of its main competitors, notably Lloyds Bank, Midland Bank, *Crédit Lyonnais* and *Société Genérale*.

Barclays as the pacesetter

Barclays' international operations can be traced back to the creation of Barclays Bank (Dominion, Colonial and Overseas) in 1925 by Frederick Craufurd Goodenough, Chairman of Barclays Bank Limited at that time.[118]

The new bank was the result of the amalgamation of the Colonial Bank, which was established in 1836 by Royal Charter to operate in the West Indies and, starting from 1916, extended its operations to the colonies of West Africa, together with the Anglo-Egyptian Bank, founded in 1864 to conduct business in Alexandria and Mediterranean region, and the National Bank of South Africa, established as *De Nationale Bank der Zuid-Afrikaansche Republiek* and renamed in 1902 after the Second Boer War.

The creation was not the result of favourable situations but, as Sir Julian Crossley and John Blandford report in their informative history of DCO,[119] the result of Goodenough's vision after the Great War of Barclays as a federation of overseas banks formed to assist British manufacturers in their expansion in the Commonwealth territories.

In order to pursue his 'imperial' vision, Goodenough started to look for possible partners. The first partner was found in the Colonial Bank, historically operating in the West Indies but with a more recent presence in Western Africa. After some discussions between Goodenough and Colonial Bank's Chairman, Lord Beaverbrook, and later Charles F. Wood, a shareholding investment of £40,000 in 1917 marked the beginning of a long partnership. In 1919 Barclays acquired full control of the bank.

The first indirect link with the National Bank of South Africa was a 'side-effect' of the acquisition by Barclays of the London Provincial and South Western Bank, which had in its portfolio substantial shares of Cox and Company (France) which in turn was participated in by the National Bank. The link with South Africa became direct in 1919 when Barclays bought 5,000 shares in that bank. That same year, the National Bank of South Africa bought 10,000 shares of the Colonial Bank, and the London manager of the National Bank was appointed to the board of the Colonial Bank, while A. B. Gillett of Barclays was appointed to the London Committee of the National Bank of South Africa.

A few months later, discussions began with the Chairman of Anglo-Egyptian Bank, R. H. Foà, to acquire control of the bank. After some negotiations, the offer from Barclays was 'strongly recommended by the board of the Anglo-Egyptian Bank to the shareholders and quickly secured wide acceptance'.[120] Undoubtedly, the board was well aware of the financial difficulties of their bank, largely because of the declining cotton business and with new and expensive ventures to recapitalise in Palestine and Sudan. Once Barclays' offer was accepted, a Barclays' director was appointed to the Anglo-Egyptian board and R. H. Foà was appointed as an advisory director of Barclays. Barclays controlled 95 per cent of the shares.

By 1925 a new and more centralised plan, compared to the original idea of a federation of overseas banks, took shape, partly as a consequence of the financial difficulties of the National Bank. The Colonial Bank absorbed the Anglo-Egyptian Bank and the 'new' bank bought the National Bank. On 27 April 1925 the 'new' Colonial Bank became Barclays Bank (Dominion, Colonial and Overseas).

Interestingly Montagu Norman, Governor of the Bank of England, was against the creation of such a large overseas bank, fearing 'it would destabilise British banking through unnecessary overseas entanglements'.[121] Fortunately for Barclays, the good contacts of Goodenough within imperialist circles assured the approval of Parliament for the merger.

The Times hailed Barclays (Dominion, Colonial and Overseas) as the 'First Empire Bank', and it truly looked to be the kind of bank a W. Somerset Maugham's character would use for his daily transactions. Through its branches the 'imperial' bank covered the greater part of Southern and Central Africa, most of the British territories in the eastern and western part of the continent, Egypt, Palestine, a number of countries in the Mediterranean region, the whole of British West Indies, the British territories in the Indian Ocean and so on.

The businesses of the three founding banks were kept almost intact. A new central board, composed essentially of Barclays Bank Limited staff, was superimposed on the three existing boards and committees. The Head Office of the DCO was located at 42 Lombard Street, just a stone's throw away from Barclays' headquarters at 54 Lombard Street. The Chairman, of course, was Goodenough.

After the first two decades of activity marked by two of the greatest tragedies of the twentieth century, the Great Depression and the Second World War, Barclays (Dominion, Colonial and Overseas) entered a period of expansion under the chairmanship of Sir Julian Stanley Crossley. The first ten years after the war were a period of unprecedented expansion in every section of the bank, the number of offices had remained fairly consistent at around 500 during the war years, but in 1952 the 700th office was opened.[122] In 1954, Barclays (Dominion, Colonial and Overseas) changed its cumbersome name to the more svelte Barclays DCO giving the opportunity to the bank's detractors to rename it 'Debits, Credits and Overdrafts' or 'Defenders of Colonial Oppression'. In the following years, the bank lost one of its founding members when Gamal Abdel Nasser nationalised the DCO's activities in Egypt, consisting of 18 full branches, 2 sub-branches and 25 agencies, and they came under the control of the newly created Bank of Alexandria. The 1960s brought a 'wind of change' in world affairs and, consequently, in the affairs of DCO. In 1960 Nigeria became independent, Ghana had already become a republic in 1958, and the path towards independence started in Kenya, Sierra Leone, Tanganyika and Nyasaland. The end of the colonial era forced DCO to diversify its activities and expand into new territories. In 1964 DCO bought a third of the Bank of London and Montreal (BOLAM), a bank created in 1958 by Sir George Bolton's BOLSA and the Bank of Montreal to operate in Central and Latin America. Sir Julian Crossley wanted to acquire a foothold in South America in particular, where DCO was almost absent and to limit the competition of BOLAM in the Caribbean. On 29 July, a press release was issued in London, Montreal and Nassau (where the head office of BOLAM was located) officially announcing the new cooperation: 'The Bank of London and Montreal will continue its operations in Latin America as before. In the Caribbean, where Barclays DCO and the Bank of London and Montreal at present compete with each other, the two banks will in future work closely together'.[123] By 1970, the triple ownership showed its limits in setting a clear direction for BOLAM and DCO would finally sell its shares to BOLSA; Latin America would remain a sort of *terrain vague* for DCO throughout the 1970s. During the Crossley era, which lasted from 1947 to 1965, DCO's offices grew from 522 to 1,416, while the staff expanded from 7,965 to 19,682. Crossley was succeeded by Frederic Seebohm, later Lord Seebohm.

The Seebohm era was marked by the decision to make DCO a 'truly, efficient, functional machine'.[124] In 1967 the consulting firm, Urwick Orr and Partners, was asked to review the bank's organisation and to suggest possible improvements. The basic goal of Seebohm was to reduce costs in order to improve profitability, but it quickly became clear that the real issue was to make fundamental changes in the management structure. A series of reports on several topics was submitted in the following two years; the most important of which was Report No. 4 submitted in February 1968 after five months of research on the organisation of the Head Office.

In its conclusions, the report suggested the adoption of a new type of organisation, at that time called 'Management by Objectives' (MBO).[125] MBO was:

A positive and systematic approach to improving the total performance of an enterprise. It involves Managers at every level in management work, that is planning, organising, directing and controlling. This involvement is brought about by predetermining and agreeing targets of performance with each Manager, and by gaining his acceptance to being held accountable for the results of his work to a single superior.[126]

The purpose of the scheme was to guide managers at all levels to work towards the objectives of the bank and to give all employees the feeling of participating collectively in achieving those goals. The adoption of MBO as the 'official' DCO philosophy in August 1968 was made possible by seminars and training courses. By setting clearly measurable objectives, the benefits brought about by MBO included increased profitability, increased morale and faster decision making. Ultimately, MBO proved a valuable management tool and in 1970 a 'pilot' project to adopt it at Barclays Limited was ratified.

In the second half of the 1960s, DCO pursued its expansion in the Commonwealth. Between 1962 and 1967 newly opened offices increased by 21 per cent from 1,317 to 1,597 while staff increased by 31 per cent from 18,265 to 23,900. The number of account holders grew by 63 per cent from 2,055,000 to 3,350,000.[127] In the late 1960s, nationalisations and 'localisations' (the transfer of the majority ownership to local subjects) followed their course. The activities in Tanganyika (today's Tanzania) were nationalised in February 1967, and Libyan activities were taken over by the Bank of the Republic after the overthrow of King Idris in 1969. The Nigerian activities were localised in November 1968, in Sierra Leone in 1971, and in Uganda, Malawi and Zambia between 1969 and 1971. Yet the bank could not be considered a global bank. The ultimate character of the bank was 'overseas', 'multidomestic' and (still) 'imperial', as Margaret Ackrill and Leslie Hannah have pointed out, rather than 'international' or 'global'.[128]

In 1970, the last year before the transformation of Barclays DCO into Barclays Bank International (BBI), the geographical spread of current, deposit and other accounts was as reported in Table 1.3.

From the table above we can clearly see why some authors have argued that 'Barclays' overseas involvement for its first half-century is best seen as 'African banking'.[129] Until the early 1970s, DCO was deriving more than 50 per cent of its profits from the African continent. Moreover, the core business had remained the same as during the previous 50 years. DCO was providing retail banking and not wholesale banking, and the extent of its cross-border activities was fairly limited. Barclays DCO represented without any doubt the most outward looking bank of the post-war years, but it took a decade more to become a global (and no longer colonial) institution with a strong presence in international financial markets. Given the fact that Barclays DCO was considered the most multinational bank since its foundation, it comes as no surprise that its competitors in the UK and France were laggards.

Table 1.3 Geographical spread of current, deposit and other accounts of Barclays DCO, 1970.

Region	Percentage
Southern Africa	38.09
Botswana, Lesotho, Mozambique, RSA, Rhodesia, South West Africa, Swaziland	
United Kingdom and West Germany	25.58
Bahamas and Caribbean	10.01
Bahamas, Barbados, British Honduras, Cayman Islands, Guyana, Jamaica, Leeward Islands, Trinidad and Tobago, Turks and Caicos, Virgin Islands, Windward Islands	
West Africa	9.40
Ghana, Nigeria Sierra Leone	
USA	6.28
California, New York	
Central and East Africa	5.36
Congo (Kinshasa), Kenya, Malawi, Mauritius, Seychelles, Zambia	
Mediterranean	5.28
Cyprus, Gibraltar, Israel, Malta	
Total	100.00

Source: Barclays DCO Annual Report 1970.

Epigones

Amongst the British clearers, Lloyds was the closest competitor to Barclays in international ventures, having created in 1911 Lloyds Bank (France) renamed in 1955 Lloyds Bank Europe (LBE) and having acquired in 1918 an interest in the London and River Plate Bank. The London and River Plate Bank was amalgamated in 1923 with the London and Brazilian Bank to form BOLSA. Lloyds Bank (Europe) was particularly active in France, Switzerland and Belgium while BOLSA had a strong presence in most Latin American countries, notably Brazil, Argentina, Uruguay, Colombia and Paraguay. It also had branches in London, Paris, Antwerp, Lisbon and New York. The third component of Lloyds' international activities was the previously mentioned BOLAM, created to explore banking possibilities in the West Indies and to develop to the fullest extent the branch network that BOLSA already had in Central America and adjacent South America. Nevertheless, the activities of the three banks remained limited to regional banking and retail activities and thus cannot be considered as examples of global banking.

The case of Midland is the case of a bank that had decided not to operate any foreign business in its own name, relying instead on correspondent banking. The decision initially paid off, since Midland came away unscathed from the turbulences of the Great Depression and the Second World War, unlike some of its competitors. Unfortunately, 'by refusing to operate overseas in its own name, Midland was left with little experience of direct international banking'.[130] Midland was not directly active overseas in the post-war years; on the other hand, it had created a complex and seemingly efficient web of correspondent banks around the world over the years. This policy traces its origins in the decision to abandon direct overseas representations after the First World War and the belief of Howard Thackstone, later Chief General Manager of Midland, that correspondent banking was best suited to conduct overseas banking, for it allowed Midland to avoid competition with domestic bankers in foreign markets. The attitude of Midland towards overseas banking would only start to change gradually in the mid-1960s. By then, Midland had started to become aware of the shortcomings of its strategy and had decided to add a timid international dimension to its character. We shall return to this point in the next chapter.

On the other side of the Channel, the situation was not much different as far as overseas banking was concerned. *Société Générale* and *Crédit Lyonnais* were large domestic banks with a marked colonial connotation, operating in Europe and in the French colonies, providing banking services to the local population and to traders. As Georges Smolarski, who entered *Crédit Lyonnais* in 1951 and in 1969 would create the Department of International Financial Operations (*Département des opérations financières internationals*, DOFI) in charge of syndicated Euroloans, pointed out:

> [i]n 1945, the international network of *Crédit Lyonnais* was one of the largest in the world: we were present in London, Spain, Geneva, Belgium, Luxemburg, Egypt, Portugal, and of course North Africa and Black Africa, which were considered as extensions of the national territory. *We practised essentially commercial banking activities, acting as intermediaries for companies* [emphasis added].[131]

The international operations were quite limited and played only a supportive role compared to domestic banking.

Crédit Lyonnais' activities in Russia, as well as the activities in the former Ottoman Empire, were closed down between the wars. In the ten years following the Second World War, a branch was inaugurated in Sarrebrück and subsidiaries in Brazil, Peru and Venezuela were opened (*Banco Frances e Brasileiro* in 1948, *Banco de Lima* in 1952 and *Banco Provincial* in 1953).[132] The activities in Egypt, Syria and Sudan were closed down between 1956 and 1957. Georges Smolarski made this interesting remark concerning the London branch of *Crédit Lyonnais* in the 1960s: 'As far as I knew this branch in the 1960s, I remember it had a *limited activity* . . . We had a sort of *diplomatic representation* which was not well entrenched in the living tissue of English and international finance [emphasis added]'.[133]

The scope of *Société Générale*'s international activities, albeit on a smaller scale than those of *Crédit Lyonnais*, was quite similar in its traits. Thanks to its subsidiary *Société Générale Alsacienne de Banque* (Sogenal), *Société Générale* was active in retail banking in Germany, Belgium, Switzerland and Luxemburg. *Société Générale* was also active in the French colonies providing banking services to the local population and expatriates. Apart from those activities, in the year of its centenary, 1964, *Société Générale* had two branches in London and New York, two subsidiaries (Francibank in Brussels, Antwerp and Charleroi, and

Sogebanque in Valencia and Barcelona), a branch in Buenos Aires, and two representative offices in Rome and Mexico City. Again, it was a large colonial and European institution operating in retail banking.

The epigones in other European countries followed a similar path. Up to the late 1950s, *Deutsche Bank*, for example, had only minority shareholdings abroad, notably in *Banco Espanol de Alemania* (15 per cent), in *Consortium Européen pour le Développement des Ressources Naturelles de l'Afrique S.A.* (16.6 per cent), in *Deltec Panamericana S.A.* (3.7 per cent), in *Handel-Maatschappij H. Albert de Bary & Co. N.V.* (19.6 per cent), in *Société Européenne de Développement Industriel S.A.* (49.4 per cent) and in *Transoceaninc Development Corporation Ltd. Toronto* (49.4 per cent) and a 52.5 per cent participation in *Deutsche Uberseeische Bank AG* (DUB), a subsidiary with operations in Argentina, Brazil and Germany. *Deutsche Bank* had only a few representative offices abroad – in Turkey, Argentina, Mexico, Venezuela, Brazil and Chile – and did not have any branches or subsidiaries abroad. Overseas operations were seen as an ancillary business geared towards foreign trade and international settlements.[134] The 'minority holding' policy persisted until the late 1960s, when a 'three-level' strategy started to be implemented. *Deutsche Bank* set up new representative offices and branches of DUB, established a subsidiary in Luxembourg (*Compagnie Financière de la Deutsche Bank*) to operate in the Eurodollar market and, finally, intensified cooperation with partner banks in Europe and participated in the creation of joint ventures outside Europe.[135]

As for American banks, the 1950s were quiet years for them too. American banks had a limited interest in international ventures up to the mid-1950s for several reasons, notably controls on capital flows, restrictions on the convertibility of European currencies, buoyant domestic demand and the expansion of American companies overseas. Consequently, when compared to the international heritage of British and French banks, US banks were laggards in international ventures. Only National City developed a considerable overseas network, but the war took its toll. In 1930 it had 83 foreign branches generating around 30 per cent of its loans, deposits and earnings while in 1955 it had only 61 branches (mostly in Latin America) generating around 15 per cent of its loans, deposits and earnings. In 1955 National City had only three branches in Europe, in London, Frankfurt and Paris.[136]

Barclays Bank through Barclays DCO was the largest multinational (or multi-domestic) bank in Europe in the post-war years, yet it remained, until the early 1970s, a bank doing more than half of its business in the African continent and operating in retail banking. Amongst its continental competitors, *Crédit Lyonnais* represented its most serious challenger but, as we have seen in this section, it was active mainly in Europe and the French colonies. Its overseas operations were not spread globally and its core business remained retail banking. Thus it appears that up to the end of the 1960s, there were no truly global European banks operating in the Eurodollar market. As we will see in the following chapters, something happened in the 1970s to make the global turn of European banks possible.

Quiet before the storm

Banking historian, Duncan Ross, remarked that:

> The British clearing banks suffered from a particular *lack of effective international strategy and presence* in the 1950s and early 1960s . . . Confined largely to domestic retail activity, the clearing banks had little direct overseas representation. Barclays and Lloyds had had subsidiaries which operated in discrete overseas markets, but *the extent of cross-border operation was minimal* [emphasis added].[137]

This state of affairs is valid not only for the British clearing banks but also for French *Banques Nationales* and, more generally, for European commercial banks *tout court*. The marginal role of international banking and financial activities was a common feature of European banking in the post-war years up to the early 1970s. This phenomenon was the natural consequence of the pro-growth policies implemented in Europe after the Second World War and the restrictive order devised by the US and UK since the early 1940s, which officially came into being at the Bretton Woods Conference in 1944.

In France 'the state wanted to be able to direct the distribution of credit',[138] and the banking system (the *Banque de France* along with the four main credit establishments) was nationalised. The banking reform of 1945, largely based on the banking reform of 1941 during the Nazi occupation, required French banks to choose between three classes of institution: deposit banks, *banques d'affaires* and medium-term banks, and put the Ministry of Finance at the top of the hierarchy. The four national banks largely dominated all other banking institutions, accounting for 45 per cent of the total assets of registered banks in 1951.[139]

Similarly in the UK, legislative measures such as the statutory reform of the Bank of England, along with the Borrowing Act of 1946 and the Exchange Control Act of 1947, gave unprecedented power to the government in monetary and financial affairs. Post-war planning and reconstruction were based on a profound (and rather justified) distaste on the part of most Western government planners for cross-border speculative financial flows and international banking, which were considered responsible for the disruptions of the inter-war years. People like Morgenthau, Keynes or White never concealed their strong opinions against the banking and financial community. Consequently, from the 1940s until the end of the 1960s, international banking remained tied to 'international trade flows and related exchange operations' and the kind of banking major European banks were doing remained 'fundamentally *similar to that seen in the nineteenth century* [emphasis added]'.[140]

The banking world started to fight back against the perceived limitations imposed on their profession by accepting dollar deposits, creating what came to be known as the Eurodollar market, followed by Eurobonds and syndicated Eurocurrency loans. Since the mid-1950s and to a greater extent after the restrictive measures on the use of sterling for external transactions and the move to external convertibility of the major European currencies, dollars came to be deposited and invested outside American jurisdiction. This market was free from regulation and could be genuinely considered the progenitor of the modern financial system.

In this chapter we have argued that despite the importance of the decade for the history of international finance and the remarkable pace of growth of the Eurocurrency market, it remained a strictly American and European affair involving very few actors. The amounts exchanged on the market were still small compared to domestic banking and banking practices were not much different from those of the early post-war period. The 1950s and early 1960s were still halcyon days.

Notes

1 Daniel Verdier, *Moving Money. Banking and Finance in the Industrialized World*, Cambridge University Press, Cambridge, UK and New York, 2003, 156.
2 Rawi Abdelal, *Capital Rules. The Construction of Global Finance*, Harvard University Press, Cambridge, MA and London, 2007, 44.
3 Howard M. Wachtel, *The Money Mandarins. The Making of a Supranational Economic Order*, M. E. Sharpe, Armonk, New York, 1990, 27.
4 Idem, 92.
5 BIS Annual Report 1964, 127.
6 Bank of England Archives (BEA), Quarterly Bulletin, Volume 10, 1970, 'The International Capital Markets of Europe-The Historical Background', 295.
7 Owen Alan Knopping, 'Why an Interest Equalization Tax?, *William & Mary Law Review*, Vol. 5, Issue 2, 1964, 230–279.
8 BEA, Quarterly Bulletin, Volume 10, 1970, 'The International Capital Markets of Europe-The Historical Background', 297.
9 BEA, 8A406/3, Speech by Sir George Bolton entitled 'The Future of the Euro-Currency Market' at the Sixth International Investment Symposium organised by P. N. Kemp-Gee & Co, King's College, Cambridge, 25–30 June 1972.
10 Idem.
11 Youssef Cassis, 'Before the Storm: European Banks in the 1950s', in S. Battilossi and Y. Cassis (eds), *European Banks and the American Challenge*, Oxford University Press, Oxford, UK and New York, 2002, 49.
12 Idem, 38.
13 A contemporary survey on the European banking sector in the early post-war period is R. S. Sayers (ed.), *Banking in Western Europe*, Oxford University Press, London, 1961. See also Benjamin Haggott Beckhart (ed.), *Banking Systems*, Columbia University Press, New York, 1954.
14 Joel Métais, 'International Strategies of French Banks', in Christian De Boissieu (ed.), *Banking in France*, Routledge, London and New York, 1990, 136.
15 For an overview of the Bretton Woods system, see for example, Bordo and Eichengreen, (eds), *A Retrospective on the Bretton Woods System: Lessons for International Monetary Reform*, University of Chicago, Chicago, IL and London, 1993. The negotiations of Bretton Woods have been the subject of many books; the most notable is the seminal work of Richard N. Gardner, *Sterling-Dollar Diplomacy in Current Perspective (New, Expanded Edition)*, Columbia University Press, New York, 1980. A more recent account can be found in Benn Steil, *The Battle of Bretton Woods: John Maynard Keynes, Harry Dexter White, and the Making of a New World Order*, Princeton University Press, Princeton, NJ and Oxford, UK, 2013. See also,

Eric Helleiner, *Forgotten Foundations of Bretton Woods. International Development and the Making of the Postwar Order*, Cornell University Press, Ithaca, NY and London, 2014.

16 Richard N. Gardner, *Sterling-Dollar Diplomacy in Current Perspective (New, Expanded Edition)*, Columbia University Press, New York, 1980, 68.

17 Idem, 71.

18 Idem, 73.

19 Idem, 74–75.

20 Ibid.

21 The reference in this field remains the *magnum opus* of Lord Skidelsky, Keynes' biographer, in three volumes.

22 *Chicago Tribune*, 'Banks Affirm Opposition to Global Plans', 30 September 1943.

23 *New York Times*, 'Post-War Program Outlined by Bank', 28 September 1943.

24 *Financial Times*, 'Bretton Woods Plan Attacked', 25 September 1944.

25 For a history of the sterling area, the reference is Catherine Schenk, *Britain and the Sterling Area. From Devaluation to Convertibility in the 1950s*, Routledge, London and New York, 1994.

26 *New York Times*, 'British Tie U.S. Aid to Bretton Woods', 28 November 1945.

27 Armand Van Dormael, *The Power of Money*, Macmillan Press, London and Basingstoke, UK, 1997, 64.

28 Fred L. Block, *The Origins of International Economic Disorder*, UCLA Press, Berkeley, CA and London, 1977, 53.

29 *New York Times*, 'Defends Bretton Woods: Morgenthau takes exception to Bankers Group's report', 6 February 1945.

30 Fred L. Block, *The Origins of International Economic Disorder*, UCLA Press, Berkeley, CA and London, 1977, 40.

31 Idem, 41.

32 Eric Helleiner, *States and the Reemergence of Global Finance*, Cornell University Press, Ithaca, NY and London, 1994, 49.

33 G. John Ikenberry, 'A World Economy Restored: Expert Consensus and the Anglo-American Postwar Settlement', *International Organization*, Vol. 46, No. 1, Winter 1992, 297.

34 Rawi Abdelal, *Capital Rules. The Construction of Global Finance*, Harvard University Press, Cambridge, MA, and London, 2007, 44.

35 Maurice Obstfeld and Alan M. Taylor, *Global Capital Markets. Integration, Crisis and Growth*, Cambridge University Press, Cambridge, UK and New York, 2004, 147.

36 In his PhD dissertation, White demonstrated that the effects of unfettered capital mobility on the prewar French economy were not unambiguously positive and that some measure of control of the volume and direction of foreign investments was desirable. See Jeffrey M. Chwieroth, *Capital Ideas. The IMF and the Rise of Financial Liberalization*, Princeton University Press, Princeton, NJ and Oxford, UK, 2010, 67.

37 G. John Ikenberry, 'A World Economy Restored: Expert Consensus and the Anglo-American Postwar Settlement', *International Organization*, Vol. 46, No. 1, Winter 1992, 300.

38 Idem, 301.

39 Richard N. Gardner, 'The Political Setting', in A. L. K. Acheson, J. F. Chant and M. F. J. Prachowny, *Bretton Woods Revisited*, Macmillan Press, London and Basingstoke, UK, 1972.

40 Scott Newton, 'Keynesianism, Sterling Convertibility, and British Reconstruction 1940–1952', in Ranald Michie and Philip Williamson (eds), *The British Government and the City of London in the Twentieth Century*, Cambridge University Press, Cambridge, UK and New York, 2004, 259.

41 Armand Van Dormael, *The Power of Money*, Macmillan Press, London and Basingstoke, UK, 1997, 66.

42   For an overview on American post-war foreign aid policies see: Robert E. Wood, *From Marshall Plan to Debt Crisis. Foreign Aid and Development Choices in the World Economy*, University of California Press, Berkeley, CA and London, 1986; Barbara Stallings, *Banker to the Third World. U.S. Portfolio Investment in Latin America, 1900–1986*, University of California Press, Berkeley, CA and London, 1987.

43   Poul Høst-Madsen, 'Changing Role of International Capital Flows', *The Journal of Finance*, Vol. 18, No. 2 (May 1963), 195.

44   Jeffry Frieden, 'Third World Indebted Industrialization: International Finance and State Capitalism in Mexico, Brazil, Algeria, and South Korea', *International Organization*, Vol. 35, No. 3 (Summer 1981), 407–408.

45   On the role of the French government on French international economic expansion, see Laurence Badel, *Diplomatie et grands contrats: L'Etat français et les marchés extérieurs au XXe siècle*, Publications de la Sorbonne, Paris, 2010.

46   On the Export-Import Bank see: William H. Becker and William M. McClenahan, *The Market, the State, and the Export-Import Bank of the United States*, Cambridge University Press, Cambridge, UK and New York, 2003.

47   Poul Høst-Madsen, 'Changing Role of International Capital Flows', *The Journal of Finance*, Vol. 18, No. 2 (May 1963), 187.

48   On the origins of the Euromarkets see, for example, Geoffrey Bell, *The Euro-Dollar Market and the International Financial System*, Macmillan, London and Basingstoke, UK, 1973; E. Wayne Clendenning, *The Euro-Dollar Market*, Clarendon Press, Oxford, UK, 1970; Paul Einzig, *The Euro-Dollar System. Practice and Theory of International Interest Rates*, Macmillan, London, 1967; C. J. Scanlon and H. V. Prochnow, *L'Eurodollar*, Calmann-Lévy, Paris, 1971; Gunter Dufey and Ian H. Giddy, *The International Money Market*, Prentice-Hall, NJ, 1978; Paolo Savona and George Sutija, *Eurodollars and International Banking*, Macmillan Press, Basingstoke, UK, 1985; Jeffry Frieden, *Banking on the World. The Politics of American International Finance*, Harper & Row, New York, 1987, 79–122; Richard Roberts (with C. Arnander), *Take Your Partners. Orion, The Consortium Banks and the Transformation of the Euromarkets*, Palgrave, Basingstoke, UK, 2001, 3–15; Catherine R. Schenk, 'The Origins of the Eurodollar Market in London: 1955–1963', *Explorations in Economic History*, 35, 221–238; Gary Burn, *The Re-Emergence of Global Finance*, Palgrave Macmillan, Basingstoke, UK and New York, 2006.

49   Armand Van Dormael, *The Power of Money*, Macmillan Press, London and Basingstoke, UK, 1997, 91.

50   Jeffry Frieden, *Banking on the World. The Politics of American International Finance*, Harper & Row, New York, 1987, 81.

51   This simple definition is borrowed from Robert Z. Aliber, *The New International Money Game* (6th edition), The University of Chicago Press, Chicago, IL, 2000, 125.

52   See for example www.federalreserve.gov/datadownload.

53   On William McChesney Martin, see: Robert P. Bremner, *Chairman of the Fed. William McChesney Martin Jr. and the Creation of the Modern American Financial System*, Yale University Press, CT and London, 2004.

54   Aaron Major, 'The Fall and Rise of Financial Capital', *Review of International Political Economy*, 15: 5, December 1943.

55   The account is reported in Armand Van Dormael, *The Power of Money*, Macmillan Press, London and Basingstoke, UK, 1997, 90.

56   Paul Einzig, *The Euro-Dollar System. Practice and Theory of International Interest Rates* (Fourth Edition), Macmillan, London, 1970, 4.

57   Ibid.

58   Banque de France Archives (BFA), 1495200501-577, Confidential Report 'The Continental Dollar Market' written by Alan R. Holmes and Fred H. Klopstock, 26 August 1960.

59   Idem.

60 Robert B. Johnston, *The Economics of the Euro-Market*, Macmillan, London and Basingstoke, UK, 1983, 10.

61 Richard Roberts (with C. Arnander), *Take Your Partners. Orion, The Consortium Banks and the Transformation of the Euromarkets*, Palgrave, Basingstoke, UK, 2001, 5.

62 A good survey of capital controls introduced in the US is John Hewson and Eisuke Sakakibara, 'The Impact of U.S. Controls on Capital Outflows on the U.S. Balance of Payments: An Exploratory Study', *IMF Staff Papers* (1975) 22, 37–60.

63 The Banking Act of 1933 established controls over deposit interest rates for commercial banks that were members of the Federal Reserve System and the Banking Act of 1935 extended the same controls over non-member commercial banks.

64 BFA, 1495200501-577, Confidential Report 'The Continental Dollar Market' written by Alan R. Holmes and Fred H. Klopstock, 26 August 1960.

65 BIS Annual Report 1964, 138.

66 BEA, 6A123/1, Confidential 'Report of Meeting of Experts on the Euro-Currency Market at the BIS', 9–11 November 1963.

67 BFA, 1495200501-578, Direction Générale des Services Étrangers, 'Deuxième Réunion sur l'Euro-Dollar à Bâle 9–11 Novembre 1963', 14 November 1963.

68 BIS Annual Report 1964, 135.

69 Idem.

70 Idem.

71 Idem.

72 Richard Roberts (with C. Arnander), *Take Your Partners. Orion, The Consortium Banks and the Transformation of the Euromarkets*, Palgrave, Basingstoke, UK, 2001, 8.

73 On the birth of the Eurobond market, its origins and impact, see Kathleen Burk, 'Witness Seminar on the Origins and Early Development of the Eurobond Market', *Contemporary European History*, Vol. 1, No. 1 (Mar. 1992), 65–87; Niall Ferguson, 'Siegmund Warburg, the City of London and the financial roots of European integration', *Business History*, Vol. 51, Issue 3, 2009, 364–382. Ferguson mistakenly affirms that the *Autostrade* bond was a six-year loan. See also, N. Ferguson, *High Financier: The Lives and Times of Siegmund Warburg*, Penguin Press, New York, 2010.

74 Robert L. Genillard, 'The Eurobond Market', *Financial Analysts Journal*, Vol. 23, No. 2, (Mar.–Apr. 1967), 144.

75 BEA, 6A123/4, 'Meeting of Experts on the Euro-Currency Market at the BIS', 6–7 July 1967.

76 Idem.

77 Idem.

78 Idem.

79 Idem.

80 Idem.

81 BEA, 6A123/5, 'Recent Trends in and Future Outlook for the Euro-Currency Market', Economic Intelligence Department, 11 April 1969.

82 BEA, 6A123/5, 'Trends in the Structure of the Euro-Currency Market in London', 23 May 1969.

83 Claudio Borio, Gianni Toniolo and Piet Clement (eds), *The Past and Future of Central Bank Cooperation*, Cambridge University Press, Cambridge, UK, 2008, 49.

84 Fred Hirsch, *Social Limits to Growth*, Routledge, London, 1977.

85 International Monetary Fund Archives (IMFA), DM 69/82, 'Some Wider Implications of the Euro-Dollar Market', Research Department, 17 December 1969, Electronic Document.

86 Bank for International Settlements Archives (BIS), 7.15 (1) G10 D22, 'Informal Record of a Meeting of the Standing Committee of Central Bank Officials on the Euro-Currency Market', 6 April 1972.

87 Lawrence Krause, 'Private International Finance', *International Organization*, Vol. 25, Issue 3, June 1971, 526.

88 *Bundesbank* Annual Report 1969, 1.

89 Ibid.

90 Ibid.

91 BEA, 6A123/6, Confidential Report of the Economic Intelligence Unit 'Euro-Currency Market', 4 June 1969.

92 *Bundesbank* Annual Report 1969, 13.

93 In a document entitled 'The Experience of the Deutsche Bundesbank with External Money Flows' (28 January 1972), sent to R. Larre, Otmar Emminger, Deputy President, wrote:

> In some of these periods [1969 to 1972], *the Bundesbank deliberately refrained from taking restrictive monetary action*, or took action not indicated by the domestic situation, in order not to stimulate even higher inflows of foreign funds. Thus during a large part of 1969 (up to the up evaluation [sic] of the DM in October 1969) the Bundesbank refrained from the necessary tightening of the monetary situation. In 1970, the Bundesbank began lowering its rediscount rate from July onward in various steps *in order to follow the downward movement of interest rates in the Euromarkets*, while publicly proclaiming that this was not justified by domestic considerations [emphasis added].
>
> (BIS Archives, 13(a)3 Vol. 9–11)

For a general account of the post-war monetary events see, for example Leland B. Yeager, 'From Gold to the Ecu: The International Monetary System in Retrospect', in *Money and the Nation State*, Kevin Dowd and Richard H. Timberlake (eds), Transaction Publishers, New Brunswick, NJ and London, 1998.

94 BEA, 6A123/7, letter from R. G. R (?) to Jeremy Morse, 'The Euro-Dollar Market and the B.I.S. Paper Joint Supervision of the Euro-Currency market', 23 December 1970.

95 Gianni Toniolo, *Central Bank Cooperation at the Bank for International Settlements, 1930–1973*, Cambridge University Press, Cambridge, UK and New York, 2005, 464.

96 Idem, 465.

97 Eric Helleiner, *States and the Reemergence of Global Finance*, Cornell University Press, Ithaca, NY and London, 1994, 105.

98 Speech of Chairman William McChesney Martin reported in BEA 6A123/7, BIS document 'Joint Supervision of the Euro-Currency Market', 10 January 1971.

99 BEA, 6A123/6, Secret Document 'Euro-Currency Meeting-Basle', 9–10 June 1969.

100 BFA, Minutes of the Board of the Bank of France, 12 September 1969.

101 BEA, 6A123/7, 'Joint Supervision of the Euro-Currency Market', 10 December 1970.

102 *Bundesbank* Annual Report 1971, 23.

103 Organisation for Economic Co-operation and Development Archives (OECDA), Documents of the WP3 1971, Confidential Note, 'Working Party No. 3 of the Economic Policy Committee Examination of the Problems Arising from Mobile Capital Flows and the Working of Euro-currency Market', CPE/WP3(71)10, 24 May 1971.

104 BEA, 6A123/7, 'The Euro-Dollar Market and the B.I.S. Paper Joint Supervision of the Euro-Currency Market', 23 December 1970.

105 Ibid.

106 BEA, 6A123/7, letter from R. C. H. Hallett to Jeremy Morse (later Chairman of Lloyds Bank 1977–93), 4 January 1971.

107 The Group of 10 (G-10) consisted of the Central Banks that had agreed to participate in the General Agreements to Borrow of the International Monetary Fund. The Group included: Belgium, Canada, France, Germany, Italy, Japan, Netherlands, Sweden, the UK and the US. Switzerland had joined the Group in 1964 as the eleventh member but the Group kept the old name.

108 BEA 6 A123/7, Note of the BIS Working Group, 17 February 1971.

109 *The Times*, 'Should the Eurodollar market be controlled?', 22 June 1971.

110 Idem.

111 Eric Helleiner, *States and the Reemergence of Global Finance*, Cornell University Press, Ithaca, NY and London, 1994, 82.

112 Geoffrey Jones, *British Multinational Banking 1830–1990*, Clarendon Press, Oxford, UK and New York, 1993, 320.

113 Youssef Cassis, 'Before the Storm: European Banks in the 1950s', in S. Battilossi and Y. Cassis (eds), *European Banks and the American Challenge*, Oxford University Press, Oxford, UK, 2002, 36.

114 John Edwin Wadsworth, 'United Kingdom of Great Britain and Northern Ireland', in Benjamin Haggott Beckhart (ed.), *Banking Systems*, Columbia University Press, New York, 1954, 780.

115 Lothar Gall, Gerald D. Feldman, Harold James, Carl-Ludwig Holtfrerich and Hans E. Büschgen, *Die Deutsche Bank 1870–1995*, Weidenfeld & Nicholson, London, 1995, 749.

116 On the history of COMIT see: Carlo Brambilla, Carlo Azeglio Ciampi, Andrea Manzella and Romano Prodi, *La Sfida Internazionale della Comit*, Il Mulino, Bologna, 2013. See also: Gianni Toniolo, *Cent'anni, 1894–1994. La Banca Commerciale e l'economia Italiana*, Banca Commerciale Italiana, Milano, 1994.

117 Stefano Battilossi and Youssef Cassis (eds), *European Banks and the American Challenge*, Oxford University Press, Oxford, UK and New York, 2002, 43.

118 Goodenough was born in Calcutta, the third son of an East India merchant. He was educated at the University of Zürich and, later, obtained the post of assistant secretary with the Hudson's Bay Company. After an experience at the Union Bank of London he was nominated as the first company secretary of Barclay & Co. In 1913, he was appointed General Manager, when Barclays' first chairman, F. A. Bevan, retired in 1916 he was the natural successor.

119 Sir Julian Crossley and John Blandford, *The DCO Story. A History of Banking in Many Countries 1925–1971*, Barclays Bank International Limited, London, 1975.

120 Idem, 8.

121 Margareth Ackrill and Leslie Hannah, *Barclays. The Business of Banking 1690–1996*, Cambridge University Press, Cambridge, UK, 2001, 83.

122 Idem, 171.

123 Barclays Bank Archives (BBA), 50/5116, General Circular No. 65/1964 'Bank of London and Montreal Limited', 29 July 1964.

124 Sir Julian Crossley and John Blandford, *The DCO Story. A History of Banking in Many Countries 1925–1971*, Barclays Bank International Limited, London, 1975, 236.

125 MBO was a managerial theory developed by Peter Ferdinand Drucker in his book *The Practice of Management*, Harper and Row, New York, 1954. Drucker proposed that bosses should set the company's overall goals and subsequently, in discussion with each employee, agree on a subset of individual goals. These individual goals had to be, in Drucker's vision, SMART (specific, measurable, actionable, realistic and time-sensitive).

126 Barclays Bank Archives (BBA), 80/5369, Urwick, Orr and Partners Report No. 9 'Organisation', 2 January 1969.

127 BBA, Barclays DCO Report and Accounts 1967.

128 Margareth Ackrill and Leslie Hannah, *Barclays. The Business of Banking 1690–1996*, Cambridge University Press, Cambridge, UK, 2001, 277.

129 Idem, 301.

130 A. R. Holmes and Edwin Green, *Midland. 150 Years of Banking Business*, B. T. Batsford, London, 1986, 249.

131 Eric Bussière, François Gallice and Roger Nougaret, 'Regards sur la politique internationale du Crédit Lyonnais, 1945–1990', in Bernard Desjardins, Michel Lescure,

Roger Nougaret, Alain Plessis, André Straus (eds), *Le Crédit Lyonnais*, Droz, Geneva, 2002, 668.

132 Crédit Lyonnais Archives (CLA), 110AH14, Exposé de M. de Montbel 'Le Crédit Lyonnais à l'étranger', 9 June 1981.

133 Eric Bussière, François Gallice and Roger Nougaret, 'Regards sur la politique internationale du Crédit Lyonnais, 1945–1990', in Bernard Desjardins, Michel Lescure, Roger Nougaret, Alain Plessis, André Straus (eds), *Le Crédit Lyonnais*, Droz, Geneva, 2002, 670.

134 Lothar Gall, Gerald D. Feldman, Harold James, Carl-Ludwig Holtfrerich and Hans E. Büschgen, *Die Deutsche Bank 1870–1995*, Weidenfeld & Nicolson, London, 1995, 749. On the activities of *Deutsche Bank* in the United States see: Christopher Kobrak, *Banking on Global Markets. Deutsche Bank and the United States, 1870 to the Present*, Cambridge University Press, Cambridge, UK, 2008.

135 Idem, 751.

136 Richard Sylla, 'United States Banks and Europe: Strategy and Attitudes', in S. Battilossi and Y. Cassis (eds), *European Banks and the American Challenge*, Oxford University Press, Oxford, UK, 2002, 56.

137 Duncan M. Ross, 'European Banking Clubs in the 1960s: A Flawed Strategy', *Business and Economic History*, Vol. 27, No. 2, Winter, 1998, 356.

138 Henry Germain-Martin, 'France', in Benjamin Haggott Beckhart (ed.), *Banking Systems*, Columbia University Press, New York, 1954, 230.

139 Idem, 234.

140 Geoffrey Jones, *British Multinational Banking 1830–1990*, Clarendon Press, Oxford, UK and New York, 1993, 320.

2 Half measures

The Eurodollar market has emerged as the largest international money market of the world. Its unique characteristic is that is a truly free market operating above national borders where deposits and loans can be negotiated without direct governmental restrictions or regulations.[1]

The changing face of international banking

From the late 1960s to the early 1970s the European banking and financial landscape gradually departed from the established banking practices of the immediate post-war years and the shape of European banking slowly started to change.

As anticipated in Chapter I, the banking practices in the UK, France but also in the US and Germany, took a clear domestic turn after the Second World War as their operations were made subservient to the reconstruction. Consequently, working in the banking and financial sector after the war was, as the former Chairman of Lloyds, Lord Franks, vividly put it, 'like driving a powerful car at twenty miles an hour. *The banks were anaesthetised* [emphasis added]'.[2]

During the early years of the Euromarket, the British banking sector was cartelised domestically (with the Committee of London Clearing Bankers functioning as its main organ)[3] and still dominated by the old practices of correspondent banking established during the inter-war period when the 'Big Five' came into being.

Despite the fact that British banks could count on around 5,500 branches in almost 70 countries, while its closest competitor, the US, only had 300 direct branches overseas in 1968,[4] British banks abroad were not of a single species. Instead, like at home, they were characterised by specialisation, with overseas banks accounting for the largest share of foreign business. These banks were mostly colonial institutions, largely involved in retail banking and operating in specific geographical regions of the former British Empire. They were active in the financing of trade on a short-term basis while refraining, in most cases, from providing long-term finance or merchant banking services.

Clearing banks had limited representations abroad, except from Europe, and focused on trade finance and advisory services for overseas businesses. Merchant banks had a well-developed web of contacts in Europe, but their structure relied more on informal relationships than direct representations.

This static context came to be progressively modified in the late 1960s and early 1970s when the 'sleeping giants' slowly started to wake up.

British banks were pushed towards increasing competition domestically, in particular with the announcement by the Bank of England of the 'Competition and Credit Control' (CCC)[5] in May 1971 (and its full operation in September 1971), which 'removed regulatory constraints on bank lending' and 'eliminated the clearing banks' right to collude in interest rates, thus ending the price-fixing cartels that the Bank of England had implicitly supported before'.[6] Consequently, as some authors have argued, the CCC was a 'policy less than welcome to what was still a semi-cartelized banking system'.[7] The Governor of the Bank of England, Leslie O'Brien, reported that the eyes of Lloyds' Chairman, Eric Faulkner, 'lit up at the prospect of entering a more competitive era in the banking field'.[8] The CCC was the response to several criticalities that had emerged in the 1960s, notably dissatisfaction with controls on lending, a desire for greater competition and the need to control monetary growth. Previous attempts to address these elements had failed because of short-term crises. The CCC marked an early shift away from the principles of embedded liberalism and 'reflected a preference for indirect rather than direct government control and a belief in market forces'.[9]

Like the CCC in the UK, a set of economic and banking reforms was implemented in 1966–67 by then Finance Minister, Michel Debré, in order to improve the competitiveness of French companies suffering under the weight of increasing international competition because of the accession to the Common Market and the penetration of American banks in Europe. The decrees removed the 'traditional demarcation lines between investment and commercial banking, thus allowing the state-owned banks to develop as full service banks, adding merchant banking and related banking services as well as commercial banking'.[10] A first series of measures reinforced the banking organisation by letting the banks participate more actively in the financing of industrial companies. A second wave of reforms pushed in the direction of an increased access by industrial companies to the financial markets.

If we look at the situation of the individual British and French banks in the late 1960s and early 1970s, we are much more struck by the similarities rather than the differences between the two experiences. Most large European banks were facing similar challenges, but also similar and interrelated opportunities. Four of them can be singled out, notably: internationalisation, internal reorganisations, cooperative banking and autonomous initiatives.

The reopening of international markets, thanks to the creation of the Eurodollar market, represented an incredible opportunity to revive the business of banking after several decades of hibernation and forced retreat inside local boundaries. As often happens, periods of innovation bring opportunities but also several challenges for those late in adapting to the new competitive environment. Because of the forced period of inactivity, the European banking system was in poor competitive shape and not entirely ready for the challenge brought about by internationalisation. British and French banks were operating in the same markets as 50 or 60 years before, the kind of services offered had not changed much since the early twentieth century, neither had their archetypal clients. Those banks were operating, of course, in their domestic markets and in the territories of their colonies, protectorates or overseas dependencies. Retail banking, international payments and trade finance were the main services provided to a clientele made of expatriates and local subjects. The Eurocurrency, the Eurobond and, later, the Euroloan business radically modified the strategies and practices of European banking.

Because of internal and external pressures, European banks were forced to find a way to deal with a world getting gradually smaller and more interconnected. As Duncan Ross has pointed out, European banks adopted two main kinds of strategy to develop their international business, i.e. banking clubs (association of commercial banks) and banking consortia (joint ventures participated in by several commercial banks).[11]

Amongst the largest British and French banks, the first to react was Midland. Starting from the early 1960s, the bank decided to abandon its policy of reliance on correspondent banking and entered what is generally defined as the 'grand design' phase, adopting a two-fold strategy towards cooperative banking. In the 1964 Annual Report, the Chairman, Viscount Monckton of Brenchley, who would die a few months later in January 1965, stated:

> For many years Midland has followed the distinctive policy of not competing in other countries with banks on their home territories, and has built its pre-eminent position in conducting the biggest foreign business in the City of London. Hence the necessity for finding means of closer association in some directions that would not weaken the friendly business relations that we have long enjoyed with thousands of banks abroad. With this end in view the Midland has moved along two paths. By the one we are linked with banks operating in Africa, Australasia and Canada . . . though a new bank to be established in London. By the other we have reached closer understandings with leading banks in Belgium, Holland and West Germany by joining in an agreement to enlarge and deepen co-operation between us in special fields.[12]

The first leg of the strategy linked Midland to *Société Générale de Belgique*, *Deutsche Bank* and the *Amsterdamsche Bank* in the European Advisory Committee (EAC) starting from 1963. The scope of the Committee was to avoid competition in the territory of the other members and to establish joint ventures and consortia to respond to a perceived 'American challenge'. The second part of the strategy pushed Midland to form in 1964 the consortium bank, Midland and International Banks Ltd or MAIBL, together with Toronto Dominion, the Commercial Bank of Australia and the Standard Bank of New York to finance 'large-scale development projects using wholesale deposits'.[13]

Barclays made some incursions into cooperative banking, participating in the creation of *Société Financiére Européenne* (SFE) in 1967 along with *Algemene Bank Nederland*, *Banca Nazionale del Lavoro*, Bank of America, *Banque Nationale de Paris* and *Dresdner Bank*. The goal of the banking consortium was to enable its shareholders to develop jointly their activities in investment banking and the medium-term Eurobond market.[14]

Banking clubs have been especially criticised for their apparent ineffectiveness,[15] but we must not forget how politically fragmented the world was when these arrangements were created. In a European context of heterogeneity in norms and regulations where 'even the largest commercial banks had little experience in international banking',[16] banking clubs represented a seminal step towards limiting the risks involved in establishing a presence abroad by allowing the systematic exchange of information between member banks through meetings and study groups. Almost all the major banks on the continent followed the example of the EAC, and new clubs were created in the early 1970s. Amongst the major banks in the UK, France, Germany and Italy, the most notable outlier was Lloyds, which never joined a banking club despite participating in cooperative banking and keeping solid links with *Crédit Lyonnais* and *Commerzbank*.

European commercial banks responded to the international challenge brought by the Eurodollar market by establishing cooperative operations but also by reshaping their own overseas network. Branches, representative offices and subsidiaries were gradually opened in targeted regions while the ties to correspondent banking were gradually severed.

The target zones did not follow univocal rules. Some banks entered or focused on particular territories because of business heritage or 'path dependence'. Some banks had an existing overseas network, like Barclays or *Crédit Lyonnais*, while others did not, like Midland Bank. Throughout the period analysed, the 'herd instinct' remained strong amongst European banks. When one bank entered a specific country or region, soon its competitors followed suit, possibly as a result of the strong asymmetries of information and regulatory barriers existing in international banking at that time.

Internal reorganisations that followed the reopening of international markets and the post-1973 financial boom represent another major axis of analysis developed in the following chapters. Between the final years of the 1960s and the very first years of the 1970s, all the major banks in our research went through a profound phase of reshaping and rationalisation of their international activities.

Barclays reshaped its foreign subsidiary, DCO, into Barclays Bank International Limited (BBI) in 1971. Lloyds merged the activities of Lloyds Bank Europe and BOLSA into Lloyds & Bolsa International Bank Limited, later renamed Lloyds Bank International (LBI) in 1973. Midland created its international division (Midland Bank International Division, MBID) in 1974.

Société Generale decided to reshape its international activities thanks to the work of its new manager, Marc Viénot, starting from 1973. *Crédit Lyonnais* first started reshaping its international activities earlier than most of its competitors in 1969 with the creation of the international office.

Deutsche Bank, like its domestic competitors, continued to rely on minority holdings, joint ventures and representative offices until the mid-1970s when a new phase of international expansion based on 'going it alone' was inaugurated. To gain an idea of the limited or inexistent direct foreign involvement of German banks, it is worth pointing out that until the end of the 1960s German banks did not have a single branch outside Germany. Thus, most of its early international expansion was strictly associated with European Banks International Company (EBIC), a club formed by the EAC members to push cooperation further, and its story is in many ways similar to those of Midland and *Société Générale*. Its expansion was articulated mainly through international banking consortia created with other EBIC members.

The American Citibank somewhat anticipated the return of international banking thanks to the arrival at the helm of the Overseas Division in 1959 of Walter Wriston. The formation of the European Economic Community (EEC) and the return to convertibility favoured new openings on European soil. A branch was inaugurated in Frankfurt in 1960; two years later branches were inaugurated in Brussels and Milan. But despite the mythology surrounding the 'American invasion', Europe was not at the core of Citibank's strategy.[17] Most of the openings were in the Far East, India and Latin America. Between 1960 and 1967, 85 foreign branches were established, 54 in Latin America and Caribbean, 14 in the Far East, 15 in Europe and 2 in the Middle East.[18] To expand in Europe, American banks preferred to buy smaller banks. Bank of America bought the *Banca d'America e d'Italia* with 83 branches in Italy; Chase Manhattan acquired a stake in the *Banque de Commerce*, with 18 branches in Belgium and in the *Nederlandsche Credietbank*, with 70 branches in the Netherlands. Nonetheless, cross-border lending was picking up slowly. Cross-border exposure in the late 1960s was no more than US$10 million in the Philippines and perhaps US$6 million in India.[19] Despite the advance of American banks in international banking, Citibank would wait until 1972 to create a vehicle devoted exclusively to the Eurocurrency market, Citicorp International Bank Limited (CIBL). In that sense, Citibank lagged behind other continental banks, as we will see in the next section.

Internationalisation and internal reorganisations

By the late 1960s, French and, particularly, British banks started to gradually move away from colonial banking to international banking. Establishing a clear pecking order to justify such a shift would be a vain effort, partly because it was a result of a perceived American challenge, partly because of domestic (deregulatory) forces, partly because of the increasing internationalisation of commerce and trade, and partly because of visionary bankers increasingly interested in overseas opportunities. What is certain is that European banks started reshaping their corporate structures with a particular focus on their international operations. Internationalisation and internal reorganisations represented two faces of the same coin: as banks gradually quit known markets, they needed new structures to better penetrate new ones. Barclays was again at the forefront of this tendency, shutting off Barclays DCO and establishing its new wholly owned subsidiary named BBI in 1971. That same year, Lloyds went through an important reconfiguration merging Lloyds Bank Europe with BOLSA to create Lloyds & Bolsa International Bank Limited. Yet, Midland waited a few more years before altering its international strategy and creating its international division in 1974. In France, *Crédit Lyonnais* created its International Affairs Division in 1969, merging two existing departments, and the following year, as we will see in the next paragraph, formed a new banking club called *Europartners* while *Société Générale* waited until 1973 to reshape its international activities.

Ultimately, a common thread can be found amongst our case studies. In each country studied, there seems to be a leader setting the pace and smaller banks following the lead. In Britain, Barclays radically reshaped its corporate structure and was followed by Lloyds and later Midland. In France, *Crédit Lyonnais* created an international office and participated in a banking club and was followed by *Société Générale*. Another common thread between Barclays and Lloyds is their need to control their international operations through wholly owned subsidiaries. To operate in increasingly interconnected markets, banks needed clear structures under a unified hierarchy, and not be competing against each other.

There are also some specificities that must be highlighted. The internal reorganisations of Barclays and Lloyds consisted of the creation of new entities, while the French banks mainly undertook reorganisations of existing structures. Midland's path was similar to the French banks, creating a division instead of a subsidiary with its own branches. Looking at the cases of Barclays and Lloyds, the reorganisations were markedly different. Barclays' reorganisation went smoothly because, despite its *envergure*, it did not involve third parties and ultimately remained an inside job between sister institutions. Lloyds' experience, on the contrary, involved the acquisition of a new bank and, subsequently, a merger between two distinct banks. The operation was clearly more complex as the two founding banks had different corporate cultures. BOLSA was a rapidly growing institution with a particular interest in the Eurodollar business, while Lloyds Bank Europe was a conservative institution operating in retail banking.

We will now turn to the individual banks to analyse in detail how British and French banks started to move away from colonial banking to international banking.

Barclays' management started to realise by the end of the 1960s, notably in 1969, that the DCO and Barclays Limited were increasingly competing for the same overseas business and clientele. The time had come for Barclays to become a truly global bank and to acquire the remaining 45 per cent shareholding outside its control. The new structure was officially recognised in October 1971 when Barclays DCO became BBI. The new name acknowledged 'a basic change of function and policy which has been taking place over the last five or six years at an accelerating pace'.[20] Figure 2.1 shows the extent of Barclays' DCO activities in 1970.

As remarked by Seebohm in his last statement as Chairman, DCO's business had remained for the previous 40 years a business centred around the Commonwealth and colonies. This state of affairs was a 'logical and economical method of operation when a high proportion of the business was in the sterling area in which funds could be moved from points of surplus liquidity to those areas where money was in short supply'.[21] The reorganisation of the international business continued in 1972 with the takeover by BBI of UK foreign branches of Barclays Limited, Barclays

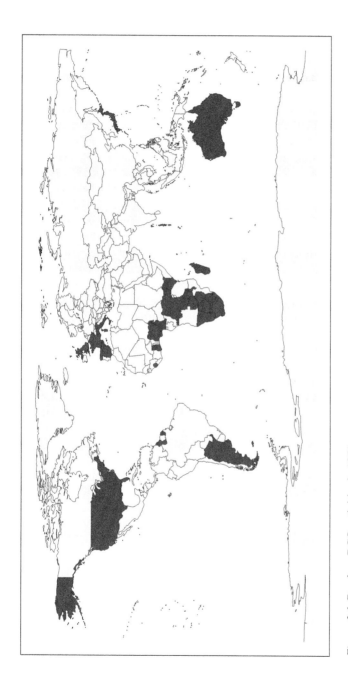

Figure 2.1 Barclays DCO activities in 1971.

Source: The image has been elaborated with the help of my colleague Cédric Chambru with QGIS from sir Julian Crossley and John Blandford, *The DCO Story*, Barclays Bank International Limited, London, 1975, xvi.

Bank SA (the French subsidiary) and some of the overseas trade investments. The final structure of the Barclays Bank Group involved a unified Group board (the Barclays Bank Limited board) under which three divisions were located: the newly created BBI, Barclays Bank UK Management Ltd., under the supervision of T. H. Bevan, and a Financial Services Division, regrouping the activities previously managed by Barclays Bank (London & International) Ltd., Barclays Bank Trust Company, Barclays Export & Finance Company and Barclays Insurance Services, under the supervision of W. G. Bryan.

The departure of Seebohm after the creation of BBI paved the way for the installation at the helm of BBI, in 1972, and of Barclays Limited, in 1973, of the most important person in the recent history of Barclays, Anthony Favill Tuke. Anthony Tuke was the grandson of W. F. Tuke, Chairman of Barclays from 1934 to 1936 and son of A. W. Tuke, Chairman of Barclays from 1951 to 1962.[22] He would remain Chairman of BBI from 1972 until 1979 and Chairman of Barclays Bank from 1973 to 1981. Given his impact on both banks, the 1970s are truly considered to be the 'Tuke years', an era marked by a rapid expansion of Barclays' overseas business and penetration into new markets. In his first statement at the 47th annual general meeting, Tuke clearly stated that the creation of BBI represented a 'transformation . . . *from what one might call an ex-colonial bank to an international bank* [emphasis added]'.[23] The transformation of DCO into BBI was a remarkably smooth process, thanks to the good relations existing between the DCO and Barclays Limited. Managers were sharing similar ideas, were coming from similar backgrounds and many of them traced their origins to the founders of the modern Barclays in 1896. In early 1971 discussions were well under way at the DCO Planning Meeting to define the international five-year plan and consequently the priority areas of the new creature. In the end, it was agreed that North America, Australia, Japan and Europe had the greatest potential for future growth.[24] Clearly, the structure was changing, but the heritage of DCO was still relevant and was reflected in the relatively conservative geographic areas of expansion.

When the BBI five-year plan was ready in August 1971, it ambitiously stated in its first line that 'we have set ourselves the objective of becoming the first British fully international bank'.[25] In order to achieve this goal, BBI had, first, to extend its international representation; second, to develop and extend the types of business undertaken and provide wider services; and, finally, to examine existing operational areas and expand where it was thought desirable.

The 1970s was also a decade of great changes for Lloyds. Until the late 1960s, Lloyds lacked an international presence and was essentially a domestic bank controlling the National Bank of New Zealand and with a minority interest of 25 per cent in National & Grindlays, which had most of its offices in Africa and India, and a minority interest of 19 per cent in BOLSA, which had almost all of its offices in Latin America.

To try to fully understand the complex process of becoming a global bank, we must go back to the last years of the 1960s and to the figure of William M. Clarke, City editor and then Financial and Industrial Editor for *The Times* from 1957 to 1966 and later, amongst many other occupations, Chairman of the Committee on Invisible Exports, the predecessor of the actual International Financial Services London.

In 1968 the Chairman of Lloyds, Eric Odin Faulkner, asked Clarke to study the position of the international activities of Lloyds with respect to its competitors. Faulkner, who would be knighted in 1974, gave a crucial contribution to radically change the business model of Lloyds Bank and push it towards a truly international dimension.[26]

After two months of research, a confidential report was prepared and presented to the Chairman in November 1968. The report, which would influence the entire international expansion of Lloyds throughout the 1970s, depicted a gloomy scenario for the bank. First of all, Clarke saw two big trends in world banking with far-reaching potential. The first was a rapprochement between the clearing banks and merchant banks, citing as an example Midland and Samuel Montagu and National Provincial and Rothschild. The second trend was the creation of international consortia. With respect to these two developments, Clarke remarked that 'Lloyds seems to be the only one of the Big Four to have participated in neither of these developments'.[27] Besides, other long-term structural changes were shaping or about to shape British banking. The first of these forces was the boom in world trade, which had increased the demands placed by firms on 'their financial mentors'. Connected to this phenomenon was the emergence of international companies with manufacturing plants all round the world, which demanded services that 'a correspondent relationship with local banks cannot provide'. The third change was the emergence of the Eurodollar market. The fourth one was the 'changing roles of the Pound and the Dollar', with the proportion of reserves held in pounds dropping from 16 to 12 per cent between 1953 and 1962 and the role of the sterling in international trade dropping from 50 per cent after the Second World War to 25 per cent.

So what lessons could Lloyds draw from this rapidly changing world? Before answering this important question, Clarke embarked on a comparison of the Big Four, and the results for Lloyds were not entirely encouraging.

He remarked that amongst the Big Four, Midland had 1,200 correspondent banks, Westminster 800, Barclays 650, Lloyds 500 and National Provincial 450. It is true that Lloyds relied more on associated banks, but the gap was still relevant. Concerning foreign subsidiaries, the most striking fact was the dominance of Barclays, thanks to its 55 per cent share in Barclays DCO. It is clear that for Clarke, Barclays was the model to pursue because 'not only is it the largest, it is also one of the best balanced, with the best representation in Europe and the United States . . . and a relatively small commitment to the less developed world'. Another advantage of Barclays was the consortium of SFE with other European and American banks.

With respect to the other clearing banks the picture was less gloomy, particularly thanks to the activities of Lloyds Bank Europe in France, the Netherlands, Monaco and Switzerland and its participations in National & Grindlays, covering the Indian Subcontinent, the Middle East and East and Central Africa, and

BOLSA, covering South America and the Iberian peninsula. Nonetheless, there was an important catch.

> This admirable spread of interest conceals the fact that in most cases the *Lloyds direct interest is relatively small*. The only internationally important subsidiary where it has a full controlling interest is National Bank of New Zealand. While National & Grindlays and Bolsa may have complementary world branch networks, Lloyds cannot yet think of these branches as part of a world-wide group as can Barclays [emphasis added].

Another weakness of Lloyds concerned consortium banking. On this point, Clarke remarked: 'In consortium banking the position appears more serious for Lloyds . . . Unlike Barclays, National Westminster, and Midland, Lloyds seem to have no direct links with banks of world stature'. Barclays had SFE, National Westminster had the International Commercial Bank and Midland had the *Banque Européenne de Credit* (BEC) in Brussels, while 'Lloyds is the only member of the big four not to be involved in the consortia banks for medium-term lending'.

Finally, the Clarke report highlighted four priorities for Lloyds: 1) developing and consolidating Lloyds Bank Europe; 2) working out relationships with existing associated overseas banks, i.e. National & Grindlays and BOLSA especially in relation to the Eurodollar market; 3) 'urgently' considering relationships with American banks; and 4) considering the addition of merchant banking and widening overseas coverage through vertical mergers.

The report made a strong impression on Eric Faulkner and the top management of Lloyds. The world of banking was changing rapidly after 40 years of (forced) lethargy, and decisions had to be taken as soon as possible to avoid the risk of losing its status as one of the top banks in the UK and Europe. Two months after receiving the report, Faulkner decided to create an 'International Banking Committee' composed of six high-ranking managers to study the practical implications for Lloyds' international strategy. The first meeting of the Committee took place in February 1969 and Clarke attended it too. The issues discussed were the American challenge, the merits of consortium banking and the four priorities mentioned by Clarke.

During the second meeting in March the creation of or the participation in a consortium was excluded for 'it offered nothing that we did not already enjoy and our participation could not be justified'.[28] In the same meeting a crucial decision was taken. A great potential was recognised in Latin American countries as purveyors of capital to European banks. In order to benefit from such developments, it was agreed that Lloyds Bank Europe and BOLSA had to jointly extend their operations on the continent. The two banks had to explore how to extend their expertise in placing Eurobonds in order not to be forced to rely on specialist brokers. Ultimately:

> The Committee agreed that priority must be given to deciding whether we should proceed alone in expanding our international business, or jointly with Barclays, forming a Lloyds-Barclays International Bank, which could

incorporate Barclays DCO and Bolsa . . . if we proceed alone, it would be initially by the development of Lloyds Bank Europe and the exploitation of Bolsa and we should consider the practicability of acquiring the whole of the Bolsa equity held by the public. Cost would be a decisive factor and an investigation will now be made to determine this.[29]

The decision was taken to act independently, and the members of the Committee did not waste time. Exploratory talks were started with BOLSA's management, a mission to South America was deployed, but the results were mixed. J. I. Kennan, who headed the mission, reported in the third meeting of the Committee in April 1969 that 'Bolsa was in no way conscious of the substantial shareholding of Lloyds Bank and did not consider itself in any sense part of the "Lloyds Bank Group"'.[30]

Despite the lukewarm reception in Latin America, the Committee was decided that 'BOLSA is poised for development and that a controlling interest appears very desirable, not only as an insurance for the future, but to give us the right to an effective control in their affairs'.[31]

The Committee agreed that the first step in building up its overseas presence was to increase its participation in BOLSA to 26 per cent, which, together with Mellon Bank (the other major shareholder since 1965), would have given joint control of the company. Before submitting a recommendation to the board, nonetheless, they had to: test the reaction of the *deus ex machina* of BOLSA, Sir George Bolton, who had joined BOLSA in 1957 after a career spent at the Bank of England; understand the views of Mellon Bank and the reaction of the Latin American financial community; look into BOLSA's books for the last five years; and, finally, have a confirmation of the benevolence of the Merger Panel.

For its part, Faulkner had already asked for the Governor's viewpoint and, fortunately, he had indicated in informal discussion that 'no question of principle was involved and that in fact such an acquisition would be encouraged'.[32]

Before the last meeting of the Committee, Faulkner met Bolton and he was given the 'true figures' (i.e. inner reserves and true profits) for the years 1964–68 on a strictly Chairman to Chairman basis, but time was running short for, as reported in the third meeting of the Committee: 'Bolsa was actively considering extending its operations in Europe in the immediate future, and unless we obtained some measure of control now it was inevitable that Bolsa would be competing directly with Lloyds Bank Europe, which was highly undesirable'.[33]

In 1969, BOLSA was a large overseas bank (much larger than LBE, as we can see from Table 2.1) with 1,200 employees in the UK and almost 7,000 abroad. It conducted three main businesses: commercial banking and financial activities, international banking and investment, and trading and commerce. It had four branches in the UK (London, Birmingham, Manchester and Bradford), seven branches in Europe (one in France, two in Portugal and four in Spain), one branch in New York. However, its activities were largely based in Latin America where it had 31 branches in Argentina, 14 in Brazil, 5 in Chile (plus 3 agencies), 2 in Paraguay (plus 2 agencies), 1 in Peru (plus 4 agencies) and 1 in Uruguay (plus 13 agencies). In addition, it had representative offices in Mexico City, Glasgow,

Table 2.1 Bolsa's and Lloyds Bank Europe revenues and expenditures (£m), 1965–69.

Bolsa	1965	1966	1967	1968	1969
Revenues	13.897	16.643	19.176	24.134	24.028
Expenditures	10.734	11.836	13.339	16.317	18.255
Lloyds Bank Europe	*1965*	*1966*	*1967*	*1968*	*1969*
Revenues	2.372	2.538	2.885	4.115	5.446
Expenditures	1.726	1.720	1.959	2.454	2.697

Source: LBA, HO/Ch/Fau/11–24, Memorandum 'Information relating to the Bank of London and South America Limited' by Cooper Brothers & Co. Chartered Accountants, 17 March 1970. LBA, HO/Ch/Fau/11–24, Memorandum prepared by Lloyds' advisor Morgan Green-fell entitled 'Apollo', 19 May 1970.

Zurich and Pittsburgh. Its deposits grew from £114 million in 1957 to £415 million in 1963 and £545 million in 1969.

The risk was then to find a new competitor on the Continent in a short space of time after the perceived American invasion started in the mid-1960s. There was another risk for Lloyds which called for immediate action:

> If we decided to dispose of our shares the Committee was in no doubt that Barclays would endeavour to acquire them, as they were clearly anxious to get a foothold in South America. This again would result in Lloyds Bank Europe facing direct competition from BOLSA in Europe.[34]

With these two daunting prospects for Lloyds Bank Europe looming on the horizon, the Committee grew stronger in its intention to act during its fourth and last meeting. The Committee agreed that the control of BOLSA was 'essential' not only to prevent them from 'queering the pitch' in Europe for LBE, but also for the 'invaluable expertise in international merchant banking that would be available to us and could be utilised for our own future international banking operations'. Finally, it was agreed to increase Lloyds's shareholding to an amount that would give the bank joint control with Mellon and preclude Barclays from 'any opportunity of gaining direct or indirect control'.[35]

During its four meetings, the Committee had set the strategy for Lloyds and its international expansion. The following months were spent pursuing the discussions with Sir George Bolton, in parallel with the Bank of England and Mellon Bank, after which in July 1969 the Board of Lloyds had agreed to Faulkner's proposal to increase its shareholding to 40 per cent.

The first step was thus to get the full approval of Bolton. After a first talk in April, a second call from Faulkner followed in August. On this occasion, Faulkner insisted that Lloyds was 'moving towards the conception of a Lloyds Group with a strong international flavour' and that '[Lloyds] had concluded that the first and most important step for Lloyds was the further investment in Bolsa and a closer partnership with Mellon therein'.[36]

Faulkner informed Bolton that he would sit on the Board of BOLSA. Bolton manifested his support for an increase in Lloyds' and Mellon's interests in BOLSA and for the proposals of Faulkner. With Bolton's approval, the second step of Faulkner's strategy was to convince Mellon to agree to its plan and to accept becoming a minority shareholder in a bank with Lloyds as the biggest shareholder.

The first serious contact with top management of Mellon arrived at the end of 1969 when Faulkner sent a letter to Mellon's Chairman, John A. Mayer. From the reply that he sent to London in January 1970, it became clear the merger was not an easy task. In Mayer's eyes, the merger would make sense because Lloyds brought a banking operation with continental branches and a stream of earnings, BOLSA brought a solid expertise in international banking and an established presence in Latin America, while Mellon provided much needed dollar capital and close contacts with an important section of North American industry which had widely invested in Europe. Nevertheless, Lloyds' ambition to acquire a controlling interest in BOLSA gave Mayer some 'fundamental concern'. The original investment in BOLSA had been justified by Mellon's will to compete with its major domestic competitors despite its limited international capabilities. The idea was to control BOLSA jointly with Lloyds. Nevertheless:

> [It] Would clearly not be workable if one partner had absolute control. When you told me in Washington that you were considering acquiring shares of Bolsa in the open market to bring your participation up to perhaps 40%, I saw no particular difficulty . . . However, with Lloyds controlling 'new' Bolsa, I think we are considering an entirely different position . . . Should we continue to maintain or even increase our investment in the merged bank with a single stockholder holding more than 51% (even where the stockholder was such a good friend as Lloyds), *we would in fact be subjecting an important part of our international competence to the control of another* [emphasis added].[37]

After this cold shower for Lloyds, Mayer was invited to London in February 1970 to discuss matters personally with Faulkner. Thanks to their good relationship and some assurances from Lloyds that the interest of Mellon would not fall below 10 per cent, the two Chairmen managed to find common ground with Mayer saying, 'I am pleased to say that Mellon Bank has no objections in seeing our discussion move forward', even though Mayer remarked that, 'I would be less than candid with you if I didn't admit to the feeling that *some hard bargaining is ahead of us* [emphasis added]'.[38]

The first approval came from Mellon in April 1970, Coopers Brothers & Co. were chosen as BOLSA's advisers, while Morgan Grenfell represented Lloyds' side. The first of a long series of monthly meetings with all the parties involved took place in May 1970 at Lloyds' headquarters in Lombard Street, with Faulkner acting as Chair. 'Operation Apollo' (probably a reference to the challenging task and to the landing on the Moon by Apollo 11 a few months earlier) could finally start even though the definitive approval from Mellon's Board did not arrive until September 1970.

After Mellon's first approval, Faulkner and his top managers thought that the hardest part was done. Unfortunately, negotiations proved to be much more complicated than expected for Lloyds and BOLSA had a very different corporate culture.

As we mentioned, Lloyds was a domestic and conservative bank with limited experience of overseas markets and the financial innovations of the last decade, while at BOLSA 'they were excited by the opportunities for world-wide growth'.[39] Lloyds was especially concerned by some matters 'arising from this speculative dealing philosophy, which extends to other areas of BOLSA's activities, sterling and international money market operations as well as trading in Euro-Bonds, off-shore funds and gilts'.[40] The bulk of BOLSA's profits was indeed coming from speculative positions on the foreign exchange market.

The clash of cultures between the two banks is one of the reasons why the merger took quite some time. BOLSA viewed LBE as a boring bank, not adapting to the changes in international banking and finance (especially concerning the Euromarket), as reported by BOLSA in the account of the joint meeting of July 1970: 'Their [LBE] philosophy was that there was no merit in taking unnecessary risks'. The views of BOLSA on LBE were crudely expressed in a paper entitled 'A Bolsa View of Lloyds Bank Europe'; the document was a shock to Lloyds' management.

BOLSA criticised Lloyds' experience on the Eurocurrency market, stating that as they had only entered the market at the end of 1967, they were therefore inexperienced. They also criticised the fact that commercial lending was static except for the business channelled from the parent bank; LBE seemed unprepared to face increasing competition by taking 'time difference risks on a major scale'; it was a sterling bank; their business in Europe was lagging; they were going for 'first class' clients and thus low margin business and that that was not a viable policy 'for the building of a bank in the future'[41].

It was a setback, and during the joint meeting in July 1970, Faulkner explained that 'the Bolsa paper on LBE had arrived without any introduction and had caused a shock, for it seemed that the previously agreed view of the need for the merger had been eroded'. BOLSA's management was not expecting such a response and they were forced to acknowledge that the scope of the paper was to get a more favourable pricing of their shares or, in their words, 'striking the right price'. Nevertheless, Sir Maurice Parson of BOLSA reiterated that 'Bolsa was still enthusiastic to establish the relationship'.[42]

The negotiations went on and, finally, by the end of the summer 1970, an agreement was found. A press communiqué was issued stating that:

> [o]n 1st September 1970 Lloyds Bank Limited ('Lloyds') and Bolsa announced that agreement had been reached in principle for a merger of Bolsa and LBE (a wholly owned subsidiary of Lloyds). The intention of the merger is to lead to the integration, as far as practicable, of the operations of

Bolsa outside Latin America with those of LBE in a new international banking company, while Bolsa continue to carry on its Latin American business
under its existing name.[43]

The new entity would be called 'Lloyds & Bolsa International Bank Limited',
Lloyds Bank would own approximately 52.7 per cent of the shares (55 per cent
when in May 1971 Lloyds acquired the shares of Barclays DCO and Barclays
Limited), while Mellon would own 10.1 per cent (Mellon also retained some sub-
scriptions obligations, share options and conversion rights until 1983 to increase
its shareholdings to approximately 25 per cent).

The successful merger managed to chase away the bad memories of 1968,
when a possible merger between Barclays, Martins Bank and Lloyds, sponsored
by the Governor of the Bank of England, Lord Cromer, was turned down by the
Monopolies Commission. Since the vote lacked a two-thirds majority, the issue
went back into Whitehall's hands, which finally decided not to allow the tripartite
merger but had nothing against Martins joining a larger bank. Since Barclays'
offer was higher than Lloyds, Martins was finally acquired on 15 December 1969.

Faulkner was rightfully very proud of its creation. Lloyds was no more the
'smallest kid' on the block; now it felt it could compete with Barclays and its
DCO subsidiary.

Faulkner suffered from being considered the Chairman of the smallest of the
Big Five/Four even though he publicly denied it when speaking to journalists.
The merger made an impression on all the banking and financial community of
that time. Writing in October 1970 to Mayer, Faulkner recalled: 'I was struck at
[the IMF meeting] Copenhagen by the welcome expressed to me for *our child*
[emphasis added]'.[44]

The final step was the vote of BOLSA's shareholders. The vote came at the
'Meeting of Members' of April 1971 and 99.7 per cent of the shareholders voted
in favour of the resolution. More than two years after the Clarke report, the new
bank with Lloyds as the majority shareholder was born.

Looking at the other side of the Channel, it must be pointed out that the situation of *Crédit Lyonnais* with respect to overseas business was in much better shape
than *Société Générale*, even during its period of '*croissance tranquille*'.[45] *Crédit
Lyonnais* had several offices overseas, but almost all foreign establishments were
in developed countries, generally in Europe (Benelux and Iberian Peninsula), or
in French colonies (North Africa, Senegal, Côte d'Ivoire) with a presence in retail
banking in South America. Their business was commercial banking for local or
French customers. Until the late 1960s, then, *Crédit Lyonnais* was a domestic
bank with some operations in Europe and French colonies. As the future President
of the bank from 1982 until 1986, Jean Deflassieux noted 'the problem was that,
unlike the time of Henri Germain [the founder of *Crédit Lyonnais*] nobody really
travelled at Crédit Lyonnais'.[46]

We can trace the first important attempt to reshape international financial
activities at *Crédit Lyonnais* back to the creation of the International Affairs
Office under the authority of Count Tanneguy de Feuilhade de Chauvin in 1969.[47]

Before that time, two offices had co-existed: the Direction of Financial Affairs (*Diréction des Affaires Financières*, DAF) and the long established Direction of Merchant Banking and Foreign Activities (*Direction de la Haute Banque et des Agences Etrangères*, DHBAE).

Under the direct responsibility of M. de Feuilhade, two new departments were also created, the first was the Department of Foreign Trade (*Département pour le Commerce Extérieur*, DCE) led by Jean Deflassieux whose objective was to 'coordinate initiatives and interventions of these [agencies, subsidiaries, associated banks and representations] in the field of international trade relations, whether imports or exports of goods, capital goods or service'.[48] The second department was the Department of International Operations (*Département des Opération Financières Internationales*, DOFI) under the control of Georges Smolarski. The mission of DOFI was to:

> Make available to communities and French or foreign companies resources gathered *outside their country of origin* [emphasis added, i.e. on the Euromarkets] to finance their expansion programs internationally; to collect stable resources currency through which our Establishment will continue to develop its role as international investment bank, to contribute to the dissemination of French and foreign securities on several exchanges . . . Accordingly, this department is responsible for the setting up, underwriting and placement of international issues; credits, called financial, for which the Credit Lyonnais extends directly medium term loans in any currency to communities and companies of international standing and, finally, stock trading on foreign stock.[49]

The structure of the International Affairs office went through some changes again in June 1972; the world was changing at an increasing pace so the Bank had to make some changes, still under the lead of M. de Feuilhade:

> Action across the globe today weighs heavy demands on us . . . The problem is whether this is indeed one of the major pathways of our future. If, in a world where borders are constantly blurring (Japan, USSR, China, Australia, New Zealand, South Africa, etc. . . . not to mention the Common Market), we believe that in order for CL to maintain its rank, it should increasingly *internationalise its activities* [emphasis added], hesitation is not allowed. We must, with the support of our European partners and, if necessary, alone pursue the establishment of a network as complete and consistent as possible, knowing that any delay in achieving this goal ultimately increases our expenses or worsens our shortfall [emphasis added].[50]

The International Affairs office was thus redesigned under a new name to reflect the changes in the international alliances, with the creation of 'Europartners', a banking club assembling *Crédit Lyonnais, Commerzbank* (both from 1970), *Banco di Roma* (from 1971) and *Banco Hispano-Americano* (from 1973). Even though

Crédit Lyonnais was the biggest bank in France at the time, it suffered from a sort of 'inferiority complex' vis-à-vis its smaller competitor, *Société Générale*, and its club, EBIC formed by the members of EAC:

> The joint projects are already important . . . But it does not seem that Société Générale could play a leading role because of the importance of its part-ners . . . We are in our opinion, the most important partner of a trio whose composition is perhaps less prestigious, but whose determination is greater.[51]

The new name chosen for the overseas department was Central Department for International Affairs and Cooperation (*Département Central pour les Affaires Internationales et la Coopération*, DCAIC). Deflassieux and Smolarski were named Directors of International Affairs under the responsibility of de Feuilhade. Each director had two responsibilities, one functional and one geographical. Functionally, Deflassieux was responsible for the DCE while geographically for LDCs. Smolarski was geographically responsible for the business in developed countries while functionally responsible for the Cooperation and the DOFI, which was divided into three sectors: General Affairs, Stock Exchange; Placements and Trading; and finally Financing. Within the DCAIC, in 1973 an International Office, regrouping the activities of the Parisian office of the *Direction des Agences de Paris* (DAPA), the short-term department of the DCE and some individual clients, was created to deal with international business mainly providing foreign exchange advances and documentary credits.

Cooperative banking

All European banks were confronted by one crucial strategic decision concern-ing their international expansion: whether or not to cooperate with other banks. Cooperating through banking clubs or joint ventures in a politically fragmented world with high information costs seemed an extremely rational strategy in order to minimise expensive and limited capital and human resources. Not all banks decided to cooperate, even though some of them would change their mind as the 1970s moved on. We can gain an idea of the number of clubs in Europe in the early 1970s from Table 2.2 below.

With regard to British banks, the main divide was between banks with interna-tional experience and banks lacking it. Barclays, until 1974, and Lloyds decided not to cooperate formally. This decision is attributable to their heritage of banks with an existing presence abroad and consequently pre-existing international know-how and structures.

Midland Bank, by contrast, was one of the members of EAC and until the creation of its international division in 1974 relied markedly on cooperation and correspondent banking to foster its international business. French banks are a dif-ferent story, because until the early 1970s they were systematically excluded from banking clubs because of the presence of the State as owner. Things started to change with the creation of Europartners on the initiative of *Crédit Lyonnais* in

Table 2.2 European banking clubs in 1973.

Group	Members	Country	Total assets in US$ billion	Total
ABECOR (Established in 1972 and reconstituted in 1974)	Algemene Bank Nederland	Netherlands	10.2	132.6
	Banca Nazionale del Lavoro	Italy	22.7	
	Banque de Bruxelles	Belgium	7.5	
	Banque Nationale de Paris	France	29.9	
	Barclays Bank Limited	UK	28.3	
	Hypobank	Germany	9.5	
	Dresdner Bank	Germany	21.0	
	Banque Nationale à Luxembourg (Associated)	Luxembourg	0.8	
	Österreichische Länderbank (Associated)	Austria	2.1	
	Banque de la Société Financière Européenne (Associated)	Consortium	0.6	
EAC/EBIC (Established 1963)	Amsterdam-Rotterdam Bank	Netherlands	9.7	104.0
	Banca Commerciale Italiana (1973)	Italy	16.8	
	Creditanstalt Bankverein (1971)	Austria	3.0	
	Deutsche Bank	Germany	24.7	
	Midland Bank	UK	19.1	
	Société Générale (1971)	France	21.6	
	Société Générale de Banque	Belgium	9.1	
EUROPARTNERS (Established 1970)	Banco di Roma (1971)	Italy	13.2	57.2
	Commerzbank	Germany	14.5	
	Crédit Lyonnais	France	24.1	
	Banco Hispano Americano (1973)	Spain	5.1	
INTERALPHA (Established 1972)	BHF-Bank	Germany	4.4	25.1
	Banco Ambrosiano	Italy	2.9	
	Crédit Commercial de France	France	4.3	
	Kredietbank	Belgium	4.4	
	Nederlandsche Middenstand-bank	Netherlands	4.3	
	Privatbanken i Kobenhavn	Denmark	1.8	
	Williams & Glyn's Bank	UK	3.0	

Source: BBA 80/6172, 'Letter of intent', 17 October 1975. The balances are consolidated figures as at the end of 1973, computed at the rates quoted in New York on 31 December 1973.

1970, as European monetary integration seemed an unstoppable force following the Werner Report presented in October 1970.[52] The decision of *Société Générale* to cooperate was a response to the activism of *Crédit Lyonnais* and the realisation of the EAC that, to enlarge the alliance, it was necessary to accept banks with public ownership, notably Italian and French banks.

Consortium banking picked up in the mid-1960s when the first joint ventures were created. Compared to banking clubs, which remained a strictly European phenomenon, consortia often involved American banks. Consortia banks operated essentially in the medium-term corporate market and their scope was much more limited than clubs, as they focused on specific markets or regions. Compared to clubs, French banks were at the forefront of consortia banking for they were amongst the first to establish joint ventures to operate in the Middle East. In 1969, *Société Générale* created the *Banque Franco-Arabe d'Investissements Internationaux* (FRAB) together with Arab investors from Kuwait, Bahrain, Oman, Dubai, Libya and Tunisia. The second important banking consortium involved *Crédit Lyonnais* and several banks from the entire Arab world; it was established in 1970 as *Union de Banques Arabes et Françaises* (UBAF). By the early 1970s, there were an estimated 60 banking consortia in the world.

The initial strategy of Barclays was to go it alone, thus refusing to cooperate systematically with other banks through clubs and consortia, but leaving freedom for associations on specific ventures or more material link-ups if they seemed desirable.

Despite the invitation, Barclays had refused to participate in the creation of Associated Banks of Europe Corporation or ABECOR with other continental bank members of SFE.

Barclays' decision was based on the consideration that it did not want to put a strait jacket on its international ambitions and because it did not want to 'offend' Bank of America, feeling that the club would isolate its long-time American friend (in an early document ABECOR was labelled as 'anti-American')[53]. Other considerations included the fact that linking up with other banks would involve 'handing over much of the profit to other parties' and 'management squabbling arising from differences of philosophy and conflicts of interest'.[54] The second point refers more or less directly to the far from satisfactory experience with BOLAM, the Central American joint venture with Lloyds and the Bank of Montreal. In an internal memo it was remarked that 'there should always be a clear majority leader firmly in control otherwise the ship just gets bogged down with all parties losing interest'.[55]

Barclays would ultimately reconsider its position in 1974. Despite not yet being a member of ABECOR, the bank participated in the creation of several projects developed by ABECOR members, for example EuroLatinamerican Bank (EulaBank) in 1973 together with 15 other banks in Europe and Latin America in order to operate in the provision of medium- and long-term Eurocurrency lending.

If Barclays had an established overseas presence and for some years it resisted the idea of becoming member of a club, Lloyds never believed in banking clubs and consortia. Throughout its foreign expansion, it kept a policy of independence from other banks, with occasional collaborations, and of direct presence in foreign markets. Midland is an interesting case because, as we have already mentioned, it followed an original path; since the early 1960s it believed in cooperative banking through alliances and joint ventures with continental and Commonwealth banks as an effective way to enter these markets. As anticipated, these different attitudes were, mainly, the result of their respective legacies.

Lloyds already had a long history of presence overseas (like Barclays), having a solid, albeit small, network in Europe and a larger one on the Indian Subcontinent. On the other side, Midland Bank was a latecomer and as Geoffrey Jones has aptly pointed out, it was a 'virgin' on the international banking arena (like National Westminster).[56] Throughout the twentieth century, its expansion abroad was limited to correspondent banking and not direct representations, a policy that can be traced back to Sir Edward Holden, elected Chairman in 1908, and his successor, Reginald McKenna, elected Chairman in 1919. In 1948, Howard Thackstone, then Chief Foreign Manager and later Chief General Manager, explained Midland's vision: 'my own bank has no branches in any other country, for we have no desire to compete on their own ground with the banks of other countries'.[57]

These views entrenched in Midland history were modified for the first time in the early 1960s. The result was a new era of cooperation and alliances, which was theorised in 1962–63 and has been called the 'grand design' phase of Midland's expansion. As we have seen earlier, the grand design pushed Midland to adhere to the EAC in 1963 in order to develop the European leg of its strategy and to create a joint venture called Midland and International Banks (MAIBL) in order to pursue its expansion in the Commonwealth market. Midland, thus, followed a policy of agreement and cooperation as opposed to Lloyds' policy of takeover and shareholding.

The grand design phase of Midland lasted a decade (1963–73). The exclusive reliance on this method of expansion through cooperative ventures came increasingly under strain during the period 1973–74 when the slack domestic demand, the recycling challenge and the need to shore up domestic industries by helping them to conquer overseas markets became crucial imperatives to remain in the banking and financial arena. The changed attitude started with the full acquisition of the merchant banks, Montagu Trust and Drayton Group Limited, in 1973.

EAC/EBIC went through two distinct phases. The first one built up from existing correspondent links and lasted from the creation of the EAC in 1963 as a way to coordinate and discuss domestic policies with the ambition to know each other better and eventually merge when Europe finally became a unified country. A second phase began in 1967, when the Committee decided to add an international dimension to its group by opening joint representative offices and creating a series of joint ventures to conquer new niches of market.[58] The new character of the EAC was officially recognised with the creation of the EBIC in 1970 as a club and not a mere committee. EAC remained as a high-level informal gathering where the guidelines for cooperation and planning were discussed, while EBIC became the juridical entity to coordinate and promote the common activities of the participating banks. EBIC also carried out joint studies in fields such as economics and automation. A major review of the founding rules of EAC in 1969 and the creation of EBIC brought in new members to the club after almost a decade of 'solitude', with the old members realising that the dream of becoming one unified bank was evaporating as monetary and economic integration in Europe started losing speed.

Nationalised banks from Italy and France, *Banca Commerciale Italiana* (COMIT) and *Société Générale*, were finally invited to join EAC/EBIC; *Deutsche Bank* exerted pressure to invite an Austrian partner; and an invitation was extended to *Creditanstalt Bankverein* too. COMIT refused, at first, to participate fully, preferring to be connected to the club while establishing its own branches. This could not be accepted by the other club members and after long discussions, COMIT fully joined EAC/EBIC while maintaining its New York branch, something that *Société Générale*, as we shall see further, did not manage to do.

Through its participation in EBIC, Midland gained membership of the foremost European banking association, a form of representation worldwide through the EAC/EBIC affiliates and participations in soundly based profitable consortium banks operations.[59] We might add: with an absence of competition from its associates.

Nevertheless, the reliance on cooperative banking was also a source of worry for Midland: in particular, it meant it was impossible to highlight its own name internationally and to emphasise its own capabilities, and it provided only minority participations in EAC/EBIC joint ventures, with only a partial say in management and a minority share of profits regardless of the contribution. Moreover, the philosophy of EAC/EBIC placed restrictions on Midland's ambitions to enter their partner's home markets.

These views reflected the changed nature of international banking in the rapidly changing context of the early 1970s, notably the explosive growth of the Eurocurrency market, enlargement of the customer base and increasing competition for business. If Midland wanted to keep pace with its English and European competitors – Lloyds was a good example – it should reconsider the entrenched philosophy of cooperative banking. Four options were considered in 1974: maintain the role of EAC/EBIC in its international strategy; adopt a 'negative stance' in EAC/EBIC and an 'aggressive development' of its own network; complete withdrawal from EAC/EBIC; adopt a 'positive stance' in the EAC/EBIC and also develop its own international initiatives.[60]

Maintaining the *status quo* had the above-mentioned drawbacks. The second option was not favoured because this alternative 'would still be reduced by the restrictions upon competing with the EAC/EBIC banks and affiliates'. The third one would have allowed Midland complete freedom of action to develop its own international initiatives and 'it would also give us the capital proceeds from the sale of the EAC/EBIC investments to finance our developments'. Was this the path to follow, then? This solution 'would have grave implications for our relationships with the other EAC/EBIC banks, and leave us virtually *without any overseas presence* or non-UK earnings ability in the short time [emphasis added]'.[61] This passage underlines a dramatic fact about Midland: until 1974 it crucially lacked any direct representations abroad. Thus, the middle solution was to remain part of the EAC/EBIC, but to start developing an autonomous international presence.

Unlike some of its British competitors, it is worth repeating that in the year of its centenary, 1964, *Société Générale* could count on only two branches (New York and London), two affiliates (Francibank in Belgium and *Sogebanque* in Spain), a subsidiary in Buenos Aires, two representative offices in Mexico City and Rome and the branches of Sogénal in Luxembourg, Switzerland and Germany. The rest of its international operations were conducted through correspondent banking. By 1969, the revenues of the overseas network represented just 11 per cent of *Société Générale*'s non-consolidated balance sheet.[62]

Despite both being members of a banking club, the two French banks considered in our study had a different strategy concerning their international expansion and deployment in international markets. The differences depended largely on the importance of their respective clubs in their overall strategic decisions. Even though *Crédit Lyonnais* was part of Europartners, it always kept a degree of independence in its strategy abroad; thus, for example, the year after the club was created, *Crédit Lyonnais* reopened its branch in New York. This attitude is probably due to the size of *Crédit Lyonnais*' foreign network and its leadership position within the club. By contrast, that same year *Société Générale*, now part of EBIC, closed its branch in the United States in order to give birth to the European-American Bank (EAB), which made headlines when it bought the ailing Franklin National Bank in 1974.[63] The branch only reopened it in 1978–79 when the EBIC experience was *de facto* already over and most of the partners, such as *Deutsche Bank* and Midland Bank, started implementing independent decisions.

The most relevant modification in *Société Générale*'s international activities was the membership of EAC/EBIC. Inviting new members to the club had been a *leitmotiv* of the EAC/EBIC throughout the 1960s. After some exploratory meetings at the beginning of 1971, *Société Générale* was officially invited to join EBIC in April 1971, the first new member in almost ten years. The proposal to invite *Société Générale* came from *Société Générale de Banque* and from Midland Bank, because the two banks were eager to limit the influence of *Deutsche Bank* within the EAC/EBIC.

The decision to join a club was greatly accelerated by three critical factors. The first element was the creation of Europartners in 1970 by its competitor *Crédit Lyonnais*. The second element was the need to grow in size in order to be able to finance multinational companies. In fact, the bank's President, Jacques Ferronnière, remarked that, without the association with other banks and excluding the merger with another French bank, *Société Générale* would not be able to reach a critical size to match the needs of French multinational companies. The third, and probably most critical element, was the realisation by President Ferronnière that foreign subsidiaries, besides being burdened by the controls imposed by the French legislation, were very expensive and usually unprofitable.[64]

Through the participation in EAC/EBIC, Ferronnière aimed at overcoming these criticalities and, once the deal was sealed, he could proudly remark that 'this agreement marks for Société Générale an important step to adapt to the evolution of the world economy and to become an integral part of the most important and prestigious group of European banks'.[65] Indeed, the participation in EAC/EBIC allowed *Société Générale* to gain an international presence with very limited direct investment and expenses. This latter element is essential to understand the cooperative phase of banking.

Before the formalisation of the association, several points had to be clarified when the parties first met in Brussels in May 1971. The first point was probably the most important one. It concerned the membership not only of EBIC but also of EAC. The most important distinction between the two institutions was that the EAC members, the fathers of the cooperation, wanted to keep the institution as a forum exclusively for privately owned companies, while EBIC would be open to state-owned banks.

Despite the reassurances by the EAC members that the Committee would not have 'any significant activity for the time being',[66] *Société Générale* feared that being invited to join EBIC but not EAC would have given its membership a secondary role status.[67] Ferronnière exposed his arguments by insisting that the creation of two categories of club members was not acceptable and that, since EBIC was only a consequence of EAC, membership of the latter was far more important than membership of EBIC. Despite the opposition of the Dutch bank Amro, which feared the loss of the original goals of the cooperation, the other members agreed that the remarks were 'understandable' and 'reasonable' and finally agreed to invite *Société Générale* to become a member of the EAC.

The second element of discussion was Japan. When *Société Générale* joined the club, it was agreed that it should give up its New York branch to EAB, so it was important to gain something in the Far East to compensate for this loss and justify it within *Société Générale* or, as the bank's executives put it: 'We must especially avoid giving the impression to the executives of our Bank that we have "dropped" our main establishment overseas without the guarantee of specific counterparties'.[68]

Société Générale asked for a participation in the new Japanese bank of *Deutsche Bank* or in the *Uberseeische Bank* (DUB).

The third point involved the participation in EAB and the closure of the New York branch. The last issue on the table was the participation in Euro-Pacific Finance Corporation. It was agreed that, pending the decision of Australian authorities, *Société Générale* should be allowed to join the entity. The admission of *Société Générale* into EAC/EBIC was not only the result of *Société Générale*'s attempts to gain an increasing overseas exposure but also of political factors within EAC/EBIC; as we have anticipated, Midland Bank and *Société Générale de Belgique* were overwhelmed by the role of *Deutsche Bank* within the club and were eager to counterbalance it. The admission of COMIT would reflect a similar wish of *Société Générale* to gain further influence in the Club by expanding the number of 'Latin' banks.

After these discussions, the association was finally formalised as 'full and satisfactory conclusions'[69] were reached. On that same occasion, the association of

Banca Commerciale Italiana was temporarily put aside because of disagreements on the terms of association (COMIT would join EAC/EBIC in 1973) and the inclusion of the Austrian bank *Creditanstalt Bankverein* was discussed; *Creditanstalt* would join later that year.

The international activities of *Société Générale* up to 1974 coincided with the activities of EBIC, much like *Deutsche Bank*. Working groups were created, a common payment system (Ebicredit) was established, ad-hoc groups on Latin America (an investment in *Banco Bradesco* of Brazil was agreed) and Asia (a joint bank European-Asian Bank was created from the demise of the *Deutsch-Asiatische Bank*, founded in 1889) were established, and representative offices were opened in Djakarta, Johannesburg and Toronto. Eurodollar operations were conducted through three main vehicles: the EAB, the Banque Européenne de Crédit and the European Banking Company. Even though *Société Générale* had decided to broaden the scope of its activities, the lack of funds crucially limited the size of its operations and forced the bank to share its activities with its partners.

Things would ultimately change in 1973–74, the year of crisis and of the arrival of a key executive in the history of *Société Générale*, Marc Viénot, a man who would radically reshape *Société Générale*'s international activities and allow the bank to become one of the big players on the international banking and financial scene.

Along with EBIC and ABECOR, the third major banking club was Europartners. The club was the second to be created on the continent when, in October 1970, *Crédit Lyonnais* and *Commerzbank* decided to cooperate together. The *Banco di Roma* that joined in January 1971 had been a second choice for *Crédit Lyonnais*, when COMIT decided to become part of EBIC because of its close ties with *Deutsche Bank*.

The original idea of the club was to become one big European unified bank. Initial successes included European Securities Corporation in New York, Transcredit (to arrange and simplify borrowing in partner countries), common representations, exchange of personnel and the creation of Europartners Nederland NV to operate in the Euroloan market.

The club came to include the *Banco Hispano-Americano* (BHA) in 1973 because of 'commercial flows between Spain and the other three countries represented', 'the efforts of our industries to penetrate that country' and 'the enormous influx of tourists to that country every year'.[70] Additionally, BHA was the second largest bank in Spain and had very close ties with the industrial sector thanks to its privileged relationship with the investment bank *Banco Urquijo*, the most important in the country.[71] Other banks contacted the partners to join the group, amongst them the *Banco Central*, *Banco de Bilbao*, *Banco de Santander* and *Banco de Vizcaya*. Nonetheless, it was thought that for both prestige and efficiency an association with BHA was to be favoured. Similarly to the creation of EBIC, the rationale for creating Europartners was the idea that Europe was definitely moving towards becoming a unified political entity: *Crédit Lyonnais*, *Banco di Roma* and *Commerzbank* imagined Europe in the late 1970s as being 'marked by individualization of European monetary space with reduced fluctuations between currencies of member countries', by the 'harmonisation in the fiscal, legal and social domains', by the 'convergence of cyclical and monetary policies' and by 'some progress in the freedom of capital movements between member states but increased capital controls between member countries and third parties'.[72]

On the last point, it is clear that the authors were referring to the on-going debate on the regulation of the Euromarkets in Basel, Paris and Washington that we mentioned in the previous chapter. This assumption is confirmed further in the same document: 'The market developments in the euro-dollar and euro-emission may encounter some limitations in Europe due to increased regulations on the continent and conversely relaxation of U.S. regulations'.[73] Commercial banks were indeed convinced that a sort of 'fortress Europe' was about to be created: a system where the Old Continent would become 'a *privileged area* . . . for industrial, commercial and financial relations'.[74]

The first results of the cooperation seemed encouraging, particularly on the Euroloan and Eurobond markets, on the listing of domestic companies on foreign stock exchanges and on the creation of joint ventures, where Europartners Securities Corporation of New York was active on the financial market, asset management and stock trading. Europartners Securities was formerly the New York branch of *Crédit Lyonnais*, which changed its name in 1970 when *Crédit Lyonnais* founded Europartners. In 1973 Europartners Bank Nederland was inaugurated.

The first half of the 1970s marked the affirmation of cooperative banking through clubs and consortia. These partnerships were a useful tool to enter new markets where management skills were limited and risks were high. Banks had resorted to them in the past. For example, in the nineteenth century British, French and German banks cooperated in their empires or other remote parts of the world. Examples include the Imperial Bank of Persia, founded in 1889, and the London & River Plate Bank, founded in 1860. The central issue with cooperative banking was to maintain the delicate balance between internal and external priorities, a task which gradually was becoming more and more challenging.

Autonomous initiatives

The rise of cooperative banking did not mean the lack of independent initiatives to enter foreign markets. The majority of British and French banks continued to implement new measures in order to reap the benefits of an increasingly interconnected world. The banks studied had different geographic focus, with the former empires still providing the platform for further expansion. Expanding outside known areas in the late 1960s was still very limited. British banks were particularly active in the Pacific basin, Western Europe and the American continent. French banks had a privileged relationship with Arab countries starting from the mid-1960s, where several consortia banks were created, with North and West Africa, and with Eastern Europe, where they became the most involved country together with West Germany.

The newly created BBI chose to focus its efforts on priority areas: the USA, Europe and the Pacific, with Latin America relegated to fourth place. The budget allocated for the first five-year plan was £50 million. Europe (notably, Holland, Belgium, West Germany, France, Switzerland, Scandinavia and Austria) was the most immediate priority area of the plan. This affirmation was justified by the imminent admission of the UK to the EEC.

The second corporate plan for 1973–77 did not radically modify the previous one. The priority areas remained the US, Europe and the Pacific Region. With regard to possible new investments, Arab countries and Brazil were timidly considered as good opportunities; a representative office was opened in Buenos Aires in 1971 and one in Sao Paulo followed suit in 1972.

These establishments were the result of a visit made during the summer of 1970 by two Barclays' representatives in Buenos Aires, Sao Paulo and Rio de Janeiro. After visiting both countries for more than one month, they invited the Group to establish representative offices in both countries and to obtain a participation in a Brazilian investment bank. The investment was justified by the need to limit BOLSA's expansion and by strategic considerations:

> At least temporarily, the U.K. economy, and with it our commercial banking system is, relatively, static, and to this extent our massive commitment of resources here, although it remains very profitable, is also likely to be fairly static. In Africa and perhaps the Caribbean, there are some signs of economic nationalism of a kind that could seriously inhibit our growth there. It makes sense therefore to direct some small part of our resources to countries that now have reasonable economic stability, favourable economic growth, and which do not at present suffer either from racial tension or antipathy to private enterprise, and which welcome foreign capital even though they may wish naturally to keep the primary banking system in their own hands.[75]

Oppressive regimes in South America complied with all of the requirements needed for sound banking practices: political stability, economic growth and antipathy to socialism. The two representatives remarked about Argentina that 'there is tolerance, no racial problems and an air of liberty, *even though there are no free elections and the military govern* [emphasis added].[76] The 'positive' aspects of Brazil were similar to Argentina's: a military dictatorship had apparently put the house in order thanks to the use of force and repression since the coup of 1964. As remarked by Deryk Vander Weyer, who failed to become Barclays Chairman in 1980, and his colleague: 'The regime is favourably disposed to private enterprise and commands the confidence of business men'.[77]

Finding new businesses was gradually becoming a central task amongst BBI's managers; the most active of them were labelled internally as 'runners'. Generally, Tuke in person was deciding who had to go where, often testing their resilience by inviting the chosen one to stay away for a month or so.

The focus of the new plan was not to further stretch BBI's operations but instead to reinforce the existing strategy and investments with further capital, marketing and, most importantly, human resources which were increasingly looking like a major constraint to BBI's policies. Another important aspect of the 1973–77 plan was the increased focus on disinvestment from 'areas which have traditionally pro-vided a disproportionately large part of our profits'.[78] The major divestment areas were South Africa (a total divestment of 50 per cent over 5 years was planned), Rhodesia, Nigeria, Sierra Leone, Ghana, Trinidad, Jamaica, Cyprus and Malta. Nevertheless, the guidelines developed in the previous plan were kept unchanged: expansion in the US, Europe and Far East and the 'go it alone' strategy.

In 1972, Barclays' presence in Asia Pacific was reinforced by the establish-ment of branches in Tokyo and Hong Kong plus several minor locations such as Fiji and New Hebrides. A majority interest was acquired in the merchant bank, Barclays Australia Limited. In New Zealand, a 20 per cent interest in the New Zealand United Corporation was taken. In Europe, Barclays Bank SA provided a good starting point with its 21 branches throughout France. In Italy, a control-ling interest of 51 per cent was bought in the *Banca Castellini*, a family-owned private bank founded in 1884, to give birth to *Banca Barclays Castellini Spa*. In the Netherlands, a 70 per cent stake in the bank *Kol & Co.* was reconstituted as *Barclays Kol & Co. NV*. In 1973 the presence in the Far East was further strengthened by the opening of another branch in Singapore; in Hong Kong a new merchant bank, named Trident International Finance, was created in coop-eration with Nomura Securities and Merrill Lynch, Pierce, Fenner & Smith. In November 1973 a 33 per cent share (the maximum allowed by local laws) was finally acquired in *Banco de Investimientos BCN SA* and *Financiadora BCN SA*, the investment banking and consumer finance companies of BCN Group of the Conde family of Sao Paulo.

It is now worth comparing the autonomous initiatives of Barclays with those of *Crédit Lyonnais*. The goals of the DCAIC for the years 1973–75 were to 'consoli-date and expand the role of *Crédit Lyonnais* internationally both in the banking and financial sector[s]' in order to improve its business with multinational French companies, to improve its share of foreign trade financing and to take advantage abroad of specialist techniques already applied in France, such as money man-agement, leasing and real estate.[79] To achieve these goals, it was important to strengthen the capacities of the foreign branches, to expand the overseas network by creating new establishments and to keep an eye on prospect countries where *Crédit Lyonnais* had not yet established an office. From the balance sheet of the overseas department, of FF419 million (almost €400 million in today's terms), FF218 million of them were set aside for capital increases and to create new offices. Priority countries were located in every world region (Europe, Eastern Europe, Arab countries and the Middle East, Africa, Asia Pacific, Latin America and North America).[80]

Despite all these efforts, *Crédit Lyonnais* was intrinsically a domestic bank until 1972. Overseas business was an accessory asset. Maurice Schlogel, Delegated Vice President since 1972, remarked during a Board meeting in September 1973:

> Most of our revenues come from Metropolitan France. We have gradually improved the ratio of profits Overseas/France, noting that we were one of the banks whose revenues were lowest not because we were investing

too much in France but because we were *not investing enough overseas.*
Nonetheless, our company must continue to focus on Metropolitan France,
the essential source of revenues, and secondly on the overseas market
[emphasis added].[81]

These promises would not be kept for long since the oil crisis radically modified
the bank's international strategy.

The programme for 1974–76 was prepared in October 1973 (unfortunate timing indeed) and largely followed the path traced by the previous programme. The
programme recognised the need of *Crédit Lyonnais* 'to be active on a global scale
in every domain of banking and financial activities';[82] in order to be able to do
that it posited to reinforce the overseas network in Europe (London, Luxembourg,
Spain and Switzerland) and the US (New York) and to expand it in the Middle
East, Far East and Comecon countries.

As for most European banks in our study, the oil crisis decisively modified the
pace and scope of the international activities of *Crédit Lyonnais*.

Legacy costs

By the end of the 1960s and the beginning of the 1970s, the European banking sector was going through a period of gradual transformation because of
internal and external pressures. Consequently, the industry was confronted with
a series of major challenges and opportunities, notably: internationalisation
and internal reorganisations, cooperative banking and autonomous initiatives.
The Eurodollar market offered European banks the opportunity to enter a new
field of business unfettered by the regulations pending on domestic markets and
activities. Nevertheless, this offshore and unregulated market also represented
a challenge after many years of hibernation and forced retreat behind domestic borders. Commercial banks in Europe had to reshape their structures and
develop new strategies.

The structures put in place during the after-war period were slowly starting to
crumble. The most notable example of this phenomenon is Barclays' decision to
eliminate, after almost 50 years, the DCO and create BBI. Other banks gradually
changed their corporate structures to respond to the imperatives of internationalisation. Lloyds formed LBI while *Crédit Lyonnais* created its international
agency. In 1972 Citibank inaugurated its international vehicle, CIBL, to expand
in the Euromarket. The geographic focus of this international expansion was still
influenced by the former imperial boundaries and, at least for European, banks
the penetration into new territories was still limited, with Europe remaining the
privileged market.

Despite the importance of the Euromarket, the scale of international banking
and financial activities of European banks until the early 1970s was held back by
three critical factors.

First, as we have seen in the previous chapter, the speculative pressures
against the Deutschmark, through the Eurodollar market, profoundly shocked the

Bundesbank and a certain unease about this unregulated market came to dominate the agenda of several European countries and controls continued to be enforced.

Second, the resources to fund ambitious plans for overseas expansion were limited. International expansion could take place only through international cooperation or through the acquisition of smaller banks, as American banks did in Europe in the mid- to late 1960s. This fact is exemplified by the reliance on banking clubs and consortia to offset costs. For example, when National Westminster had to decide whether to enter into a joint venture with Chase Manhattan and Royal Bank of Canada or build its international business from scratch, the working party rejected the latter option because 'to achieve a truly international position and to match the US giants in the banking field, National Westminster cannot go it alone for reasons of: *cost*; *time*; *staff*; and *know-how* [emphasis added]'.[83] When the decision to form a joint venture was passed in September 1969, the working group remarked that:

> [b]y pooling their individual contributions of geographic coverage, banking and financial services, customer connections and information sources . . . the three partners acting together could achieve their international objectives effectively and at an acceptable cost; whereas, acting individually and competitively, *the task might well prove prohibitively expensive* [emphasis added]'.[84]

Similarly, Midland Bank explicitly stated that 'for each bank to open up competing branch networks throughout Europe would be counter-productive, and be *prohibitively expensive in capital and staff terms* [emphasis added]'.[85] The case of *Deutsche Bank* is similar, as remarked by Gall *et al.*, 'the main problem, however, was the *scarcity of capital* [emphasis added]'.[86]

Third, there was a lack of incentive to expand in uncharted territories and operations given the still favourable European economic and political context in the 1960s and the risks involved in international ventures. As we have illustrated, Europe represented a privileged terrain for all the major European banks. In the following chapters, we will see how the oil shock and the imbalances it created would help to overcome these limits by pushing Western governments to fully support the Euromarket and ease certain regulations, by providing huge funds to invest in overseas operations and by providing powerful incentives to internationalise through creating a formidable pool of customers, especially in the developing world.

Because of the limitations mentioned above, the strategies of European commercial banks started to change, but were not radically modified by the early 1970s. As had been the case for other large European banking institutions, like *Deutsche Bank*,[87] the phase of limited international presence lasted until around 1967 before yielding to an intermediate phase of intensified presence abroad through minority holdings and some representative offices mostly in connection with clubs and consortia. These were 'half measures' and they would not last in the face of the impact of events in the oil sector.

Notes

1 BEA, 6A123/7, Paper delivered by Minos A. Zombonakis at the Eurofinance in 1971 Conference in London, 18 March 1971.
2 Anthony Sampson, *The Money Lenders. Bankers in a Dangerous World*, Viking Press, New York 1981, 108.
3 See David A. Alhadeff, *Competition and Controls in Banking. A Study of the Regulation of Bank Competition in Italy, France, and England*, University of California Press, Berkeley, CA, 1968.
4 Lloyds Banks Archives (LBA), HO/D/Int/1, 'International Banking: An Inquiry for Lloyds Bank' prepared by William M. Clarke, November 1968.
5 On CCC see chapter 10 in Forrest Capie, *The Bank of England: 1950s to 1979*, Cambridge University Press, Cambridge, UK and New York, 2010 and Charles A. E. Goodhart, 'Competition and Credit Control. Some Personal Reflections', *Financial History Review*, Volume 22, Issue 02, August 2015, 235–246.
6 David Rogers, *The Big Four British Banks*, Palgrave Macmillan, London, 1999, 27.
7 David Kynaston, 'The Bank of England and the Government', in Richard Roberts and David Kynaston (eds), *The Bank of England. Money, Power and Influence 1694–1994*, Clarendon Press, Oxford, UK, 1995, 51.
8 Reported in Forrest Capie, *The Bank of England: 1950s to 1979*, Cambridge University Press, Cambridge, UK and New York, 2010, 491.
9 Gordon T. Pepper and Michael J. Oliver, *Monetarism under Thatcher. Lessons for the Future*, Edward Elgar, Cheltenham, UK, 2001, 5.
10 Derek F. Channon, *Global Banking Strategy*, John Wiley and Sons, Chichester, UK and New York, 1988, 20. On the Debré reforms see also Laure Quennouelle-Corre, 'Les réformes bancaires et financières de 1966–1967' in VA, *Michel Debré, un réformateur aux Finances 1966–1968*, Comité pour l'histoire économique et financière de la France, Paris, 2005.
11 See for example: Duncan M. Ross, 'Clubs and Consortia: European Banking Groups as Strategic Alliances', in S. Battilossi and Y. Cassis (eds), *European Banks and the American Challenge*, Oxford University Press, Oxford, UK, 2002. On banking consortia see also Charles Ganoe, 'Banking Consortia: Are They Here to Stay?', *Columbia Journal of World Business*, Vol. 7, August 1972, 51–57 and Michael Von Clemm, 'The Rise of Consortium Banking', *Harvard Business Review*, Vol. 49 (May–June 1971), 125–141.
12 Midland Bank Archives (MBA), Report of the Directors and Accounts 31st December 1964 and Statement to the Shareholders by the Chairman.
13 Geoffrey Jones, *British Multinational Banking 1830–1990*, Clarendon Press, Oxford, UK and New York, 1993, 269.
14 SFE was a joint venture aimed at expanding in the Eurobond business at the end of the 1960s. Towards the end of 1960s, SFE's European members (extra-European members included Bank of America and Sumitomo Bank) split into an 'inner circle' (known as the 'Camu Club' from the name of the president of the *Banque de Bruxelles*, Louis Camu), willing to push cooperation and integration further like EAC had shown, composed of *Dresdner Bank, Bayerische Hypotheken und Wechsel Bank, Algemene Bank Nederland* and *Banque de Bruxelles* and an 'outer circle' which, despite remaining active members of SFE, had decided to opt out of the new vehicle, composed of Barclays, *Banque Nationale de Paris* and *Banca Nazionale del Lavoro*.
15 Duncan M. Ross, 'European Banking Clubs in the 1960s: A Flawed Strategy', *Business and Economic History*, Vol. 27, no. 2, Winter, 1998, 353–366.
16 Richard Roberts (with C. Arnander), *Take Your Partners. Orion, the Consortium Banks and the Transformation of the Euromarkets*, Palgrave, Basingstoke, UK and New York, 2001, 20.

17 Stefano Battilossi and Youssef Cassis (eds), *European Banks and the American Challenge. Competition and Cooperation in International Banking under Bretton Woods*, Oxford University Press, Oxford, UK and New York, 2002.

18 Harold van B. Cleveland and Thomas F. Huertas, *Citibank 1812–1970*, Harvard University Press, Cambridge, MA, and London, 1985, 264.

19 Phillip L. Zweig, *Wriston*, Crown Publishers, New York, 1995, 221.

20 BBA, Barclays Bank DCO Report and Accounts 1971, Statement by the Chairman, Sir Frederic Seebohm.

21 Ibid.

22 Tuke was educated at Magdalene College, Cambridge, before joining the Scots Guard in 1940. He joined Barclays after the end of the Second World War in 1946 working in London's West End before leaving for South Africa in 1948. Back in England he climbed all the stairs of Barclays' *cursus honorum*, getting appointed to the board of DCO in 1966.

23 BBA, BBI Report and Accounts 1972, Statement by the Chairman Mr Anthony Favill Tuke.

24 BBA, 80/5904, Strictly Private & Confidential 'Minutes of Planning Meeting', 5 February 1971.

25 BBA, 80/5906, Strictly Private & Confidential 'Barclays Bank International Five-Year Plan 1971/6', August 1971.

26 Faulkner was educated at Corpus Christi, Cambridge, and at 22 joined the merchant bank Glyn, Mills & Co. He returned to Glyn, Mills & Co. in 1946 becoming its Chairman in 1963 until 1968 when he joined Lloyds Bank as Director and became its Chairman the following year until 1977. In the meantime, he was nominated President of the British Bankers Association (BBA) when it was reconstituted in 1972.

27 LBA, HO/D/Int/1, Confidential Report by W. M. Clarke 'International Banking: An Inquiry for Lloyds Bank', November 1968. The following quotes are from the same document.

28 LBA, HO/D/Int/1, 'Minutes of the International Banking Committee', 4 March 1969.

29 Idem.

30 LBA, HO/D/Int/1, 'Minutes of the International Banking Committee', 8 April 1969.

31 Idem.

32 Idem.

33 LBA, HO/D/Int/1, 'Minutes of the International Banking Committee', 16 May 1969.

34 Idem.

35 Idem.

36 LBA, HO/Ch/Fau/11–24, Secret Memorandum 'Bank of London and South America –Lloyds Relationship', 19 August 1969.

37 LBA, HO/Ch/Fau/11–24, Personal and Confidential Letter from John A. Mayer to Eric Faulkner, 8 January 1970.

38 LBA, HO/Ch/Fau/11–24, Letter from Mayer to Faulkner, 2 April 1970.

39 Geoffrey Jones, *British Multinational Banking 1830–1990*, Oxford University Press, Oxford, 1993, 329.

40 LBA, HO/Ch/Fau/11–24, 'Bolsa-Some Matters for Further Consideration' (no other information provided).

41 LBA, HO/Ch/Mor/ 11–24, 'Summary of Significant Points from "A Bolsa View of Lloyds Bank Europe"', 17 July 1970.

42 LBA, HO/Ch/Mor/ 11–24, 'Summary of the Meeting held on 22nd of July 1970, at Lloyds Bank Limited Head Office'.

43 LBA, HO/Ch/Mor/ 11–24, Internal Letter of the Chief General Manager to Managers of Branches and Heads of Departments, 14 October 1970.

44 LBA, HO/Ch/Mor/ 11–24, Letter of Faulkner to Mayer, 2 October 1970.

45 For an exhaustive work on the history of the Crédit Lyonnais see Jean Rivoire, *Le Crédit Lyonnais. Histoire d'une banque*, Le Cherche Midi éditeur, Paris, 1989 and Bernard

Desjardins, Michel Lescure, Roger Nougaret, Alain Plessis, André Straus (eds), *Le Crédit Lyonnais, 1863–1986*, Droz, Genève, 2006. On the origins of *Crédit Lyonnais* the reference is Jean Bouvier, *Le Credit Lyonnais de 1863 à 1882. Les années de formation d'une banque de dépôts*, 2 Vols., SEVPEN, Paris, 1961. For a short overview on *Crédit Lyonnais'* international activities in the 1960s and 1970s, see E. Bussière, 'European Aspirations and Market Reality: Paribas, the Crédit Lyonnais, and their European Strategies in the 1960s and 1970s', in S. Battilossi and Y. Cassis (eds), *European Banks and the American Challenge*, Oxford University Press, Oxford, UK and New York, 2002.

46 Bernard Desjardins, Roger Nougaret and Alain Plessis 'Des études financières à la Présidence. Entretien avec Jean Deflassieux': 'Le problème était que, contrairement à l'époque d'Henri Germain, personne ne voyageait vraiment au Crédit Lyonnais'. In Bernard Desjardins, Michel Lescure, Roger Nougaret, Alain Plessis and André Straus (eds), *Le Crédit Lyonnais, 1863–1986*, Droz, Geneva, 2003, 82.

47 Count de Feuilhade would mark the first ten years of international expansion of *Crédit Lyonnais*. He entered *Crédit Lyonnais* in 1951 after Law studies in Paris and work experiences at the Ministry of Agriculture (1943–45), at the Ministry of Finance as *Inspecteur* (1945) and at the Organisation for European Economic Co-operation (OEEC) (1948–51).

48 Crédit Lyonnnais Archives (CLA), 332AH180, Letter of the General Director to the employees, 18 February 1969.

49 Idem.

50 CLA, 110AH10, Programme des Affaires Internationales 1973–75, 23 May 1973.

51 CLA, Board Minutes, 7 October 1971.

52 On the Werner Report and the story of European monetary union, see Harold James, *Making the European Monetary Union*, Harvard University Press, Cambridge, MA, and London, 2012; Emmanuel Mourlon-Druol, *A Europe Made of Money. The Emergence of the European Monetary System*, Cornell University Press, Ithaca, NY and London, 2012.

53 BBA, 80/3173, 'Note for the Group Policy Committee', 15 April 1970.

54 BBA, 80/5850, Memo 'International Strategy to A. F. Tuke', 25 April 1972.

55 BBA, 80/5850, Memo 'International Strategy', 20 April 1972.

56 Geoffrey Jones, *British Multinational banking 1830–1990*, Oxford University Press, Oxford, UK, 1993, 330.

57 As reported in A. R. Holmes and Edwin Green, *Midland, 150 Years of Banking Business*, B. T. Batsford Ltd, London, 1986, 250.

58 *Banque Européenne de Credit* (BEC) founded in 1967, European Banking Company founded in 1973, European American Bank founded in 1968, Euro-Pacific Finance Corp. founded in 1971, European Arab Banks in Brussels, Frankfurt founded in 1972 and London founded in 1976, European Asian Bank founded in 1972.

59 MBA, 0200/0749b, 'The Strategy of Midland Bank Group and International Banking', November 1974.

60 Ibid.

61 Ibid.

62 *Société Générale* Archives (SGA), Rapport Annuel 1974.

63 On the history of Franklin National Bank see Joan E. Spero, *The Failure of the Franklin National Bank: Challenge to the International Banking System*, Columbia University Press, New York, 1980.

64 SGA, 81466, Letter of President Ferronnière to Branch Directors, 4 June 1971.

65 Idem.

66 SGA, 81466, EBIC Invitation Letter, 20 April 1971: 'Nous voulons éviter d'être considérés comme un partenaire de second rang'.

67 SGA, 81466, 'Compte rendu de la réunion du 8 mai 1971'.

68 'Il faut notamment éviter de donner le sentiment aux cadres supérieurs de notre Banque que nous avons "lâché" notre implantation principale à l'étranger sans avoir l'assurance de contreparties suffisamment précises'.

69 SGA, 81466, EBIC-Minutes of Emergency Meeting, Brussels, 8 May 1974.
70 CLA, 143AH7, 'Relations avec le Banco Hispano Americano', 20 December 1971.
71 On Banco Urquijo see, for example: Nuria Puig and Eugenio Torres, 'Managing Succession within Spanish Financial Dynasties: A Study of Uruquijo Bank (1850–1983)', in Anders Perlinge and Hans Sjögren (eds), *Biographies of the Financial World*, Gidlunds Förlag, Stockholm, Sweden, 2012.
72 CLA, 143AH8, 'Perspectives de la coopération interbancaire: Réflexions préliminaires concernant les besoins de services bancaires et financiers', no other information probably 1972.
73 Ibid. 'Les développements du marché de l'euro-dollar et des euro-émissions pourraient rencontrer certaines limites en Europe du fait des règlementations accrues sur ce continent et au contraire du relâchement des règlementations américaines'.
74 Ibid.
75 BBA, 80/3173, 'Visit to South America by Mr G. G. Money and D. V. Weyer' 13 July 1970–5 August 1970.
76 Idem.
77 Idem.
78 BBA, 80/5907, Strictly Private & Confidential 'BBI Corporate Plan-Projections 1973–77', no date.
79 CLA, 110AH10, Direction Centrale des Affaires Internationales-Programme 1973–75, 14 November 1972.
80 The target areas were: Europe, notably GB, Switzerland, Belgium-Luxembourg, The Netherlands, Austria, Scandinavian countries, Spain, Portugal, Greece; Eastern Europe, in particular URSS, RDA, Poland; Arab countries and the Middle East such as Saudi Arabia, UAE, Kuwait, Iran, Libya; Africa, especially Côte d'Ivoire, Senegal, Cameroon, Gabon, Zaire, Nigeria, South Africa; Asia Pacific, Japan, Indonesia, Singapore, Malaysia, Hong Kong, Australia, China, North and South Korea, the Indian subcontinent; finally Latin America, Brazil, Mexico, Peru, Venezuela, Colombia, Cuba and North America, USA, Canada.
81 SGA, Board Minutes, 7 September 1972: 'L'essentiel de nos revenus provient de la Métropole. Nous avons progressivement amélioré le rapport de nos profits Étranger/France, constatant d'ailleurs que nous étions sans doute l'une des banques dont les revenues étaient les moins élevés non point parce que nous faisions trop d'efforts sur la France mais parce que nous n'en faisions pas assez à l'étranger. Il n'en demeure pas moins que notre Maison doit continuer à être préoccupée d'abord par la Métropole, source essentielle de ses revenus, et en second lieu par l'international'.
82 CLA, 110AH10, Direction Centrale des Affaires Internationales, 'Programme 1974 – 76', 30 October 1973.
83 Quoted in Richard Roberts (with C. Arnander), *Take Your Partners. Orion, the Consortium Banks and the Transformation of the Euromarkets*, Palgrave, Basingstoke, UK, 2001, 44.
84 Ibid.
85 MBA 0200/0749b, The Strategy of Midland Bank Group and International Banking November 1974.
86 Lothar Gall. Gerald D. Feldman, Harold James, Carl-Ludwig Holtfrerich and Hans E. Büschgen, *The Deutsche Bank 1870–1995*, Weidenfeld & Nicolson, London, 1995, 750.
87 See Lothar Gall, Gerald D. Feldman, Harold James, Carl-Ludwig Holtfrerich and Hans E. Büschgen, *The Deutsche Bank 1870–1995*, Weidenfeld & Nicolson, London, 1995.

3 The impact of oil

I have never been a very rich man, Mr. Holmes – never made but one investment in my life, as Dr. Trevelyan would tell you. But I don't believe in bankers. I would never trust a banker, Mr. Holmes.

(Sir Arthur Conan Doyle, 'The Resident Patient',
The Memoirs of Sherlock Holmes, 1894)

Bankers have a wealth of experience in judging the merits of investment, the quality of management, and the risks involved.[1]

Changing times

In 1973 an earthquake of epic proportions shook the foundations of Western economies. The cuts in oil production, the increase in oil prices and the embargo declared by the Organization of the Petroleum Exporting Countries (OPEC) led to the first energy crisis and gave the *coup de grâce* to the period usually called the 'golden age' of economic growth.[2]

The shock created huge monetary imbalances in the world economy. On the one side, OPEC countries experienced vast inflows of dollars looking for a place to go; on the other, both developed and developing countries experienced balance of payments deficits. A need to rebalance such a situation emerged as the crucial issue in international circles. Many possibilities were considered as to how to deal with these imbalances and who would be responsible for the adjustment of the world economy. In the end, the task was delegated to private actors, more precisely to Western (US, European and Japanese) commercial banks.

The International Monetary Fund in particular, but also the Bank for International Settlements and the Organisation for Economic Co-operation and Development, decided not to counteract but to accept oil-induced imbalances and pushed for a 'recycling', i.e. a transfer of oil money through private channels, delegating the task of channelling these funds from surplus to deficit countries through the unregulated Euromarket.

After initial hesitations, the banking sector accepted the task because after the first oil shock their domestic business was facing a sluggish demand from local customers. Since developed countries were able to receive funds directly from

OPEC countries or through the Eurobond market, commercial bank credit came to play a crucial role especially amongst LDCs.

Thus, starting in 1973, Western commercial banks found themselves in a peculiar situation. On the one hand, they were facing a gloomy scenario in their home countries with unsatisfactory rates of growth and profit, and on the other, they were flooded with money from OPEC countries and pressured by international organisations such as the IMF to smooth the rebalancing of monetary imbalances acting as intermediaries between OPEC countries and LDCs.

In this context, the non-oil developing countries 'faced the choice of draconian reductions in economic growth and standard of living, with the probability of serious social and political upheaval or financing balance of payments deficits by borrowing from private sources e.g. transnational banks through the Euromarkets'.[3] Ultimately, the latter option was preferred.

This privatisation of capital flows represented a whole new phenomenon taking place after years of official control over financial flows and institutions and of official aid going to LDCs. This delegation of power had a two-fold implication.

In the shorter term, it tied once and for all the destiny of developing countries to Western banks. In the longer term, it triggered the process of empowerment of the banking and financial sector after years of financial conservatism that characterised the system of Bretton Woods[4] and inaugurated a neo-liberal phase in economic policies, where neo-liberalism is intended as 'the reestablishment of the domination of finance after a period of retreat'.[5]

To our knowledge, the recycling of petrodollars through the Euromarket has not yet received an extensive analysis from historians and other social scientists. One notable exception is the seminal work of David E. Spiro. Despite being extremely informative, the author tells a story relying exclusively on American sources and adopting an American point of view.[6] This chapter will strive to offer a more transnational, comparative and historical perspective in order to describe the broader (economic, political and social) tendencies that shaped the recycling process and the rise of global finance. The first section will describe the battle over the destiny of the Euromarket between those wishing to control it and those against. The second section will illustrate how the oil crisis changed the ball game by shifting the priorities of policymakers. The final section will conclude the chapter.

The battle of Basel: controllers vs. free-marketeers

The creation of the 'Standing Committee on the Euro-currency Market' in April 1971, which we illustrated in Chapter 1, represented the most serious challenge to the survival of the Euromarket and, consequently, to the foundations of modern finance. The debates of the Standing Committee are of capital importance and worthy of thorough analysis in order to understand how perceptions and priorities were modified by the oil crisis. If we consider the Euromarket as the progenitor of modern finance, the battle around its control has to be considered as a battle to decide whether the whole international financial architecture had to be controlled or not. Eric Helleiner mentions that 'the West European and Japanese representatives stressed the need to control such flows', while the US 'continued to oppose controls'.[7] The evidence provided in this chapter somewhat alters this well-established narrative and adds a new layer of complexity to the existing literature.

When the first meeting of the Standing Committee took place in May 1971, the first decision was the agreement by central banks of the G-10 not to increase official placements on the Euromarket in order to limit its growth. This decision had been pushed forward, not surprisingly, by Germany and the Netherlands. In fact it is difficult not to remark that in March 1971 a paper from Professor G. A. Kessler of the Dutch Central Bank was circulated 'at the suggestion of the Chairman [Otmar Emminger]' entitled 'The United States Deficit, the Euro-Currency Market and World Inflation' (the Bank of England labelled it 'a tendentious note'). In the conclusion of this paper it was explicitly stated that 'the existence of the Euro-currency market, as this market has been functioning up to now, has considerably reinforced the inflationary effects of the big U.S. monetary deficit'. In order to fight inflation, the paper continued, it was vitally important that 'the U.S. monetary deficit is drastically reduced' and that 'an international co-operative effort be made *to put restraints on the expansion . . . of the Euro-currency market* and in particular on the foreign lending activity of R.W. [rest of the world] commercial banks [emphasis added]'.[8]

Nevertheless, the Germans were not the only ones behind this decision. Contrary to the popular argument that the Americans wished to undermine any kind of controls on finance, the decision to stop official placements on the Euromarket was actively supported by the United States. In an internal memorandum of the Bank of England relating to the first meeting of the Standing Committee, it is clearly stated that:

> Zijlstra . . . put on the table a proposal (made strongly . . . *by the Americans and the Germans*) that pending a further report by the Standing Committee . . . the central banks present should decide not to increase the total of their placements, direct or through the BIS, in the Euro-currency market [emphasis added].

The revealing paper continues:

> Burns [Arthur, Chairman of the federal Reserve from 1970 to 1978], who had been very hectoring in a private discussion with us, was almost as heavy in the meeting, chiding those central banks who, in unworthy pursuit of profit, had unwittingly invented 'a new dollar creating mechanism of great power' and so jeopardised the whole of international monetary co-operation.

Burns even brought 'a personal message from the President [of the United States], to the effect that he is determined to fight inflation as when he came into office and that he repudiates the doctrine of "benign neglect" of the balance of payments'.[9] New archival evidence, thus, offers a much more complex picture than the current narratives, suggesting that there was much more contention about the future of the Euromarket than existing accounts would imply and that the US had a much more ambivalent attitude towards this market, while the Bank of England emerges clearly as the strongest advocate of the Euromarket. The above raises questions about Jeffrey Chwieroth's account which argues that:

> *The French Government – in two initiatives taken in 1971 – promoted the use of cooperative controls.* The first initiative . . . produced agreement among the Group of 10 (G-10) central bankers to limit their placements of funds in the Eurocurrency market to help stem its growth, marking the first attempt to curb the expansion of this market [emphasis added].[10]

We argue instead that the first measures to regulate the Eurodollar market were promoted by the Federal Reserve and the *Bundesbank*, particularly through Otmar Emminger, and the President of the *Bundesbank*, Karl Klasen (who remarked that if the G-10 did not establish a Standing Committee on the Euromarkets 'our whole Western system would be in jeopardy'[11]), while France played only a supportive, albeit not negligible, role. These assumptions are substantiated not only by the above-mentioned document but also by various documents at the BIS archives on the origins of the Standing Committee and at the IMF. In a personal memorandum explicitly entitled 'Controlling the Euro-Dollar Market', the European Department noted that:

> The issue [of controlling the Eurodollar market] has been obfuscated from two different directions. On the one hand, there are those who instinctively feel that dealings in international currencies on the scale which now takes place should in principle be brought *under some form of inspection and control*. Because it is almost impossible to see how this could be done by a single central bank, we are led to seek an international mode of control. On the other side there are those (*the Governor of the Bank of England being an outstanding example*) who instinctively feel that any form of interference with an institution which works well and (because it provides a needed service) is highly profitable is on the face of it a bad thing [emphasis added].[12]

At this point, it seems that, at least in certain departments of the Fund, the attitude of the IMF towards free capital flows was less univocal than expected. The author of the memorandum indicated that on the issue of controls: 'It will be clear that my own prejudices lie in the direction of seeking some form of control'. A report dated August 1972 clearly stated that: 'It has been suggested that foreign currency banking [i.e. the Euromarket business], which in most countries is not subject to extensive regulation, should be subjected to some form of coordinated control'. The object of these measures would be to 'limit the extent to which disturbing short-term flows could be financed through these markets'.[13]

At the IMF, the reason to seek a regulation of the off-shore market was twofold. First, there had never been a market as large as this without a lender of last resort that had not at some time produced a financial crisis. Consequently, as the size of the market expanded to become significant compared even to the U.S. money supply, this problem became larger and more urgent.

It seems that the IMF was still, at least until the late 1960s and very early 1970s, the guardian of fixed parities and, more generally, of a 'Keynesian' orthodoxy and not yet a prophet of financial liberalisation as is usually represented by a growing literature in recent years.[14] The second reason to regulate the market was that the Euro-currency markets as they had been operating had increased short-term currency flows and therefore made international crises larger, notably between 1969 and 1973.

The 'Brave New World' which was, maybe too quickly, starting to appear on the horizon after years of controlled markets and Keynesian compromise seemed somewhat to baffle the established beliefs of the IMF staff: 'Perhaps crises are healthy, and perhaps patterns of exchange rates devised by international bureaucrats need disturbances from market forces from time to time. But *if you believe in fixed parities your affection for short-term capital flows cannot be very warm* [emphasis added]'.[15]

German monetary authorities appear clearly as the leaders of the 'conservative wing' within the G-10, receiving support particularly from strong-currency countries such as the Netherlands and Switzerland, while the United Kingdom appears as the flag-bearer of the more liberal wing, with the support of smaller countries such as Belgium and Luxembourg (where the Eurodollar business was actively supported to foster the region as a financial hub) and the US had a nuanced position. In all the documents related to the Standing Committee, the German's will to regulate this off-shore market is evident:

> There were certain major markets for Euro-funds, such as London and Luxembourg, where the banks' foreign currency liabilities were not subject to any regulations whatsoever. That had been a disturbing element, and might in future be more so . . . *There was no doubt in his* [Ottmar Emminger] *mind that the banks' foreign currency business should be subject to the same conditions as their domestic credit operations* [emphasis added].[16]

In particular, Germany was proposing to recreate on a European scale what had been in place domestically throughout the 1960s. In fact, liabilities to non-residents (including foreign banks) were subject to reserve requirements similar to those on the banks' liabilities to domestic non-banks. This attitude was one of the reasons why Frankfurt never became a Euromarket centre.

At the BIS, the reason to study the Eurocurrency market was two-fold. One problem, at the national level, was represented by the obstacles with which the central banks 'monetary policy is faced as a result of inflows of funds from the Euro-currency market'. On the international level, the issue was 'the disturbing effect of Euro-currency operations on the smooth working of the international monetary system'.[17] The rationale for setting up of the Committee is summarised in a paper from 1972 prepared by Milton Gilbert, Head of the Economic Department of the BIS, which embarks upon a difficult exercise of tightrope walking between the hardliners of more regulation (Germany) and those wishing a benign neglect of the Eurodollar phenomenon (UK). Gilbert remarked that the growth of the Euromarket had caused far-reaching changes in monetary conditions at both national and international level. In fact, by linking together the money markets of different countries, notably of Europe and the US, the market had greatly increased cross-border capital mobility. This internationalisation of world liquidity appeared to a number of central banks as a 'source of trouble' for, as we have previously seen in the German case, it facilitated speculative movements of funds frustrating the monetary authorities' efforts to combat inflation. Moreover, central banks found themselves with the dilemma of either bringing their interest rates into line with the Euromarket, without regard for the requirements of the domestic situation, or setting off large inflows or outflows of capital with their contractionary or expansionary effects on domestic liquidity and monetary reserves. Ultimately, these developments 'have led to calls for the operation of the Euro-currency market to be controlled'.[18]

In Basel, the debate inside the Committee was long and often difficult as the two antagonistic positions were facing each other. These two positions represented not only distinct political implications but, more generally, two distinct visions about the future of the monetary and financial system. The Bank of England in a document sent to the BIS, aptly defined the issues at stake as 'philosophical'.[19]

The 'controllers', saw the world in a not too dissimilar manner to the officials of Bretton Woods, a world where private financial flows were to be controlled in a cooperative way and embedded within a broader set of economic and social norms, where domestic priorities would prevail over international ones. The 'free-marketeers' envisioned a brave new world where capital flows would be free to move from one country to another, where finance was a second-class citizen no more, but, instead, would play a positive and equilibrating role in our economies, directing capital where due without the distortions of the public hand. In this sense, the debate around the Euromarket at the BIS acquires the role of a defining moment in modern financial history, even more so than the election of Margaret Thatcher or Ronald Reagan, in the rise of global finance and neoliberalism.[20]

The debate between controllers and free-marketeers can be further historicised by seeing it as a decisive moment between two different kinds of societies, one based on a 'solid' form of capitalism and a new one 'liquefied, flowing, dispersed, scattered and deregulated'. If we agree that the post-war monetary and financial order built on the Keynesian 'middle-way' and on the embedded liberalist paradigm was a 'panoptical' order where the people at the helm were 'in the controlling tower' monitoring and directing capital flows, the financial and monetary order which started to take form in the early to mid-1970s is a disembedded and 'post-panoptical' one. An order where:

> [t]he concept of basing the international financial system once again on the model of a self-regulating market has increasingly dominated the agendas both of the major financial powers, especially the United States and the United Kingdom, and of the main economic actors in the international system, especially financial services firms and multinational corporations.[21]

A world, where the controller abdicates its prerogatives and responsibilities in favour of a disengaged attitude towards the international financial and monetary architecture.[22] This trust in the efficiency of market actors is clear from documents found at the Bank of England. In one document, for example, it is written that 'our tradition in Britain is of a much less formal system of supervision of banks than is customary elsewhere . . . Ultimately, *the stability of the market depends on the judgement and self-discipline of those who participate in it* [emphasis added]'.[23]

The origin and natural consequence of a post-panoptical world is what Susan Strange calls the 'retreat of the State', seen as a reversal of the state-market balance of power.[24]

The developments of the early 1970s could be interpreted as a fundamental moment in the secular shift towards the empowerment of the banking and financial sector and a decisive period to understand why 'where states were once the masters of the markets, now it is the markets which, on many crucial issues, are the masters over the governments of states'.[25] Contrary to some authors, such as Walter Wriston, former CEO of Citibank, who said that 'policymakers are discovering that many of the events that are altering the world come not in response to their actions, but are *driven by technologies* which they may only dimly understand [emphasis added]',[26] we do not see this evolution as something inevitable, perhaps because of the unstoppable advances in information technology.

Such a vision, quite common in the economic profession, is inaccurate at best and fatalistic at worst seeing the governments as powerless actors in an ever-changing world driven by anarchic forces. We disagree with such views and argue instead that governments and international institutions have played a central role in the *unleashing* of finance, in the *empowerment* of the banking and financial sector and in the *perpetuation* of their influence in economic matters with their decisions since the early 1970s. Geoffrey Underhill[27] argued that the relationship between states and markets is one of symbiosis, a 'condominium', and it is in the early 1970s that the condominium was built. The post-1973 relationship between states and private actors, especially banks, can be best described as a principal-agent relationship that, in the course of events, evolved into an increasingly asymmetrical one where 'States, having set up the conditions in which more open international financial markets were established in the 1970s and 1980s, are now having *difficulty controlling their own creations* [emphasis added]'.[28]

It was up to Milton Gilbert to summarise the positions within the Standing Committee on the Euro-currency market:

> The fundamental difference between the various central banks represented on the Committee was that *some believed that there was a problem and others did not*. They could not have a solution without a problem. All members of the Committee believed that Euro-currency flows could create problems for their own countries and that the central bank and the government authorities had the power to take action to help deal with them. However, some

countries considered that there was no need to go beyond that and that there was no kind of problem for which a combined effort was needed, while others believed that there were such problems [emphasis added].[29]

All in all, the balance of power seemed to swing in favour of the 'conservative' faction within the Committee, especially after the breakdown of the Bretton Woods system in 1971 which further contributed to highlight the speculative pressures coming from the Euromarket. At the end of 1972, four papers regarding the Euromarkets were on the table of BIS General Manager, Réné Larre, one from Italy, one from Germany, one from the UK and one from the US. The issues addressed in each paper were: first, the exchange rate instability; second, the interference with national monetary policies; and third, the general problem of inflation. The headline of the *Financial Times* below (Figure 3.1) gives us an idea of the centrality of the debate for the financial community. A special survey of the *Financial Times* clearly stated that:

> *The pendulum may now be swinging against the Euromarkets.* After more than a decade of virtually uninterrupted growth, the international money and capital markets could be entering an era during which their development will be retarded by a combination of internal and external pressures. Probably the most serious threat to the markets' role as the largest source of international liquidity is that of the control imposed by national and international organisations. A growing number of politicians and central bankers appear determined to *tame the 'Euromonster'* which they hold responsible for the monetary upheavals of the past year [the breakdown of Bretton Woods] . . . [emphasis added].[30]

The four papers had little agreement on each of these topics, but two clear lines of thought can be traced. On the one side, some members of the Committee, wishing to control this off-shore market, saw the role of the Euromarket in recent macro-economic disturbances as quite relevant. Some members were particularly worried about rapid rate of growth, the absence of regulations on this market, the

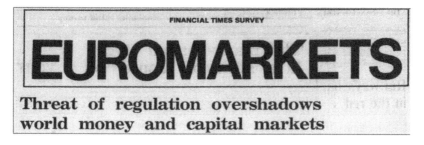

Figure 3.1 The 'threat' of regulation of the Euromarket.

Source: *Financial Times*, 13 March 1972.

'artificial' competitiveness of the Eurobanks compared to domestic banks and, finally, the potential for credit creation. On the other side, some members insisted on the fact that 'even without the intermediation of the Euro-currency market, international movements of short-term funds would still take place on a substantial scale because of exchange rate uncertainties and interest rate differentials'.[31]

The disagreement on such fundamental issues ultimately produced two antagonistic sets of policy measures. One proposal (elaborated by the UK and US) was that every country would take *national* defensive measures to offset short-term movements of funds; the second proposal pushed for *coordinated* controls on the Eurocurrency markets. Within this line of intervention, two proposals were being analysed, the first one coming from Germany and the second from Italy. The German proposal involved the coordinated reserve requirements on foreign currency liabilities, while the Italian proposal called for the creation of a regulated area (essentially the European Economic Community, EEC) where the overall rate of growth of the Euromarkets and the distribution of Eurocurrencies between different countries of the regulated area would be controlled. Moreover, vis-à-vis the outside area, the controls of the regulated area countries would consist of reserve requirements on deposits taken by their banks, and a *Bardepot* (a cash deposit) on borrowings of their non-banks. The proposal also involved open-market operations: if the problem were one of flows between countries inside the regulated area, the international agency which absorbed the funds from the market would deposit them with the central banks of the countries from which the outflow had occurred. This recycling would protect countries from losing reserves as a result of currency flows within the area. If the problem were an inflow from the outside area, the funds absorbed by the international agency would be placed outside the regulated area.

The Bank of England moved two main criticisms against this proposal. First, open-market operations could not be effectively undertaken unless the countries forming the regulated area had reached a fairly advanced stage of monetary integration. Second, it was remarked that it could sometimes be difficult to distinguish between temporary flows and those resulting from underlying payment disequilibria. Third and foremost:

> [t]he proposed reserve requirement on Euro-currency deposits received from the outside area would put the banks of the regulated area at a disadvantage in competing with outside-area banks both in bidding for, and therefore also in lending, funds outside the regulated area.[32]

A new plan, comprising some German and some Italian elements and also taking into consideration British criticisms, was presented in January 1973 and put the Bank of England in great difficulty. The intention of the scheme was to tax foreign-currency liabilities without placing banks at a disadvantage compared with banks in non-regulated countries. It involved a uniform reserve requirement to be imposed on foreign currency liabilities of banks situated in the regulated area, supplemented by a reserve requirement on borrowing by non-banks in the regulated area from outside. The reserve requirement would

be imposed on liabilities of banks in the regulated area in all foreign currencies owed to any non-bank resident of any country of the regulated area, while
liabilities to other banks in the regulated area would be excluded. The reserve
requirement would also include net liabilities of banks in the regulated area to
the outside area (whether owed to banks or non-banks and whether in domestic or foreign currency). Finally, the reserve requirement would affect gross
liabilities of non-banks in the regulated area to the outside area (whether owed
to banks or non-banks and whether in domestic of foreign currency). The regulated area was not specified but it seemed to coincide with an eventual European
monetary union, as Kit McMahon put it 'the scheme in fact involves something
much wider than regulating Euro-currency banking operations. It would be a
first step towards creating an exchange control ring fence around the EEC'.[33]

The new plan addressed the major criticism moved by the Bank of England,
that is displacing business to off-shore centres, by restricting the requirement to
net liabilities to the outside area and imposing a tax on non-bank's borrowing
from outside. A bank inside the area could borrow, from inside or out, without
paying the tax; if it lent to the outside area, a bank outside the area could borrow
from inside or outside the area without paying the tax; but if it lent inside the area
it would have to absorb some of the tax imposed on the borrower.[34]

The unease of the Bank of England was clearly visible. The Economic Section
labelled the document as 'the *most coherent* which we have seen, and the *hardest
to resist*, since it contains a *neat solution* to the problem of migration of business
[emphasis added]'.[35] In an internal note along the same lines, it is stated that:

> [t]his scheme is going to be much more difficult for us to controvert than
> any of the previous propositions . . . It presents, in other words, an *entirely
> coherent framework* for dealing with problems of monetary flows between
> the regulated and the outside world [emphasis added].[36]

The only way to undermine the discussion was to argue that the Standing
Committee was not the appropriate forum to discuss such an ambitious scheme
involving international short-term capital flows and not simply the Eurocurrency
market. According to the Bank of England, the appropriate forum for the problems of capital flows was the Committee of Twenty (C-20) of the IMF,[37] while the
question of harmonisation of banking controls was a matter for the EEC. Despite
such a line of argument, the final BIS proposal to control the Euromarket was sent
to the Governors and was discussed during their June meeting.

In the end, the battle was harsh between those who considered the Euro-currency
market as an integral and interchangeable part of international capital movements
and '*do not favour specific controls of Euro-banking* as such' and those who felt
that without the facilities offered, foreign currency banking international capital
flows and the problems associated with them would be considerably smaller and
thus '*favour an international approach aimed specifically at the regulation of the
Euro-currency* [emphasis added]'.[38] From the heated debate described above, we
can see that the smooth functioning and the liberty of the Euromarket (and, more

generally, international finance) were at stake up to the summer of 1973. Then, a stroke of good luck came to save the world of finance.

A new ball game: the first oil shock and the liberalisation of finance

The oil shock that followed the Yom Kippur war in October 1973 changed the course of recent financial history not only by introducing huge amounts of money into the financial system but, in particular, by bringing the regulatory agenda to an end and shifting the priorities of national and international monetary authorities.

The Yom Kippur war served mainly as a pretext to justify a unilateral increase in the price of oil, something the OPEC countries had been asking for without success at the meeting between OPEC and oil companies in Vienna in April 1973 and before that at the Geneva meeting of January 1972. It was at this latter meeting where OPEC producers managed at least to obtain compensation after the dollar devaluation by receiving a 8.5 per cent increase in the price of oil and a permanent indexation of its price based on the value of the dollar. These attempts were the continuation of the early initiatives of 1970–71, under the aegis of Libya's new ruler, Colonel Gaddafi (along with Algeria and Iraq), which constituted the first break with the cheap oil policies of the post-war era.[39]

When war was declared, OPEC countries agreed to reduce their production by 25 per cent on average in November 1973. A committee composed of Saudi Arabia, Algeria, Libya and Kuwait was created to divide oil-importing countries into 'friendly', 'neutral' and 'hostile' states and to enforce the embargo on the latter ones. The US, South Africa, Rhodesia, Denmark, the Netherlands[40] and Portugal were embargoed. France, Italy and West Germany, for example, were considered 'friendly' states. The embargo on the US would be lifted in March 1974 at the OPEC meeting in Vienna thanks to Henry Kissinger's 'shuttle diplomacy', which contributed crucially to the disengagement agreements between Egypt and Israel, known as 'Sinai I' in January 1974 (which would be followed by 'Sinai II' in September 1975), and between Syria and Israel in May 1974.[41]
The shock was of epic proportions, particularly because of the increasing post-war dependence of Western countries on oil as opposed to solid fuel. As historian Tony Judt reminded us, in 1950 coal and coke accounted for 83 per cent of Western Europe's energy consumption, while oil accounted for just 8.5 per cent. These figures changed entirely in the 1970s, when the figures were 29 per cent and 60 per cent respectively. The post-war consumer boom greatly increased the dependence of Western countries on cheap oil.[42] Countries like Italy and Portugal imported up to 80 per cent of their energy requirements.

The shock was a defining moment in recent economic history, for it marked the definitive end of the gilded age of capitalism and left permanent marks on the surface of Western economies from which, with the benefit of hindsight, they never recovered, as borne out by GDP figures and productivity growth in Europe and the US. Overall GDP growth of the seven largest OECD economies was drastically cut, from an average of 5.1 per cent during the period 1960–69 to 3.6 per cent during the period 1969–79 and 3 per cent for the period 1979–1990.[43] Between 1973 and 1974, OPEC revenues increased from around US$35 billion to US$113 billion. According to the OECD, the landed price of Arabian light crude in Europe and North America, which stood at around US$3.45 per barrel before the crisis, and at around US$5 before Christmas 1973, reached US$9 on 1 January 1974 before stabilising at around US$12. The current account balance of industrialised countries was in surplus by US$3 billion in 1973, while in 1974 it experienced a deficit of US$33 billion. It must be pointed out that the crisis of 1973 intervened at the end of a long wave of post-war expansion in Western Europe, when the level of industrial output was already well below the long-run average of the previous 20 years.[44] As historian Robert Brenner has remarked, average rates of growth of output, capital stock, labour productivity and real wages after 1973 have been one-third to one-half of those for the period 1950–73, while the average unemployment rate has been more than double.[45]

All Western countries implemented extraordinary measures to save oil. In the US, Sunday petrol was prohibited and many European countries prohibited Sunday driving (except UK, France and Ireland). Sweden, Norway and the Netherlands introduced rationing of oil by late 1973/early 1974. Governmental control of energy supplies was implemented in Germany and Japan. Measures concerning capital flows were also implemented.

Any possible regulation of the Euromarket was subdued and watered down not only at the BIS but also at the WP3 and the IMF. In a letter dated April 1974, found at the Bank of England, written by the Governor of the Bank, it is clearly stated that 'at the Working Party 3 meeting in Tokyo there was some discussion over the possibility of exchange of information over conditions in the euro-markets. It was readily agreed that the *plans for international capital issues control . . . were impracticable* [emphasis added]'.[46]

At the meeting of the Standing Committee on the Euro-currency market in Basel, Milton Gilbert, interrogated about the state of the harmonisation schemes, 'rightly observed that *the oil crisis had changed the ball game* [emphasis added]' and that 'the pressing question now was the soundness of the [Eurodollar] market'.[47] The shift in priorities was epochal.

Even countries with strong currencies were now faced with huge monetary imbalances and deficits. The issue now was not how to insulate from the rest of the world but how to open up to international financial flows and get the money that was missing at the national level. As pointed out in a paper of the Overseas Office of the Bank of England in March 1974:

> Many Continental European countries, with the recent large increases in oil prices, are now facing the prospect of having to finance oil-induced balance of payments deficits. In the recent past, these countries, having experienced high levels of economic growth, have been recipients of substantial speculative inflows of international capital, particularly during the many currency crises of the seventies. Given that such inflows tended during times of monetary restraint to undermine domestic monetary priorities, measures were taken

to stem speculative inflows in many of these countries. Now, *faced with the changing economic situation* – the need to finance oil-induced deficits – some countries have taken initial steps to relay these controls [emphasis added].[48]

Emminger's priority shifted accordingly, from an unattainable regulation towards a more realistic exchange of information on a confidential basis during the meetings in Basel. Again, the Bank of England was sceptical about giving 'true' confidential information, but agreed to share details on interest rates, maturities and spreads.[49]

As Charles Goodhart has pointed out, the oil shock of 1973 had the effect of:

[r]eversing (official) concerns about the Euromarket, from worries about whether it was *too expansionary* (to be consistent with the Bretton Woods pegged exchange rate system), to worries about whether it was *too anaemic* and unstable to play a major role in recycling petrodollars from oil-exporting countries to oil importers [emphasis added].[50]

Almost all Western countries took measures to ease controls on non-residents' bank deposits and non-residents' investments in domestic securities. What was considered until the beginning of the year a source of disequilibrium was now a much welcome source of finance.

As to the first point, several countries took measures to ease or abolish minimum reserve requirements against non-resident bank deposits and to ease limitations on the payment of interest to non-residents. On the second point, new measures to facilitate inflows of international capital took the form of relaxations of controls restricting foreign investments in domestic securities.

This point was particularly evident in Germany, Switzerland and the Netherlands, precisely the countries that had pushed for more regulation. The general tendency towards a more relaxed approach towards international capital movements was even more evident in weaker currency countries such as Italy and France. In the latter, various measures were introduced in January 1974 to encourage capital inflows and to stem outflows. In France, the maximum amount of funds which could be raised abroad without the authorities' prior approval was increased from FF2 million to FF10 million. The dual exchange market system, introduced in August 1971 to stem capital inflows, was abolished in March 1974. Moreover, the French government announced in February 1974 that it had arranged to borrow US$1.5 billion from the Eurodollar market. Similarly, in Italy several measures were taken to discourage capital outflows and induce inflows. The basic discount rate was raised from 6.5 per cent to 9 per cent in March, while the dual exchange system was abolished in January.[51] Thus, the first borrowers on the Euromarket in 1974 were not LDCs, for the recycling mechanism took a few months to be implemented, but developed countries. Overall, Western economies accounted for 60 per cent of total Euroloans. Developing countries accounted for 35 per cent, Mexico being the largest borrower with US$1.25 billion and Algeria the second with US$1 billion. LDCs accounted for the rest.[52]

Countries such as Belgium, Germany, the Netherlands and Switzerland relaxed the restrictions imposed on inflows of funds imposed at the beginning of the 1970s at the height of the Bretton Woods' turbulences.

All of a sudden, after the boom of the early 1970s, the world was confronted with a new situation: growth, which was already slowing down by the late 1960s, disappeared, as did balanced budgets, while huge deficits made their appearance. On top of that, the era of stable oil prices was over (we must not forget that the price of oil had been almost unchanged for 20 years).

Periods of crises are a fertile ground for new policies and ideas. There is a natural human tendency to attribute present failures to past behaviours, and the oil shock with the imbalances it created turned out to be a strong catalyst for changes in economic policies.

IMF Managing Director, H. J. Witteveen, pointed out in a speech at the Economic Club of Detroit that the new deficits and surpluses were of a peculiar character for they had come about very suddenly and they could not be eliminated '*by any of the traditional policy responses* which the Fund and its members have come to regard as normal over the past twenty-five years [emphasis added]'.[53]

What was the traditional policy response of Western countries? Witteveen was referring to the policies implemented in the 1930s, i.e. internal deflation and import restraint. Nevertheless, according to Witteveen, in the context of an oil-induced deficit each of these policies would be wrong because deliberate exchange rate depreciations by industrial countries would risk a return to the 'beggar-my-neighbour policies which proved so harmful in the 1930s'.[54] This speech reflected the views expressed by the C-20 in January 1974 during the Finance Ministers' meeting and, particularly, by the WP3 of the OECD in an informal meeting held on 16 January just before the Ministerial Conference of the C-20 (17–18 January). In this fundamental meeting, two main points were on the agenda of the WP3. The first one was the impact on the balance of payments, the appropriate policy responses and balance of payments aims; the second one was the issue of financing problems and particularly how far the deficits should be financed out of reserves and how far by borrowing.[55]

What was emphatically decided was bound to have long-lasting consequences on the rest of the decade.

Ultimately, three important points emerged from the discussion. First and foremost, OECD countries had to 'accept the oil deficit' whatever it would turn out to be. Second, countries recognised that deficit countries had to make structural efforts to correct that part of their balance of payments deficit which had nothing to do with oil. Finally, there was considerable concern about the consequences of the oil rise for the developing countries which 'were not fortunate enough to have their own oil'.[56]

Because of the confidential character of the WP3, it was up to the IMF to lay down officially the foundations for the new world economic order. Banks would play a crucial role in it as a fundamental vehicle between Western governments and developing countries. The basic ideas of the policies to come were stated in the final communiqué issued by the C-20. The Committee agreed that:

In managing their international payments, *countries must not adopt policies which would merely aggravate the problems of other countries.* Accordingly they stressed the importance of avoiding competitive depreciation and the escalation of restrictions on trade and payments. They further resolved to pursue policies that would sustain appropriate levels of economic activity and employment, while minimizing inflation. They recognized that serious difficulties would be created for many developing countries and that their needs for financial resources will be greatly increased; and they urged all countries with available resources to make every effort to supply these needs on appropriate terms [emphasis added].[57]

A few days after the Rome meeting, the Secretary-General of the OECD, Emile van Lennep, singled out the three main threats faced by the developed world at the annual address to the Consultative Assembly of the Council of Europe. First of all, the rise in oil prices would almost certainly influence the price-wage spiral. A second threat was represented by 'an unwanted contractionary effect on the general level of economic activity and of employment', as income which would have been spent in local economies was being transferred to oil-producing countries. The third danger involved the impact of the oil crisis on the balance of payments of OECD countries, as developed countries gradually plunged into the red. The central issue was to avoid a spiral of competitive – and mutually frustrating – devaluation, deflation and trade restrictions – the disastrous spiral which had been witnessed between the two World Wars. Consequently, it was crucial to:

[c]onsider what steps need to be taken to enable the very large amounts of capital that will . . . be flowing out of oil-producing countries to be made available in the geographical locations . . . that will *most facilitate the continued expansion of world trade and employment* [emphasis added].

The ideal customer was found quickly by van Lennep: 'One obviously important group of countries to whom part of these funds should be channelled is the less-developed countries'.[58]

A basic agreement was reached on the idea that OPEC surpluses could not and should not be fought; on the contrary, developed countries had to accept these surpluses and elaborate together a mechanism to transfer their deficits to the developing world – the last missing element was how to achieve that.

At that time the IMF did not have enough funds; its quotas as a percentage of total imports declined from 11.2 per cent in 1955 to 3.7 per cent in 1982.[59] Two oil facilities were developed by Witteveen in 1974 and 1975 for a total amount of 6.9 billion SDR (corresponding to around US$8 billion), but, given the size of balance of payments' deficits, the IMF was not in a solid position to be the main protagonist of the story. Moreover, the oil facilities never gained favour in the eyes of the US, who considered them too benevolent towards the 'aggression' of OPEC. The IMF knew that, as did other international organisations such as the

Bank for International Settlements. In a signed letter addressed to the Governor of the Bank of England dated June 1974 it is stated:

> I had a word with Zijlstra [Governor of the Netherlands Bank and Chairman of the Board of Directors of the BIS] in Luxembourg about recycling and a possible role for the BIS. Zijlstra said his own feelings were much in line with ours: viz., it was natural and right that the *intermediation job should start with the banking system . . . The IMF facility was useful but would never amount to much.* The BIS would, he was sure, have a *real role* [emphasis added].[60]

In the aforementioned speech, Witteveen continued by recognising the 'basic role' of private markets as the main protagonists in financing balance of payments disequilibria. Witteveen remarked that *'the Euro-currency markets may be expected to be the main channel* [emphasis added]' because they were well equipped to handle large volumes of funds and offered the *'flexibility* and the *anonymity* that the lenders desire [emphasis added].[61]

With slight variations, this is the policy that would be followed during the decade up to the debt crisis of 1982. This is not to say that international organisations never questioned the privatisation of the recycling mechanism, for example in a WP3 document of 1981 it is stated that:

> [g]iven the position of banks which evolved following OPEC-I and the large potential recycling needs associated with OPEC-II, bank regulatory and supervisory authorities have indicated (to varying degrees) concern about the international exposure of banks, the adequacy of bank capital and the need for increasing attention to be paid to limits on country risks, maturity matching and consolidation of balance sheets.

Despite these elements, the top priority remained the smooth functioning of the recycling process and controls always remained on the side lines. Official expressions of concern, while they sometimes resulted in direct intervention in banks' international lending activity, did not alter lending decisions given the need for banks to continue to play an important role in recycling. Consequently, 'regulatory or supervisory practices should not be tightened so abruptly as to lead to a substantial pull-back in the international lending activity of banks with corresponding adverse macro-economic effects'.[62]

We can get an idea of the huge amounts of Euro-currency bank credits and the burden of debt on LDCs economies from Tables 3.1 and 3.2. The first table shows us how the conditions of private flows towards developing countries were markedly different from official ones. Private commitments had much shorter maturities than official ones, while charging also markedly higher interest rates. Given the inflation rates prevailing in the mid- to late 1970s, real interest rates remained favourable to borrowers but, as rates started to increase and inflation was reduced, the burden of debt became much heavier starting from 1979.

Table 3.1 Average term of commitments for 94 non-oil LDCs, 1972–79.

	1972	1973	1974	1975	1976	1977	1978	1979	Average 1972–79
Interest Rate (%)									
Official Creditors	4.3	4.2	4.4	4.9	5.5	5.2	5.0	5.0	4.8
Private Creditors	7.3	9.1	9.7	8.8	7.9	8.0	9.4	11.6	9.0
Average	5.6	6.7	7.0	6.9	6.8	6.8	7.9	9.3	7.1
Maturity (years)									
Official Creditors	24.2	25.4	23.4	23.5	22.1	22.6	24.8	25.0	23.9
Private Creditors	8.9	10.8	10.1	7.8	8.1	8.0	8.9	8.9	8.9
Average	17.6	18.0	16.9	15.3	14.3	14.0	14.5	14.6	15.7

Source: IBRD, World Debt Tables, retrieved from OECDA, CPE/WP3(81)5.

From Table 3.2 we can appreciate how identified gross indebtedness of non-OPEC LDCs to the BIS reporting banks went up, from US$32 billion to US$247 billion, a sevenfold increase, between 1973 and 1982. According to the BIS, this increase represented more than twice the growth of these countries' aggregate gross national product and more than twice the growth of their aggregate exports over the same period. Consequently, their external bank debt increased from 60 to 130 per cent of their exports. In the case of Eastern Europe, external banking debt increased from US$10 billion to US$61 billion between 1973 and 1982, compared to an increase from US$14.5 billion to US$50 billion in their exports to Western countries.

The main vehicle for the recycling mechanism was found in the Euroloan market. A Euroloan was a credit, issued by several banks at flexible interest rates (generally LIBOR plus spread), on a medium-term basis (five to ten years on average), generally in dollars, for large amounts which enabled international banks to absorb much larger deposits. These loans were used for a variety of purposes, to pay for imports and to finance infrastructures, etc. The advantage of Euroloans compared to official credits, was their relative simplicity and lack of conditionality. The drawbacks were the variable interest rates which made the debtor vulnerable to increases in interest rates in developed countries and the shorter maturity than official loans.

Euroloans brought two critical innovations in the field of international bank lending: floating interest rates and syndication. The so-called rollover technique had been around for a few years, but its application to Eurocurrency loans exploded in 1973; it allowed the banks to offer high-interest yields on short-term deposits to investors who were unwilling to invest in fixed-interest securities in a period of rising inflation.

Table 3.2 Estimated flows between the BIS reporting banks and groups of countries outside the reporting area (LDCs, Eastern Europe and OPEC countries, 1974–82, US$bn at constant end-quarter exchange rates).

	Stocks at end-1973	Flows 1974–77 Yearly average	Stocks at end-1977	1978	1979	1980	1981	1982	Stocks at end-1982
Non-OPEC LDCs									
Gross deposits	27.6	8.1	60.7	14.6	12.3	4.0	9.4	4.2	101.0
Gross borrowings	32.0	14.3	97.2	22.4	36.3	38.9	39.9	19.7	246.9
Net deposits	-4.4	-6.2	-36.5	-7.8	-24.0	-34.9	-30.5	-15.5	-145.9
Eastern Europe									
Gross deposits	4.5	0.7	8.4	1.7	4.6	0.9	0.1	1.9	16.4
Gross borrowings	9.5	5.1	38.3	5.7	7.1	6.8	4.8	-4.7	53.3
Net deposits	-5.0	-4.4	-29.9	-4.0	-2.5	-5.9	-4.7	6.6	-36.9
OPEC countries									
Gross deposits	16.0	14.8	77.9	3.3	37.4	41.8	3.3	-18.3	135.2
Gross borrowings	6.5	7.0	39.1	16.7	7.2	7.0	4.3	8.1	78.6
Net deposits	9.5	7.8	38.8	-13.4	30.2	34.8	-1.0	-26.4	56.6

Source: BIS Annual Report 1983, 120.

Additionally, it allowed banks to limit the risk of holding fixed-term securities in case of a rise in deposit rates. The borrowers enjoyed the liberty of avoiding being stuck with high interest rates in case of a slowdown in inflation and the flexibility of being able to repay the loan before the end of commitment period without penalty. Syndication consisted of sharing the loans amongst several banks and had existed for bonds since the nineteenth century, but was never systematically applied to bank loans. Syndication allowed banks to offer larger and larger amounts to customers, a timely innovation in the context of increasing balance of payments deficits. In fact, in the early 1970s, the Eurobond market was able to raise amounts of around US$100 million maximum, while the Euroloan market could raise ten times or more this amount.

The priority of national and international institutions was no more to regulate a possible source of instability, totally outside the control of monetary authorities, but to use the Euromarket to channel funds from OPEC countries to deficit countries, mainly in the developing world.

The stance of international institutions such as the WP3 of the OECD towards developing country indebtedness is quite clear. In a document written in January 1974, just a few months after the oil shock, it is clearly stated that:

> [f]rom the global point of view *it would seem very desirable for at least part of the increased savings of the oil producers to be passed on to the non-oil developing countries.* This would also help to reduce both the external and internal imbalance created in the OECD area [emphasis added].[63]

From international institutions such as the OECD and IMF, the policy of privatising credit through the recycling of petrodollars spread to national institutions. One of the clearest descriptions of the recycling mechanism can be found at the *Banque de France* archives where the Balance of Payment Department rapidly recognised the new challenges ahead:

> The OPEC countries will see in the coming years the opportunity to earn substantial capital . . . A significant portion of the surplus accumulated by OPEC countries will be at the expense of OECD countries that consume the largest share of world energy produced and whose supply of oil is mainly dependent on the Middle East.

They continued by describing the international scenario in the context of newfound economic instability:

> If we see it as a game with three agents, OPEC, OECD and the USA, where from the point of view of the trade balance one is a neutral (USA), and another in surplus (OPEC), it is obvious the third can only be in deficit . . . For this 'threesome' to lead to a sustainable balance in the medium term it would require the absorption capacity of OPEC countries to grow significantly: but if for some countries (Iraq, Iran, Algeria, Egypt) this ability is perhaps

currently underestimated (or at least could be stimulated), others such as Saudi Arabia, Libya and the Emirates of the Persian Gulf live permanently in a situation of *rentiers* and in these circumstances *only the introduction of a fourth economic agent can break the squared circle* [emphasis added].

A fourth economic agent was much needed to help European countries to alleviate their critical state – but where to find such an important element? The answer came quickly enough:

> *This agent will be called for convenience 'LDC'* [developing countries]. To redraw the map of balance of payments deficits and since this is to redress the balance of payments of the OECD and therefore *'transfer' to LDCs OECD's deficit*, it is important a) to give positive consideration to the deficits that developing countries will accumulate, b) to increase trade among developing countries and other agents (including OECD) since the volume of international trade will be the vehicle of this deficit [emphasis added].[64]

Essentially, LDCs had to accumulate debt in order to keep the world economy going and to avoid a world recession as in the 1930s. Borrowing by LDCs reflected not only the growing trust of international organisations (IMF, BIS and OECD) in private markets or the need to shore up earnings by commercial banks but also a demand coming from developing countries' regimes, generally 'one-party democracies' or military juntas, to finance productive investments in industrial sectors deemed strategic.

Banks again became a central actor in the world economy after the conservative years of Bretton Woods, and they experienced a major redeployment on global markets, which we shall illustrate in the following chapter. It is crucial to stress again that the empowerment of banking could not have been possible without the role of international institutions and the backing of national governments (generally through the central banks) to push them to embark on a risky adventure such as the recycling process.

Institutions like the BIS, the IMF and the Bank of England played a crucial role in shaping the modern financial landscape in the early 1970s. The Bank of England was the staunchest free-marketeer and played a fundamental role in influencing the policies of the IMF and, particularly, the BIS thanks to its privileged position at the centre of the Eurodollar business and main provider of (not always unbiased) statistics. Explaining the attitude of the Bank would require an entire chapter;[65] what it can be said here is that, especially amongst the Treasury and the Bank of England, 'there was a consensus that London should remain an important financial centre and that restricting the new business through invasive action was inadvisable'.[66] This attitude is largely corroborated by the archival evidence from the Bank of England. Amongst the numerous examples, the secret document sent from R. A. O. Bridge, Adviser to the Governors, to Maurice Parsons, Executive Director and later Deputy Governor, is particularly revealing:

> *The Euro currency market is in most ways a 'good thing' and it is a source of profit to London.* Like other forms of banking it involves the taking of some risks. The Discount office . . . exercise a general supervision over the banking community as a whole but not over a bank's foreign currency operations in particular, nor is there any regular supervision of this business carried out elsewhere in the Bank [emphasis added].[67]

Again, the benevolent attitude of the Bank towards the Euromarket is clear looking at the memorandum prepared by the Economic Intelligence Department to Downing Street:

> By their participation in the market the banks in the U.K. earn profits in foreign exchange on the margins between their borrowing and lending rates and from time to time switch currency assets into sterling for lending in the U.K. (the dollar counterpart accruing to the reserves) . . . London was a pioneer and remains a leader in the market, and *the City can be congratulated* on the role it has played in the development [emphasis added].[68]

Banks were a cautious actor in the period immediately following the first oil shock. Sir Philip de Zulueta, one of the two British delegates at the Trilateral Commission (the discussion group created by David Rockefeller in July 1973) and Chief Executive of the merchant bank Antony Gibbs and Sons, wrote in June 1974 to the Governor of the Bank of England after the meeting of the Trilateral in Brussels that:

> At the Brussels meeting we had among other things a discussion about the re-cycling of Arab oil money. The bankers present, of whom the most important were David Rockefeller himself and Alan Hockin [Executive Vice President of the Toronto Dominion Bank] but included some Europeans, expressed considerable worry about the capacity of the private banking system to re-cycle the extra Arab oil money into medium term credits . . . *I must say that I was surprised to find my own worries so strongly shared* [emphasis added].[69]

Ethan Kapstein wrote that Rockfeller was particularly worried about four possible impediments to recycling petrodollars: first, the maturity mismatch between assets and liabilities; second, the credit exposure problem; third, the 'fact that Arab investors would ultimately seek alternative investments to their short-term deposits in low-yielding accounts'; and, finally, 'the simple fact that most developing countries were not credit-worthy'.[70]

Thus, the attitude of commercial bankers towards recycling is less clear-cut than commonly assumed. For example, the hesitancy of the banking sector to intermediate oil funds on a large scale does not fit well with the assumption that 'the first to embrace the new role of banks in development finance [after the first oil shock] were the bankers themselves'.[71] More precisely, banks saw in the recycling mechanism, in the Euromarkets and in the international expansion *potential* sources of profits, but they were conscious of the associated risks and needed to be reassured on the fact that they would benefit from certain safety-nets or guarantees. As Kapstein rightly remarked, 'the banks were hesitant to place their funds in developing countries in the absence of government support for this undertaking';[72] essentially they expected to be bailed out if necessary. The Bank of England recognised this challenge, thanks to its frequent meetings with City bankers, and wrote in a memorandum on the role of central banks in financing oil deficits that:

> [i]t is the job of central banks to ensure the effective operation of a highly leveraged banking system and *above all to prevent its collapse*. The prospect of back-stopping, even without any direct action, will go a long way toward providing such assurance [emphasis added].
>
> . . .
>
> The task of recycling oil revenues will fall in the first instance on the leading 20 to 30 commercial banks of the world, if they can carry the burden. They will take in the funds, and they will have to lend them to the countries that need the funds and that normally have access to the market for medium-term credit. *Without assurances . . . they will feel themselves unable to perform this role* [emphasis added].
>
> . . .
>
> Central banks must make it clear to the public at large that they *stand behind these large banks*, both as receivers of deposits and as lenders of funds . . . The commitment could be undertaken by the Group of Ten countries or . . . it could be undertaken by the central banks that meet monthly at Basle . . . They should issue a communiqué soon before financial markets get too jittery to function well as the volume of oil funds grows rapidly in the next few months [emphasis added].[73]

This view was first applied to the case of the troubled German bank, *I. D. Herstatt Bankhaus*,[74] and revealed a profound difference of views between the British and the Americans, who were willing to support domestic banks engaged in risky activities abroad, and the controllers, notably Germany. The President of the *Bundesbank*, Karl Klasen, particularly feared that any indication on the part of central banks of their readiness to intervene on the market would be self-defeating, because it would 'hang a security net under the banks whose position is shaky'.[75] We do not know whether this document was released when the news about the collapse of the German bank, *Herstatt*, had already been disclosed (the date of the document is the same as that of the collapse), but what the document hoped became reality in September 1974. At the meeting of the governors of the G-10, a crucial communiqué was issued reassuring the markets of their responsibilities as lenders of last resort on the Euromarket.[76] The seemingly trivial communiqué had huge importance for the financial community as they received 'the support they were looking for from the central bank governors of the Group of Ten nations'.[77]

The changing attitude of the Americans towards banking supervision is difficult to explain without direct access to American sources. Possible explanations include a gradually less restrictive policy concerning inflation after the oil shock compared to the early 1970s, as unemployment grew from 5 per cent to reach 9 per cent between May 1974 and May 1975 and the fact that part of the petrodollars were flowing into the US Treasury bill market financing the US deficit. The policy of backing dubious banking activities pushed forward by the free-marketeer countries was highly risky. Providing guarantees against insolvency to large banks while taking all restraints off lending was a recipe for disaster by favouring moral hazard on a large scale.

It is striking to see how the picture was radically changed in the short space of two or three years. By late 1974, commercial banks had a market free from regulations as opposed to a strictly regulated domestic market, a powerful incentive to expand abroad because of the stagnating economy in their home markets, large pools of money to invest, support from international organisations and support from central banks. All the ingredients were laid for the biggest transfer of money in recent world history.

The recycling challenge

Recession years

As mentioned earlier, the C-20 reached a consensus in Rome not to fight the oil-induced deficits but to accommodate them and re-equilibrate the imbalances through a recycling, or transfer, of dollars from surplus to deficit countries. The rationale was not to replicate the mistakes of the 1930s and to keep the world economy going by creating an artificial demand through credit.

The Eurodollar market was 'blessed' by the oil shock and priorities shifted. If, up until late 1972/early 1973 the priority was the regulation of this off-shore and unregulated market, now the IMF clearly stated that despite the fact that banking activity had been left 'largely unsupervised'[78] the trust in the banking sector 'had not been misplaced', because new techniques to improve decision-making processes had been developed, such as syndicated lending. The *U-turn* of regulators becomes even clearer by continuing the analysis of this most revealing document:

> In principle, for the overwhelming majority of the banks operating in the Euro-currency market, *detailed monetary authority supervision* of their operations *is out of the question* . . . the essence of the system has to remain one in which the *responsibility for avoiding losses rests with the banks themselves* [emphasis added].[79]

Along the same lines, the Bank of England recognised the changed views on regulation:

Until about a year ago the main thrust of official criticism of the euro-markets (especially from Germany) was that they added substantially (through a high euro-market credit multiplier) to world credit, thereby aggravating world inflation and disequilibrating capital flows as well as the domestic monetary problems of particular countries. A specific complaint was that the euro-markets are not subject to any of the monetary controls (e.g. reserve requirements) that apply to national banking systems.[80]

As we have shown, the UK consistently objected that the Euromarket was a supplement to other sources of credit, that the imposition of controls would drive the business to tax havens and that national controls on residents' foreign currency transactions would suffice to handle flows between euro and domestic markets. The document continued by saying that:

> [a]rguments for monetary controls have not been pressed recently in the light of the recognised role of euro-markets in recycling; and in July the UK reserved its right to resume official placements [on the Euromarket], partly in relation to a possible need to ease the euro-markets' present liquidity problems [emphasis added].[81]

Thus, the system that starts to take form by the end of 1974 is a system where regulation is not a priority, where commercial banks are entrusted with the re-balancing of international monetary imbalances, while at the same time they have the sole responsibility for evaluating their own risks. A risky (but profitable) recipe indeed.

The final support from G-10 countries in September 1974, as expected from the Bank of England, managed to reassure the banks after the banking debacles of 1974.

In an Office Memorandum from the European Department to the Managing Director and Deputy Managing Director, relating a visit to commercial and central banks in Europe and to the BIS and OECD, it is stated: 'We gained the impression that the market was rather well on the way toward regaining its self-confidence' and:

> [t]here was . . . remarkably little sign of attention to the overall growth of the market. Broadly, the authorities seemed to feel that the likely market growth was not excessive – that in fact in a depressed world with recycling problems a somewhat greater growth would be welcome'.[82]

This is a crucial point in this work, for it summarises a central issue of the post-1973 world. After the end of the gilded age of Fordist capitalism, a new compact for growth had to be found. The compact that started to take place in the Western world (Europe for the purpose of our work) in the early 1970s, after the crumbling of Bretton Woods and, particularly, after the first oil shock, was a compact based on less and less regulation on financial movements and institutions. It was based on the centrality of the banking and financial sector as opposed to the public hand and industrial sector as the engines of growth, and, finally, was based on the collusion between controllers and controlled, which increased the moral hazard. All these elements appear in the 1970s, degenerating in the following decades into 'financialisation' or 'financial globalisation'.

The mood in the international financial and banking community continued to improve after the events of 1974 despite (or maybe thanks to) the longest recession since the 1930s during 1974–75. Gross external foreign currency liabilities of the eight European reporting countries increased by US$28 billion or 14 per cent year-on-year to US$220 billion, less than the growth of US$60 billion or 45 per cent experienced in 1973. On a net basis, the size of the Eurocurrency market (including banks in places outside the European reporting area) grew by US$55 billion, compared to US$50 billion in 1973, to more than US$210 billion. Eurocurrency loans went up by US$45 billion to US$177 billion.[83]

The year of 1975 marked the apex of the recession and the beginning of a gradual recovery, with growth rates improving despite persistent disequilibria in the monetary and financial system. Economic growth showed timid signs of improvement, thanks in particular to increased spending by families and governments, starting from the spring of 1975 notably in Japan (February 1975), the US (April 1975) and Germany (July 1975). Overall, the first period of recycling of oil surpluses seemed to work well. The BIS could write in its Annual Report of 1976 an entire paragraph entitled 'From Recession to Recovery: A Success Story' and in October 1975 Mr Karlstöm of the European Department of the IMF could write in a confidential memorandum after discussion with the Bank of England and private banks that the Euromarket was functioning well as maturities were lengthening both on the deposit and on the lending side and 'there are no indications of a new crisis like the one in late 1974 and early 1975'.[84]

The recovery of industrial output in 1975 reversed three-quarters of the decline of the recession in Belgium, France, Germany, Japan, Switzerland and the United States, while Italy and the Netherlands recovered by roughly one-half. Among the major countries, activity was lagging only in the United Kingdom and Canada, but these countries had not been hit by as deep a recession as the others.

Growth in other parts of the world proved to be more resilient. In Comecon countries, growth was spurred by money pouring into fixed industrial investments, and increases in industrial production ranged from 7.5 per cent in Soviet Russia to 12.4 per cent in Romania. In non-oil developing countries, growth came mostly from rising prices of export commodities well into 1974 before the decline in prices by late 1974 and early 1975.

A major reconfiguration of international capital flows and banking strategies was also seen in 1975. The recession of 1974 and early 1975 dramatically slowed the demand for funds by developed-country borrowers and pushed Western banks to focus on overseas business as never before. We will analyse in the following chapter the banking strategies of individual banks; for the moment, we will focus on the macro-economic picture. One side effect of the recession was to improve the balance of payments of most developed countries by limiting their imports;

that was not the case for non-oil developing countries and socialist countries (and smaller industrial states). Thus commercial banks found a profitable business in the financing of sovereign deficits. This element gave the international banking community an incredible leverage on international economic matters after the years of Bretton Woods. Nevertheless, in 1975, some elements of concern about developing country indebtedness started to surface, albeit timidly. The BIS remarked that although bank lending in 1974 and 1975 'was to be welcomed' for it had prevented the recession from becoming even worse by limiting the fall in the import capacity of LDCs, it entailed a 'very sharp increase in the short and medium-term indebtedness of the borrowers [developing countries]'.[85]

Thus preoccupations concerning indebtedness started to emerge at a very early stage of the recycling process. Nevertheless, these worries had very limited practical implications. On the contrary, we shall see how recycling would continue unabated until the Mexican default of 1982.

External assets in domestic and foreign currencies increased by US$50 billion or 18 per cent to reach US$300 billion, while liabilities increased by US$37 billion. Banks in the UK accounted for 40 per cent of the overall growth of Eurocurrency assets and liabilities. The main sources of funds continued to be OPEC countries and a handful of developed countries. Direct deposits by oil-producing countries went up to US$25.5 billion in 1975 compared to over US$20 billion in 1974. The contribution of the G-10 countries remained more or less stable at US$15 billion.[86]

How is it possible that developed countries were at the same time borrowers and lenders? There are three main explanations for this apparent paradox. First, part of the funds borrowed on the Euromarket by the public sector of Western countries for balance of payments was re-deposited on this market. Second, oil companies, resident in the European reporting area, built up their reserves in Eurodollars in anticipation of royalty payments. Third, large supplies of euro funds were coming from reporting countries such as Switzerland, which served essentially as an intermediary between off-shore trustee accounts and users.

Eastern Europe and non-oil developing countries (Latin America, South-East Asia and a handful of African countries) were net fund users. Compared to the earliest phase of the shock where the largest borrowers were developed countries such as Italy and Great Britain, in 1975 the largest borrowers became Mexico and Brazil, which accounted for half of gross claims on developing countries. Banks became more and more involved in balance of payment financing on a global scale and this represented a crucial shift for the history of the 1970s. Total gross claims outstanding vis-à-vis developing countries amounted to about US$63 billion at the end of 1975. This constituted an increase of around US$17 billion compared to 1974.[87]

The turbulences of 1974 and early 1975 had brought about some changes in international banking operations. Interbank activity had been reduced as credit lines were severed, the Euromarket came to be divided between bigger and smaller players, with the former still able to obtain and loan funds at competitive rates and the latter less likely to do so. Maturities decreased while spreads increased. The situation persisted in 1974 but, by 1975, the list of banks participating in the interbank market increased and the interbank market started to function again, with smaller banks able to obtain money from bigger names. As the economic situation did not improve as quickly as expected in Europe and the US, the demand for new loans in this part of the world declined, while the financial needs of the developing world and socialist countries, thanks to favourable terms of trade and ideological reasons, continued to grow. The 'long wave' of crisis of 1974 influenced the spreads of the loans and the maturities. For prime borrowers, the spreads tended to decrease, but for 'subprime' borrowers the terms deteriorated and fees increased.

Maturities in 1975 were reduced. While in 1974 more than two-thirds of the Euroloans carried original maturities of seven to ten years, and 10 per cent maturities of over ten years, most of the credits reported in 1975 had maturities of between one and six years and only one per cent of more than ten years.[88]

Eurobond issues experienced a short revival too. In 1975 total new issues amounted to US$10.4 billion, more than twice the volume of 1974, but the geographical scope remained limited to OECD countries, leaving only the Euroloan market available to developing countries and non-prime borrowers. Much of the revival in Eurobond issues was a result of more expansionary policies in 1975 and declining interest rates across Europe and the US. It must be noted that inflationary fears brought about shortening maturities and an increasing percentage of issues at flexible rates.

The IMF reported that 'there seems to be *little official concern over the size of the Euromarket*' and that '*there are few suggestions from official quarters at present that would call for measures of specific monetary control of the Euro-market* [emphasis added]'.[89]

The future seemed to look brighter for banking after the jitters of 1974. The IMF document was able to say that:

> In general, the situation in the international financial markets appears to be psychologically better now than it was in 1974–75. Bankers are generally much less concerned over possibly disruptive effects of large short-term shifts, or over the size of oil-related balance of payments deficits. *There is a broad consensus that the banking industry was on the whole well able to weather the crisis in 1974 and to play an important role in the recycling effort* [emphasis added].[90]

Disappointed expectations

1976 showed how weak the Western recovery really was compared to the expectations. Investment activity had already stagnated by late spring in 1976, and unemployment showed no particular signs of slowing down after the illusion of late 1975 and early 1976, mainly due to the growth of exports, the rebuilding of stocks of intermediate products and increased purchases of consumer durables. By February 1977, output in several countries was still below the pre-recession levels of 1974. The prolonged effects of the recession and the sluggish recovery puzzled policymakers.

In its 1977 Annual Report, the BIS noted that the protracted economic pause after mid-1976 was a 'perplexing phenomenon that took policy-makers by surprise' differing both from the cycle of the 1930s and from most post-war recessions. The Report concluded by asking: 'Is the weakness of the current recovery due to an abnormal cyclical response of public policy? Or are more fundamental structural factors at work?'[91]

The albeit slow recovery managed, nonetheless, to increase the OPEC current account surplus by US$10 billion to a total of US$45 billion, the deficits of developed countries increased by US$17 billion to a total of US$29 billion, while the deficits of developing countries, partly due to better prices for export materials and increased borrowings, declined by US$12 billion to reach US$20 billion. This amount was largely covered by US$12 billion in official flows and US$15 billion in private lending. OPEC funds available for investment remained stable compared to 1975 at around US$35 billion.[92]

What about international finance? Simply put, the diverging paths of the industrial and financial sectors persisted and grew larger. In a memo of the IMF it is noted that 'the impression already gained through our contacts in New York that the international banking community has largely rebuilt its self-confidence, was strengthened'. The memorandum well illustrates the *zeitgeist* amongst the international financial and banking community remarking that '*bankers did not seem overly concerned* with the immediate dangers of defaults or debt rescheduling' and, rather interestingly:

> [b]ankers felt that while they might have to accept refinancing of some loans they were *unlikely to have to sustain very severe losses.* Some bankers bluntly indicated that they would *look to the Fund* to provide the debtor countries with the resources to meet their obligations if serious difficulties were to arrive [emphasis added].[93]

Moral hazard was gradually becoming a central element of international banking.

The Euromarkets experienced a 'boom year' in 1976 thanks to a favourable combination of large-scale deficits and ample supplies of funds, with BIS reporting countries' new international bank lending amounted to US$70 billion. External claims in foreign currencies of the European reporting countries plus Switzerland increased by US$47 billion in 1976 to reach a total estimated amount of US$305 billion, while liabilities increased by US$52 billion to a total of US$310.7 billion. Banks in the UK accounted for US$19.8 billion (42 per cent) of the total growth of Eurocurrency assets.

Net of double-counting, the total volume of Euroloans outstanding through the reporting European centres may be estimated to have expanded from US$205 to US$247 billion, or by about 20 per cent, in 1976. According to the IMF, new international lending by banks amounted to US$65 billion in 1976, which represented a nominal rate of expansion of 25 per cent and 20 per cent in real terms.

The principal sources of funds in the market were private depositors in developed countries, monetary authorities in non-oil LDCs and monetary authorities in OPEC countries such as the Saudi Arabian Monetary Authority (SAMA). The latter institutions accounted for US$10.6 billion of bank deposits compared to US$5.5 billion in 1975. Markets continued to stabilise, the interbank market was functioning well again, the tiering in interest rates became less pronounced than in 1974–75 and uneasiness on capital standards and borrowers' risk diminished.

American banks were doing more and more business from tax heavens in the Caribbean and less from London. The currency composition of the Euromarket remained almost unchanged, with the dollar accounting for two-thirds of all foreign currency claims to non-residents.

International banking and financial business were thriving because domestic banking in Western countries was not experiencing the revival everybody anticipated. The IMF remarked that international bank lending was affected by the 'continued weakness in domestic loan' in most industrial countries, 'the continued high level of demand for balance of payments financing' and 'the ample availability of funds' because of slow economic activity and sluggish internal demand for corporate loans which pushed banks to accelerate their international lending to 'maintain overall growth targets for assets and earnings'.[94]

The favourable climate for international expansion of banking and financial activities was accentuated by favourable interest rates, which remained quite low reflecting ample supplies of capital, and sluggish demand at home. Maturities on Euroloans lengthened and spreads narrowed in early 1976, to widen again towards the end of 1976 and early 1977. Compared to current standards, spreads were quite acceptable for borrowers: a 'wide' spread in the terminology of the 1970s reflected spreads of around 2 per cent over LIBOR. For example, countries like Mexico and Brazil were borrowing at the same rate as Sweden or Denmark. Besides, in 1976 declining interest rates more than compensated for wider spreads. All in all, borrowing terms remained extremely favourable to borrowers until 1979.

Lending came to be highly concentrated among a small number of countries, with Mexico and Brazil accounting for 50 per cent of claims to reporting banks by non-oil LDCs, while, according to the IMF, the ten largest borrowers accounted for 71 per cent of gross debt to banks.[95] Bank claims on Comecon countries increased by US$6 billion on a net basis, the biggest borrowers being USSR, Poland, GDR and Hungary. Claims on off-shore banking centres, another vehicle to finance LDCs, increased by US$20 billion.[96] Loans extended on the Euromarket became bigger and bigger, with an amount of US$1 billion not uncommon (the so-called 'jumbo loans').

The picture for international banking definitely looked rosier. The optimism of international organisations such as the IMF seemed to be justified by three elements in particular. First, loans/loss experience in international lending had been better than domestic experience. Second, the majority of international bank lending to LDCs was concentrated in the supposedly higher income and higher growth countries. Third, a large proportion of loans was guaranteed by Western governments through informal or formal agreements. Banking supervision looked sclerotic, as on the one hand, a bit more supervision was put into place after the crisis of 1974 notably through the Basel Concordat, and on the other, the attitude of monetary authorities was one of benign neglect, as reported by the IMF document:

> Banking supervision has been strengthened, both by paying increasing attention to international lending and country exposure and by providing bank examiners and supervisors with improved information about foreign borrowers. However, there does *not appear to be any systematic guidance to banks by monetary authorities regarding country situations* and there is a division of opinion as to the desirability of such guidance [emphasis added].[97]

All in all, the BIS viewed more and more benevolently the involvement of private actors in the international monetary and financial scene, apparently overlooking the clouds on the horizon because the banks' heavy involvement in recent years in international financing and particularly in lending to developing countries was considered '*a stabilising factor* in the world economy [emphasis added]'.[98] The benefits related to the greater involvement of private actors in the financing of world imbalances were considered to outweigh the risks, while the experience of international banking on sovereign lending was considered better than the experience with private borrowers (probably because sovereign lending was almost frozen for 40 years).

In stark contrast to the booming banking and financial sector, the world economy in 1977 was faltering again despite decreasing oil surpluses as a result of adjustment policies in the oil-importing world. This adjustment occurred in three ways: a reduction in the consumption of oil per unit of gross national product in many large industrial countries, more through the substitution of other energy sources than through conservation; a decline in the 'real' price of oil since 1974; and a sizable absorption of imports of goods and services by the oil producers.[99]

The lacklustre economic performance was mainly a result of low private and public investments, resulting from contingent reasons such as inflationary fears, but also from what increasingly looked like a deep break with post-war economic performances. In fact, the share of profits in national income continued its downwards spiral, fixed capital expenditures stopped growing and large excess capacity emerged in some key industries such as shipbuilding (mainly in Scandinavian countries and England), steel and textiles. Growth was strong only in the US, but this contrasted with a soaring public deficit, rising to US$20.2 billion in 1977 compared to just US$1.4 billion in 1976, and a larger trade deficit, since exports were rising by only 2 per cent while imports were rising by more than 10 per cent.[100]

As had happened with the short-lived revival of late 1975 (which came to an end in spring 1976), the revival of late 1976 and early 1977 came to a halt by the end of 1977. In particular, Japan and Germany failed to be the 'locomotives' of the world economy as had been expected from their solid balance of payments and relatively low inflation rates. For example, Germany's imports of goods and services increased at the same rate as that recorded by exports (around 4.2 per cent); thus its impact on the world economy was neutral. Japan increased its volume of imports by 2 per cent, while exports increased by 10.4 per cent, so that its impact on the world economy was contractionary. Industrial production in Europe continued to fall.

Four years after the oil shock, Europe was failing to achieve the four pillars of post-war economic growth: productivity growth, high employment, stable prices and external equilibrium. In 1977, international financial markets continued to grow strongly thanks to the larger balance of payments deficit of the US and sluggish investment activity and credit demand in Europe.

In a BIS report prepared for the November 1978 meeting of the WP3 it is stated that 'the twelve months ending in June 1978 . . . were a period of rapid growth in international bank lending'. The sources of growth were mainly supply-driven.[101] First and foremost, the US payment deficit produced a liquidity-creating effect on the rest of the world; second, the slack demand for credit from domestic customers in the principal surplus centres gave rise to a large volume of funds seeking outlets on the international financial markets.[102]

The eight European countries reporting to the BIS reported the sharpest increase in external bank claims in 1977. Foreign loans in foreign and domestic currencies increased by 23 per cent year-on-year (or US$81 billion, 85 per cent of which was in foreign currency loans) to a total of US$434 billion.[103] Also, European banks led the way with regard to foreign lending: the rate of increase in external non-bank claims of US banks and their branches abroad was 15 per cent while foreign lending by European countries of the G-10 rose by 27 per cent. European banks were at the forefront of the international financial arena. This state of affairs reflects the fact that domestic demand for loans in the US picked up in 1977 because of favourable borrowing terms, while the economic situation in Europe remained sluggish and the fact that European banks had more room to accommodate large foreign borrowers compared to American banks, which had already gained large exposures to foreign customers. External assets of US banks slowed from US$11.7 billion in the first nine months of 1976 to only US$2.6 billion in 1977. New lending to non-oil developing countries amounted to US$11.3 billion compared to US$18 billion in 1976.[104] New credits to Brazil contracted from about US$6.5 billion in 1976 to US$1.7 billion and those to Mexico from around US$4.5 to US$1.5 billion, indicating not more conservative lending practices but simply that lending was becoming gradually more widespread amongst developing countries. New lending to Eastern Europe amounted to US$4.1 billion, about US$3 billion less than in 1976. Hungary and Poland were the largest borrowers, obtaining about US$1.2 billion and US$0.9 billion respectively, whereas claims on the Soviet Union showed only a marginal increase, after a US$2.5 billion rise in 1976.[105] OPEC countries started borrowing on the market to increase their reserves and ceased to be net suppliers of new funds to the international banking system. With regard to Euroloans, industrial countries were good customers with Italy and UK as the biggest borrowers, followed by France. New international bond issues amounted to US$35 billion, US$19.4 billion of which were

Eurobonds, benefiting from sluggish credit demand at home and depressed equity markets. Spreads were declining and maturities lengthening while new borrowers were now able to enter the international financial arena: the circuit was becoming bigger and bigger. As noted by the IMF document:

> Foreign ('cross-border') loans now represent a substantial proportion of the portfolio of many major banks and are an important source of banks' earnings, as *the sharp increase in the demand for international bank loans coincided with the considerable slackening in investment activity and domestic loan demand in several major financial market countries* [emphasis added].[106]

Moral hazard was reaching new heights. Because of increasing competition amongst bankers, the Euromarket was quickly becoming a highly liquid borrower's market. This was reflected in narrower spreads: prime borrowers could borrow at just 60 basis points (bp) over LIBOR; if we include front-end fees, the total cost for prime borrowers was just 113 bp over LIBOR in 1977 compared to 153 in 1976. The tendency towards accepting thinner spreads (i.e. below 1 per cent) was particularly visible amongst European and Japanese banks. As mentioned before, this reflected increasing competition in the international arena and a higher demand for domestic loans in the US. The size of the loans was becoming bigger and bigger and customers more numerous, while creditworthiness was becoming less of an issue.

The decrease in spreads pushed European, but also some American, banks to extend loans to subprime, or marginal, borrowers in order to increase profitability while feeling protected against possible risks. As remarked in the IMF paper:

> Discussions with bankers revealed instances of lending by first-name banks to a few countries already facing serious payments difficulties. The banks involved believed that such lending constitutes a *reasonable risk* because national authorities and international organizations ultimately will ensure that the countries in question do not default on their external obligations and also because an abrupt stop in new loans could precipitate exactly the type of crisis both parties would wish to avoid [emphasis added].[107]

At the same time that spreads had narrowed, maturities continued to lengthen. Immediately after the collapse of *Herstatt* and Franklin National Bank in 1974, maturities had shortened visibly, but in 1977 maturities on Eurocurrency commitments rose so that 78 per cent were of five years and more compared to just 33 per cent in 1975 and 42 per cent in 1976. After the annual visit of IMF staff to European financial centres, the IMF could conclude that:

> There is a general recognition that *private financial markets will have to play a major role* in the financing of payments imbalances for the foreseeable future and that, on balance, *the process has worked reasonably well*. There are concerns that market conditions have been, and are, permitting some

countries to finance unsustainable current account positions, thus delaying
needed adjustment measures. However, in general, monetary authorities *do
not believe* that it would be appropriate to take initiatives at this time through
the bank supervision process to direct bank lending so as to force some deficit countries into more effective adjustment policies. In some cases this is
viewed largely as a *self-correcting problem* [emphasis added].[108]

The changing role of commercial banks and the gradual shift of power from
national and international institutions to private market actors is well summarised
in a discussion paper of the Research Department of the IMF: 'commercial banks
have been carrying out some of the functions which have often been thought of as
more in the province of central banks, governments, and international organiza-
tions'.[109] From being second-class citizens during the pre-1973 world, commercial
banks were now considered at the same level as governments. The rise of international finance was definitely on its way and governments, central banks and
international institutions were not doing much to stop it.

The recycling process through commercial banks via the Euromarkets continued in the second part of the 1970s. A most revealing internal discussion paper
dated 25 January 1977 entitled 'The Fund and the Commercial Banks', reported
that commercial banks had played a growing role in international capital movements, receiving both an increasing share of the foreign assets of surplus countries
and financing a growing share of aggregate capital flows to deficit countries. The
paper remarked that in principle '*the scope of their activities could be reduced* by
changes in national official policies, but *governments are reluctant to consider
curbs*' because they recognized that, given the size and difficulty of the recycling
process, '*it is considered unwise to seek any sharp reduction in the scale of commercial bank operations*'.[110]

The reluctance to 'consider curbs', and the push towards a liberalisation of
finance, was more or less a common attitude in the Western world after the oil
crisis, as we have shown previously, but, as reported in a study prepared by the
Research Department on the Eurocurrency market, it is important to understand
once and for all from where in particular this reluctance came:

> Broadly speaking, we found that in *Washington, New York, London* and
> *Basle* the most widely accepted view was that Eurobanking was not a seri-
> ous threat to stability. In *Frankfurt* and *Paris*, on the other hand, views were
> rather different. While it was not felt that under existing conditions of eco-
> nomic slack there was any imminent danger, there was generally a certain
> amount of uneasiness about the potential for expansion at some future time
> [emphasis added].[111]

Thus as illustrated before, the main actors in the liberalisation of international
finance, at least in the early 1970s, are the IMF, the UK, the BIS and, to a
lesser extent, the US. The 'weakness', in political or economic terms, of states
with more conservative views in pushing towards a regulation of finance was

a precipitating factor in the unleashing of finance in the 1970s and was conducive to the disaster of 1982.

New turbulences

The year of 1978 was marked by two major events: first, the dollar crisis of 1978 and second, the resurgence of inflationary tendencies.

The dollar crisis of 1978 involved a steadily depreciating dollar starting from the last quarter of 1977 until October 1978 and, more generally, turbulences on the foreign exchange market only comparable to the break up of the Bretton Woods regime in 1971–73. From September 1977 to March 1978, the dollar lost 24 per cent against the Swiss Franc and 14 per cent against the DM. The biggest decline occurred towards the end of May 1978, with the dollar declining not only against the strong European and Asian currencies but also against the French franc, the Italian lira and the British pound. By the end of October, the dollar had fallen from late May by about 23, 25, 18, 14, 13 and 9 per cent, respectively, vis-à-vis the Japanese yen, the Swiss franc, the DM, the French franc, sterling and the Italian lira as a consequence of huge speculative movements against it resulting from balance of payment deficits and expansionary monetary policies. It was considered to be the first currency crisis of the post-Bretton Woods regime. In fact, the crisis of 1978 was the first crisis to take place in a regime of floating exchange rates, and it dismantled the belief, strongly held in the early 1970s by monetary authorities, that one of the key advantages of a flexible regime compared to a fixed exchange one was its supposed capacity to avoid currency crises. That was not the case.

The decline of the dollar ceased when US monetary authorities committed to defend its value by mobilising large resources on the foreign exchange market. Some of the measures included US$3 billion of IMF drawings; SDR sales totalling US$2 billion; increases in the Federal Reserve System's swap-lines with the *Bundesbank*, the Bank of Japan and the Swiss National Bank from a total of US$7.4 to US$15 billion; and the intention to issue up to US$10 billion of US Government securities denominated in foreign currencies.[112] On top of that, the Federal Reserve increased its discount rate by 1 per cent.

The situation of the dollar improved by the end of 1978 and early 1979, when US monetary policy became tighter. A far-reaching side effect of the dollar crisis was the acceleration of the process of creation of the European Monetary System (EMS) in March 1979.[113]

Inflation manifested its resurgence in the US as well as in many countries in Western Europe. In the US, consumer prices, on a December-to-December basis, which had risen by only 4.8 per cent in 1976, rose by 6.8 per cent in 1977 and 9 per cent in 1978. In the first three months of 1979, it was increasing at a rate of 13 per cent, while in the G-10 countries inflation averaged 12.5 per cent compared to 7 per cent at the end of 1978.

With regard to balances-of-payments, the BIS reported that the combined current account of the G-10 plus Switzerland swung from a US$5 billion deficit in

1977 to a surplus of US$18 billion in 1978. At the same time, the combined deficit of the other developed countries, which had averaged more than US$20 billion in the years since 1974, was reduced to US$11 billion. In part, this improvement in the developed countries' current position, totalling US$3.5 billion, was mirrored by a deterioration in the position of the non-oil developing countries because of worsening terms of trade for primary products. Following reductions in the two preceding years, their current deficit rebounded by an estimated US$9 billion in 1978 to a total of US$24 billion, largely because of the relative fall in primary product prices.[114] In Comecon countries, the picture was no rosier: their trade deficit reached US$5 billion from just US$1 billion in 1977 and their net indebtedness of Eastern European countries to the banks in the BIS reporting area increased by US$7 billion.

The surplus in G-10 countries was largely a result of strong balances-of-payments in Germany, Switzerland and Japan. In Japan the current payment surplus increased from US$10.9 to US$16.6 billion; in Germany from US$4.3 to US$9 billion; and in Switzerland from US$3.5 billion to more than US$5 billion.

1978 was a pivotal year in the decade: as reported by the BIS, the expansion of foreign business in the banking sector reached 'unprecedented proportions'[115] and Henry C. Wallich, Governor of the Federal Reserve, could proudly say that:

> [t]he Euromarkets are one of the *success stories* of our day, which needs a few successes. In difficult times, they have helped to keep trade flowing, they have financed investment and development, they have enabled countries to deal with their balance of payments problems. *The Euromarkets serve as a reminder of what a market system can achieve when it is allowed to operate freely* [emphasis added].[116]

In light of the events of the 1980s and beyond, these words assume an uncomfortable connotation.

The main tendencies that pushed international banks to internationalise their activities more and more – sluggish demand at home and increased liquidity – became even stronger in 1978, and the interbank competition, particularly in Euroloan business became extremely tough. Margins compressed to levels that 'seemed to be based on the assumption of a future without problems or losses'.[117] Countries, especially LDCs, were borrowing on extremely favourable terms both to cover their financing needs and to shore up their reserves, while lending margins were almost back 'to their pre-*Herstatt* levels of 1974'.[118] Thus, a large fraction of the amounts borrowed was re-deposited with Western banks, thereby reinforcing the borrowing frenzy that would almost bring down the entire financial and economic system in four years' time. The BIS reported that total external assets of banks in the G-10 countries, Austria, Denmark, Ireland (a novelty in BIS statistics) and Switzerland and of the branches of US banks in offshore centres expanded by US$213 billion in 1978, or by nearly twice as much as in 1977.[119] This is a staggering amount even taking into consideration the depreciation of the US dollar. On a net basis, this increase to US$110 billion compared to US$75 billion in 1977. Banks in the European reporting area increased their foreign currency liabilities by US$99 billion or 25 per cent compared to 1977.

The Euroloans extended by banks in the European reporting area expanded by US$75 billion. The international bond market was less buoyant and new issues amounted to US$36.7 billion. Eurobond issues dropped from US$19.5 billion to US$15.9 billion, essentially because of a sharp drop in dollar issues due to the weakness of the dollar and rising US interest rates. The explanation for the explosion of international financial markets is well resuméd by the BIS:

> Finding it difficult to achieve the desired rates of expansion at home, *the major banks continued to step up their international business*, particularly through their low-cost affiliates in the Euro-markets. Moreover, *the freedom of the international markets from regulatory constraints* that add to the cost of intermediation meant that part of the banks' credit business which would otherwise have shown up in their domestic books was accommodated through the Euro-markets [emphasis added].[120]

In 1978, new deposits of OPEC countries dropped from US$13.4 billion to US$5.9 billion reflecting shrinking OPEC surpluses while borrowing over US$14 billion. Non-oil LDCs were, once again, recipients of vast sums of money, with new lending to those countries sky-rocketing from US$11.1 billion in 1977 to US$24.7 billion, mirroring the worsening current account situation of these countries. Latin America was the largest recipient with US$14.9 billion; new borrowing by Comecon countries doubled compared to 1977, reaching US$9.3 billion, with Poland as the largest recipient of funds.

The picture of the international economy looked rather gloomy by the end of the 1970s. Debt levels in the developing world were piling up, growth was continuing to falter in Europe and US, but matters became even worse in late 1979 when oil prices started to rise, again creating a second oil shock, and interest rates in the US rose dramatically as a consequence of the 'Volcker Shock' of October 1979, when the Federal Reserve decided to target monetary aggregates instead of setting interest rates (e.g. the three-month Treasury bill yield rose from 9½ per cent in March 1979 to 15 per cent in March 1980). As Joseph Treatster wrote:

> [Paul Volcker's] solution, which now seems breathtakingly simple, was to take the cutting-edge decision out of the hands of the members of the Fed – or at least make it seem that way. Under Volcker's new plan, the Federal Open Market Committee would end the practice of setting the most influential interest rate. Instead, the members would establish targets for the supply of money in the American economy and permit the supply of money to determine the federal funds rate. The board would retain the discount rate as a largely symbolic tool, but the *emphasis would be on the money supply* [emphasis added].[121]

By not intervening on the interest rate but leaving the demand for money to determine the rate, the Federal Reserve started to operate 'closer to the ideas of the economist Milton Friedman'.[122] The policies implemented by Volcker pushed American interest rates (and consequently Eurodollar rates) sky-high and LDCs one step closer to the edge of collapse, since the greatest part of their debt had been contracted in dollars at floating interest rates.

The increase in interest rates had three devastating consequences. First, it imposed greater cash cost on indebted countries. Second, it deepened the recession in individual countries and in the OECD as a whole. Third, it increased the real cost of developing countries' debt by increasing the cost of funding it in relation to the economic return that could be obtained on individual projects or on governments' spending programmes.[123]

The second oil shock started in late 1978 and early 1979 when the regime of the Shah was overturned in Iran in favour of a Shia theocracy which decided to curtail oil exports (at that time Iran accounted for about one fifth of the entire oil production) and continued in late 1979 to most dramatic effect. This second crisis differed in many respects from the first one: one notable difference is the fact that the shock was more gradual than in 1973.

In mid-December 1978, the OPEC member countries met in Abu Dhabi and announced their decision to raise the price of Arab light crude oil through 1979 on a quarterly basis, from a base of US$12.70, by 5 per cent on 1 January, 9 per cent on 1 April, 11.5 per cent on 1 July and 14.5 per cent on 1 October.[124] The average annual increase amounted to 10 per cent. But, in March, in the wake of the upheaval in Iran, the OPEC countries decided that the full planned increase should come into effect from the second quarter of 1979 and that, in addition, some countries would be free to charge premium prices higher than the mutually agreed basic price. The result was price anarchy.

The oil price increase intervened at a time when OPEC surpluses were rapidly decreasing as a result of low global demand, increasing deficits in oil exporting countries and the decreasing value of the dollar.

The word 'shock' to refer to the oil price increase of 1979 is not entirely accurate. As anticipated the so-called second oil shock was more a series of agreements to increase the price of oil, remarkably stable in 1977 and 1978, finalised at the OPEC meeting of December 1978 in Abu Dhabi. By the end of November 1979, the price per barrel was US$40 compared to US$15 at the beginning of 1979 and it continued to rise until 1981, when the recession hit Western economies.

The fall in Iranian exports was made up by increasing exports from more cooperative oil producers such as Saudi Arabia, but the tensions intervened in a period when a larger number of countries were competing for oil in a highly fragmented market with less and less spare capacity available. Thus, 1979 saw a scramble for oil, where customers were more focused on increasing their supplies than the price they were paying. This is confirmed in the archives of the OECD, where the Director General of the Swiss National Bank, Pierre Languetin, remarked in the WP3 meeting of December 1979 that: '[the scramble for stocks] had aggravated the oil price problem and had helped to support the psychosis of continued oil price increases'.[125] Uncertainty in oil supplies was a crucial element in triggering the second oil crisis. Other elements included the fact that the increase in Saudi supplies 'failed to help those who had been affected' while improving 'the position of those least affected by the Iranian situation'[126] since the Aramco partners (the Saudi Arabian national oil and gas company), the least affected by Iran's decision, were the main beneficiaries of the Saudi intervention and, conversely, British Petroleum and Shell had no direct benefits from it. Consequently, many companies found themselves competing for limited supplies of oil. Further stress on the market came from the need to prepare for winter and replace oil stocks and by the development of a two-tier price structure in the market, one tier made up of Saudi crude in the hands of Aramco partners, and a second tier forced to pay higher oil prices.

For these reasons, the second shock is sharply different from the first one, even if too often the differences are overlooked in historiography. In 1979:

[i]t was the loss of the previous flexibility in the supply system (based on the existence of a cushion of spare capacity), coupled with an overreaction by some buyers of oil, that largely explained the sharp increases in oil prices and disorderly conditions in the oil market during the past two years.[127]

As after the shock of 1973, oil surpluses of OPEC countries experienced an incredible surge, reaching almost US$60 billion in 1979 and more than US$120 billion in 1980.[128] As a result of doubling prices, new deposits amounted to US$38 billion compared to just US$6 billion in 1978. By contrast, G-10 countries experienced a combined deficit of US$23.5 billion compared to a surplus of US$34 billion the previous year. Non-oil developing countries suffered a deficit of US$38 billion compared to US$24 billion in 1978. The appearance of new huge amounts of money required a new recycling mechanism and commercial banks had, again, a role to play in it.

From Table 3.3 we can see the details of OPEC's investments in the UK and US. Around 60 per cent of assets in the two countries were held in the form of bank deposits and Treasury bills. Direct investment and investment in property remained very small, while portfolio investments represented around 20 per cent of total OPEC's assets in those countries. By 1979, around 77 per cent of the amount held in bank deposits was in Eurocurrency markets, over half of this in the UK. After four years in which OPEC's external assets had been increasing more rapidly than their short-term investments, the bulk of their investments in 1979 took the form of bank deposits and money-market investments. This could be explained by the rapid increase in the surplus and the consequent difficulty in swiftly arranging long-term investments and by the rise of short-term interest rates in the main financial centres in 1979.

Another important difference compared to the first oil crisis was the attitude of OECD countries towards macro-economic disequilibria and especially inflation. If, as we have previously illustrated, in 1973–74 the priority was to shore up international demand while accepting oil-induced deficits *and* a higher degree of inflation, in 1979 the priority was given to fighting inflation, which was averaging 7 per cent in G-10 countries, through a tightening of monetary policies and the

Table 3.3 Estimated deployment of investible OPEC surpluses in the UK and US (US$ bn), 1974–79.

Items	1974	1975	1976	1977	1978	1979	Levels end-1979
Bank deposits and money-market placements							
Dollar deposits in the US	1.9	1.1	1.8	0.4	0.8	4.9	6.0
Sterling deposits in the UK	1.7	0.2	−1.4	0.3	0.2	1.4	1.0
Deposits in foreign currency markets	22.8	9.1	12.1	10.6	3.0	31.2	57.6
Treasury bills in the US and UK	4.8	0.6	−1.0	−1.1	−0.8	3.4	2.5
Total	31.2	11.0	11.5	10.2	3.2	40.9	67.1
Long-term investments							
Special bi-lateral arrangements and other investments	11.8	12.4	12.2	12.7	8.7	11.8	57.8
Loans to international agencies	3.5	4.0	2.0	0.3	0.1	−0.4	9.9
Government securities in the US and UK	1.1	2.2	4.1	4.5	−1.8	−0.9	10.1
Other	8.7	6.1	8.5	5.8	3.3	2.4	32.4
Total	25.1	24.7	26.8	23.3	10.3	12.9	110.2
Total new investments	56.3	35.7	38.3	33.5	13.5	53.8	177.3

Source: BIS Annual Report 1980, 101.

return to 'monetary conservatism'. 'Without exception – the IMF pointed out – the authorities of the larger countries have committed themselves to giving *top priority* to the containment of inflation [emphasis added]'.[129] The BIS was even more explicit in differentiating the post-OPEC I and post-OPEC II experiences:

> In the light of their experiences following the 1973–74 outburst of global inflation, policy-makers have this time generally tended to give much greater weight than before to the need to prevent the spread and intensification of inflationary forces. Although unemployment is still high, and in some cases increasing, the policy focus everywhere has been on containing the momentum of price/wage inflation.[130]

Thus, if the policies of OECD countries had been expansionary in 1973–74, they became contractionary in 1979 in order to fight inflation. The priority of fighting inflation was made clear in Belgrade in October 1979 at the Annual Meeting of the Fund's Board of Governors where 'there was a clear agreement that inflation poses a grave threat to our economic and financial system, and that it must be tackled with greater determination and accorded higher priority among the objectives of economic policy'.[131]

The international financial market experienced a terrific year in 1979, recycling the greatest amount of the new OPEC surpluses. Conditions for borrowers became even more favourable than in 1978 as maturities continued to lengthen and spreads to decrease; only by the end of 1979 and early 1980 did some concerns start to emerge in international monetary circles with respect to the sustainability of this borrower's market. The BIS reported, referring to the syndicated loan market, that the margins charged to borrowers by OECD banks decreased from an average of 0.7 per cent in the last quarter of 1978 to an average of 0.5 per cent in the autumn of 1979. External claims of banks in G-10 countries, Austria, Denmark and Ireland and of the branches of US banks in the offshore centres of the Caribbean and Far East expanded by US$218 billion (an underestimation since it did not include the offshore activities of banks in Bahrain nor the business done by non-US banks in the offshore centres of the Caribbean and Far East), or 24 per cent, during 1979 to reach a total of US$1,111 billion. This increase was, of course, the result of new OPEC deposits but also from deposits of oil importing countries, attracted by rising interest rates. If we consider bank lending and new bond issues and exclude double counting, the total amount of new credit intermediated by international financial markets amounted to US$150 billion, an increase of 13 per cent compared to 1978 (Table 3.4).

Table 3.4 Estimated lending in international markets, changes in external claims of banks in domestic and foreign currencies and international bond issues (US$bn), 1975–79.

Lenders	1975	1976	1977	1978	1979	Amounts outstanding 1979
Banks in the European reporting countries and Switzerland	50.5	55.7	80.6	145.2	164.8	776.2
Of which Euro-currency market	42.9	47.2	68.5	117.2	137.9	639.9
Banks in Canada and Japan	−0.3	4.8	0.8	16.2	15.0	71.0
Banks in the US	13.6	21.3	11.5	37.8	17.1	136.0
Branches of US banks in offshore centres	15.0	23.8	16.2	15.4	21.2	127.7
Total	78.8	105.6	109.1	214.6	218.1	1,110.9
Due to redepositing among the reporting banks	38.8	35.6	34.1	104.6	88.1	445.9
A = Net new international bank lending	40.0	70.0	75.0	110.0	130.0	665.0
Eurobond and foreign bond issues	22.8	34.3	36.1	37.3	37.1	–
Minus redemptions and repurchases	3.3	4.3	5.1	8.3	9.6	–
B = Net new international bond financing	19.5	30.0	31.0	29.0	27.5	–
A + B = Total new bank and bond financing	59.5	100.0	106.0	139.0	157.5	–
Minus double counting	2.5	3.5	4.0	6.0	7.5	–
Total net new bank and bond financing	57.0	96.5	102.0	133.0	150.0	–

Source: BIS Annual Report, various years.

Liabilities showed an even stronger increase of US$264 billion, or 31 per cent. A very important characteristic of the second oil shock was that banks in the European reporting countries accounted for the majority, over 75 per cent according to the BIS, of the increase in external claims.

The largest borrowers were in Latin America with US$23.6 billion of reporting banks' claims on these countries. Mexico (US$7.5 billion), Argentina (US$6.5 billion) and Brazil (US$5.5 billion) were the heaviest borrowers. Countries in Asia accounted for US$8.8 billion with South Korea (US$3.4 billion), the Philippines (US$1.4 billion) and China (US$ 1.2 billion) as the largest borrowers.[132] Most of the Eurocurrency business was done from London, which accounted for more than 40 per cent of the whole business.

The main influences behind such buoyancy of international banking can be located in the second oil shock, higher interest rates in national markets, declining appeal of the Eurobond market and, as pointed out by the BIS, by:

> *The eagerness of the major banks in the industrial countries to expand their international business, particularly through their affiliates in the principal Euromarket centres.* This was particularly true of *Japanese and European-owned banks*, whereas US banks' share in international lending declined. Moreover, their relatively good loan-loss experience in recent years may have led to a lowering of the banks' perception of the risks involved in their international lending business [emphasis added].[133]

Because of its wholesale character, low unit costs and privileged regulatory status, the banks still found Eurobusiness quite attractive, notwithstanding the thinness of lending margins in the syndicated loan market. In addition, front-end fees and the payment of rates below LIBOR to non-bank depositors continued to make for higher margins than might have appeared from published figures.

The trust in the foresight and efficiency of private capital markets (and commercial banks) continued during the second recycling and dominated the IMF 'ideology' even after the end of the Witteveen mandate. Consequently, the privatisation of credit could continue unabated. During a speech at the annual assembly of the Federal Association of German Banks in Bonn in 1980, Jacques de Larosière, new Managing Director of the IMF, said:

> *The banking system has proven to be an efficient vehicle for the transfer of financial savings internationally* and it is extremely important that this process be allowed to operate smoothly and effectively. Prudential regulations must keep pace with market developments, but without causing disruptions in the process of international intermediation . . . I believe that the market mechanism is basically sound and that banks should be playing a major role in the current phase of recycling, without facing undue strain. *Bankers have a wealth of experience in judging the merits of investment, the quality of management, and the risks involved* [emphasis added].[134]

Unfortunately, in less than two years' time, Mexico would default on its debt triggering the worst economic crisis since the Great Depression. In this regard, our story is somewhat different from Rawi Abdelal's account of the IMF attitude towards private financial flows during the De Larosière mandate. In his book *Capital Rules*, he argues that 'De Larosière's authority within the Fund appears to have been a moderating influence among an increasingly liberal-minded staff'.[135] Our evidence suggests that De Larosière followed the liberal path of Witteveen without any major re-examination of the ideology which came to dominate the Fund in the years following the end of Bretton Woods.

A brave new world

A pivotal contribution to the rise of international finance was given by the two oil crises, the payment imbalances they created and the subsequent growth in financial flows from OPEC countries to developing countries through Western commercial banks. The cash surplus of OPEC countries reached US$60 billion in 1974 and 1979 and almost US$120 billion in 1980, while averaging around US$40 billion during the rest of the 1970s. This money provided essential and much-needed fuel to the engine of international finance. The oil crisis played a crucial role in putting the regulatory agenda to an end and shifting the priorities of national and international monetary authorities from regulation to assuring the smooth functioning of this market. The impact of the oil crisis in liberalising international finance has been mostly overlooked by existing scholarship. On the contrary, the crisis was fundamental in keeping the Euromarket unregulated and to triggering the rise of international finance by providing much needed funds to the Western banking and financial sector and pushing banks to find new markets and customers to compensate for sluggish domestic performances.

The lack of regulation of the Euromarket and the subsequent privatisation of petrodollar recycling represented a boon for some and a hindrance for others. Without any possible doubt, the biggest winner of this story is the banking and financial sector.

Banks were marginal actors in the world economy compared to the industrial sector throughout the Bretton Woods period. Private financial flows were modest and official controls on capital movements and exchange rates omnipresent in Europe and the US.

When private capital movements became visible on the radar of Western governments and regulators, policies started to be elaborated, notably in Basel, to limit and control these flows. A battle between controllers and free-marketeers ensued and, ultimately, a comprehensive regulatory scheme arrived on the table of G-10 Governors in the summer of 1973. The regulatory proposal represented a most serious challenge to the existence of the Euromarket and, more generally, international finance, as regulations would have radically reduced its attractiveness as a haven for international capital.

Thanks to the oil shock, there arose a need to transfer wealth from surplus to deficit countries. As we have seen, channelling these funds through the Euromarkets via commercial banks became the official policy of developed countries since the meeting of the Committee of Twenty in January 1974. Consequently, priorities shifted from a possible control of the Euromarket to assuring its soundness in order to transfer huge amounts of capital on a global scale.

The privatisation of the recycling mechanism had a two-fold implication for the banking and financial sector. First, it allowed commercial banks to free themselves from any kind of regulations and gain influence in international monetary and financial affairs as never before, thus putting to a definitive end the Keynesian 'middle way'[136] and the embedded liberalist regime of Bretton Woods, and paving the way for a new regime based on the discipline of (euro)markets and banks, as their most important participants. Second, the privatisation of credit allowed a 'renaissance' of the banking profession. Banks expanded in new territories and developed new products, setting the stage for a second globalisation of finance, as we shall see in the next chapter.

What about the governments? As we have already pointed out, their contribution was essential to understanding the empowerment of the banking sector in the 1970s.

Through the IMF, OECD and BIS, Western governments put in place the recycling mechanism and empowered again the banking sector after many years of repression. The result was a system where 'the *role of governments . . . has weakened* and could be described by saying that governments now participate as partners with commercial banks in a *market-based monetary system* [emphasis added]'.[137] Additionally, they finally decided not to regulate the Euromarkets, creating a *de facto* asymmetrical regulatory standard in official regulations and policies, where international activities were free from regulations and domestic activities strictly controlled. In the next chapter, we shall see how commercial banks across Europe benefited from such an opportunity.

Notes

1 IMFA, European Department-EURAI Subject Files Box 146, Address by J. de Larosière on the Occasion of the Annual Assembly of the Federal Association of German Banks in Bonn, 29 October 1980.
2 On oil and the energy crisis see, for example: Anthony Sampson, *The Seven Sisters. The Great Oil Companies and the World They Made*, Hodder and Stoughton, London, 1975; Tadeusz M. Rybczynski (ed.), *The Economics of the Oil Crisis*, Macmillan Press, London, 1976; Raymond Vernon (ed.) *The Oil Crisis*, W. W. Norton & Company, New York, 1976; Robin C. Landis and Michael W. Klass, *OPEC. Policy Implications for the United States*, Praeger, New York, 1980; and Ian Skeet, *Opec: Twenty-Five Years of Prices and Politics*, Cambridge University Press, Cambridge, UK and New York, 1988.
3 Richard Bernal, 'Transnational Banks, the International Monetary Fund and External Debt of Developing Countries', *Social and Economic Studies*, Vol. 31, No. 4, Regional Monetary Studies (December 1982), 78.
4 Some authors have talked of 'financial repression', see: Ronald McKinnon, *Money and Capital in Economic Development*, Brookings Institutions Press, Washington,

DC, 1973 and Edward Shaw, *Financial Deepening in Economic Development*, Oxford University Press, New York, 1973. See also Carmen M. Reinhart and M. Belen Sbrancia, 'The Liquidation of Government Debt', *NBER Working Paper Series*, WP 16893, March 2011, 1–64.

5 Gérard Duménil and Dominique Lévy, *Capital Resurgent. The Roots of the Neoliberal Revolution*, Harvard University Press, Cambridge, MA, and London, 2004, 156.

6 David E. Spiro, *The Hidden Hand of American Hegemony. Petrodollar Recycling and International Markets*, Cornell University Press, Ithaca, NY, 1999.

7 Eric Helleiner, *States and the Reemergence of Global Finance*, Cornell University Press, Ithaca, NY and London, 1994, 106.

8 OECDA, WP3 Documents 1971, CPE/WP3/71(5), 12 March 1971, Note by Professor Kessler titled 'The United Sates Deficit, the Euro-Currency Market and World Inflation'.

9 BEA, 6A123/7, Brief 'Euro-Currency Market' (no further information).

10 Jeffrey M. Chwieroth, *Capital Ideas. The IMF and the Rise of Financial Liberalization*, Princeton University Press, Princeton, NJ and Oxford, UK, 2010, 139.

11 BEA, 6A123/7, Brief 'Euro-Currency Market' (no further information).

12 IMFA, European Department Division Files-EUR Division Subject Files Box 11, Letter from M.V. Posner to Mr. Rose, 'Controlling the Euro-Dollar Market', 5 November 1971.

13 Reported in Margaret Garritsen de Vries, *International Monetary Fund 1972–1978*, Vol. III, International Monetary Fund, Washington, DC, 1985, 50.

14 See for example Joseph E. Stiglitz, *Globalization and its Discontents*, Penguin Books, London, 2002; Kevin Danaher (ed.), *50 Years is Enough. The Case Against the World Bank and the International Monetary Fund*, South End Press, Boston, 1994; Ngaire Woods, *The Globalizers. The IMF, the World Bank and Their Borrowers*, Cornell University Press, Ithaca, NY and London, 2006.

15 IMFA, European Department Division Files-EUR Division Subject Files Box 11, Letter from M. V. Posner to Mr. Rose, 'Controlling the Euro-Dollar Market', 5 November 1971.

16 BIS, 7.15(1) G10 D22, 'Informal Record of a Meeting of the Standing Committee of Central Bank Officials on the Euro-Currency Market', 12 February 1972.

17 BIS, 13(a)3 Vol. 9–11, 'Introduction to the Second Part of Standing Committee's Work: Euro-Bank Operations', 19 December 1971.

18 BIS, 7.18(23) GILB 1, 'The Euro-Currency Market' (no further information available).

19 BEA, 6A123/8, 'The Euro-Currency Market in London', June 1972.

20 See, for example: David Harvey, *A Brief History of Neoliberalism*, Oxford University Press, Oxford, UK, 2005; Monica Prasad, *The Politics of Free Markets. The Rise of Neoliberal Economic Policies in Britain, France, Germany, & the United States*, The University of Chicago Press, Chicago, IL and London, 2006; Daniel Stedman Jones, *Masters of the Universe. Hayek, Friedman, and the Birth of Neo-liberal Politics*, Princeton University Press, Princeton, NJ and Oxford, UK, 2012.

21 Philip G. Cerny, 'The Dynamics of Financial Globalization: Technology, Market Structure, and Policy Response', *Policy Sciences,* 1994, Vol. 27, Issue 4, 319.

22 Zygmunt Bauman, *Liquid Modernity*, Polity Press, Cambridge, UK, 2000, 149. Also, the previous terminology is drawn from Bauman.

23 BEA, 6A123/7, Note (not signed), 'Convertibility and the Eurodollar Market', 3 March 1971.

24 Susan Strange, *The Retreat of the State. The Diffusion of Power in the World Economy*, Cambridge University Press, Cambridge, UK, 1996. See also: Susan Strange, *Mad Money. When Markets Outgrow Governments*, The University of Michigan Press, Ann Arbor, MI, 1998.

25 Idem, 22–23.

26 Walter B. Wriston, 'Technology and Sovereignty', *Foreign Affairs*, Vol. 67, No. 2, Winter, 1988, 63.

27 Geoffrey R. D. Underhill, 'State, Market, and Global Political Economy: Genealogy of An (Inter-?) Discipline', *International Affairs*, Vol. 76, No. 4, 2000, 805–824. See also, Geoffrey R. D. Underhill, 'The Changing State-Market Condominium in East-Asia: Rethinking the Political Underpinnings of Development', *New Political Economy*, Vol. 10, No. 1, March 2005, 1–24.

28 Philip G. Cerny, 'The Dynamics of Financial Globalization: Technology, Market Structure, and Policy Response', *Policy Sciences*, 27, 322. In this quote, Cerny is referring to: Geoffrey R. D. Underhill, 'Markets Beyond Politics?: The State and the Internationalization of Financial Markets', *European Journal of Political Research*, 19, 197–225.

29 BIS, 7.15 (1) G10 D22, 'Informal Record of the Meeting of the Standing Committee of Central Bank Officials on the Euro-Currency Market', 9 December 1972.

30 *Financial Times*, 'Euromarkets: Threat of regulation overshadows world money and capital markets', 13 March 1972.

31 BIS 7.18 (16) HAL.4, 'Progress Report on the Work of the Euro-currency Standing Committee', 3 April 1973.

32 Idem.

33 BEA 6A123/9, Note by Kit McMahon 'BIS Scheme for Regulating Euro-Currency Banking', 16 January 1973.

34 BEA 6A123/9, Confidential Note 'The BIS Scheme: An Outline of a Co-Ordinated System of Euro-Currency Regulation', 11 January 1973.

35 Idem.

36 Idem.

37 The Committee on Reform of the International Monetary System and Related Issues (Committee of Twenty or C-20) was formed in July 1972. Its first meeting was held in Washington DC in September 1972 and its final report was sent to the Board of Governors of the IMF in June 1974. The Committee of Twenty would be followed by the Interim Committee of the Board of Governors on the International Monetary System in October 1974.

38 Ibid.

39 On the 'ascendancy' of OPEC see Chapter 3 in Ian Skeet, *OPEC: Twenty-five years of prices and politics*, Cambridge University Press, Cambridge, UK, 1988.

40 On the impact of the oil crisis on the Netherlands see: Duco Hellema, Cees Wiebes and Toby Witte, *The Netherlands and the Oil Crisis. Business as Usual*, Amsterdam University Press, Amsterdam, Netherlands, 2004. The embargo on the Netherlands and Denmark would be lifted on 10 July 1974.

41 For a thorough analysis of US-Middle East diplomacy and the role of Kissinger see Kenneth W. Stein, *Heroic Diplomacy. Sadat, Kissinger, Carter, Begin, and the Quest for Arab-Israeli Peace*, Routledge, New York and London, 1999.

42 Tony Judt, *Postwar. A History of Europe since 1945*, Penguin Press, New York, 2005, 455.

43 Robert Brenner, *The Economics of Global Turbulence*, Verso Press, London and New York. 241.

44 On the long-term origins of the crisis of Western capitalism see the *opus* of Fernand Braudel, *Civilization and Capitalism, 15th–18th Century* (3 vols.), University of California Press, Berkeley, CA, 1992. See also Giovanni Arrighi, *The Long Twentieth Century: Money, Power, and the Origins of Our Times*, Verso Press, New York, 2010.

45 Robert Brenner, *The Economics of Global Turbulence*, Verso Press, London and New York, 2006, 4.

46 BEA, 8A406/6, Letter by the Governor, 29 April 1974.

47 BEA, 6A123/10, Note on 'Basle-Euro-Currency Standing Committee', 13 December 1974.

48 BEA 8A406/5, 'Europe: Measures Adopted to Relax Controls on Inward Direct Investments – An Assessment ', 19 March 1974.

49 BEA 8A406/6, Internal Document, 29 April 1974.
50 Charles Goodhart, *The Basel Committee on Banking Supervision. A History of the Early Years, 1974–1997*, Cambridge University Press, Cambridge, UK and New York, 2011, 31.
51 OECDA, Documents of the WP3 1974, Confidential Document 'The Implications of the Oil Situation for Domestic Monetary Management', CPE/WP3(74)10, 5 April 1974.
52 Data are from BEA 8A406/5, 'The International Capital Movements-1973', 25 January 1974.
53 IMFA, European Department-EURAI Subject Files Box 145, 'Speech by H. Johannes Witteveen at the Economic Club of Detroit', May 6 1974.
54 Idem.
55 OECDA, Documents of the WP3 1974, 'Informal Meeting of Working Party No. 3 in Rome on 16th January 1974-Brief Summary', 17 January 1974.
56 OECDA, Documents of the WP3 1974, 'Statement by Mr Marris at the EPC Meeting on the 18th–19th February 1974 Reporting on the Last Two Meetings of WP3', 25 February 1974.
57 IMFA, European Department-EURAI Subject Files Box 145, 'Speech by H. Johannes Witteveen at the Economic Club of Detroit', May 6 1974.
58 Annual Address to the Consultative Assembly of the Council of Europe, Strasbourg, 23 January 1974, in OECD, *Fifteen Years of International Economic Co-operation. Selected Speeches of Emile van Lennep Secretary-General 1969–1984*, Paris, 1984.
59 David Lomax, *The Developing Country Debt Crisis*, Palgrave Macmillan, London, 1986, 9.
60 BEA, 4106/1, Signed Letter to the Governor of the Bank of England, 7 June 1974.
61 IMFA, European Department-EURAI Subject Files Box 145, 'Speech by H. Johannes Witteveen at the Economic Club of Detroit', May 6 1974.
62 OECDA, Documents of the WP3 1981, CPE/WP3(81)5, 'Recycling', 29 April 1981.
63 OECDA, WP3 Documents 1974, 'The Increase in Oil Price', CPE/WP3/74(1), 12 January 1974.
64 BFA, 1489200304–15, 'Quelques réflexions sur les excédents accumulés par les pays de l'O.P.E.P. et le recyclage des balances des pays de l'O.C.D.E.', Direction Générale des Services Etrangers, Balance des Paiements, 4 December 1974.
65 The literature on the City-Government relationship is vast, a good starting point is Ranald Michie and Phillip Williamson (eds.), *The British Government and the City of London in the Twentieth Century*, Cambridge University Press, Cambridge, UK and New York, 2004. On the Bank of England, the reference is Forrest Capie, *The Bank of England. 1950s to 1979*, Cambridge University Press, Cambridge, UK, 2010.
66 Catherine R. Schenk, 'The Origins of the Eurodollar Market in London: 1955–1963', *Explorations in Economic History*, 35, 1998, 234.
67 BEA, 6A123/1, Secret Letter from R. A. O. Bridge to Maurice Parsons, 'Euro-Dollar Market', 6 March 1964.
68 BEA, 6A123/5, 'The Euro-Dollar Market', 24 October 1968.
69 BEA 8A406/6 Letter from Sir Philip de Zulueta to Governor Gordon Richardson, 27 June 1974.
70 Ethan B. Kapstein, *Governing the Global Economy*, Harvard University Press, Cambridge, MA, and London, 1994, 65.
71 Robert Devlin, *Debt and Crisis in Latin America. The Supply Side of the Story*, Princeton University Press, Princeton, NJ, 1989, 61.
72 Idem, 66.
73 BEA 8A406/6 'Memorandum on the Role of Central Banks in Financing Oil Deficits' 27 June 1974.
74 Herstatt was the largest private bank in Germany with important bets on the foreign currency market (*Bundesbank* Annual Report 1974, 18–19). When the bank became

insolvent by the end of June 1974, German authorities shut the bank and appointed a receiver after German markets had closed *but before the US markets had closed*. The failure of Herstatt (and of the Israel-British Bank in July and Franklin National Bank in October) led to the creation of the Basel Committee on Banking Supervision (BCBS) in December 1974, responsible for the Basel Accord of 1988 (Basel I). On the Herstatt crisis see: Catherine Schenk, Summer in the City: Banking Failures of 1974 and the Development of International Banking Supervision, *English Historical Review*, Vol. CXXIX, No. 540, October 2014, 1129–1156.

75 IMFA European Department-EURAI Subject Files Box 70, 'Confidential Note of the European Office of the IMF in Paris to the Managing Director Witteveen', 11 July 1974.

76 The final press communiqué issued the 10 September 1974 stated:

> At their regular meeting in Basle on 9th September, the Central-Bank Governors from the countries of the Group of Ten and Switzerland discussed the working of the international banking system. They took stock of existing mechanism for supervision and regulation and noted recent improvements made in these fields in a number of major countries. They agreed to intensify the exchange of information between central banks on the activities of banks operating in international markets and, where appropriate, to tighten further the regulations governing foreign exchange positions. The Governors also had an exchange of views on the problem of the lender of last resort in the Euro-markets. They recognized that it would be not practical to lay down in advance detailed rules and procedures for the provision of temporary liquidity. But they were satisfied that *means are available for that purpose and will be used if and when necessary* [emphasis added].

The communiqué is reported in Charles Goodhart, *The Basel Committee on Banking Supervision*, Cambridge University Press, Cambridge, UK, 2011, 41.

77 Ethan Kapstein, *Governing the Global Economy*, Harvard University Press, Cambridge, MA and London, 1994, 66.

78 IMFA, Western Hemisphere Department-WHDAI Economic Subject Files Box 25, 'Immediate Issues in the Euro-Currency Market', 24 September 1974.

79 Idem.

80 BEA 8A406/6, Brief on 'Criticisms of the Euro-Markets', 5 September 1974.

81 Idem.

82 IMFA European Department-EURAI Subject Files Box 70, 'Office Memorandum Euro-Currency Market-Staff Visit to Europe', 28 February 1975.

83 BIS Annual Report 1976, 80.

84 IMFA European Department-EURAI Subject Files Box 70, Confidential Memorandum, 'Euro-Currency Markets', 14 October 1975.

85 BIS Annual Report 1976, 80.

86 BIS Annual Report 1976, 83–84.

87 BIS Annual Report 1976, 85.

88 IMFA, SM/76/138, Paper prepared by Staff Team to the Executive Directors, 'International Banking – Recent Developments and Present Outlook', 24 June 1976, Electronic Document.

89 Idem.

90 Idem.

91 BIS Annual Report 1977, 15.

92 Data are from the BIS Annual Report 1977

93 IMFA European Department-EURAI Subject Files Box 70, Office Memorandum, 'International Banking-Staff Visit to Europe', 9 April 1976.

94 IMFA, SM/77/111. 'International Banking and Bond Markets-Recent Developments and Prospects for 1977', 11 May 1977, Electronic Document.

95 Idem. The largest borrowers at that time were Brazil, Mexico, Liberia, S. Korea, Argentina, Peru, Philippines, Taiwan, Israel, and Colombia.

96 Idem, 12.

97 IMFA Report by the Staff Team to the Executive Directors, SM/77/111, 'International Banking and Bond Market-Recent Developments and Prospects for 1977', 11 May 1977, Electronic Document. Previous data are also from the same document.

98 BIS Annual Report 1977, 101.

99 BIS Annual Report 1978, 5.

100 BIS Annual Report 1978, 9.

101 External claims of the banks of the G-10 amounted to US$657 billion, an increase of US$109 billion over 1976.

102 OECDA, WP3 Documents 1978, 'The Development of International Bank Activity Since Mid-1977 and Currency Unrest', Document prepared by the BIS for the WP3 meeting, 27–28 November 1978, CPE/WP3 (78)12.

103 IMFA, SM/78/160, 'International Banking and Bond Markets-Recent Developments and Prospects for 1978', 21 June 1978, 10, Electronic Document.

104 BIS Annual Report 1978, 91.

105 Data are from the BIS Annual Report 1978.

106 IMFA, SM/78/160, 'International Banking and Bond Markets-Recent Developments and Prospects for 1978', 14 June 1978, Electronic Document.

107 IMFA, SM/78/160, 'International Banking and Bond Markets-Recent Developments and Prospects for 1978', 14 June 1978, Electronic Document.

108 IMFA, SM/78/160, Exchange and Trade Relations Department Staff Memo, 'International Banking and Bond Markets-Recent Developments and Prospects for 1978', 14 June 1978, Electronic Document.

109 IMFA, Western Hemisphere Department, WHDAI-Economic Subject Files Box 25, Discussion Paper 'International Commercial Banking and World Economic Stability', Research Department, 14 September 1976.

110 IMFA, Exchange and Trade Relations Department, ETRAI-Director Ernest Sturc Subject Files, Box 3, Internal Discussion Paper 'The Fund and the Commercial Banks', 25 January 1977.

111 IMFA, European Department-EURAI Subject Files Box 70, Document prepared by the Research Department, 'The Eurocurrency Market', 24 May 1978.

112 BIS Annual Report 1979, 136.

113 On the EMS negotiations see Chapter 5 'Negotiating the European Monetary System', in Harold James, *Making the European Monetary Union*, Harvard University Press, Cambridge, MA, and London, 2012; Emmanuel Mourlon-Druol, *A Europe Made of Money. The Emergence of the European Monetary System*, Cornell University Press, Ithaca, NY and London, 2012.

114 BIS Annual Report 1979, 82.

115 BIS Annual Report 1979, 103.

116 IMFA, Exchange and Trade Relations Department-ETRAI Subject Files Box 4, 'Speech of Henry C. Wallich at the 1978 Euromarkets Conference', London, 8–9 May 1978.

117 BIS Annual Report 1979, 103.

118 OECDA, Documents of the WP3 1978, 'The Development of International Bank Activity since Mid-1977 and Currency Unrest', Prepared by the BIS for the Meeting of the WP3 (27–28 November 1978), CPE/WP3 (78)12.

119 BIS Annual Report 1979, 103.

120 BIS Annual Report 1978, 107.

121 On the monetary policies implemented by Volcker in 1979 a useful reading is Joseph B. Treaster, *Paul Volcker: The Making of a Financial Legend*, Wiley, Hoboken, NJ, 2004, 148 and William L. Silber, *Volcker. The Triumph of Persistence*, Bloomsbury Press, New York and London, 2012.

122 Judith Stein, *Pivotal Decade. How the United States Traded Factories for Finance in the Seventies*, Yale University Press, New Haven, CT and London, 2010, 228.

123 David Lomax, *The Developing Country Debt Crisis*, Palgrave Macmillan, London, 1986, 44.

124 Ian Skeet, *Opec: Twenty-Five Years of Prices and Politics*, Cambridge University Press, Cambridge, UK, 1988, 158.

125 OECDA, Documents of the WP3 1979, 'Confidential Summary Record by the Secretariat of the Working Party 3 of the Economic Policy Committee held on 12th and 13th December 1979'.

126 Ian Skeet, *Opec: Twenty-Five Years of Prices and Politics*, Cambridge University Press, Cambridge, UK, 1988, 161.

127 IMFA, 'World Economic Outlook-World Oil Situation', 10 April 1981, ID/81/6, Electronic Document.

128 BEA, Quarterly Bulletin, December 1981.

129 IMFA, 'World Economic Outlook-The Current Picture', 3 January 1980, ID/80/1, Electronic Document.

130 BIS Annual Report 1980, 24.

131 IMFA, European Department-EURAI Subject Files Box 146, 'Remarks by J. de Larosière at the Annual Dinner of the U.S. Council of the International Chamber of Commerce in New York City', 5 December 1979.

132 BIS Annual Report 1980, 118.

133 BIS Annual Report 1980, 110.

134 IMFA, European Department-EURAI Subject Files Box 146, 'Address by J. de Larosière on the Occasion of the Annual Assembly of the Federal Association of German Banks in Bonn', October 29 1980.

135 Rawi Abdelal, *Capital Rules. The Construction of Global Finance*, Harvard University Press, Cambridge, MA and London, England, 2007, 135.

136 Jonathan Kirshner, 'Keynes, Capital Mobility and the Crisis of Embedded Liberalism', *Review of International Political Economy* Vol. 6, No. 3, Autumn, 1999, 313–337.

137 IMFA, OMD-Jacques de Larosière Papers Box 14, 'Developing a New International Monetary System: A Long-Term View, Lecture by H. J. Witteveen, Chairman of the Group of Thirty before the Per Jacobsson Foundation', Washington, DC, 25 September 1983.

4 Full measures

It was the best of times, it was the worst of times, it was the age of wisdom, it was the age of foolishness, it was the epoch of belief, it was the epoch of incredulity, it was the spring of Light, it was the winter of Despair.

(Charles Dickens, *A Tale of Two Cities*, 1859)

Since 1973, the involvement of private banks in the recycling process has provided a formidable boost to the expansion of their international activities. The emergence of unprecedentedly large payments imbalances requiring financial intermediation on a world-wide scale brought a massive increase in both the supply of funds to the international banking system and the demand for balance-of-payments finance.[1]

The 'paradox' of the 1970s

The banking expansion was dramatically accelerated by the imbalances created by the oil crisis. The sharp increase in the world market price of oil caused a sudden and large rise in the demand for private international capital, while the surplus oil-exporting countries placed a sizeable proportion of their disposable funds with banks in the major capital market countries. Thus, 'the *demand for the intermediary services of banks rose sharply* [emphasis added]'.[2] The oil shock provided the banking sector with vast new loanable funds and stimulated their international activities by relaxing the three already mentioned constraints that still limited their expansion: lack of support by international organisations, lack of capital to fund new ventures and lack of incentives to expand abroad given the favourable domestic context.

As remarked by Richard Roberts, petrodollar recycling, especially after the reassurances of the G-10 Governors of September 1974, presented opportunities for banks to provide a range of fee-earning advisory services, such as asset management, or to launch joint ventures with the common idea of matching OPEC financial resources with Western financial expertise.[3] The geographical expansion of European commercial banks was astonishing, particularly after the first oil crisis, when the imperatives of recycling the oil surpluses pushed banks into new territories (such as the Gulf region, the Far East and socialist countries), into new products, for example wholesale banking, and towards new customers, notably governments.

Overall, European commercial banks went through a phase of significant structural transformation. In the ten years following the oil crisis, commercial banks re-entered the international arena after a decades-long hiatus by setting up networks of branches, subsidiaries and affiliated companies to operate in foreign money and the Euromarket, while the scope of the Eurocurrency market widened both geographically, to become a global market, and in the range of financial instruments and facilities provided. As Joel Métais remarked:

> We can probably consider the twenty years from the mid-1960s to the mid-1980s as the second most significant wave of foreign expansion of French commercial banks after the first, experienced from 1860 to 1905. And *the decade starting around the first oil shock probably witnessed their most tremendous ever foreign involvement* [emphasis added].[4]

The same was true for the British clearers, as authors like Geoffrey Jones or David Rogers have noted in their studies.

Despite the importance of the decade for an understanding of the changes in international banking and finance, the 1970s have received scant interest from the financial historian. This is mostly due to limited access to archival evidence. This limitation inevitably affects the depth of existing analysis, failing to provide us with important information behind the international expansion of the major European banks. More precisely, several crucial details on the motivation and process of international expansion are neglected or overlooked by current narratives. In this chapter, we will try to offer new archival-driven understandings of the motives behind the simultaneous expansion of several large European banks, using recently disclosed documents to illustrate how and where these banks expanded, the challenges they faced and their responses.

Thus, after having illustrated how the Euromarket was saved by the oil crisis and how the recycling challenge was delegated to commercial banks, we will now illustrate how European commercial banks responded to this increased demand for their services and entered a formative period that marked the beginning of a new era of financial globalisation. The new era of overseas expansion was characterised by the rise and fall of cooperative banking, especially banking clubs, and the increasing importance of direct representations around the world.

The transformation of the European banking sector after the oil crisis is a particularly interesting phenomenon, because the years stretching from 1973 to 1982 are unanimously considered by the historiography as years of crises and broken dreams. In the short space of ten years, the world witnessed a series of monetary crises which destroyed the Bretton Woods regime, two energy crises in 1973 and 1979, and the worst debt crisis since the 1930s, sprawling across the developing world in 1982. Logically we would have expected the banking sector to be forced to remain behind local boundaries and to adapt to slower growth. Instead, those years represented some of the most innovative years for the banking and financial sector and they also marked the beginning of what Andrew Haldane, Simon Brennan and Vasileios Madouros ironically call the 'productivity miracle' in the

American and European banking and financial sector to refer to the remarkable growth of financial intermediation compared to the rest of the economy.[5]

Let us quantify the impact of the oil crisis on the banking sector by looking at the French case. Between 1968 and 1973, French banks had set up 27 overseas representative offices, 23 branches and 37 subsidiaries. Over the next five years, between 1974 and 1979, the pace became hectic. They established 81 representative offices, 48 branches and 63 subsidiaries.[6] As Métais has remarked, it is undeniable that 'The pace of foreign expansion markedly gained momentum after the first oil shock'.[7]

Is it really possible to consider the simultaneous decline of the industrial sector and the rise of finance simply as a coincidence – or a paradox? After having illustrated the response of Western countries to the recycling challenge, we are now better positioned to argue that the same causes underlying the end of the post-war miracle are at the origins of the rise of finance, as commercial banks became fundamental to the creation of new markets for Western export through Euroloans to importing regions such as Latin America.[8]

Crucially, the crisis brought along a *realignment of interest* between public and private institutions after the Bretton Woods break, provided *huge capital* to finance international ventures and *powerful incentives* to expand overseas. A new relationship between banks and Western governments was forged after the oil crisis. As most governments in industrial countries felt the pressure of deteriorating balance of payments, they looked desperately to potential new buyers for their exports in order to transfer their deficits. Most of the time, potential buyers did not have the money to pay for their imports and at that point commercial banks became the crucial link to help industrial companies win export orders. Everyone was 'passing the buck': governments to commercial banks and banks to borrowers through syndicated Euroloans. Philip A. Wellons has argued that governments and banks can have one of four kinds of relationships: liberal, mercantilist, playing-the-system and alliance.

A 'liberal' relationship would posit strong and independent banks in their home government; a mercantilist relationship would entail weak banks subject to the government (essentially the situation under Bretton Woods); a 'playing-the-system' relationship would involve the banks and the government using each other to pursue their own interests. A final position is the 'alliance'. The alliance involves governments and banks allying 'either formally or tacitly to achieve goals both sides want'.[9] We argue that after the oil crisis the relationship between governments and banks steadily moved towards an alliance, as banks became the *trait d'union* between surplus and deficit countries.

As political scientist, Michael Loriaux, has remarked: 'Foreign borrowing, both on the market and through foreign institutional lenders, provided a panacea that addressed nearly all the problems that the monetary and energy crises had aggravated or created'.[10] Banks became important tools in the policy adjustment to the oil shocks, with most Western countries responding to the shock by improving their balance of payments, increasing exports and slowing imports.[11]

The side effect of that panacea was the delegation of more and more power to the banking and financial sector by privatising the monetary and financial circuit.

The oil crisis not only put commercial banks at the centre of the monetary and financial system as purveyors of credit to LDCs but also as purveyors of capital to developed countries suffering increasing deficits. Gérard Aubanel of the Overseas Department (*Diréction Générale des Services Etrangers*, DGSE) of the *Banque de France* noted:

> If we take France, for example, the coverage of its budget deficits, since 1974 – in conjunction, moreover, with its capital requirements in the long run that the domestic financial market could not meet – has required use of external markets, with its foreign debt, on December 31, 1979, standing at 66 billion francs in Euro-credits and 27 billion francs in Eurobonds, which under-lines the *crucial role of the Euro-credits* even for a country like ours [emphasis added]'[12]

It is now important to appreciate how the decisions taken at the international level (IMF, OECD, BIS) and processed by resourceful bankers shaped the course of European banking by revolutionising the scale and scope of the continental banking and financial sector. The Chairman of the international subsidiary of Lloyds Bank was adamant in recognising the crucial role of the oil crisis in unleashing international finance. Sir Reginald Verdon-Smith remarked in its annual statement that, despite the years since Lloyds Bank International's formation in 1974 being marked by the rise in oil prices, balance of payments problems, uncertainty in the international markets and the deepest recession since the 1930s:

> [t]he fears of the pessimists have so far proved unfounded . . . For all its dangers, the situation created by the oil price rise provided an *opportunity* for the commercial to play a part in international financing that was perhaps *more important than ever before* . . . banks were able to respond quickly to the new situation and, by taking part in the recycling process, to sustain world trade and, in particular, to make possible the continued growth of the non-oil-producing developing countries. Lloyds Bank International (LBI) shared fully in these developments which have resulted in a *lasting increase in the scale and range of our business* [emphasis added].[13]

The gradual transformation of the British, as well as the French, banking sector from a domestically focused and low-risk industry to a more globalised and riskier one could aptly be summarised under the headline 'Big is Beautiful'. Essentially, this meant an obsession with *asset growth* and *geographic expansion* at all costs with scarce attention to the quality of its sources and the impact on the welfare of its shareholders.

The post-1973 years represent a crucial decade for understanding the process that has created the modern banking and financial landscape dominated by global institutions spanning across the globe in a seamless web of transactions. As we have seen, until the late 1960s and early 1970s several factors still limited the international ambitions of European banks.

It was only in the 1970s, when all major obstacles (risk of control, lack of funds and lack of incentives) had been overcome, that commercial banks were finally able to be 'engaged once more in the international activities they had largely refrained from since the Depression era'.[14]

It is true that the tendency towards international expansion had been latent in the European banking sector since the mid-1960s, but it is also true that, without the turbulences of the 1970s, the evolutionary process of European banks from sheltered and conservative institutions to global and highly innovative ones would have taken a much longer period. As some authors have pointed out: 'Petro-currency recycling and large-scale borrowings by deficit countries for balance-of-payments purposes were the *fundamental forces* driving the expansion of the Euromarkets in these years [emphasis added]'.[15] As the Euromarket was the driving force behind the transformation of the European and Western banking and financial sector, the study of international banking in the 1970s is, inevitably, a study of petrodollar recycling.

The goal of this chapter is to analyse the transformation of the European banking sector during the 1970s by explaining why and how the sector moved from being fundamentally similar to that seen in the nineteenth century to a more complex, more competitive, more integrated but also a much riskier one.

The first part will analyse the organisational changes and the subsequent wave of internationalisation, focusing on Lloyds, *Société Générale* and Midland Bank. The second section will illustrate the new autonomous initiatives to enter new markets put in place by Barclays, Midland Bank and *Crédit Lyonnais*. European banks entered new regions on a scale never reached before. The final section will present direct evidence on the 'promiscuous' relationship between commercial banks and the IMF and between commercial banks and dictatorships around the world.

Further organisational changes and a new wave of internationalisation

The oil crisis brought along a new wave of internal changes and internationalisation for European banks. These two elements must be seen as two sides of the same coin. The timid efforts of the earlier part of the decade were insufficient to sustain the new role of commercial banks as intermediaries between deficit and surplus countries and new structures had to be devised as international banking was radically different from domestic banking in terms of scope, risk and know-how. Consequently, Lloyds bought the remaining shares of its international company to create LBI in April 1974. Midland Bank abandoned its grand designs and correspondent banking by directly entering foreign markets through its newly formed International Division, created in July 1974. Midland reshaped its management structure by establishing a two-headed leadership, with one general manager in charge of the domestic business and one devoted to the international side. *Société Générale* reshaped its international activities between 1974 and 1975 by replacing its functional structure with a geographical one.

Barclays and *Crédit Lyonnais*, which had already effected profound changes to their corporate structures to respond to the international challenge, did not alter their internal structures radically, but the pace of expansion was greatly accelerated. New regions were explored by bankers, notably Latin America, the Pacific Basin and the Middle East, while Europe gradually became a residual market for most banks.

New vehicles for Lloyds and Midland

After the merger with BOLSA, Lloyds' management had rapidly started to realise that having 25 or 55 per cent of a bank was not a suitable solution to achieve the grand design of a 'world-wide bank, offering the widest possible range of financial services to wholesale customers'.[16]

In December 1971, a 'Special Project Team' was set up to advise the Executive Directors on the future strategy of the new bank; they submitted a report in February 1972. Some of the information contained in the report proved extremely interesting in indicating how the Bank was seeing the future and appreciating how the shock of 1973 radically changed the strategy and accelerated the process of change of Lloyds and BOLSA International. Incredibly, they got almost everything wrong. The Special Project Team saw in the EEC and the Far East the major areas of growth while 'Latin America is not expected to afford growth prospects for foreign banks' and 'the Eurodollar market is expected to be relatively stagnant [in the coming years]'.[17]

Even if the direction was not exactly right, to use a euphemism, the general idea that the new Bank needed a new structure was accepted. After the report of the Special Project Team, Lloyds and BOLSA International asked for the assistance of the consulting firm, McKinsey, to devise a new strategy and structure. McKinsey's plan entitled 'Setting a New Direction for the Bank' was submitted in October 1972. It was an ambitious one, albeit an impossible one to realise without the full control of Lloyds and BOLSA International. It involved targeting subsidiaries of multinational companies, local companies with international operations, governments and government bodies and other banks in the EEC, the Pacific Basin and the US and offering them local currency loans, international currency loans, investment and merchant banking services and a wide range of non-banking services.

The new Bank was in a deadlock; the transformation of Lloyds from a domestic to a predominantly international one needed full ownership to implement bold ideas; Mellon Bank had to leave the boat. For its part, we can assume that Mellon realised, in a context of increasing competition on the international arena, that owning 15 per cent of a bank would not make much sense and fighting to keeping its shares would not be worth the effort.

As the Chairman of Lloyds and BOLSA International, Sir Reginald Verdon-Smith, pointed out, 'a total identity of interest'[18] between Lloyds Bank and LBI was needed. First, the minority interest of Mellon Bank was acquired and, subsequently, a public offer for the remainder was launched.

In April 1974, the new Bank was officially renamed Lloyds Bank International or LBI, Lloyds Bank now had 100 per cent of the company and the total bill for the operation amounted to £85 million.

In 1974, the strategy outlined in the late 1960s seemed to be largely complete. Lloyds now had its Overseas Department within Lloyds Bank (focusing on the international needs of UK branches) and LBI, which included BOLSA (it kept its name for the Latin American market), the Bank of London and Montreal (BOLAM), the National Bank of New Zealand and Lloyds Bank California (active in retail banking, bought from World Airways as First Western Bank for US$115 million when US regulatory authorities made it clear that they would not permit its acquisition by Wells Fargo).

Nonetheless, the shock radically modified the priorities and strategies of LBI as it did for most of the large European banks, giving a whole new role and dimension to what was not much more sophisticated than an old-style overseas bank.

If, just two years before, the top management did not see any growth in Latin America and the Euromarket was seen as stagnant, now everything changed. Latin America, the Middle East, Far East Asia and the Euroloan business, what we shall call the 'recycling circuit', became the main drivers of LBI's growth.

The Middle East, which had been a *terrain vague* for Lloyds, was rapidly occupied. A representative office was opened in Beirut in 1974 and subsequently closed in 1976 because of the civil war. A Teheran office was opened in 1976, an offshore branch was established in Bahrain in 1977, a full branch in Dubai in 1977 and a foreign currency branch in Cairo that same year. In October 1976 the Middle East and Africa Division was established as a separate entity and profit centre. Target customers came to be regrouped under three categories based on geographical sub-regions. The branches in Bahrain, Dubai and Cairo concentrated on the private sector, on the public sector and on ancillary business such as foreign exchange and letters of credit. In South Africa, target customers included the private sector financing, notably subsidiaries of UK companies, and the public sector. In the rest of the Division, LBI was principally active in the sovereign risk market.

Commercial banks became essential actors, in a context of stagnant growth at home and thus of fiscal crisis, in helping exporting industries (especially in developing countries). The usual loans in domestic currency at fixed interest rates backed by official guarantees were increasingly insufficient and expensive for the central government to ensure given the high inflation rates, depreciating sterling and increasing competition from abroad. Thus the solution became to provide trade finance in Eurocurrencies; the Secretary of State for Trade, for example, introducing the 'Foreign Currency Buyer Credit Facility' in 1976.

Even if the most important guidelines remained as outlined in 1969, LBI's strategy, along with the rest of the Group, was reviewed for the first time in 1976 and for a second time in 1979 (and for a third time in December 1982 when the debt crisis erupted and at increasingly short intervals throughout the rest of the 1980s). The focus of the reappraisals in the 1970s was always growing in size: the *mantra* (or obsession) of almost all major banks during that decade.

In August 1976 the 'Framework for the Future' prepared by B. H. Piper, Chief Executive of Lloyds Bank, confirmed Lloyds' intention of achieving a secure place as a major international bank. As for LBI, Piper posited that the subsidiary should 'provide a comprehensive international banking capability, establish a physical presence for the Group in the major financial centres of the world and serve . . . the needs of Group customers *in as many different countries as possible* [emphasis added]'.[19]

The growth of the international activities of Lloyds during these years is by any means impressive, as we can see from Table 4.1. If, until 1972, domestic business gave the main contribution to Lloyds' asset growth, since 1973 Lloyds started to really look like an international or global bank, especially thanks to the contribution of LBI's activities. According to the 1976 Report, it had more than 11,000 employees in more than 40 countries; 7,000 of them were employed in Latin America, 320 in North America, 2,000 in Continental Europe, 1,400 in the UK and 100 in the East and Australasia.

LBI's managers, with the assistance of Lloyds' new Chairman, Sir Jeremy Morse, were travelling the globe to seek new funds and customers to build a cross-border lending business. Sir Jeremy is a particularly important character in Lloyds' history, having been its Chairman from 1977 to 1993. Like Faulkner, he was trained in banking at Glynn, Mills & Co., becoming a director in 1964. After studying at Oxford, he then moved to the Bank of England from 1965 to 1972. After the end of Bretton Woods, he was selected as Chairman of the Deputies of the Committee of Twenty in charge of the elaboration of a new monetary system. With such a curriculum, he was an ideal choice for an ambitious bank such as LBI. He arrived at Lloyds in 1975 as Deputy Chairman, before being nominated as successor to Faulkner in 1977.

After the presence in Latin America was consolidated with over 130 branches through BOLSA and BOLAM, from the mid-1970s onwards priority was given to re-balance the profit contribution between Latin America and other regions. Special consideration was thus given to the Middle East and the Pacific Rim.

Table 4.1 Composition of assets of Lloyds Bank (£bn), 1971–81.

Year	Assets Group £ bn	Domestic %	International %
1971	3.8	63	37
1972	5.1	65	35
1973	6.7	55	45
1974	8.3	48	52
1975	9.4	46	54
1976	10.8	43	57
1977	12.6	40	60
1978	14.1	38	62
1979	16.2	41	59
1980	19.5	43	57
1981	24.5	38	62

Source: LBA, HO/Ch/MOR30, 'Lloyds Bank's Expansion of International Operations', Strategic Planning Unit, 7 September 1987.

Europe, in particular after 1973, became a residual market for LBI, and the *mot d'ordre* became to diversify away from domestic dependence much more than following the customers ('This was not a very powerful motive for us'[20]), as generally accepted by the existing literature.

In general, the opening of a branch and, to a lesser extent, a representative office, followed a similar path. The opening of the Seoul branch of LBI in 1977 when South Korea was under the control of the authoritarian President (for life) Park Chung-hee, provides a good illustration of this path.

A visit to the Republic of Korea (ROK) by M. J. Young (Chief Manager Operations, Asia, Australasia, Middle East and Africa Division) and G. H. Campbell (Executive for Asia and Australasia, Economics Department) was arranged from 9–11 December 1974. The objectives of the visit were to familiarise themselves with the conditions of the ROK, establish contact with leading companies and banks, update the Bank's knowledge of the political and economic background and review the lending policy in light of current observations.[21] The two managers produced, as was the norm, a report outlining the present situation and future prospects of the country. The British found 'energetic people, with a certain basic dynamism, industrious, adaptable and ready to work long hours, with management prompt in making decisions'.[22] They were impressed by the stability (at a high cost for human rights, we might add) of the country under the rule of President Park Chung-hee and the remarkable results achieved by a strongly export-led economy. They concluded their report by saying:

> For the foreign businessman or banker, the political risk in the Republic of Korea is considered good-to-moderate; there is currently no alternative in sight to the authoritarian rule of President Park, who still seems to enjoy the necessary degree of support from the forces backing him [Park-Chung-hee would be assassinated in 1979 by the Director of the Korean intelligence]. It seems unlikely that attempts by the DPRK [Democratic People's Republic of Korea] to subvert order in the Republic will be successful. The economic risks should remain good . . . Our conclusion for the medium-term is that the ROK leadership will make the necessary changes to its development strategy to support an expanding economy, remaining, as the IMF Representative considered, a good prospect in the medium-term.[23]

They mentioned an IMF representative. In fact, during their visit, like all the other exploratory visits, the members of the Bank met a wide array of individuals and institutions. In the Korean case, for example, Young and Campbell visited the British Embassy, the IMF office, Chartered Bank, the Economic Planning Board, the Bank of Korea, the Korea Exchange Bank, the Korea Development Bank, the Commercial Bank of Korea, First National City Bank, Korea Electric, Hyundai Motor and the Korean Traders Association.

After the first report was submitted, Lloyds was informed by the British Embassy that requirements to open a branch in the country were to be relaxed; a second visit followed and Young was asked to express a formal recommendation whether or not to open a representation or branch in South Korea. In 1976, a 'Recommendation to Open a Branch in the Republic of Korea' was issued. In its conclusions and recommendations, Young stated:

> The visit confirmed our understanding that for the time being the authorities have adopted an 'open door' policy towards foreign bank involvement in the Korean banking system ... Both the Ministry of Finance and the Bank of Korea have indicated that an application for a full branch from LBI would be looked upon favourably.[24]

On the type of the new establishment, many elements pointed in favour of the creation of a full branch. The reasons included the fact that none of the alternatives would have generated such a volume of profitable business.

Since a representative office did not handle business directly itself, but was used only when full branches were not allowed or where greater knowledge of local banking conditions was required, it was not considered a viable alternative. Therefore, the final recommendation to LBI's Board concluded that the best option was to open a full branch. The branch's activities should include short-term financing in local currency; routine banking business; Eurocurrency lending; fee-based business, especially related to project finance and export finance; acting as a source of business for other LBI branches in the Pacific Basin, for example by directing and receiving documentary business or directing Korean customers with overseas operations to them. As we can see from Table 4.2, the branch was finally authorised and opened in 1977.

In 1975 the international merchant banking activities were brought under the new Merchant Banking Division, which contained the departments responsible for loan syndication, international bond issues and corporate advisory services. The early to mid-1970s were hectic years for LBI, as shown in Table 4.2. As we mentioned earlier, Sir Jeremy played a crucial role in this expansion, travelling personally all around the world by Concorde to meet potential new customers and foster new alliances. During his long years at the helm of the Bank, he travelled the globe from Uruguay to Hong Kong, from South Korea to Australia. In a world that was becoming smaller and more connected, he was one of the best examples of the new breed of international bankers.

Table 4.2 International expansion of LBI, 1973–77 (branches and representative offices).

	1973	1974	1975	1976	1977
Representative offices	Hong Kong (finance company, branch in 1978)	Manila	Toronto Moscow Cairo	Teheran Kuala Lumpur	Houston
Branches			Singapore Tokyo	Chicago	Düsseldorf Bahrain	Cairo Dubai Seoul

Source: LBI Annual Reports, various years.

The international strategy was reviewed again in 1979. The position of LBI was a complex one, as stated in the 'Review of Corporate Strategy' of July 1979: 'LBI has now reached a point where it is too big to be just a Latin American specialty bank, but *not big enough* to compete with the major international banks [emphasis added]'.[25]

LBI had to get even bigger because in all important markets they were still smaller than their major competitors and the size of their corporate resources relative to theirs put LBI and the Lloyds Bank Group at a competitive disadvantage. But, according to LBI, size was not an end in itself; it was only a means to an end. The end itself was 'improved profit performance'.[26]

In the post-oil crisis financial market, a larger size was essential to meet the growing needs of governments and multinational corporations, to participate in the syndicated loan market and to have larger country limits.

The new LBI should not only be a larger bank by assets but also geographically. Representation in a larger number of countries had two crucial implications: first, it enabled a bank to take advantage of global opportunities; second, it provided a better spread of risk.

Getting bigger very fast posed a dilemma to LBI's management between the need to maximise opportunities and the need to avoid excessive concentrations of risk.[27] The strategy review involved the following major objectives. First, recognising growth as a measure of strength and a requirement for survival, to make a major contribution towards improving the Lloyds Bank Group's position in the world league of banks. Second, to develop globally a diversified financial services organisation, adjusting to changing circumstances and continually seeking new opportunities for growth. Third, to avoid excessive concentration of capital, assets and earnings in any single country, industry, product or market in order to enhance consistency of performance. Finally, to achieve profitable growth in real terms; and to achieve a return on equity capital and a compound rate of growth in earnings per share sufficient to place Lloyds' performance in the top 30 banks in the world. The objectives were supposed to shape LBI's strategy for the 'coming decades'.

The priority areas were confirmed and they were the Middle East, the Far East and Africa. The target customers were multinational corporations, local companies with international business and governments and government bodies. In some areas in Europe (namely France, Belgium and the Netherlands) core business should move away from retail banking to wholesale banking.

From being the smallest and one of the most conservative of the Big Four, by the end of the 1970s Lloyds, thanks especially to LBI, was at the forefront of international banking. This new status brought, as expected, increased risk as the international expansion of Lloyds was getting out of control. It committed more and more human capital and organisational resources in the build up and maintenance of its cross-border lending business to LDCs. Between 1978 and 1982, outstanding cross-border lending grew by 52 per cent, from US$12.5 billion to US$19 billion.

In fact, the whole process of international expansion increasingly looked like an end in itself. Replicating the dynamics of almost all the major banks in Europe, the ambition to put a flag on the world map predated considerations on profitability and shareholder value. Within Lloyds, these considerations would be challenged only in the second half of the 1980s and their demise would give birth to one of the most profitable banks in Europe, but this is an intriguing and fascinating phenomenon that we shall analyse in the following chapter.

The wind of change was also blowing in Poultry, where Midland had its headquarters. The realisation of the inadequacy of Midland's strategy to face the new challenges of the 1970s logically involved a second major strategic reconfiguration after the grand design era that took place in 1974–75, when it was recognised that special priority should be given on 'increasing the long term profit contribution from international activities'.[28] The grand design phase was replaced with a new strategy named 'Own Initiative'. A Midland's Director's Committee was created to draw up the new corporate plan and it soon realised that:

> The Bank's traditional attitude towards its international business (which had avoided direct involvement outside the United Kingdom) had probably been right when it was adopted and had brought benefits to the bank by way of foreign banking business in London; it felt, however, that these advantages had been eroded by the recent very rapid growth in the number of foreign banks established in London. Moreover, other British Banks had now *followed Barclays lead into conducting operations overseas* . . . The Committee had suggested that a balance would have to be found between the need for expanding income from international business and upsetting relationships with the other members of the EAC and that, initially, *consideration might be given to direct representation* where none of the other EAC banks were involved – e.g. the Middle East and the Philippines [emphasis added].[29]

The result of this fundamental reconfiguration of Midland was the creation of Midland Bank International Division (MBID) in July 1974, which regrouped the Overseas Branch, the Export Finance Division and currency lending activities, and the appointment of two Chief General Managers, one for the domestic activities, Stuart Graham, and one for the international activities, Sir Malcolm Wilcox, who worked at Midland for 46 years until his retirement in 1981.[30] The 'two-headed' structure would ultimately prove detrimental for Midland's destiny but, at that time, the decision seemed rational and the most important decision was where and how to expand.

The process of reorganisation was a long one. At the time of the formation of the International Division, Midland had no branches or subsidiaries outside the UK and only four representative offices in Brussels, Frankfurt, Tokyo and Zürich. Given the limited banking capacity of a representative office, we could safely say that international banking was almost a clean slate for Midland.

The structure and mission of MBID were only finalised in the first quarter of 1975, when the overall development and organisational plans were outlined at the Board meeting of 14 February, and an International Credit Control Committee established in March.

The future strategy of MBID was based on the following objectives: first, to ensure that Midland would be recognised as a major international bank; second, to obtain from international activities an increasing share of total Group profits; and, finally, to improve the quality of Group revenue by increasing the proportion of earnings from abroad, and by extending their geographical spread.[31]

At the organisational level, the structure of MBID was reorganised in order to provide a fair degree of independence for the Division, but with the use of central services in appropriate areas, to establish the concept of a separate profit centre and to provide a style of management structure to accommodate the Division's responsibilities.[32] The strategic reconfiguration was in good measure the result of the report of the consulting firm, Stanford Research (now, SRI International), commissioned by Wilcox in 1974.

MBID had an Eastern International Region (Middle East and Africa area, Asia and Pacific area, Money and Exchange), a Central International Region (European area, Latin American area, Banking Operations), a UK Region (Corporate Finance, Trade and Development) and a Central International Region (North American area, Export Finance).

The post-1974 'Own initiative' strategy of Midland recognised after more than 50 years that minority stakes and correspondent banking were incompatible with the new corporate objectives of becoming a major international bank. In particular, Wilcox recognised that Midland had to be represented under its own name through branches and representative offices or through wholly owned subsidiaries. Since the interests in consortium banking were not relinquished, MBID ultimately adopted two parallel strategies of cooperating while establishing direct representations in specific areas or types of business.

Growing without revolutions, the case of Société Générale

As with Lloyds, Midland and Barclays, the international expansion of *Société Générale* in the second half of the 1970s is inextricably linked to the figure of a key executive, in this case Marc Viénot. Mr Viénot arrived at *Société Générale* in the defining year of 1974, after a career in the French civil administration[33] and in several international organisations (IMF, IBRD, OCDE 1970–73). By the time he entered *Société Générale* in 1974, the overseas network accounted for 20 per cent of the non-consolidated balance sheet of the Bank.

Viénot's profile is very similar to other international managers of that time. The combination of domestic and international experiences was probably the main reason why the Chairman of *Société Générale*, Maurice Lauré, recruited him in early 1974 as Deputy General Director and then General Director in 1977. Viénot would spend the rest of his career at *Société Générale*, becoming Chairman in 1986 and Honorary Chairman in 1997, a career path similar to several bankers of his generation.

As (Deputy) General Director, he supervised the Foreign Department (*Diréction de l'Etranger et de la Trésorerie*, DEIT). Before the arrival of Viénot, the Foreign Department had a mixed functional/geographical structure. Viénot did not criticise this double structure *per se*, but he was very critical of the results of this organisation within *Société Générale*. He thought that repartition of charges between the two poles, as it stood, was 'wasting energies' and 'creating conflicts'.[34] The balance between functional and geographical services had to be modified in favour of the latter.

The arrival of Viénot at the Foreign Department ushered the reorganisation of February 1975 because of 'the development and the increasing complexity of international commercial, banking and financial operations'.[35] The reorganisation of the Foreign Department was probably the most significant accomplishment of Viénot during the 1970s and the most relevant change in *Société Generale*'s structure of that decade. From an organisational point of view, the reason behind the reorganisation was twofold. First, it was necessary to reinforce the administrative side by creating a secretariat to manage the human resources and administrative tasks. Before the reform, DEIT did not have a centralised secretariat in charge of administrative tasks and human resources. Second, it became crucial that the Foreign Department be reorganised on a geographical basis in order to pursue the overseas expansion of *Société Générale* and assist domestic customers willing to export. This last aspect is without any possible doubt the most important legacy of the reorganisation of 1975. From then on, each geographic sector became the basic vehicle to conduct business overseas, taking over the business of the Branches and Subsidiaries Office, which was suppressed in January 1975. The geographic unit was responsible for managing the Bank's implantations in its country of responsibility and mediating between the foreign establishments and the Parisian headquarters. The new organisation of DEIT included a secretariat and a service for foreign exchange, treasury and international credits. Two geographic zones were created: International Relations Department (Zone I), comprising Central and South America, Africa, Socialist Europe, Near and Middle East, Far East and Australasia. Zone I included at that time the Tokyo branch; the representative offices in Mexico City, Rio de Janeiro, Caracas, Moscow and Berlin; and several affiliated companies in Latin America and the Middle East. The International Relations Department (Zone II) comprised Europe and Anglo-Saxon countries. Zone II included the London branch, the representative office in Milan and several affiliated companies in Europe.

The Branches and Subsidiaries Office was eliminated and its functions absorbed by the two International Relations departments and the cooperation service. A newly created European cooperation service was created to deal with the other EBIC banks and joint ventures. Finally, a Risk Management service saw the light.

Geographic sectors were pivotal in Viénot's reform. Their role abroad consisted first, in managing all the relations with their country of responsibility (e.g. control of representative offices and branches, contacts with local powers and French powers in that country, contacting French firms, promoting the Bank's products); second, in looking for new markets for French exporters; and third, in monitoring possible competitors. Their role in the Parisian office consisted of: a) taking charge of correspondent banking, dealing with foreign banks in Paris and with correspondent banks; b) keeping in constant touch with the French administration involved in foreign business; c) controlling overseas branches and subsidiary companies; and d) dealing with ancillary services such as the finance direction or loan services.[36] In early 1976, the two geographic zones were merged under one single zone under the supervision of Louis Buttay.

In 1976, still under the leadership of Marc Viénot, and because of the increasing importance of medium-term, syndicated Eurodollar credits after the oil shock, two services were merged. Historically, Euroloans were the domain of DEIT and Eurobonds of the Financial Department (*Direction Financière*, DF). In early 1976, the service for international credits (of DEIT) and the service for international issues (of DF) were merged to create the International Financing Department (*Service des Financements Internationaux,* SFI) associated to DEIT. The reason for this decision by Mr Viénot is clear: the activities of the Finance Department, Eurobonds, were declining while the activities of the Foreign Department, Euroloans, were prospering 'beyond the reasonable', putting strains on the manpower of the department.

The numbers justified the creation of the SFI. In 1972 *Société Générale* granted 20 Euroloans for US$61 million, while in 1975 it granted 86 of them for US$307 million, occupying the 10th place in the syndicated Eurodollar market.[37] Particularly notable was the Euroloan of US$1.5 billion (a record sum at that time) arranged for the French Republic in 1974.

The efforts to improve the performance of the Foreign Department continued unabated. In March 1976, Viénot created a special committee, composed of himself and three other top managers, to analyse the position of *Société Générale* and the results achieved in the different domains of international banking with respect to its competitors at home and abroad, to improve its performance in international banking and finally to estimate its needs in terms of human capital and resources. A report was prepared by May. The report showed that foreign establishments accounted for almost 18 per cent of the total balance sheet compared to just 10 per cent in 1970. More generally, international activities were showing very strong growth rates compared to the metropolitan network. This contribution compared favourably with its French competitors but very unfavourably with its British and, especially, American competitors. For example, Citicorp derived 70 per cent of its profits from its operations overseas in 1975, while Barclays accounted for 30 per cent. This resulted mainly from the limited direct presence abroad of *Société Générale* compared to its French competitors, as we can see from Table 4.3.

Looking at the number of branches, the inferiority of *Société Générale* in terms of its foreign network becomes evident. The Bank was relatively strong in the US, UK, Japan, Spain, Iran and, for historical reasons, Francophone Africa. With some exceptions, these were not the most promising places to do business. Critically, *Société Générale* was very ill-suited for the post-1974 world because it lacked offices in Central and Southern America, Anglophone Africa (especially South Africa and Nigeria), South East Asia (except for its 14 per cent stake in Euras Bank) and other important Commonwealth territories such as Canada and Australia. One important reason for this slow expansion of branches abroad was

Table 4.3 Foreign vehicles of French banks in 1976.

	SG	BNP	CL
Branches	4	30	31
Participations in commercial banks	33	31	24
Participation in financial companies	17	12	21
Representative offices	11	19	21
Total	65	92	97

Source: SGA, 81156, Confidential Report 'Le développement des activités internationales de la Société Générale', 3 May 1976.

the colonial heritage, but we must also mention the constraints imposed by the EBIC membership, a situation similar to that of Midland.

In fact, it was difficult to implement a clear strategy abroad when the interests of the Bank had to be constantly balanced with the interests of the club and its vehicles (joint ventures, subsidiaries, representative offices, etc). Often when an EBIC office of subsidiary was present in one country, the only solution possible to enter a new market was to settle for second best, in general a representative office or a finance company. The volume of business going through these vehicles was much lower than could be achieved by branches.

In order to compensate for its weaknesses abroad, some priority areas were singled out: Latin America, South East Asia, Eastern and Northern Europe, Africa and the Middle East. With regard to Latin America, the most promising countries in which to expand were Mexico, Brazil and Venezuela. Panama was also considered, especially for its tax-haven status and liberal policies. In South East Asia, where *Société Générale* had only a regional office in Jakarta and a participation in Euras Bank, it was decided to focus on Hong Kong, the Philippines and Singapore. In Europe, efforts were to be concentrated on West Germany, Switzerland, the Netherlands and Scandinavian countries. In Africa, South Africa and Nigeria were considered the most promising markets. Other important areas were the Middle East and Comecon countries. Existing operations in the Middle East were reoriented towards investment banking; this is the case especially of FRAB, which, until the end of 1972, was essentially devoted to deposit taking in the Arab world and to short- and medium-term commercial loans.

The structure of the international operations of *Société Générale* was modified again at the end of the decade when DEIT became the Department of International Affairs and Treasury (*Direction des Affaires Internationales et de la Trésorerie*, DAIT) under the direction of Léopold Jeorger, who reported directly to Mr Viénot. The new name reflected the creation in September 1978 of an International Office to increase deposits from other banks and to cater more precisely for the needs of international companies. Under their joint supervision, DAIT had a Department for International Banking and Commercial Relations (divided into three zones: Africa, Latin America and Japan; European socialist countries; continental Europe and Anglo-Saxon countries), a Department for Treasury and International Financing (comprising the recently created SFI) and an administrative department.

In addition to the strategic and managerial context, it is now crucial to analyse in more detail why *Société Générale* decided to increasingly internationalise its operations from 1973–74 onwards. Viénot had very clear ideas on that aspect, since every time he had to talk about the subject he mentioned the same elements. For example, in a letter addressed to Finance Minister Jacques Delors, Viénot wrote:

> Among the factors that has led Société Générale, like other large banks, to engage strongly in international operations over the last few years are: a) the development of international trade, b) the emergence and development of Euromarkets, c) the slowing rate of growth in domestic banking.[38]

In the same letter, Mr Viénot gave more details on the mission of *Société Générale* on the international markets. Amongst the services offered in the international arena, he mentioned settlements in foreign transactions, foreign exchange operations, helping the export sector and international financing. These last two elements are of particular interest because they highlight the central role of banks in the financing and survival of the French manufacturing and industrial sector after the post-war years dominated by state financing.[39] In a previous document, Viénot was even more explicit when mentioning the three reasons why *Société Générale* decided to internationalise its activities, mentioning the rise in international commerce and the explosive growth of the Eurodollar market, but adding that:

> The third reason which pushed the French banks to internationalize, is that this sector is *more conducive to bold new initiatives and it is not regulated* . . . there is in the country some saturation of banking facilities and since 1973, an almost constant supervision of credit. So it is not surprising that French banks have sought to pour their energies into the area of least resistance, i.e. overseas [emphasis added].[40]

With regard to support for the export sector, banks became a fundamental actor in the context of increasing competition from new competitors, especially Japanese firms backed by their respective banks. For example, in September 1974, the Bank of Tokyo and the newly created (by President Carlos Andrès Perez) Venezuelan Investment Fund (*Fondo de Inversiones de Venezuela*, FIV) signed a cooperation agreement whereby Japanese companies would provide capital, technical assistance and human capital to foster development in the country. In a note from Mr A. Sicard of the International Department to Buttay it was noted:

> *The Japanese are willing to do anything*, presumably by investing up to 20%, through the provision of technical assistance, the transfer of know-how, the assignments of patents and, where applicable, of consumer durables. For the rest – ie for capital good itself – the sales would be in cash if possible, with short or medium term facilities if necessary. Such offers look interesting to the . . . Venezuelans, without that meaning an exclusive agreement with the Japanese. However, up to now, nobody is on the ranks.

> We can therefore ask ourselves whether a large French bank . . . would not gain something by taking inspiration from the initiative taken by the Bank of Tokyo [emphasis added].[41]

Since the economic situation in Western countries started deteriorating in the early 1970s and especially since the first oil shock, exporting became the Holy Grail of most governments. Furthermore, as the fiscal crisis did not allow them to directly help domestic companies, they resorted to the banking and financial sector, which, after the development of the Eurodollar business, was able to create money without affecting their increasingly shaky domestic balances. For French banks, the Euromarket and other international operations allowed them to escape domestic regulations such as the infamous *encadrement du crédit*.[42]

Société Générale, as with the other banks in France, assumed a crucial role for exporting industries by extending further credits to possible buyers, not satisfied with the old system of *Crédits-acheteurs*, which were export credits in French francs given to the buyers. These 'extra' credits were called financial credits or *crédits financiers d'accompagnement* and they were credits in Eurodollars given directly to LDCs, not guaranteed by the COFACE (the state-owned export company). These credits covered expenses such as local costs, refinancing of previous state-guaranteed credits, etc. Often they were just bribes given to local élites, interlopers or corrupt state officials. The amount and the interest on these financial loans became the crucial element to win contracts in LDCs, as did the role of banks in the financing of the private or semi-private sectors. The other important element mentioned by Mr Viénot to Mr Delors was international financing. This was another factor that fostered their expansion and at the same time gave them prominence in the economic sphere. The strategy on this market was two-fold: on the one hand, *Société Générale* had clients in LDCs and on the other, it had clients in developed countries where the balance of payments problems and the problems of growth of internal money supply had led to a '*sustained reliance on international financial markets* [emphasis added]'.[43] The 'first leg' of the strategy pushed *Société Générale* in the short span of a decade to territories never previously explored, while the second helped the Bank to gain a previously unprecedented prominence in the economic sphere.

The internationalisation of *Société Générale*'s activities during the 1970s is summarised in Table 4.4. From the table we can trace *four* axes in *Société Générale*'s international expansion. The first one is composed of emerging international financial centres: Tokyo in 1972, Bahrain in 1975, Hong Kong in 1977 and Singapore in 1979. The second one consists of traditional exporting areas for *Société Générale*: Francophone Africa, the EEC and Eastern Europe. The third axis consists of North America (European-American Bank before and then fully owned branches). The fourth and last axis consists of LDCs (oil and non-oil), especially Latin American countries, Gulf countries and the Far East. But not all the axes are of the same importance when we consider that two-thirds of the representative offices and half of the branches were opened in countries involved in the recycling circuit, i.e. Latin America, Far East, Comecon countries and Gulf

Table 4.4 The internationalisation of *Société Générale*'s activities, 1972–1981.

	1972–75	1976	1977	1978	1979	1980	1981
Representative Offices	Bangkok Berlin (East) Beirut Caracas Jakarta Moscow Teheran	Warsaw Johannesburg	Bucharest Cairo Sao Paulo Stockholm Sydney	Athens Belgrade Bogota Lagos New Delhi Manila	Buenos Aires Oslo	Edinburgh Hong Kong Huston Nairobi Rome Sofia	Seoul Tokyo (Financial Services)
Branches	Tokyo	Birmingham Manama	Amsterdam Frankfurt Hong Kong	Bristol New York	Leeds Singapore	Athens Bucharest Manila Milan Rotterdam Taipei	Los Angeles Panama
Subsidiaries			Sogeko (South Korea) SG S.A (Canada)	Hudson Securities (USA)		SG Strauss urn-bull(UK) SG Australie	
Affiliates	Beal Bradesco Ebc Erab Euras Union Congolaise de Banque Uab cominif(Iran)	Coframex AL Bank Al Ahli Al Omani	Sogefinance (Côte d'Ivoire) SG Nigeria	Frab Bank (Bahrain)	Sudanese Investment Bank National SG Bank Egypt	Central European International Bank (Hungary) Trade Credit Ltd Australia	Industrial and Mining Development Bank of Iran

Source: Société Générale Annual Reports, various years.

countries. A clear break in *Société Générale*'s expansion abroad occurred in 1974. During that year, the Cominif (*Compagnie d'Investissement Irano-Française*) was created to promote cooperation between France and Iran: Sofimo was created in Lebanon as a merchant bank; the United Arab Bank in Sharjah (UAB); and representative offices were opened in Teheran, Caracas and Moscow.

The Middle East was at the centre of *Société Générale*'s strategy. In 1976 three new branches of the UAB were inaugurated in Abu Dhabi, Deira and Ras Al Khaimah. An offshore branch was opened at Manama in Bahrain. That same year, the Bank Al Ahli Al Omani was founded in Oman.

Additionally, a regional office was established in Cairo with the responsibility for covering Egypt, Sudan, Saudi Arabia and the two Yemen.

Latin America was an important market too. In 1976, a new bank, Coframex, was created in association with the Mexican development bank, *Nacional Financiera*. In Venezuela, the office opened in 1975 co-managed a US$1.5 billion Euroloan. In Eastern Europe, a new representative office, inaugurated in Warsaw, backed the Berlin and Moscow offices. In the Far East, the Korean French Banking Corporation (Sogeko) was created in 1977. The opening was preceded by a new branch in the form of a 'Deposit Taking Company' in Hong Kong and was followed, in 1978, by a new branch in Manila.

An important element in appreciating the increasing relevance of the international operations for *Société Générale*'s business is given by the number of employees working on overseas activities. In 1981 DAIT employed 1,500 people in Paris, 400 of them in the International Financing Department, to which we have to add 1,800 people working on international operations from branches in the rest of France and 320 expatriates in overseas branches and 4,000 foreign employees. In total, 7,600 people were working on international operations, which represented more or less 10 per cent of the total workforce. The number of foreign establishments amounted to just 30 in 1971, but 92 in 1981, representing more than 30 per cent of the total Group's balance sheet. This important growth in a very short period would not have been possible without an extensive number of visits to almost every corner of the world, from Brazil to South Korea, from Cameroon to the Philippines. The typical visit involved Viénot and other top managers of the Foreign Department travelling to target countries, especially LDCs, in order to illustrate their financial proposals. In other cases, *Société Générale* was approached by the governments themselves during state visits or international meetings. For example, in May 1975, a ten-day visit to South America was organised by the Foreign Department. The countries visited were Brazil, Mexico, Venezuela and Santo Domingo. The visit involved meetings with all the most important members of the economic establishment (Ministry of Finance, Development Bank, e.g. *Nacional Financiera* in Mexico, Central Bank) and French representatives. Competition for business was harsh, with Western commercial banks eager to 'escape' domestic markets and pushed by their governments to do so (directly or indirectly). The representative of the Brazilian Ministry of Finance, for example, remarked that he was 'overwhelmed by propositions from all sides, USA, Japan and Europe'.[44] In this context, devising more complex operations, taking more risks and resorting to corruption became important expedients for gaining new business. In 1976, in a second visit to Latin America and while in Mexico, Viénot pointed out proudly during a meeting with the Minister of Finance during the Echeverria administration, Mario Ramon Beteta, nephew of former Minister Ramon Beteta Quintana, that 'our exposure towards Mexico had tripled since 1974'.[45]

Sometimes, gala dinners, public relations and political pressure were not enough. In the archives of *Société Générale* we found clear evidence of bribes being paid to facilitate overseas expansion with reference, for example, to the proposed opening of a branch in Jakarta in 1982. We will revert to this interesting story further in this chapter when we discuss the dangerous relationships between commercial banks and dictatorships throughout the developing world.

By the late 1970s, the organisational and strategic efforts were proving profitable. Table 4.5 shows that even though *Société Générale* was the smallest of the Big Three, its performance in the Euroloan market was comparable to that of the much bigger *Banque Nationale de Paris*, while *Crédit Lyonnais* was still way ahead.

A very important decision taken in the latter part of the decade was to return to the United States. *Société Générale* had been the first French bank to enter the US in 1940, and the branch was active until 1971, when it merged with the European-American Bank. The decision to re-open the branch had already been considered by Viénot in late 1977 when *Deutsche Bank* and Midland considered opening independent branches in New York. Faced with this possibility, Viénot remarked that 'if Midland follows Deutsche Bank [in opening a branch in New York] it seems clear that we should open one too'.[46] Once its partners decided to go ahead (*Deutsche Bank* received the authorisation from US authorities in July 1978), *Société Générale* received authorisation in December 1978, started operations in February 1979 and officially inaugurated the branch in June 1979. As Viénot wrote in a letter to L. Jeorger, the opening was justified by the fact that:

> This reopening appeared to us necessary given both the recent establishment in New York of our main French competitors and the necessity for our company, which ranks among the largest 7 or 8 banks in the world, to appear in its own name in the United States. It should enable us to increase our influence in this country, to strengthen our relationships with banks and American clientele, to access advantageous dollar funding and better serve our French clientele.[47]

Table 4.5 Volume of managed or co-managed Euroloans by the Big Three (US$m), 1977–79.

	1977	*1978*	*1979*
SG	5.345	11.497	11.793
BNP	5.752	13.848	12.104
CL	1.236	10.022	21.247

Source: SGA, 81093, 'Réflexions sur les provisions de 1980', DCAIT, 15 April 1981.

As a result of this opening, conflicts broke out within EBIC, given the presence of EAB in the US market. This probably marked the beginning of the decline of the cooperative phase of the international expansion of *Société Générale* and, given the prominence of EBIC in the world of banking clubs, the decline of these original creatures as well.

From Table 4.6 we can see how the growth of 'peripheral' markets as important customers was by any measure phenomenal. Between 1978 and 1980, total claims towards Mexico increased by 267 per cent; towards Brazil by 337 per cent; towards Argentina, 446 per cent; towards South Korea, 318 per cent; and towards the Philippines, by an astonishing 2,050 per cent. If we consider the ten biggest exposures (Mexico, Brazil, Singapore, Spain, Hong Kong, Argentina, Philippines, Côte d'Ivoire, China and South Korea) total claims increased by 294 per cent in just the two years from 1978 to 1980.[48] As the geographical spread of *Société Générale*'s operations increased, so did the risks, since its activities became increasingly reliant on LDCs, especially Latin American and Far Eastern countries involved in the recycling circuit. Risk gradually became more and more concentrated with the ten biggest clients: in 1978 the ten countries accounted for 35.4 per cent of the total exposure towards LDCs; by 1980 they accounted for 63.3 per cent.

Société Générale entered the Euromarkets and overseas markets quite late because of its implication with EBIC and its subsidiaries such as *Banque Européenne de Crédit*, European-American Bank, Eurasbank, EuroPacific Finance Corp, etc. In the first part of the decade it followed a path similar to Midland by becoming a member of EAC/EBIC in 1971 and following a cooperative strategy. Like Midland, it created increasingly bigger margins of manoeuvre within the strategy of its club, pursuing, in the second half of the decade, a much more independent strategy of development overseas. By adopting this double

Table 4.6 Société Générale ten biggest exposures by country 1978–80 (Opec excluded, 2012 million euros, all maturities).

	End 1978	End 1979	End 1980	1978–80 Growth
Mexico	611.893	803.318	2.245.39	267%
Brazil	204.717	411.967	894.464	337%
Singapore	442.349	463.327	1.071.33	142%
Spain	312.502	304,906	771.127	147%
Hong Kong	105,614	207.611	720.129	582%
Argentina	74.87	320.459	409.073	446%
Philippines	18.084	45.211	388.819	2050%
Côte d'Ivoire	47.019	147.208	388.095	725%
China	13.382	252.099	313.587	2243%
South Korea	55.7	68.359	232.929	318%
Total Exposure	1886.13	3024.465	7434.94	294%

Source: SGA, 81093, Letter or M. Viénot to M. Delors, 31 July 1981. Original data were in FF, the data in the table have been actualised through http://www.insee.fr/fr/themes/calcul-pouvoir-achat.asp on 16 April 2013.

strategy, *Société Générale* had accumulated enormous risks by the late 1970s, since it gradually lost control of its own and its affiliates' exposures. After the second oil shock and two more bonanza years, things at the periphery and on the Euromarkets started to become increasingly shaky. *Société Générale's* total portfolio increased from US$89.911 million in 1978 to US$412.030 million in 1979.[49] Premises were not good and the situation got increasingly out of hand as the fateful year of 1982 approached.

New horizons and new threats

Compared to the late 1960s and early 1970s, the period immediately following the oil crisis was a period marked by international expansion through direct representations abroad. Once the internal structures had been readapted to respond to the needs of recycling, a new phase of intense expansion could finally begin. New branches, affiliates and subsidiaries were established throughout the globe. Barclays, through its subsidiary BBI, continued to focus on Europe, the US and the Pacific Basin. The decision, which would spare Barclays from the misadventures of its peers, was the result of wise management and sheer luck. BBI was boycotted by Arab countries for several months, limiting its expansion in the region and, subsequently, failed to acquire Lloyds. The latter element spared Barclays from the huge exposure of Lloyds to that region. As we anticipated in the previous section, Midland entered the international arena quite late, establishing its International Division, MBID, in the summer of 1974. After the creation of MBID, the Bank expanded enormously overseas, becoming one of the most exposed banks to LDCs. Midland and its General Manager, Wilcox, grew increasingly obsessed with international expansion and, especially, into the United States and tied up several options to enter the North American market. Midland also expanded vigorously in the developing world, notably in Latin America and Eastern Europe. As *The Times* noted about Wilcox: 'he tramped the world opening representative offices and branches and generally putting Midland's name on the map'.[50] Not surprisingly, the Bank was badly affected by the defaults of the early 1980s.

The tendency towards autonomous initiatives was common to most European and American banks. *Deutsche Bank*, after acquiring minority holdings and creating joint ventures, inaugurated a 'third phase' of international expansion based on setting up branches and or subsidiaries and acquiring majority holdings in order to 'gain strong access to international financial centres and to open up markets with growth potential in lending and securities business'.[51] Branches were set up in London and Tokyo in 1976; in Paris in 1977; Brussels, Antwerp, Buenos Aires, Sao Paulo and Asuncion in 1978; and Madrid, Milan, Hong Kong and Tokyo in 1979.

Every national banking system had its privileged areas. German banks were particularly active in Eastern Europe, because of political and historical reasons, and OPEC countries, as important importers of German products. American banks continued to focus on their home market while also paying special attention to Latin America. French banks continued to serve their country as providers of financial resources to the government and French borrowers and focused on OPEC countries and Eastern Europe. British banks had a more diversified focus: they expanded in the Pacific region and OPEC, but also in the US and in Eastern Europe, where they trailed Germany and France.[52]

Dodging bullets: the international expansion of Barclays

The first BBI corporate plan after the oil crisis was presented to the Board in April 1974. As remarked in the plan: 'The 1974 Plan has been prepared at a time of unprecedented economic crisis caused by a critical shortage of energy resources, monetary uncertainty and global inflation'.[53] Consequently, the extraordinary turbulences invalidated most of the forecasts of the plan. High commodity prices and their positive effect on the economies of several territories where Barclays was involved were to be largely offset by the rising cost of oil and imported capital. The corporate objectives of BBI were first, to achieve the representation, recognition and status of a dynamic international bank and challenge its competitors in market share and rate of growth of both balance sheet and profits. The target was a 25 per cent compound growth rate per annum in operating profits. Second, it was important to maintain close liaison with its parent and associates and develop common services; and third, to temper BBI's short-term profit and growth goals with the social responsibilities of a large corporation, especially where 'we are a major bank in a small country'.[54] The plan envisioned £166 million in further investments, and priority was given to developing merchant banking activities. The policy of disinvestments was pursued in South Africa, Swaziland, Kenya, Ghana, Sierra Leone, Mauritius, Jamaica and Rhodesia, while in Zambia and Trinidad control was surrendered. Undoubtedly, oil money was at the centre of BBI's preoccupations in early 1974. The corporate plan recognised that oil-producing countries in the Middle East, notably Saudi Arabia and the Gulf States, had become 'a *major force in international economic affairs*' and that '*very large sums* are going to be available for placement [emphasis added]'.[55] Nonetheless, despite the importance of capital flows from OPEC countries, Barclays was in a peculiar situation. In fact, despite not being on the official boycott list, it was under investigation by the Boycott Office because of its involvement in the Barclays Discount Bank in Israel. The turbulent relations with the Arab world would mark the mid-to-late 1970s strategy of BBI.

Barclays continued to develop autonomous initiatives despite joining the banking club, ABECOR. In order to penetrate the Arab market without too much attention, Barclays decided to adopt a 'low key' approach in order to stay clear of the Boycott Office. In Barclays' terms, it was agreed that the best thing to do was 'to try to ride both horses at once'.[56] A final report prepared by V. T. Tudball called 'Wild Ishmaelite Ideas' was prepared on 3 January 1974 and by the end of January, Tuke started to arrange a team to visit the Middle East. Sir Ronald L. Prain, who spent his life in the copper industry at the Rhodesian Selection Trust (RST) until his retirement in 1972, was personally invited by Tuke to lead the team on their visit. A 12-day mission composed of 5 officials was arranged in March 1974 to visit Egypt, Saudi Arabia, Kuwait, Bahrain, Abu Dhabi, Dubai and Lebanon. At the end of the visit, the team concluded that 'we should embark on a carefully planned and phased extension of our group activities in the Middle East and we have formed the view that there is *minimal risk* of our being placed on the Boycott list [emphasis added]'.[57]

Unfortunately, despite the opening of a branch in Teheran, several branches in the United Arab Emirates, a representative office in Bahrain and the Cairo Barclays International Bank in partnership with the *Banque du Caire*, the proposed expansion in the Middle East by riding two horses at the same time soon proved trickier than expected. The most important obstacle was that, contrary to Prain's expectation, Barclays came under Arab scrutiny by mid-1975. In June 1975, the Central Bank of Kuwait sent a letter seeking explanations of a loan made by Barclays to the Industrial Development Bank of Israel for £840,000 and Barclays' association with the Israel-based Barclays Discount Bank. A confused series of letters between Barclays and the Arab countries followed. The dialogue was made more difficult by the lack of direct communication between the parties involved. Often Barclays was receiving documents through third parties and had no direct access to the Boycott Office. The Central Boycott Committee met in Alexandria in March 1976 and urged Barclays to terminate its participation in Barclays Discount Bank within six months on pain of inclusion on the black list. Barclays now had to decide whether to wait and see or to comply with the Committee's request. In September BBI's General Manager G. A. O. Thomson, prepared a memorandum providing: 'authenticated evidence of the extent to which Barclays Bank is involved in international business with Arab countries and to indicate the extent of financial assistance which Barclays Bank provides to the Arab world'.[58] In its heartfelt plea, Thomson tried to defend Barclays' position by trying to demonstrate that:

> Barclays Bank has a long and friendly association with the Arab world going back to the days well before the State of Israel was created, and is anxious to play its part in helping the development of Arab countries . . . *the assistance rendered to Arab countries is many times greater than that extended by the Bank to Israel* [emphasis added].[59]

In fact, financial commitments made by Barclays to Arab clients amounted to more than US$360 million while financial commitments to Israeli banks amounted to just US$30 million and its investment in the Discount Bank to just US$684,000.

The hesitancy of Barclays to comply with the Arabs' request put the Bank in a tight corner in November 1976, when the Central Boycott Office finally put Barclays on its blacklist. The verdict had been almost unanimous, with the exception of Egypt.

By 1975, the outward business from BBI UK branches towards Arab countries totalled £130 million while the average balance with BBI totalled US$49 million.[60] Barclays found itself in a precarious position at a time when its competitors were expanding at a fast pace in the Gulf region.

Barclays did not waste time licking its wounds and developed a clever way to circumvent the boycott by secretly putting in place 'Operation Diversion'. With the assistance of its 'frenemy' Midland Bank, Barclays set up a special department, the Diversion Department or DD, at 168 Fenchurch Street, to process the boycott business. Branches were instructed to direct to the DD 'that business with the Arab countries which were actively implementing the boycott and where we were fairly certain that the transactions concerned would be rejected if sent'.[61] The operations were then routed through Midland in exchange for a commission. In the event that a transaction was refused by an overseas bank, the branch had to 'cleanse' the documents as far as possible and re-route the item to the DD.

Since 'Operation Diversion' was secret, everybody thought that Barclays had taken a hard stance towards Arab countries and letters of support were received from the Governor of the Bank of Israel praising 'the courageous stance' and from the Board of Deputies of the British Jews extending their gratitude 'for your courage and determination in standing firm against the Arab boycott of Israel' and hailing Tuke for showing 'that morality and fairness are not incompatible with sound business practice'.

Meetings at the highest level between Barclays and Midland continued in early 1977 despite some minor complaints. In April 1977, Lord Armstrong,[62] Midland's Chairman, remarked to Barclays' Chairman that they were happy to continue to deal 'though they felt they were being slightly under-paid for the service they were rendering'.[63]

Nonetheless, as the months passed, Barclays' situation was becoming more and more uncomfortable. In May 1977, Tuke met privately with the Governor of the Bank of England to express his frustration in being 'in the murky world of Arab politics' and in seeing that some large clients were receiving invitations to refrain from dealing with Barclays.[64] At the lowest point of Barclays' fortunes in the Arab world, something finally happened thanks to the unexpected visit of the famous tycoon R. W. 'Tiny' Rowland.[65]

Rowland came to visit Tuke, introduced by Sir Kenneth Cork, one of the greatest British experts on receivership. Rowland offered to introduce Tuke to Sheikh Kamal Adham, head of the Saudi Arabian intelligence agency *Al Mukhabarat Al A'amah* (later renamed General Intelligence Presidency or GIP). In exchange for its services, Rowland 'wanted . . . information and help on getting the Arabs accepted into the Edward Bates bank'. Edward Bates and Sons was a London merchant bank going through very bad times because of unfortunate investments made in the mid-1970s in the property and tanker markets as well as the £5.5 million investment in Welfare Insurance in 1973.

Tuke accepted Rowland's offer and in late May 1977, when Kamal Adham was accompanying then Crown Prince Fahd of Saudi Arabia to Washington, they had a 'long and useful talk' in London. The Sheikh agreed to meet the parties again on his flight back and a meeting was finally arranged at 77 Eaton Square for 7 p.m. Tuke reported that the meeting was 'strange'.[66] After making his way through the bodyguards, Tuke sat down with Rowland and the Sheikh, nobody spoke for long minutes then the Sheikh asked why Barclays was in this unfortunate situation. Tuke explained the Bank's position and, after listening carefully, the two walked together to the lift. The Sheikh promised to get back to Tuke within three days. The meeting had to remain secret of course, as Tuke reported: 'They are all particularly anxious that *none of us should admit that this meeting took place*, and I promised that we would keep quiet about it and not, particularly in the next week or so, do any lobbying elsewhere' [emphasis added].[67]

The Sheikh spoke to the 'persons who mattered' in Riyadh and Barclays was finally taken off the blacklist by the end of June 1977. A visit to Egypt, Saudi Arabia and Bahrain was arranged in July. In Saudi Arabia the dominant themes were:

> [s]urprise that we had got off so quick, congratulations, a desire to return to normal relations as soon as possible, and a hope that we will get official blessing shortly by way of publication in the official gazette that we are off the list.[68]

After more than six months of boycott, Barclays could again continue its expansion in the Middle East.

As we have mentioned before, the overall expansion of BBI into the rest of the world had not stopped since the early 1970s. In 1974, representative offices were opened in Malaysia, Indonesia and the Philippines. In 1975 three new branches were opened in the Arab Emirates (Abu Dhabi, Dubai and Sharjah), a 50 per cent stake in the Cairo Barclays International Bank was acquired and representative offices were opened in Bahrain and Mexico. That same year, the Western Hemisphere line of business was split into two divisions, one covering the Caribbean and Latin America and a second one covering the US, Canada and the Virgin Islands. The presence in the US of Barclays Bank of New York was strengthened by the opening of three new branches, bringing the total to 27 while Barclays Bank of California opened 5 new branches giving a total of 45.

In 1976 a representative office was opened in Istanbul. The presence in South East Asia was reinforced by the acquisition of a 20 per cent interest in the Malaysian Merchant Bank Berhad; by the acquisition of the Hong Kong subsidiary of the United Dominions Trust; and Barclays bought the shares of Merrill Lynch in Trident International Finance, bringing its participation to 66.7 per cent. The presence in the US was additionally strengthened through a BBI office in Atlanta and new offices of Barclays Bank of New York and Barclays Bank of California.

BBI's sixth anniversary, and the fifth year since the foreign branches of Barclays Limited had been taken over, were marked by striking results. Since 1972, pre-tax profits had grown according to plan at a compound rate of around 25 per cent per annum. In July 1977, the banking business of the merchant bank, Edward Bates, was taken over by Barclays together with several Arab partners, as the basis of a new bank called Allied Arab Bank Limited. Branches were opened in Manila and Seoul, a representative office was inaugurated in Houston and new branches were added in California and New York.

By 1977, BBI's geographical pre-tax profits' spread was as shown in Figure 4.1. The changes are evident: less business came from the African continent while activities in the rest of the world surged.

The end of the decade brought new plans in continuation with the previous ones. Priority areas in 1977–81 remained Western Europe, North America, the Far East (including Australasia) and the Middle East. Remarkably, Latin America remained outside the list, which would have a great influence in sparing Barclays from the hardships of the debt crisis. In terms of individual countries, the highest priority was given to Belgium, the Netherlands, Spain, Denmark, Greece, Ireland, Switzerland, France and West Germany in Europe; to Canada and the US in America, and to Australia, Japan, Singapore, New Zealand, South Korea, Hong Kong and the Philippines in the Far East.

In term of vehicles, priority was given to the development of wholly owned subsidiaries and wholesale branches. In 1978 a new branch was inaugurated in Bahrain, while a new branch of the Cairo Barclays International was opened in Alexandria.

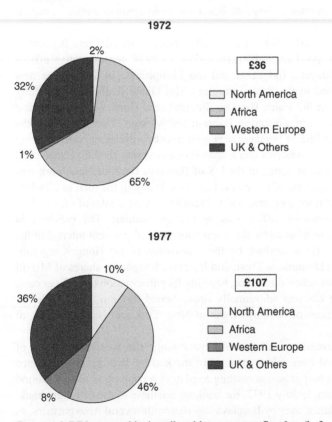

Figure 4.1 BBI geographical attributable pre-tax profits, £m, (before loan stock interest and extraordinary items), 1972–77.

Source: BBA, 80/2521, 'An informal look at the international side of the group', no date.

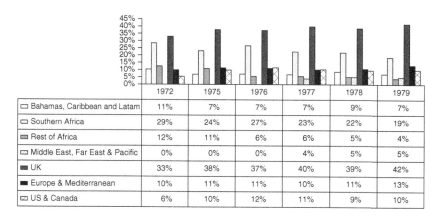

	1972	1975	1976	1977	1978	1979
☐ Bahamas, Caribbean and Latam	11%	7%	7%	7%	9%	7%
☐ Southern Africa	29%	24%	27%	23%	22%	19%
▣ Rest of Africa	12%	11%	6%	6%	5%	4%
☐ Middle East, Far East & Pacific	0%	0%	0%	4%	5%	5%
▬ UK	33%	38%	37%	40%	39%	42%
■ Europe & Mediterranean	10%	11%	11%	10%	11%	13%
▥ US & Canada	6%	10%	12%	11%	9%	10%

Figure 4.2 BBI geographical spread of current, deposit and other accounts by amount, 1972–79.

Source: BBA, BBI Annual Report, various years.

By 1979 BBI was almost a new bank in terms of size, scope and complexity compared to its ancestor DCO. It now had 2,000 offices in 75 countries compared to just 40 in 1970. In 1979 Tuke decided to step down from his post as Chairman of BBI to focus on the chairmanship of Barclays Limited; Henry Uvedale Antrobus Lambert took his post. The years spent at the helm of BBI had been the most 'adventurous' that the former DCO had lived in many years. The departure of Tuke did not radically change BBI's ambitions and priorities.

The long experience on international markets and, especially, the 'family ambience' reigning at Barclays, with the heirs of the founding families sitting in the boards of BBI and Barclays Limited, contributed to the development of a more coherent and long-term oriented strategy than most of its competitors.

Nonetheless, Barclays was not immune from some *faux pas*. For example, in 1976–77 Barclays became one of the preferred targets for organisations such as the Anti-Apartheid Movement and the End Loans to Southern Africa (ELTSA), given its subscription of £6.6 million South African defence bonds as part of a mandatory investment in governmental securities. A 'National Day of Action against Barclays' was even organised on 1 March 1978.

Despite its size, Barclays was comparatively less exposed to LDCs and notably Latin America not just because of the international heritage and the family ambience, even though these two factors played an important role. It was also a question of favourable coincidences. In fact, the destiny of Barclays could have been very different had it decided to merge with Lloyds in the mid-1970s. It is an as yet unknown story compared to the famous attempt to merge Barclays, Martins and Lloyds in 1968, but an important one to understand why Barclays escaped the 1982 trap better than Lloyds and Midland. In a strictly private and confidential paper from April 1975, the idea of merging the parent banks was evaluated and eventually discarded in favour of a kind of merger between LBI and BBI activities 'principally on the grounds of geographical fit, the wastefulness of conflict and the importance of size in international banking'.[69] The idea of an outright purchase of LBI by BBI was discarded for financial reasons and because LBI would have never agreed to such a decision. Thus, the favoured option was to create a jointly owned holding company. The two Chairmen, Anthony Tuke and Eric Faulkner, met on May 1975. Tuke asked Faulkner whether he thought there was any merit in having a general discussion on some form of cooperation abroad between BBI and LBI. Tuke emphasised the weakness of sterling and the risk of competition between British banks. Faulkner agreed on many points with Tuke's analysis, nonetheless he knew very well who was the stronger party of the two. Thus:

> His people therefore would be bound to feel that any merger was in effect a takeover and they would be absorbed . . . The result of all this is that we go our separate ways, but keep in close touch and if necessary exchange views at Chairman level from time to time.[70]

The merger, therefore, never took place and this was ultimately a good thing for Barclays in view of the aggressive overseas expansion of Lloyds in the 1970s.

The disadvantage of backwardness: Midland and its international ventures

Unlike Lloyds with LBE or Barclays with DCO (and later BBI), Midland did not have an existing presence abroad. In continental Europe, the decision was taken to develop not only representative offices but asset-creating representations. The clearest example is to be seen in France, the most important market for Midland in Europe. In 1978, the subsidiary Midland Bank France SA (MBFSA) was created to deal in money-market and foreign exchange business, corporate finance, syndicated loans and correspondent banking and other investment activities. MBFSA was to complement the newly established Paris branch and the recently bought *Banque de la Construction et des Travaux Publics* (BCT), later renamed BCT Midland Bank, which specialised in residential mortgage business.

Other areas of interest in Europe included Spain, where a representative office and later a branch were opened in Madrid; Greece, where a representative office would be opened; and West Germany, where a representative office had already been opened in Frankfurt in 1973. As we can see, the original agreement of the EAC members not to compete on their home ground was falling apart by the late 1970s.

The United States was the *idée fixe* of Sir Malcolm Wilcox like many other colleagues at that time. By 1977, 16 Group companies were already contributing £10 million of pre-tax profits, while the American activities of MBID contributed £3.6 million. But the strategy lacked long-term vision, with each part of the business independent of each other and not cohesively structured. Thus, Wilcox recognised that the strategy needed some coordination and that the 'overriding factors' in Midland's strategy were to 'obtain direct commercial banking presence' and 'fill the gap' in US earnings after the demise in 1978 of Midland's interests in broking insurance through Bland Payne Group (acquired in 1973 when it bought Montagu Trust).

The three top priorities for the US were commercial banking, commercial finance, and savings and loans. This ambitious strategy pushed Midland towards some of its riskiest gambles, and the losses incurred in these operations would give a crucial contribution to its inglorious end. A first attempt to penetrate the American market was made in 1978, when Midland bid US$520 million for 100 per cent of Walter E. Heller International Corporation (the largest US acquisition proposed by a UK bank up to that time). In August 1979, Wilcox visited the target bank premises in Chicago where he was impressed by the 'competence and the keenness' of Heller's staff and, particularly, by the 'friendly reception he had been accorded by the President of the Federal Reserve Bank in Chicago, who had expressed his bias in favour of the success of Midland's application'.[71]

Heller would have allowed Midland to enter the first two priority areas of commercial banking and commercial finance given the fact that the commercial finance subsidiary of Walter Heller & Co. operated 51 offices in 25 states and that on the commercial banking side, the Chicago-based American National Bank and Trust Company ranked fifth in Illinois. Unfortunately, negotiations were abruptly terminated in October 1979, once the survey undertaken by Ernst & Whinney (which merged with Arthur Young in 1989 to form Ernst & Young) revealed much larger loss provisions than expected. Despite this cold shower, the debacle did not deter Midland's management and the chase for a new prey in America continued.

Of course, the international strategy of Midland was not limited to Europe and the US. In Australia in 1979, it bought Associated Securities Finance (ASF), offering Midland the opportunity to enter the Australian market despite the impossibility of opening full branches. Other interests 'down under' by the end of the decade included the Group's and LAICO's (the Australian subsidiary of Thomas Cook) representative offices, the EuroPacific Finance Corporation and Samuel Montagu's share in the merchant bank Capel Court.

Up to 1973, overseas expansion was associated mainly with European markets, but after 1973 the emerging markets of the Far East, the Middle East, Latin America and Comecon countries represented an increasingly crucial area of development. In July 1974, an internal memorandum remarked: 'Midland Bank receives very substantial and increasing . . . deposits from a Middle Eastern oil producer'.[72] That same year saw a participation in the Latin American-based *Banque Européenne pour l'Amérique Latine* (BEAL), which managed a respectable network of branches in Brazil and Argentina. Hectic years soon followed.

In 1975 the strategic investment in Standard Chartered was increased from 5 per cent to 16 per cent. This investment was liquidated in mid-October 1979. The decision was possibly a result of the Heller bid, since US legislation prevented a bank holding company to control banks in more than one state, and Standard Chartered had recently accomplished the acquisition of Union Bancorp in California, while the Heller Group included, as stated above, the Chicago-based American National Bank and Trust Company. In May 1975, a representative office to cover the Middle East was opened in Beirut and another one in Teheran; but that same year the Beirut office had to be closed because of the eruption of the Lebanese civil war. In 1976 representative offices were inaugurated in Moscow and Sao Paulo. A replacement for Beirut was found in Bahrain, where an Offshore Banking Unit (OBU, essentially a branch) was opened. In 1977 new representative offices were opened in Cairo, Manila and Madrid.

The Eurocurrency loan portfolio increased by 20 per cent in 1978; the Tokyo office, opened in 1973, was converted into a full operating branch, while further representative offices were added in Sydney and Hong Kong. The Tokyo branch represented a milestone in Midland's history for it was the first branch established overseas. As remarked by the Board in May 1976: 'The Board appreciated the significance of the Bank establishing a Branch overseas, and the change thereby being made in the Bank's traditional policy of not establishing operating Branches overseas'.[73] The reason to upgrade the representation in Japan was made clear by G. W. Taylor, Assistant Chief General Manager, to the Chairman's Committee:

> In competitive terms we are finding that only having a Representative Office in Tokyo, with a very small staff, places us at a pronounced disadvantage . . . it is the firm view of the International Division that our office in Tokyo should be accorded full branch status at the earliest opportunity. The fact that such a step is recommended in an important financial centre such as Tokyo would not only be a clear indication to the banking community that we propose to aim for a higher degree of significance in world banking terms but it would also be of considerable benefit to the prestige of Midland Bank Group in Japan.[74]

In 1980 a new representative office was opened in Beijing. Midland was the first European bank to take this step, thanks to its long-standing relationship with the Bank of China. In the same year, new branches were added in Hong Kong and Singapore. The efforts put into the implementation of the great strategic review of 1974–75 were remarkable.

As for country exposure compared to the rest of the UK banking sector, by the mid-1970s Midland enjoyed a larger proportion of business with Comecon countries, a higher-than-average exposure with Latin American countries and a much larger exposure with the South African regime (a point to which we shall return further in this chapter).

Brazil provides us with a particularly interesting case to further illustrate what we meant when we mentioned that commercial banks after the first oil shock came to play a crucial role in shoring up exporting industries in the context of economic stagnation in Europe, increasing balance of payments difficulties for Western governments and an increased scramble for markets amongst Western powers.

During the state visit to the UK in May 1976 of the then President of Brazil, General Ernesto Beckmann Geisel, a memorandum of understanding was signed by the Brazilian Railway Company (RFFSA), the General Electric Company (GEC) and NM Rothschild covering the proposed electrification of the Belo Horizonte-Itutinga-Volta Redonda railway (the so-called 'Steel line'). The contract involved the provision of goods and services imported from the UK on a negotiated basis, i.e. without an international tender offer. Like the old days, the ECGD agreed to guarantee a sterling loan of £115 million, but, unlike the old days of export finance, there was a catch. The Brazilians now wanted dollars and in the agreement it was stipulated that 'Rothschild should seek to raise in the market euro-dollar loans in a ratio 1:1 with the sterling loans'. The two operations were 'inextricably linked'. This meant that 'the GEC contract will only become effective to the extent that the euro-dollars are forthcoming and in turn the first drawing on the euro-dollar loan will be made to pay the down-payment under the contract between RFFSA and GEC'.[75] These increasingly important loans in Eurodollars were officially justified by the need to meet the local costs of the project. In reality, large shares of these loans were bribes given to corrupt local and governmental authorities to procure the contracts in a context of increasing competition between Western companies.

The Brazilians were adamant in their intentions. They made it extremely clear that they would not place major contracts with countries whose banks were not prepared to support their industry. The Brazilians pointed out the fact that German banks had undertaken to provide US$700 million in Eurodollars in support of nuclear power stations and the French had promised substantial financial credits to complement COFACE insured financing. Thus, both the French and the Germans had 'accepted, though obviously with reluctance, that *their respective contracts are tied to the euro-loans being forthcoming* [emphasis added]'.[76]

Nevertheless, the business was a risky, if quite lucrative, one. Midland and the three other clearing banks were supposed to lend US$50 million each; Rothschild would keep 1/16 of one per cent as a management fee while the Big Four would share the rest. In addition:

> In view of the help which would be afforded to GEC if the four banks agreed to underwrite the euro-dollar loan, GEC had indicated that they would pay an additional front-end fee to the four banks out of the down-payments received . . . from the Brazilians.[77]

Midland and the other banks were doubtful. They felt that the deal amounted to 'blackmail' by the Brazilians and that 'the amounts involved presented serious "country limit" problems for all the banks'. Midland thought that 'HMG [the British Treasury] should do more if the deal was really "pro bono public"'; thus 'Rothschild's proposal was not . . . acceptable *judged on normal commercial criteria* [emphasis added]'. But during the 1970s, and perhaps not only then, normal commercial criteria were not very well enforced and, moreover, 'A number of very important "political" considerations were involved'.[78]

One thing should be clear: Eurodollar financing was crucial to shore up exporting industries. At this point, nobody at the national or international level was interested in regulating the Euromarket; commercial banks, as the central actors in this market, achieved unparalleled leverage in international monetary and financial affairs. In short, governments now needed them. Banks, then, were indeed lending larger and larger sums of money to LDCs and it is true, as some authors[79] have argued, that they pushed the 'game' too far, with dire consequences for the people of the developing world. Yet to understand the banks' behaviour we have to recognise the reality of the 1970s and, more importantly, its political and economic scenario. Without the collaboration of governments, in not regulating the Euromarket and not delegating to private actors the process of re-equilibration of global monetary imbalances, the monetary and financial order would have changed at a slower, and perhaps different, pace.

The expansion of MBID continued unabated throughout the 1970s. One of the problems of this expansion is the fact that it was based on unrealistic assumptions. In the 'Strategic Plan' for 1978–82 it was stated:

> Our view . . . is that *no fundamental changes in the political or financial world structures will take place*. It is likely that in the western world there will be a continuance of the slow and cautious economic recovery led by the USA, Germany and Japan [emphasis added].[80]

Unfortunately, the world was not moving towards a recovery and fundamental changes in the political and financial world were indeed about to take place. But these changes were, if not impossible, difficult to anticipate.

By the end of the decade, the international ambitions of Midland outlined in the 'Own Initiative' strategic review of 1974–75 were almost fulfilled. By 1979, Midland had representative offices in Brussels, Cairo, Frankfurt, Hong Kong, Madrid, Manila, Moscow, Sao Paulo, Sydney, Teheran, Toronto and Zürich; and branches in Manama, Tokyo and Paris. It had two operating subsidiaries, Midland Bank France and Midland Financial Services, in Canada. Even the utmost symbol of accomplishment seemed almost achieved when Midland found a new prey in the Californian bank, Crocker National Bank, to finally gain access to a source of dollars. In the next chapter, we shall see the detrimental consequences of this investment.

New regions and new risks: the overseas expansion of Crédit Lyonnais *and* Société Générale *after the oil crisis*

The impact of oil came to be felt by *Crédit Lyonnais* also. Between 1971 and 1974, the Bank started to receive large amounts of dollars from Arab banks, as we can see from Table 4.7.

In the 1973–75 programme, the Department of International Financing (DOFI) expected medium-term foreign currency assets to reach US$600 million, while in reality they reached more than US$1 billion. DOFI pointed out that expectation had been 'pulverised'. Thus, in October 1974 the biannual programme had to be updated in the light of the new turbulences.

Table 4.7 Arab banks' deposits with *Crédit Lyonnais* (US$m 2014), 1971–74.

Year	Growth from previous year (US$m)	Growth from previous year (%)
1971	61,584	
1972	110,151	79%
1973	143,675	30%
1974	255,040	78%

Source: CLA, Board Minutes, 6 February 1975.

As noted in the updated plan, the new circumstances in the world economy demanded of *Crédit Lyonnais* and the other big French banks an increased support to French companies for their operations abroad and in particular their exports and a 'parallel effort to raise funds in the context of the recycling of petrodollars'.[81]

Given these tasks, geographical priorities came to be modified and oil-exporting countries became the priority *par excellence*, particularly Gulf countries, Lebanon, Libya and Iran. But other areas were of great importance for *Crédit Lyonnais* as important customers for French companies: the US, because of the dollar; socialist countries; and South East Asia and Latin America, especially Brazil, Mexico and Argentina. A total of FF112 million was allocated to existing branches and representative offices and to create new ones.

The programme for 1977–79 was a continuation of the previous ones. Risk control was always a priority, but immediately after that came the search for profitability. Given the tremendous expansion of *Crédit Lyonnais* during the decade, we can safely assume that the latter prevailed over the former.

In a context of increasing competition, the pressure to secure results became stronger, and the balance between risk control and profits gradually became unstable. DOFI in particular was pushing to increase its exposure on the Euroloan and Eurobond markets in order not to lose ground against its domestic and international competitors. To give an idea of the tremendous growth of the Euromarkets business, it is worth pointing out that DOFI employees doubled in number in just five years, from 111 in 1972 to 219 in 1976.[82]

Existing networks had to be consolidated, while at the same time new areas had to be penetrated by transforming representative offices into branches (e.g. the Tokyo representative office became a branch in 1977) and by creating 'antennas' in promising cities.

Important organisational modifications took place in July 1978 because of the departure in June of the mastermind behind *Crédit Lyonnais'* internationalisation, Count de Feuilhade, and 'to adapt this device to the considerable development of our locations and international banking and financial activities'.[83] On that occasion, Jean Deflassieux, ('a man of character, very attached to the House', remarked President Pierre-Brossolette) became responsible for DCAIC. Geographic areas were reinforced by taking over the responsibilities previously held by the Department of Foreign Establishments and Participations (*Direction de Etablissements et Participations à l'Etranger*, DEPE); two directors were chosen to assist Deflassieux and manage the two newly created geographic areas. One was responsible for Latin America, Far East, Near East and Arab countries and the other for North America, Western and Eastern Europe and non-Arab Africa. Georges Smolarski became the deputy of Deflassieux, responsible for operational services. Despite all the talks about risk management, until the reforms of 1978 no one was really in charge of risk control. Nonetheless, by the late 1970s, the risks associated with lending to LDCs through the Euromarkets became more visible after the rescheduling of some peripheral countries such as Peru. A Department for the Administration and Control of Foreign Affairs (*Département pour l'Administration et le Contrôle des Affaires Internationales*, DACI) was thus created. The department was in charge of functions previously held by the DEPE (audit and overseas budgets), and by the General Secretariat of DCAIC (general administration, cooperation budget). A Committee on International Affairs under the responsibility of the President was also established.

A new plan for 1978–80 was prepared. Special attention was devoted to newly established operations, notably in Canada, Zurich, Tokyo and Panama and new operations were to be established in Greece and Italy (two branches were opened in Milan and Rome), the United States (where business development offices were established in Houston and San Francisco) and in Canada, but especially in LDCs. Since the beginning of the 1970s, *Crédit Lyonnais* had established branches in the US (New York in 1971, Los Angeles in 1974, Chicago in 1975, San Francisco and Houston in 1978), in Canada (Montreal in 1974, Toronto in 1976), in the Gulf with the inauguration in cooperation with Riyad Bank of Gulf Riyad Bank and in Asia (Tokyo in 1977, Hong Kong and Seoul in 1978, Singapore in 1979). An offshore branch covering the Latin America region was inaugurated in 1977 in Panama.

In the latter part of the decade, the priority areas remained unchanged relative to 1974. Latin America represented one of the areas where *Crédit Lyonnais* was the strongest: Brazil, Mexico, Venezuela and Argentina remained the most important countries. Despite the increasing indebtedness of the regions, the programme for the region recorded that: 'Remarkable results have been achieved . . . in the fight against inflation and in the pursuit of the equilibrium of commercial balance and of the balance of payments'.[84] The results achieved in the region since the beginning of the decade were remarkable by any means. In the export credit business, *Crédit Lyonnais* had a share of 22 per cent in 1976 amongst French banks compared to 15 per cent in 1974. The Bank managed to become a preferred partner for the Mexican oil giant PEMEX and its Brazilian counterpart PETROBRAS, and it was a manager in many of the most important projects on the continent, such as the Caracas metro and the project Technip-Copesul for a chemical plant in Argentina.

The share of foreign currency operations in *Crédit Lyonnais* balance sheet moved from FF50 billion in 1975 to more than FF200 billion in 1980 (Figure 4.3).[85]

Brazil remained the number one priority in Latin America, followed by Mexico and Argentina. In order to increase the profits from overseas, it was posited to 're-evaluate the policy of restraint with respect to direct investments and

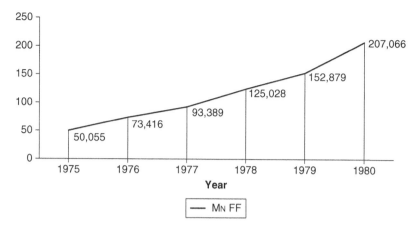

Figure 4.3 Crédit Lyonnais' total foreign currency balance sheet (FFm) 1975–80, year end.

Source: CLA, 110AH2, DCAIC, tableau de bord, 'Activité en devise-ressources et emplois, 20 March 1981.

financial credits of the past three years'.[86] Despite the far from perfect situation of the public finances of Mexico and Brazil, the programme stated that: 'Despite a critical economic and financial situation in the short term, *significant risks can be taken* on the long and medium term in these two countries, particularly Brazil [emphasis added]'.[87]

At the operational level, it was important to favour large direct risks in sovereign entities, or those guaranteed by governments or central banks; to maximise investments and profits; to increase the share of foreign trade business; and to develop a stronger cooperation with DOFI with respect to Euroloans and Eurobonds so as to maximise the benefits (to help raise funds for a company often implied getting collateral business from that company).

The programme was mobilised in 1979 because of the second oil crisis. Notably, intervention in the Middle East was reinforced: the programme for Latin America reported that 'although the area is booming and could be the theatre of messy events, we must be present and reinforce our presence'.[88]

The first goal was to increase *Crédit Lyonnais'* share in collecting resources from central and commercial banks and sovereign funds, trade credits and financing operations with local or international groups active in the region. In order to preserve its profit margins in the Euroloan market, DOFI decided to focus on getting manager or co-manager roles in international loans and on 'complex financing', because they allowed the Bank to perceive larger management fees and margins compared to classic financing. Moreover, these operations contributed to the prestige of the institution and they allowed *Crédit Lyonnais* to be present in a market niche where North American and English banks were leaders.[89]

In the Eurobond market, the goal was also to gain roles as managers or co-managers by implementing more aggressive marketing techniques:

Greater aggressiveness in terms of conditions and presence among potential clientele is indeed an indispensable imperative to manage a greater number of operations and improve our profitability and our market position. The context of active competition from foreign banks, as well as our French competitors, represents an extra incentive to strengthen our *commercial attack* on potential borrowers [emphasis added]. [90]

The second goal was to reinforce the placing power of DOFI, particularly by implementing the 'bought deal' technique.[91] The priority areas did not change, but efforts were doubled. Missions to LDCs were multiplied, new products devised and new offices opened. The efforts produced remarkable results: between January 1978 and March 1980 rollover syndicated Euroloans increased from US$1.1 billion to US$2.3 billion. Interestingly, these numbers represented just 38.4 per cent of the overall exposure of *Crédit Lyonnais*, indicating that overseas branches were contributing more and more to the growth of this line of business.

From 1976 to 1986, the number of branches and affiliates sky-rocketed from 106 to 272 and investments in foreign branches and affiliates from FF350 million to FF3.3 billion. A rough but meaningful description of this frantic activity outside France is noticeable in Figure 4.4, which measures over a period of 100 years the number of subsidiaries and affiliated banks (but not branches) of *Crédit Lyonnais*. It is evident that the 1970s marked a watershed in the international activity of the company, with more office openings than ever before.

The efforts expended on the Euromarkets were extremely satisfactory, as can be seen in Table 4.8. In 1980 *Crédit Lyonnais* led or co-led 48 Eurobonds for US$3.6 billion and 136 Euro-credits for a total of US$23.5 billion, taking the number one spot in Europe and the third spot in the world. The last huge

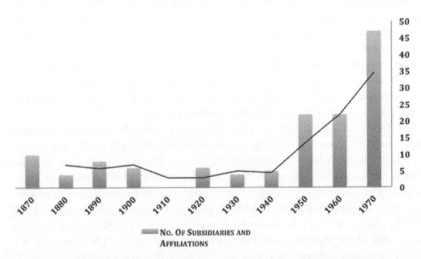

No. OF SUBSIDIARIES AND
AFFILIATIONS

Figure 4.4 Number of subsidiaries and affiliations of *Crédit Lyonnais*, 1870s–1970s.

Source: CLA, *Crédit Lyonnais* annual report, various years.

Table 4.8 Eurobonds/loans lead or co-led by *Crédit Lyonnais* (US$m), 1975–80.

	1975	1976	1977	1978	1979	1980
Eurobonds	860	1,600	2,400	1,700	2,900	3,600
Euroloans	2,200	3,000	1,250	10,000	21,000	23,500

Source: CLA, *Crédit Lyonnais* Annual Report, various years.

Euroloans issued or co-issued under the direction of one or more Europartners was accorded to PEMEX in April 1982, just four months before the debt crisis, for an amount of US$2 billion.[92]

As with the other banks in our research, the international expansion of *Crédit Lyonnais* was not only developed by autonomous decisions but also by cooperative efforts.

The zenith of cooperative banking

Cooperative banking through clubs and consortia reached its zenith in the mid-1970s and after that time entered a spiral of decline. Almost all major banks ultimately entered a banking club by the mid-1970s, and banking consortia focusing on specific regions or sectors flourished.

Cooperative banking represented an important step in preparing European banks for their new role as international banks, but as time passed and commercial banks gained the needed know-how, the usefulness of clubs and consortia was put into question. As strategic alliances based on competitive collaboration, banking consortia quickly suffered from increasing competition amongst its members, which ultimately precipitated their demise. Clubs suffered from the same intestine wars.

A peculiar problem involved Arab-European banking consortia such as FRAB and UBAF. FRAB was dominated by *Société Générale* (despite the presence of a number of Arab shareholders), but towards the end of the 1970s several problems emerged between FRAB's management and Paris. FRAB was increasingly competing for the same customers as *Société Générale* while also increasingly refusing to accept the authority of Paris over its activities. Moreover, internal clashes became routine at the top level of the Bank between the Chairman and the General Manager: the clash between the two became so violent that *Société Générale* threatened to liquidate FRAB unless the two were to alter their positions. In 1978 a new Chairman and General Manager were chosen but the problems persisted, as FRAB continued to be viewed in a bad light by Western and Arab customers alike and its shareholders remained very heterogeneous.

At UBAF, the problem was the growing litigiousness amongst the Arab shareholders and the declining influence of *Crédit Lyonnais* with only 30 per cent of the votes. In 1979 a clash between the Libyan and Palestinian candidates to the presidency erupted; moreover, UBAF was increasingly competing for the same business as *Crédit Lyonanis* (Count de Feuilhade, new UBAF administrator, described it as 'shameless competition').[93]

The era of cooperative banking constituted an indispensable bridge between correspondent banking and full-blown international banking by allowing the European banking sector to limit the costs associated with international banking, to share knowledge of international markets amongst its members and, at least in some cases, to limit competition on domestic markets. The experiences of Barclays and *Crédit Lyonnais* are particularly interesting for evaluating the highs and lows of cooperation.

Barclays finally joined ABECOR in 1974, not coincidentally a few months after the shock, leaving Lloyds as the only large European bank outside a club. A meeting was arranged in February 1974 to assess the future of ABECOR and decide whether it was meaningful to continue with an inner and an outer membership. In fact, it was recognised that this division amongst banks was impacting negatively on the club's image, giving an impression of disunity compared to its competitors, notably EBIC. The meeting was therefore called to review the whole question of the future of ABECOR and, if possible, to find 'a formula which would overcome our present differences and thereby bring the seven banks closer together'.[94] After considerable discussion, the seven members decided to draft a new letter of intent for the new ABECOR. In June 1974, a memorandum of understanding was signed and a steering committee, composed of two senior executives from each bank, and a coordinating committee, composed of high-ranking officials, were created, assisted by the respective secretariats and a central secretariat in Brussels. The five goals of the cooperation were: first of all, to cooperate closely whenever possible in the international loan and syndicate business as well as in the fields of international commercial and merchant banking; second to assist each other as far as possible in the promotion of new developments and new business; third to undertake common research in areas such as automation and marketing; fourth to collaborate in collating and exchanging economic intelligence; and fifth to exchange personnel and organise regular meetings between officers operating in the same field.[95] Since cooperation in the field of international loans and Euroloans figured in the first place, and since the decision to become part of the club intervened in 1974, we can safely assume that the opportunities related to the shock and the recycling of petrodollars played a decisive role in changing the strategy of Barclays and the other outer members of *Société Financière Européenne*. In October the new letter of intent was drawn up and signed by the members. In November 1974 a company was established in Brussels under the name Associated Banks of Europe Corporation SA. Far from being useless, ABECOR like EBIC or Europartners became a very useful forum to exchange views and take decisions on important matters such as the adoption of the payment network SWIFT and automation.

At the time when ABECOR was reconstituted, Europartners had entered its fourth year and, after the enthusiasm of the early years, several problems had started to surface. Smolarski of *Crédit Lyonnais* remarked: 'Among the various banking groups Europartners appears as the least structured of all' and 'the functioning of the cooperation does not appear entirely satisfactory despite some positive achievements'.[96] The 'political' decisions concerning the cooperation were undertaken at the periodic meetings of the Directors General and of a Cooperation Committee. Cooperation Secretariats and a set of working groups dealt with the day-to-day management. Nonetheless, there were no common secretariats or a central coordination structure like those of other clubs (EBIC and ABECOR) and consortia (ORION[97]). Moreover, unlike other clubs, there was no common international bank. With regard to this latter aspect, in March 1974 *Crédit Lyonnais* elaborated a proposal to create a joint bank active on international markets given 'the new and considerable expansion of the Euromarket'.[98] Neither the Bank nor the secretariat would ever become a reality because of financial concerns (the Bank) and because of organisational disagreements (the secretariat).

In a letter to President Jacques Chaine (killed by an anarchist in May 1976), Smolarski singled out all the main problems of cooperation. Primarily, common achievements were few and of inconsistent quality when compared to those of groups like EBIC and ABECOR. He laid the blame on difficulties overcoming divergent interests and policy; conjunctural problems; structural differences amongst the four banks; on the fact that, 'Crédit Lyonnais was essentially the only member bank to have a vast international network'; and, finally, on 'the lack of consultation among members'.

The end result was that everyone was acting independently.[99] Radical decisions had to be taken: 'we cannot leave things as they are and it would be better to end the cooperation at the international level or reshape and clarify our relations'.[100]

The first option was set aside because of the bad publicity it would create and because *Crédit Lyonnais* had no interest in becoming isolated in the international banking world. It was clear that the process of European integration was not moving as planned and that differences (in ambitions, results, balance sheets) amongst members were slowing the process of expansion. Mr Cambon of the Cooperation office remarked that 'each of us has the feeling that the Cooperation is not going well. Some even fear that it might die'.[101]

But the cooperation did not die; it was gradually restructured into something else: it moved from exclusivity to *preferentiality*. The new rules of the game were that 'cooperation is not an end in itself but an instrument to facilitate the international expansion of its members. It should not be binding but it should give the opportunity to create without exclusivity a *preferential club* [emphasis added]'.

The new cooperation was institutionalised during the May and November 1976 Directors General's meetings: 'We opted for a pragmatic cooperation, the need to integrate giving place to a simple principle of preferentiality'.[102] Ultimately, French banks started to open branches in Germany and vice versa; the era of the banking clubs was rapidly fading.

From then on, the creation of common representations or joint ventures had to be justified by numbers and not ideals. Thus, a new proposal by *Crédit Lyonnais* to *Commerzbank* to create a joint financial company to operate on the Euromarkets was refused by the Germans, Italians and Spaniards, because of the costs and because it would compete against existing vehicles. A branch of *Crédit Lyonnais* was opened in Frankfurt and branches of *Commerzbank* and *Hispano-Americano* were opened in Paris. Also the meetings became more rare (for example meetings of the Directors General were reduced from four times per year to just two).

On top of all that, the macro-economic situation started to deteriorate by the end of the decade after the second oil crisis, but the member banks agreed that the 'the current situation, although unfavourable, cannot alter the long-term strategy of major international banks or lead them to abruptly stop credits from going abroad'.[103]

Liaisons dangereuses?: commercial banks, the IMF and oppressive regimes

As we have illustrated, starting with the oil crisis of 1973 the contacts between commercial banks and the IMF intensified and morphed. From the possible regulation of the early 1970s, the relationship gradually transformed into an alliance, with the Fund acting in support of the banking and financial sector. The Fund and commercial banks developed an increasingly promiscuous relationship, more and more information was transmitted to commercial banks and we can legitimately question whether the Fund was operating in favour of the interests of the Western financial community or serving the interests of the developing world.

The business of banking also pushed commercial banks into forging strong relations with oppressive regimes around the world: in Latin America, in Asia, in the Middle East and in Africa. Bankers were ultimately prepared to 'tolerate a certain level of malfeasance if the leadership seemed willing and able to formulate good macro-economic policy'.[104] Such open-mindedness involved paying bribes and doing business with some of the worst dictators of the period.

How close is too close? Commercial banks and the IMF

The relationship between the IMF and Western commercial banks after 1973 became increasingly promiscuous. We can glimpse that by looking at some 'not for public use', declassified documents held at the archives of the Fund in Washington DC.

The first changes in the relationship between the Fund and commercial banks took place in 1974 when 'the earlier concern about the possibly excessive growth of the Eurocurrency markets tended to be overshadowed by concerns about the viability of the markets'.[105] That year, for the first time, a staff team made systematic, informal contacts with bankers, supervisory/monetary authorities and the BIS to discuss a number of issues relating to the underlying stability of the markets and the prospects for their effective role in the recycling process. After these visits, the staff team prepared a document on the 'Immediate Issues in the Euro-Currency Market', which was the first occasion when the Board's attention 'was directed to various issues relating to the role of the Fund vis-à-vis private market international lending activities'.[106] On that occasion, it was agreed to expand the research on the recycling process and to collect more statistical information on international bank lending but also not to intervene in the direction of capital flows.

The discussion continued in January 1977 when the banking turbulences of 1974 had proved to be temporary and the Euromarket activity had picked up again by mid-1975. A paper explicitly entitled 'Fund Relations with Commercial Banks',[107] which provided a basis for several Executive Board discussions, recognised that banks had come to play, in recent years, 'a growing role in international capital movements' receiving both an increasing share of the foreign assets of surplus countries and financing a growing share of aggregate capital flows to developing countries.

A follow up paper was prepared in mid-1977. The central issue of the paper was that commercial banks were continuing to provide the major portion of balance of payments financing for a large group of Fund members, and that in present circumstances a continued large role was to be expected and welcomed. In assessing the creditworthiness, 'the banks rely on their own judgement. The major banks, whose judgements in practice dominate the flows, have wide access to current information and are confident in their ability to make independent judgements on the appropriate level of lending'.[108]

As the role of the commercial banks was growing in international monetary and financial affairs, they sought more confidential information from the Fund and more and more often, such confidential information was leaked.

On the one hand, this practice posed a dilemma to the institution because all the staff papers and reports were strictly confidential and for internal use only. On the other, commercial banks were at the centre of the recycling mechanism and their role could not be stopped without serious problems for deficit countries: 'the issue remains that everything possible should be done to improve the flow of information to banks, so improving the basis for their action and lessening the danger of abrupt and disruptive shifts of lending'.[109] These were the key proposals of the document:

- continue the existing arrangements and practices with respect to 'parallel' lending operations whereby the banks, at their own discretion, link in various ways their own lending operations to financial programmes supported by the Fund;
- permit member countries, at their own option, to release Recent Economic Development reports (REDs) prepared in their own country outside official channels to private institutions when it would facilitate their relations with the private market;
- reaffirm that Fund papers containing staff assessments be kept strictly within official channels;
- participate in debt restructuring discussions between members and private banks, at the request of the parties, along the same lines and with the same safeguards associated with the Fund's role in multilateral renegotiations of official debt.[110]

However, the issue of transmission of confidential RED reports was left aside because of pressure from the representatives of developing countries. The

Chairman did not insist on the publication of the reports because he knew that they were leaking out anyway remarking that:

> [i]n practice, staff reports on countries . . . find their way into unofficial chan-
> nels, at the convenience of the interested authorities. In fact, it is not uncom-
> mon in loan agreements between the banks and member countries that the
> latter are obliged to make such documentation available.[111]

Executive Director, Lamberto Dini, was extremely clear in acknowledging that the issue of the Fund's relations with commercial banks had arisen because '*the Fund and governments had lost control* over international liquidity creation and global balance of payments financing [emphasis added]'.[112] This is an astonishing quote, pointing out clearly the fact that after the oil crisis, commercial banks were at the helm of international finance.

Dini continued: 'bankers had come to feel that their new role entailed some risks, and they wished to cooperate with the Fund to minimize it . . . *The Fund should do all it could to assist private banks* . . . [emphasis added]'.[113] In an inter-nal office memorandum addressed to Leslie Whittome, head of the European Department, Hans O. Schmitt was adamant in acknowledging that:

> [o]ver the last decade or two *the international monetary system has in
> large measure been privatized* . . . The international monetary system has
> evolved in a way that has given the private banks an increasing role to play.
> It is now time perhaps for the Fund once more to be placed at its center
> [emphasis added].[114]

Executive Directors had different views on how to assist commercial banks, with some in favour of sharing internal documents and others who believed that the Fund was not responsible for providing information to commercial banks. Byanti Kharmawan, who represented the South East Asian region, remarked that 'the developing countries felt that the distribution of papers to the private sector would not be in their interest'. Witteween was particularly in favour of exchanging more information with the private sector. Jacques de Groote from Belgium remarked that 'the Chairman's proposals were ill-timed . . . The proposals under discussion might give the impression that the Fund was embarking upon a new practice of giving increasing amounts of information to commercial banks'.[115]

But what were commercial banks and the Fund talking about? Let us con-sider the reference year of 1977. From 10 February to 15 August 1977, there were 306 recorded contacts with commercial banks, private financial and other institutions and public export credit agencies. Around two-thirds of the con-tacts were made by phone, while the remaining third were by visits. American commercial banks accounted for half of the contacts, while the remaining ones were made by banks from Belgium, Canada, France, Germany, Japan and Great Britain. There were 368 inquiries, 29 on Turkey, 19 on Zaire, 10 on Egypt, 42 on Mexico, 29 on Peru and 11 on Argentina. Out of the 306 contacts, Fund staff at the level of division chief or above handled 119. More than 40 per cent of the queries involved requests for economic and financial data, 30 per cent were of a 'less routine nature', for example on financial programmes supported by the Fund or recent economic developments. The remaining 30 per cent of the enquiries involved six highly leveraged countries, namely Argentina, Egypt, Mexico, Peru, Turkey and Zaire. Topics of discussion involved payments prospects, foreign exchange developments, creditworthiness, etc.

As some authors have pointed out: 'Economic crises do not take place in a political vacuum'.[116] Archival evidence seems to suggest that the political will to delegate the recycling mechanism to private actors played a critical role in pushing developing countries towards their 'lost decade'. The IMF had an important role in paving the way for the debt crisis of 1982 by not resisting those political pressures.

Business with the enemies: commercial banks and oppressive regimes

Since 'as late as the 1970s, autocracy was more common than democracy',[117] it comes as no surprise that doing business with developing countries in the 1970s involved dealing with military dictatorships, racist regimes, one party 'democracies' and so on. These ranked amongst the most important customers for European commercial banks, and their respective governments were more than happy to use commercial banks as tools to penetrate peripheral markets in the context of the global scramble for customers so as to shore up domestic industries and employment.

In this paragraph we shall illustrate four short but particularly informative empirical studies, one involving Barclays and the oppressive regimes in Latin America, one on Midland Bank and the South African racist regime, another one involving *Société Générale* and the Iraqi President Saddam Hussein, and the final one involving the payment of bribes to the Suharto regime in Indonesia by *Société Générale*. These cases have been chosen because of their historical relevance, but many others could have been considered, since almost all the developing countries of that time were ruled by dictators *et similia*.

Despite the fact that Latin America was not Barclays' core region, this did not mean that the Bank was not active on the continent. Given the number of new military dictatorships in Latin America in the 1970s (Bolivia in 1971, Chile and Uruguay in 1973, Argentina in 1976) the interests of Barclays in that region came under increasing scrutiny. As reported in an internal document in June 1977, BBI's Vice Chairman, Steve Mogford, had been 'asked by one our detractors [sic] whether we are "ploughing money into some of the military regimes in South America"'.[118] Following this episode, a document entitled 'Oppressive Regimes in Latin America' was drawn up collecting all the information on the exposure of Barclays towards Latin American countries considered to be under the rule of authoritarian regimes.[119]

The document revealed that Barclays was particularly compromised with the military regimes in Argentina, Bolivia, Brazil, Chile, Paraguay and Uruguay. The

Table 4.9 BBI exposure to Latin American oppressive regimes as of July 1977 (£m).

Country	Government	Private	Total
Argentina	53,062	21,988	75,050
Bolivia	143	1,530	1,673
Brazil	276,450	124,987	401,437
Chile	3,610	11,128	14,738
El Salvador	–	603	603
Guatemala	–	1,294	1,294
Nicaragua	784	503	1,287
Uruguay	5,709	842	6,551
Total	339,758	162,875	502,633

Source: BBA, 80/6284, Note 'Oppressive Regimes in South America', 23 June 1977.

data shown for the first time in Table 4.9 indicate a total exposure of more than £500 million; in current terms, this would represent an exposure of more than £2.5 billion. Most of these amounts were in the form of medium-term Euroloans and export credits guaranteed by the ECGD. We can safely assume that at least some of this money was invested by oppressive regimes to reinforce national security, to buy more sophisticated arms and to strengthen the repressive apparatus.

Barclays, of course, was not the only bank involved in dubious practices. Midland Bank was very active in Southern Africa: it was so active that in 1974 the pressure group ELTSA was founded by the Reverend David Haslam. The group's goal was to pressurise British banks into putting an end to their South African business; Barclays and Midland were particularly targeted. The pressure was already mounting in 1974. Nevertheless, 'the Board did not feel that such loans assisted the apartheid regime, and saw no reason to discontinue the Bank's present policy in this regard'.[120]

In the Board meeting of 14 March 1975, it was reported that the Chairman had advised the Board that mounting pressure was being made by certain religious bodies objecting to the lending of money to the South African Government by the Bank and its overseas associates, and that as a result:

> [h]e and Mr Graham had recently seen a deputation led by Lord March, the Church of England representative on the World Council of Churches, and the Chairman of the Finance Committee of the Church Commission. The Board agreed that the Bank should not yield to such pressure but that it should without publicity, avoid provocative action and proceed cautiously in regard to further loans to South Africa.[121]

Controlling the complex web of operations was no easy task considering that Midland was involved in international financial operations not only through its own branches but also through a vast number of affiliates and subsidiaries. In 1974 the *Sunday Times* conducted an investigation into a loan to Rhodesia by European-American Finance based in Bermuda and arranged by the European-American

Bank. The article alleged that, while the loan was ostensibly for the importation into Europe of steel from South Africa, it was in reality for the purpose of extending steel works in Rhodesia. This was against the sanctions imposed by the United Nations in 1966 against Ian Smith's white supremacist regime targeting the sale of arms, oil, motor vehicles, airplanes, etc. An internal investigation on this operation was launched after the embarrassing revelations of the *Sunday Times* and the 'enquiry had shown that the allegations were correct, and further that, when the proposal had been submitted to Midland Bank for approval, information regarding the true purpose of the loan had been suppressed'.[122] Was this the true story? Did Midland really ignore the true purpose of the Rhodesian loan? Or was this the only way out once the illicit operation had been revealed to the public?

The end of the story was that Midland's Chairman wrote 'in strong terms' to H. E. Ekblom, Chairman and President of EAB, in which he 'tendered full apology'.[123] As a side note, another similar loan was made by the Vice Chairman of EAB, Mr K. Jacobs, without the knowledge of Mr Ekblom. It is a story of ingenuity or bad faith, possibly both. Jacobs resigned after the operation was discovered.

At both the General Meetings in 1976 and 1977, a Special Resolution called on Midland to make no further loans to the South African Government, its departments, agencies and state corporations. The Chairman was always against these resolutions and the Board was with him. The vote of the shareholders followed the indications of the management and the resolution was defeated both times on the grounds that:

> [i]n our lending, we should follow normal banking principles, and, in particular, that we should not allow ourselves to be influenced either by our own personal opinions, or by opinions expressed to us by others, about a borrower's conduct outside the commercial field.[124]

In its board meeting of 7 October 1977, it was remarked that press reports issued by the ELTSA campaign 'were inaccurate and should be ignored'.[125] Nevertheless, facing mounting pressures, the Chairman decided to meet the pressure groups. He reassured them that new loans were not planned, but that the Bank did not envisage ceasing to grant conventional banking support to those commercial customers who had South African interests.[126]

In conclusion, Midland kept a very positive attitude towards the South African regime, enjoying much larger exposure towards that region compared to its competitors. Comparing the claims of Midland on overseas residents in foreign currency areas with those reported for all the banks represented in the Bank of England Quarterly Bulletin, it appears that Midland's exposure to South Africa accounted for 4.4 per cent of its total exposure compared to an average of 1.7 per cent for all other banks.[127] In 1976 Midland had claims for £40.4 million, more than its claims on the Far East (excluding Japan), which amounted to £37.4 million.

Of course, dealing with dubious regimes was common practice during the decade analysed in this book. The decision was often the result of greed, political pressures and lack of appropriate controls.

Société Générale, BNP and *Crédit Lyonnais* were very active on the Arab market, in line with a historically strong French-Arab alliance since the de Gaulle presidency. Amongst the most interesting commercial relations in the Arab world, especially given the tragic developments of the late twentieth and early twenty-first centuries, we should certainly mention the one with the Iraqi President from 1979 to 2003 (and Vice-President from 1968 to 1979), Saddam Hussein.[128]

In 1974 Prime Minister Jacques Chirac, who would later be nicknamed 'Jacques Iraq' for the special relationship with the Iraqi regime, and President Valéry Giscard d'Estaing visited Iraq. In 1975 Saddam Hussein reciprocated and was welcomed in Versailles as a true friend of France; he was even invited to Chirac's country house for the weekend. The visit of Saddam Hussein represented a very good opportunity for *Société Générale*, even though it was remarked that 'President Saddam has a very tight schedule'.[129]

The contacts with Hussein were limited but he was accompanied in his visit by Adnan Al Kindy, President of the Central Plan Organization and Vice-President of the Follow Up Committee (the latter was created in December 1973 to accelerate the pace of industrialisation by bypassing some regulations). Al Kindy was probably the most important target and the Middle East department remarked that he was 'maybe more important to meet "and conquer" than President Hussein himself'.[130]

Saddam Hussein was also accompanied by Adnan Al Hardan, Director of the High Council of Agriculture, and two nuclear specialists, Dr Khaled Ibrahim Said, Director of the Nuclear Research Institute, and Dr Abdul Razak Al Hashimy, representing the national metal industry. The commercial aspects of the visit involved four points: oil and gas; nuclear energy; information technology and agricultural development. Another important topic of discussion was international borrowing to finance these operations.

In historical terms, the most important outcome of these discussions was the decision to sign a nuclear cooperation agreement, finalised in 1976, to finance and build a nuclear reactor in Iraq, named Osiraq.

Osiraq was an Osiris-class nuclear reactor ('the most advanced nuclear reactor in the Arab world'),[131] officially conceived for research purposes. Unfortunately for Saddam Hussein, Israel did not think the same and, seeing the reactor as a first step towards the first Arab atomic bomb and a threat to its national security they launched 'Operation Babylon', sending eight F-16 Falcon aircraft and six F-15 Eagles on 7 June 1981 to destroy it. The attack killed a French technician and caused a major international uproar as the first pre-emptive strike against a nuclear facility in recent history.[132] In the end, the financing of the Osiraq project was entrusted to *Crédit Lyonnais*' UBAF and *Banque Française pour le Commerce Extérieur*. The decision not to include *Société Générale* through its 'Arab' bank FRAB in favour of UBAF was justified by the fact that the former had amongst its shareholders Rafidain Bank, the most important nationalised bank of Iraq. Nevertheless, we are able to get a glimpse of the delicate transactions in which commercial banks were implicated.

The links between the French banking elites and the Iraqi government continued to be intense and profitable after the Osiraq affair. Throughout the 1970s and

1980s, Iraqi dignitaries paid visits to *Société Générale* and vice versa. In January 1983, Vice-President Tareq Aziz visited Paris and was received by President Mitterrand and several key ministers. A war with Iran had erupted in September 1980 and, after more than two years of fighting, Iraq was destitute (the cost was estimated at US$1 billion per month) and in desperate need of new and more modern arms to strike at Iranian oil facilities in the Gulf. Logically, Iraq turned to its ally, as it was estimated that by early 1983 40 per cent of all of France's arms exports were going to Iraq.[133] Aziz asked for a moratorium on debt repayments, saying explicitly that 'you cannot abandon us, *if we sink you will sink too* [emphasis added]'.[134] During his visits, Aziz also requested FF4 to 5 billion and sophisticated arms. A final agreement was reached in May, when France agreed to settle FF2.5 billion for outstanding debt and to triple its purchase of Iraqi oil.[135] The French support also involved military equipment: in 1983 five *Super Etendard*, a carrier-borne strike fighter jet built by Dassault-Breguet, were sold to Iraq with the help of the nationalised banks.

Dealing with dictators and tyrants sometimes involved resorting to non-conventional business practices, often bribes. Some authors have argued that 'personalist and personalist-hybrid regimes have higher average corruption rankings than do other forms of dictatorship, including monarchies'.[136] By mid-1982, just before the eruption of the debt crisis, *Société Générale* was looking with great interest at opportunities in Indonesia, since 'Indonesia is indeed one of the main countries of South East Asia because of its population . . . and its natural resources, notably oil'.[137]

Indonesia had not authorised foreign banks since 1969, but this policy was about to change. The question was whether *Société Générale* should wait for the visit of President Mitterrand or whether it should force its way in. Waiting was a risky option because there was no assurance that they would be chosen: 'we do not have more chances than our competitors to be the national bank selected'.[138]

The solution to all problems came in June 1982 when Mr Meraud of the Asia-Australasia office reported in a confidential note that two intermediaries 'working for people close to President Suharto' had approached him to help *Société Générale* to establish a presence directly in Indonesia.[139]

Buttay of the International Department remarked that he was not surprised by such proposal, but that the 'credibility' of the intermediaries had to be verified. Thus, before starting the negotiations, it was important to know whether the deal had been 'invented' by these intermediaries or whether the initiative came from above. The document continued: 'We do not lack the means to carry on this investigation at the highest levels of Indonesian politics'. We have here a clear admission of close contacts with the Suharto administration. *Société Générale* knew that this was a risky business and Buttay remarked that it was important not to leave written traces of the transaction, pointing out that 'we must refuse any writing commitment, *we have already acted this way on other occasions* with great success [emphasis added]'.[140]

The archival evidence we are presenting here is some of the few traces left clearly showing the wide-spread practice of bribing officials to open branches abroad and the close relationships with dictatorships around the world: a topic that deserves careful attention by historians in the future.

Société Générale started negotiations with a certain Mr Iskandar, a man with supposedly good connections in the Suharto administration. The middleman asked for a conspicuous amount of money for its good services, US$7.5 million. Nonetheless, Mr Meraud believed that 'we should recover this amount in three years'. Despite the assurance of quickly recovering the bribe paid, the offer was to be attentively pondered since the price asked was very high and there was a political risk involved. The opportunity of opening a branch in the country was very appealing to *Société Générale*, so it decided to carry on the negotiations.

Receiving the approval from the French Treasury was the next step: 'Because of the unusual importance of this entrance ticket, and its not less unusual amount, we think that it would be better to *inform the Treasury and ask for its green light* [emphasis added]'.[141] Thus the problem was not the bribe but its amount and we can safely assume from this document that paying bribes was a common practice to speed up some operations in LDCs. The complicity of the government is surprising at first glance, but less so if we read this chapter: political backing has been a critical asset for the rise of the banking and financial sector in Europe.

It was specified that the matter should be dealt with 'confidentially but firmly'. A letter was sent to the Finance Minister Delors and in October 1982 he replied positively to President Mayoux about the request. A bank guarantee was prepared in favour of Mr Iskandar payable 'in the event that approval has been granted by the appropriate authorities to the application'.[142]

Lone wolves or herd mentality?

The international expansion of European banks clearly entered a whole new dimension after 1973 as the imbalances created by the first oil shock brought along a *realignment of interest* between public and private institutions after the Bretton Woods break and provided *huge capital* to finance international ventures and *powerful incentives* to expand overseas.

These elements explain why the international expansion of European commercial banks did not take place in the 1960s and also why, not coincidentally, all the banks in this book experienced tremendous growth in general through new products, new customers and new alliances from the early 1970s.

As we have illustrated, even before the first oil shock, international expansion through new branches and Euromarkets was under way, but efforts were sporadic and frustrated by lack of capital. As noted in the 1983 Annual Report of the Bank for International Settlements:

> While the international banking sector, especially the Euro-currency market, had been growing rapidly during the 1960s, it was only following the 1973 oil price increase and the removal of all restrictions on bank lending out of the United States in January 1974 that banks came to play the predominant

role in net international capital movements. They began to provide general balance-of-payments finance for oil-importing countries on an unprecedented scale, as well as development finance particularly for non-OPEC LDCs.[143]

Some continental alliances were institutionalised through the creation of clubs and consortia. The most important and structured of them was EBIC of which *Société Générale* and Midland were members, followed by ABECOR where Barclays was a member and Europartners of which *Crédit Lyonnais* was a member. The only major bank outside a club was Lloyds, a decision that was a double-edged sword: being more independent, Lloyds was able to expand at a very fast pace, but this proved to be a risky bet given their losses incurred on loans to LDCs.

Despite the limits of these institutions, we should see them more as rational institutions created to minimise costs than simply inefficient ones. They certainly failed in the long term, but they represented a first and crucial step towards creating continental players able to compete with the American heavyweights of that time in a context of very high asymmetries of information. Another advantage of the clubs was to limit competition in Europe, thereby allowing the members to focus on international ventures.

Despite some differences in strategies, European banks followed a similar pattern of expansion, a pattern not really in line with some well-established theories of multinational expansion. For example, the Uppsala Model posited a negative correlation between 'psychic distance' and foreign establishments, intended to be 'factors preventing or disturbing the flows of information between firm and market',[144] such as differences in language, culture, political system. On the contrary, commercial banks expanded sooner in regions further away from them than in closer ones. Besides, as we have illustrated, 'mundane' factors, like political pressures and the fear of competitors, pushed banks into risky ventures. These elements are only seldom considered by mainstream theories and existing literature, highlighting the important contribution of business history to management topics.

Looking at the pattern of international expansion, we see clearly that European banks had a tendency to adopt a herd mentality, with Barclays being a partial outsider because of sheer luck, boycott problems, international heritage and its family and conservative ambience. When one close competitor moved to one country or increased its exposure towards certain clients, there was an immediate response from its competitors. In this sense, commercial banks adopted a herd mentality rather than behaving as lone wolves. This tendency to move in herds explains why, at the end of the decade, exposure on LDCs was massive. As we shall see in the next chapter, the strategy of moving in herds and embarking on riskier bets was justified: a lone wolf can be left aside but an entire herd has to be rescued.

Given the fact that commercial banks came to play a critical role in rebalancing the global monetary imbalances after the first oil shock by acting as intermediaries between surplus and deficit countries, it is not surprising to see that they had to deal with tyrants and dictators. As we have illustrated, commercial banks were on good terms with racist regimes in Southern Africa, with authoritarian regimes in the

Arab World and in South East Asia, as well as with military dictatorships in Latin America. We must point out that this was often the result of political pressures or political agreements, as occurred between the French government and Saddam Hussein. Perhaps more surprising is the closeness of relations between the Fund and commercial banks in the US and Europe, but if we go back to the previous chapter we would see how international organisations played a crucial role in the delegation of power to the banking sector after the first oil crisis.

By the late 1970s, the macro-economic context was looking increasingly unstable. Interest rates were soaring, the prices of commodities were plunging, debt levels were reaching all-time highs and the exposures of commercial banks were gradually becoming unmanageable. Thus, the last aspect we shall investigate in the following chapter is how the 'perfect storm' of 1982 approached, from the viewpoint of international organisations, national regulators and commercial banks.

Notes

1   Rinaldo M. Pecchioli, *The Internationalisation of Banking*, OECD, Paris, 1983, 22.
2   IMFA DM/80/48, Exchange and Trade Relations Department, 'The Response of International Capital Markets to the 1973–74 Oil Price Increases' Prepared by Ulrich Baumgartner, 15 July 1980.
3   Richard Roberts (with C. Arnander), *Take Your Partners. Orion, the Consortium Bank and the Transformation of the Euromarkets*, Palgrave, Basingstoke, UK, 2001, 96.
4   Joel Métais, 'International Strategies of French Banks', in *Banking in France*, Christian de Boissieu (ed.), Routledge, London and New York, 1990, 137.
5   Andrew Haldane, Simon Brennan and Vasileios Madouros, 'What is the Contribution of the Financial Sector: Miracle Or Mirage?', in Adair Turner *et al. The Future of Finance: The LSE Report*, London School of Economics and Political Science, London, 2010.
6   Joel Métais, 'International Strategies of French Banks', in *Banking in France*, Christian de Boissieu (ed.), Routledge, London and New York, 1990, 138.
7   Ibid.
8   On the importance of commercial banks to shore up domestic economies through financial credits, see Philip A. Wellons, *Passing the Buck. Banks, Governments, and Third World Debt*, Harvard Business School Press, Boston, MA, 1987.
9   Idem, 6.
10 Michael Loriaux, *France after Hegemony. International Change and Financial Reform*, Cornell University Press, Ithaca, NY and London, 1991, 35.
11 Phillip A. Wellons, *Passing the Buck. Banks, Governments, and Third World Debt*, Harvard Business School Press, Boston, MA, 1987, 59.
12 BFA 1415200610–24, Speech at the University of Dijon, 11 August 1980.
13 LBA, Lloyds Bank International Limited, Reports and Accounts 1978.
14 Harold James, 'Central Banks and the Process of Financial Internationalization: A Secular View', in S. Battilossi and Y. Cassis (eds), *European Banks and the American Challenge*, Oxford University Press, Oxford, UK and New York, 2002, 209.
15 Richard Roberts (with C. Arnander), *Take Your Partners. Orion, the Consortium Banks and the Transformation of the Euromarkets*, Palgrave, London, 2001, 111.
16 LBA, HO/Ch/Fau/23, Letter signed G. F. T, 4 February 1971.
17 LBA, HO/Ch/Fau/34, 'Report and Recommendations of the Special Project Team', 11 February 1972.
18 LBA, F/1/D/Com/2.4, 'Chairman's Statement and Review of Activities', 7 December 1973.

19 LBA, HO/Ch/Mor/30, 'Framework for the Future', August 1976.

20 LBA, HO/Ch/Mor/30, 'Minutes of a Meeting of the International Strategy Working Party', 30 July 1987.

21 LBA, F/1/Bd/Far/1.6, 'Visit to the Republic of Korea', 9–11 December 1974.

22 Idem.

23 Idem.

24 LBA, F/1/Bd/Far/2.4, M. J. Young, 'Republic of Korea- Recommendation to Open a Branch', no date.

25 LBA, F/1/Ce/Off/1, 'Review of Corporate Strategy', July 1979.

26 Idem.

27 Idem.

28 A. R. Holmes and Edwin Green, *Midland: 150 Years of Banking Business*, Batsford, London, 1986, 257.

29 MBA, Board Minutes, 21 June 1974.

30 Wilcox entered the Midland Bank in Liverpool in 1938 but, when war broke out, he served in the Territorial Army, with the Royal Artillery, the Royal Horse Artillery and the General Staff. After the war he continued his career with Midland, becoming its Joint General Manager in 1967, its Assistant Chief General Manager and, as we mentioned earlier, Chief General Manager for the international side.

31 MBA, Board Minutes, 14 February 1975.

32 Idem.

33 *Inspection des finances* 1953–56, *Chargé de mission* at the Paul Ramadier's and later Félix Gaillard's cabinets, 1957, *Direction du Trésor*, 1958 and 1965–70, French embassy in the US and Canada.

34 SGA, 81120, 'Note sur les principes d'une réorganisation de la Direction de l'Étranger', 15 May 1974.

35 SGA, 81120, Ordre de service relatif à l'organisation de la Direction de l'Étranger, 28 January 1975.

36 SGA, 81120, Memorandum of Marc Viénot 'Nouvelle organisation de la Direction de l'Étranger', 22 November 1974.

37 SGA, 81156, 'Rapport pour le Comité "Développement des activités internationale"', May 1976.

38 SGA, 81093, Letter from Marc Viénot (General Director) to Jacques Delors (Minister of Finance), 31 July 1981.

39 On the role of the French state in the financing of the economy, see for example, Laure Quennouelle-Corre, 'The state, banks and financing of investments in France from World War II to the 1970s', *Financial History Review*, Volume 12, Part 1, April 2005, 63–86.

40 SGA, 81119, Speech of Marc Viénot to the Directors 'L'activité internationale de la Société Générale', 26 April (1976?): 'La troisième raison qui a poussée les banques françaises à s'internationaliser, est que ce secteur d'activité est d'autant plus propice aux initiatives nouvelles et hardies qu'il n'est pas règlementé . . . il existe sur le territoire national une certaine saturation des installations bancaires et depuis 1973, un encadrement quasi permanent du crédit. Aussi n'est il pas étonnant que les banques françaises aient cherché à deverser leur energies dans la zone de moindre résistance, c'est à dire vers l'étranger'.

41 SGA, 81161, Letter from Mr Sicard to Mr Buttay, 13 November 1974: 'En d'autres termes, les japonais sont prêt à tour faire, vraisemblablement en participant aux investissement à la hauteur de 20% par des prestations d'assistance technique, des transferts, de savoir faire, des cessions de brevets et, le cas échéant, de biens de consommation durable. Pour le reste – c'est à dire pour les biens d'équipements proprement dits – il y aurait vente, au comptant si possible, avec facilités à court ou moyen terme si nécessaire. Pareille offre intéresse . . . les vénézuéliens, sans que cela les incite pour autant à se satisfaire d'un tête à tête avec les japonais. Or, jusqu'à présent, personne ne s'est mis

sur les rangs. On peut donc se demander si une grande banque française . . . n'aurait pas d'intérêt à s'inspirer de l'initiative prise par la Banque de Tokyo'.

42 The *encadrement du crédit* became the central element of the French monetary policy since 1973 in order to stem the growth of monetary aggregates to fight inflation.

43 SGA, 81093, Letter of Mr Viénot to Mr Delors, 31 July 1981.

44 SGA, 81145, 'Mission en Amérique Latine', 27 May 1975.

45 SGA, 81119, Note pour M. Jeorger by M. Viénot on his business trip to Mexico, 31 March 1976.

46 SGA, 81121, Letter from M. Viénot to President Lauré, 19 December 1977.

47 SGA, 81147, Letter from M. Viénot to L. Jeorger, 1 February 1979: 'Cette réouverture nous est apparue indispensable compte tenu à la fois de l'implantation récente à New York de nos principaux concurrents français et de la nécessité pour notre Établissement, qui se classe désormais parmi les 7 ou 8 premières banques mondiales, de figurer en nom propre aux États-Unis. Elle doit nous permettre d'accroître notre influence dans ce pays, de renforcer nos relations avec les banques et la clientèle américaines, de recourir à des financements en dollars avantageux et de mieux servir notre clientèle française'.

48 SGA, 81093, Note for the Minister of Finance Jacques Delors 'Note sur l'activité internationale de la Société Générale', 31 July 1981.

49 SGA, 81093, 'Évolution du portefeuille', No date.

50 *The Times*, 'Obituary Sir Malcolm Wilcox', 29 May 1986.

51 Lothar Gall, Gerald D. Feldman, Harold James, Carl-Ludwig Holtfrerich and Hans E. Büschgen, *The Deutsche Bank 1870–1995*, Weidenfeld & Nicolson, London, 1993, 760.

52 Information on the geographical spread of Western banks in the late 1970s can be found in P. Wellons, *Passing the Buck. Banks, Governments, and Third World Debt*, Harvard Business School Press, Boston, MA, 1987.

53 BBA, 80/5908, 'BBI Corporate Plan 1974–1978', April 1974.

54 Idem.

55 Idem.

56 BBA, 80/3175, Confidential Memorandum 'Our Strategy Vis-à-Vis Arab Countries', no date.

57 BBA, 80/5902, 'Report on the Middle East', 1 April 1974.

58 BBA, 80/5859, Confidential Memorandum by G. A. O. Thomson, September 1976

59 Idem.

60 BBA, 80/5859, 'Note for the Chairman', 10 November 1976.

61 BBA, 80/5859, 'Minutes of the First Meeting of the "Boycott Committee" (Operation Diversion)', 29 November 1976.

62 Lord Armstrong, born in Clapton, London, and educated at Exeter College, Oxford, entered the civil service in 1938 in the Board of Education. In 1943 he became private secretary to Sir Edward Bridges, secretary of the war cabinet. After the end of the war, he moved to the Treasury becoming the principal private secretary of three Chancellors of the Exchequer, Sir Stafford Cripps, Hugh Gaitskell and R. A. Butler. In the following years, he climbed the echelons of the Treasury becoming, in 1962 and until 1968, the joint permanent secretary to the Treasury, aged forty-seven. In 1968, he became the first permanent secretary of the Civil Service Department. He became the 'right hand' of Prime Minister Edward Heath, giving a crucial contribution to many of the economic policies of that time such as the 1972 Industry Act or the so-called 'Barber boom'. After leaving the public scene at the zenith of its power because of health issues, in 1974 he joined the Board of Midland and in 1975 he became chairman. Barran, born in Knightsbridge, London, and educated at Winchester and Trinity College, Cambridge, took the helm and remained Chairman for two years. After graduating in history, he was recruited by the Asiatic Petroleum Company, a subsidiary of Royal Dutch-Shell, and spent the greater part of his career within the Shell group, first in Africa, Middle East and India and, then, in London.

63 BBA, 80/5859, 'Confidential Memorandum-Barclays, Midland Meeting', 26 April 1977.

64 BBA, 80/5859,Tuke's Note to Group's and BBI Chair, 3 May 1977.

65 Rowland was born Roland Fuhrhop from a German father and an Anglo-Dutch mother in a detention camp in British India, was enlisted in the Hitler Youth before moving to the UK and was detained in the Isle of Man with his parents for pro-German sympathies, where his mother would die of cancer. He then moved to Southern Rhodesia in 1948, becoming a farmer despite his elegant taste and immaculate dress-sense. From these modest beginnings, Rowland started to build a small fortune by acquiring the Rhodesian franchise for Mercedes Benz, two goldmines and an option to build an oil pipeline in Mozambique. When, in 1961, the London and Rhodesia Mining and Land Company (L&R), later renamed Lonrho, acquired an important shareholding in his company, Shepton Estates, he became an important shareholder of the company and was appointed joint managing director. Lonrho gradually became a multi-faceted conglomerate with interests ranging from hotels, to car distributorships, to food. In the early 1970s, Lonrho became more and more involved in the Arab world, opening offices in Sudan and Egypt, and a 22 per cent interest was bought by a Kuwaiti consortium. Richard Davenport-Hines, 'Rowland, Roland Walter [Tiny] (1917–1998)', Oxford Dictionary of National Biography, Oxford University Press, Oxford, UK, 2004 [http://www.oxforddnb.com/view/article/70253, accessed 17 Sept 2013]. On Lonrho see: Chibuike Uche, 'Lonrho in Africa: The Unacceptable Face of Capitalism or the Ugly Face of Neo-Colonialism', *Enterprise & Society*, Vol. 16, Issue 2, April 2015, 1–27.

66 BBA, 80/5859, Strictly Confidential Tuke's Note to Group and BBI Chair, 9 June 1977.

67 Idem.

68 BBA, 80/5859, 'Visit to the Middle East', 22 July 1977.

69 BBA, 80/5894, Strictly Private and Confidential Note on 'BOB-British Bank Overseas', 15 April 1975.

70 BBA, 80/5894, Confidential Note from A. F. Tuke, 27 June 1975.

71 MBA, Board Minutes, 7 September 1979.

72 MBA, 0141/0033, Memorandum 'Arab Oil Money in the London Money Market', 8 July 1974.

73 MBA, Board Minutes, 7 May 1976.

74 MBA, 0200/0760d, Note from G. W. Taylor to the Chairman's Committee, 4 May 1976.

75 MBA, 0200/0759, 'Brazilian Railway Electrification General Electric Company Ltd. and Other Companies', 6 September 1976.

76 Idem.

77 Idem.

78 Idem.

79 See for example Robert Devlin, *Debt and Crisis in Latin America. The Supply Side of the Story*, Princeton University Press, Princeton, NJ, 1989.

80 MBA, 0528/0008, 'Strategic Plan 1978–1982', April 1977.

81 CLA, 110AH10, Direction Centrale des Affaires Internationales, 'Programme Intérimaire 1975', 30 October 1974.

82 CLA, 111AH11, DOFI-Program 1977, 8 October 1976.

83 CLA, 332AH180, 12 June 1978.

84 CLA, 110AH11, 'Program 1978–80-Latin America/Greece/Portugal Zone', 6 October 1977.

85 CLA, 110AH2, DCAIC Tableau de bord, 'Activité en devise-Ressources et emplois, 20 March 1981.

86 CLA, 110AH12, 'Programme 1979–82-Zone Amérique Latine', 31 May 1978.

87 Idem.

88   CLA, 110AH12, 'Programme 1979–80' Middle East Region, 12 June 1979: 'Bien que la zone soit en pleine effervescence et puisse être le théâtre d'évènements désordonnés nous devons y manifester et y renforcer même notre présence . . . '.

89   CLA, 110AH12, 'Programme DOFI 1980', 10 May 1979.

90   Idem: 'Une plus grande agressivité, en matière de conditions et de présence auprès de la clientèle potentielle, constitue en effet un impérative indispensable pour diriger d'avantage d'opérations et améliorer notre rentabilité ainsi que notre position sur le marché. Le contexte de concurrence très active de la part des banques étrangères, aussi bien que de nos confrères français, constitue une incitation supplémentaire à renforcer notre attaque commercial des emprunteurs potentiels . . . '.

91   A firm commitment by the underwriter of a secondary offering to buy the entire share issue from the issuing company, and then re-sell the shares to investors.

92   CLA, *Crédit Lyonnais* Annual Reports, various years.

93   SGA, 81283, Note to M. Viénot, 29 November 1979.

94   BBA, 80/6148, 'ABECOR Meeting in Brussels', 8 February 1974.

95   BBA, 80/6148, 'Memorandum', 20 June 1974.

96   CLA, 143AH9, 'Projet de création de nouvelles structures de la coopération', no date.

97   ORION was a consortium bank created in 1970. It had six shareholders: Chase Manhattan, Royal Bank of Canada, National Westminster, *Westdeutsche Landesbank*, *Credito Italiano* and Mitsubishi Bank.

98   CLA, 143AH9, 'Projet de création d'une banque internationale pour les Europartenaires', 25 March 1974.

99   CLA, 143AH10, Memorandum by G. Smolarski, 'Quelques réflexions sur la cooperation dans le domaine international', 9 January 1975. Smolarski remarked: 'Chacun tire la couverture vers soi'.

100   Idem.

101   CLA, 143AH10, 'Réunion du mardi 21 octobre', 8 October 1975: 'Chacun de nous a le sentiment que la Cooperation ne va pas bien. Certains craignent meme qu'elle ne meure'.

102   CLA, 143AH12, 'Réunion des Directions Générales du 12 juillet 1977': 'On a opté pour une coopération pragmatique, le souci de rechercher une certaine intégration faisant place à un principe de simple préférentialité'.

103   CLA, 143AH13, 'Compte rendu de la réunion des Présidents et Directeurs Généraux des Europartenaires du 13 Juin à Rome', 4 August 1980: 'La conjoncture actuelle, bien que défavorable, ne saurait modifier la stratégie à long terme des grandes banques à vocation internationale ni les amener à arrêter brutalement les crédits vers l'étranger'.

104   Phillip L. Zweig, *Wriston*, Crown Publishers, New York, 1995, 434.

105   IMFA, European Department-EURAI Subject Files Box 30, 'The Fund and International Lending by Commercial Banks: Possible Avenues of Fund Guidance', 15 September 1981.

106   Idem.

107   IMFA, Exchange and Trade Relations Department-ETRAI Director Ernest Sturc Subject Files Box 3, 'The Fund and the Commercial Banks' (Internal Discussion Paper), 25 January 1977.

108   IMFA, European Department-EURAI Subject Files Box 30, 'Fund Relations with Commercial Banks', 6 June 1977.

109   Idem.

110   Idem.

111   IMFA, European Department-EURAI Subject Files Box 30, 'The Fund and International Lending by Commercial Banks: Possible Avenues of Fund Guidance', 15 September 1981.

112   IMFA, European Department-EURAI Subject Files Box 30, 'Minutes of the Executive Board Meeting 77/90', 22 June 1977.

113 Idem.
114 IMFA, European Department-EURAI Subject Files Box 30, Office memorandum 'The Fund and the Banks', 14 April 1982.
115 Idem.
116 Blanca Heredia, 'The Political Economy of the Mexican Crisis', in Dharam Ghai (ed.), *The IMF and the South*, Zed Books on behalf of the United Nations Research Institute for Social Development (UNRISD) and the Institute of Social and Economic Research (ISER), London, 1991, 117.
117 Erica Frantz and Natasha Ezrow, *The Politics of Dictatorship. Institutions and Outcomes in Authoritarian Regimes*, Lynne Rienner Publishers, Boulder and London, 2011. 1.
118 BBA, 80/6284, Note 'Oppressive Regimes in South America', 23 June 1977.
119 Using the categorisation of the Human Rights Report prepared by the US Department of State submitted in March 1977 to the subcommittee on Foreign Assistance of the United States Senate.
120 MBA, Board Minutes, 20 December 1974.
121 MBA, Board Minutes, 14 March 1975.
122 MBA, Board Minutes, 3 May 1974.
123 MBA, Board Minutes, 3 May 1974.
124 MBA, Report and Accounts, December 1977.
125 MBA, Board Minutes, 7 October 1977.
126 MBA, Report and Accounts, December 1977.
127 MBA, 0200/0759 a, b, 'International Exposure', 9 April 1976.
128 On the France-Iraq relations see, for example David Styan, *France & Iraq: Oil, Arms and French Policy Making in the Middle East*, I. B. Tauris, London and New York, 2006.
129 SGA, 81183, 'Visite du Président Saddam Hussein', 9 September 1975. It was remarked that: 'Le President Saddam Hussein a un emploi du temps très minute'.
130 Idem: 'peut être plus important à voir "et à conquerir" que le President Hussein lui-même'.
131 Ghassan Bishara, 'The Political Repercussions of the Israeli Raid on the Iraqi Nuclear Reactor', *Journal of Palestine Studies*, Vol. 11, No. 3, Spring, 1982, 58.
132 The literature on this famous attack is vast, see, for example, Donald G. Boudreau, 'The Bombing of the Osirak Reactor', *International Journal on World Peace*, Vol. 10, No. 2, June 1993, 21–37; Shai Feldman, 'The Bombing of Osiraq-Revisited', *International Security*, Vol. 7, No. 2 (Autumn, 1982), 114–142; Jed C. Snyder, 'The Road to Osiraq: Baghdad's Quest for the Bomb', *Middle East Journal*, Vol. 37, No. 4, Autumn 1983, 565–593.
133 David Styan, *France and Iraq. Oil, Arms, and French Policy Making in the Middle East*, I. B. Tauris, London and New York, 2006, 142.
134 SGA, 81183, Note pour Monsieur Viénot 'Visite du Vice-President Tarek Aziz à Paris', 13 January 1983.
135 David Styan, *France and Iraq. Oil, Arms, and French Policy Making in the Middle East*, I. B. Tauris, London and New York, 2006, 143.
136 Natasha M. Ezrow and Erica Frantz, *Dictators and Dictatorships. Understanding Authoritarian Regimes and Their Leaders*, Continuum, New York and London, 2011.
137 SGA, 81146, Note of Mr Jeorger to Mr Mayoux, newly appointed Chairman and CEO of SG, 'Feu vert du Trésor pour le paiement de droit d'entrée en Indonésie', 2 August 1982: 'L'Indonésie est en effet l'un des principaux pays de l'Asie du Sud-Est en raison de sa population . . . et de ses ressources naturelles, notamment le pétrole . . . '.
138 SGA, 81146, Note of Mr Buttay to Viénot, Jeorger, Mayoux, 29 June 1982: 'nous n'avons pas plus de chances que nos concurrents d'être la banque nationale choisie'.
139 SGA, 81146, Confidential Note of Pierre Meraud to Jeorger and Buttay, 28 June 1982.

140 SGA, 81146, Note of Mr Buttay to Viénot, Jeorger, Mayoux, 29 June 1982: 'Nous refuser à tout engagement écrit quel qu'il soit, nous avons ainsi procédé, avec succès, en d'autres circonstances'.
141 SGA, 81146, Note of Mr Jeorger to Mr Mayoux, Viénot, Auberger, Buttay, 2 August 1982.
142 SGA, 81146, Telex to Mr Meraud from *Société Générale* Jakarta containing the proposed text of a bank guarantee in favour of Mr Iskandar, 9 July 1982.
143 BIS Annual Report 1983, 118.
144 Jan Johanson and Finn Wiedersheim-Paul, 'The Internationalization of the Firm – Four Swedish Cases', *Journal of Management Studies*, Vol. 12, Issue 3, October 1975, 305–323.

5 Wuthering heights

It is not the creation of wealth that is wrong but love of money for its own sake.[1]

Approaching the brink

The events of the late 1970s and early 1980s rate amongst the most eventful of contemporary history. As we have anticipated in the last part of Chapter 3, the world was bracing, just six years after the first shock, for a new period of turbulence.

Ultimately, the depressive impact of the first oil crisis had been alleviated through the creation of a debt spiral in which developing countries came to be gradually but viciously entangled.

The issue at stake after the second oil crisis was whether commercial banks would be able to cushion against the depressive impact of the oil crisis without harmful effects to the world economy and the international monetary system. As the Bank of England noted in a secret document in December 1979:

> [m]any non-oil LDC's [sic] enjoy reserve levels which in gross terms are high by historical standards, but these have only been achieved by means of market borrowing. Aid flows are not likely to increase on the scale required, while the contribution of the IMF may be relatively modest despite the greatly increased resources which it is now in the process of obtaining. *Thus the private capital markets will again be called upon to shoulder the major part of the recycling burden* [emphasis added].[2]

Ultimately, the reliance on the Euromarket to recycle oil surpluses continued unabated during the fated years approaching 1982, and the task of intermediating the new OPEC funds was, again, delegated to commercial banks.

The IMF, the BIS and the WP3 of the OECD never questioned in a credible way the approach adopted to deal with the first oil crisis, and commercial banks in the West continued to expand their operations in the developing world.

The Mexican default was not the first default in recent years. Zaire, which had received large sums of money as an ally against pro-communist Angola, defaulted in 1976; Turkey and Peru, the latter had borrowed greatly under the 'Revolutionary Government of the Armed Forces', defaulted in 1978; Poland in

1981; and several more . . . But Mexico was the largest debtor, and its default triggered a regionalisation syndrome affecting many LDCs. At the end of 1982, Brazil asked for help and throughout the 1980s more than 50 developing countries would start the procedure to reschedule their debt. What we might ask now is whether or not the international financial community was aware of the incoming payment problems.

On that point, some authors have argued that 'the crisis had largely caught policymakers by surprise'[3] – was this *really* the case? Such an assumption is only partly correct. As mentioned earlier, the level of indebtedness of LDCs was an issue of debate amongst bankers and officials in monetary circles. The first preoccupations emerged after the hot summer of 1974 but diminished when markets started to function again in 1975. All in all, the first recycling was perversely successful in the eyes of the international financial community, newspapers were talking of the recycling miracle and officials of the IMF and other international organisations were commending the efficiency and effectiveness of private channels in recycling the petrodollars.

Nevertheless, preoccupations started to surface again after the second oil crisis. During the summer of 1979, the Governors of the G-10 met in Basel to discuss whether the rapid growth of their banks' international business, especially through the Euromarkets, '[was] giving rise to problems which called for corrective action, either by individual countries or on an internationally co-ordinated basis'.[4] The main topics of the debate were the worldwide macro-economic effects of the growth of international banking; its effects on the ability of national authorities to control liquidity in their own economies; and the prudential questions raised by the growth of banks' international operations, including those carried out by their foreign branches and subsidiaries.[5] The rather inconclusive results of this debate, which were summarised in a communiqué by G-10 Governors in April 1980, are not relevant enough to be included in this chapter; what is important to note is the fact that the international financial community was not completely unaware that some risks were on the horizon. A secret paper was redacted in January 1980, more or less one year before the default of Poland, entitled 'The International Banking System: The Effect of an Eastern Bloc Default'.[6] Another example is a document prepared by the Bank of England in June 1980 entitled, quite explicitly, 'Apocalypse Now' (Francis Ford Coppola's film had just came out a few months earlier) on the consequences of the default by a developing country. Thus, the possibility of a default had been contemplated several times, but what really caught policymakers by surprise was not the default in itself but the *scale* of these risks.

To explain this colossal failure of common sense we have to go back to Philip Wellons' study on governments and bank relations. After the oil crisis, a tacit alliance was formed between governments and banks. The former agreed to bail out banks in case of need and would not regulate the Euromarket, while the latter would continue to intermediate funds on a global scale and would continue to finance exporting industries.

The debt crisis represented for many countries across the globe a changing experience. Its effects proved particularly detrimental for Latin American countries, which went through 'the worst economic crisis since the world-wide depression of the 30's'[7] and 'put an end to a period of more than a century during which Latin America had been gaining ground in the world economy'.[8]

The impact on the European banking sector was exceptional. Chapter 2 has shown the still relative triviality of the European banking and financial sector in the Bretton Woods era. In the short space of ten years, that torpid state of affairs was radically modified by the turbulences of the decade. As Wellons has aptly pointed out:

> Barriers to entry were still high in 1960. The Eurocurrency market, outside the ambit of national controls, was tiny. International banking was a *stable, slow-growth market* populated by *cautious banks and investors*. By 1980, international banking had *altered beyond recognition*. Hundreds of new entrants had opened foreign offices . . . Many banks linked financial markets around the world . . . The entire industry became *more complex, more competitive, more integrated*, and *more public* [emphasis added].[9]

The transformation started in the early 1970s and continued in the latter part of the decade. Despite increasing risks, and under the aegis of international organisations, European commercial banks continued their transformation towards becoming global institutions able to compete in every corner of the world, offering complex products to a wide variety of customers, thus 'moving outside their traditional spheres of influence (historically confined . . . to the home market and countries carved out of their own nation's colonial empires) and targeting the international arena as a source of growth and profits'.[10]

As a counterpart to this astonishing expansion, several criticalities emerged. Amongst them were the large amounts of debt accumulated by the developing world in a short period of time, their debt-servicing ratios, the banks' country exposures and, finally, their capital ratios which had eroded throughout the decade under the weight of a persistent borrower's market.

In the early 1980s, the developing world was struck, albeit not homogenously, by a three-fold shock: an increase in real interest rates, the reduction of world GDP and the weakness of commodity prices after a very favourable decade. Even though the crisis which started in 1982 can be considered as the first contemporary global crisis, it particularly affected those countries which exported raw products, notably Latin American, African and less industrialised Asian countries, but less so those countries exporting final products, notably the newly industrialised countries (NIC) of the Asian continent, such as South Korea, which had a lower ratio of debt to GDP.

Differences between developing countries broadly reflected different economic models: between what economist, Bela Balassa, termed 'inward-oriented' and 'outward-oriented' development strategies in order to identify strategies based on satisfying a domestic market or conforming to world-market opportunities.[11] East Asian NICs relied on a domestic industrial base capable of generating competitive products and the incentives and marketing experience needed to sell them, thus managing to capture growing world markets' shares, thereby earning revenues to finance higher import bills. By contrast, East European and Latin American countries 'were saddled with a structural dependence on imports, a domestic industrial base that was largely non-competitive on world markets, and a lack of expertise in world marketing'.[12] For Latin American countries in particular, the effects of the crisis and the 'medicine' of the IMF imposed severe strains on their economic and social tissue. Latin American countries would lose more than a decade, in economic, social and political terms, under the weight of harsh austerity measures before timidly recovering.

In this chapter, we will start by analysing the view of the IMF, the BIS and the OECD on the global economic situation after the second oil crisis in order to understand their attitude towards increasing risks in international finance. In the second section, we will consider how commercial banks in the UK and France behaved in the latter part of the 1970s and early 1980s. In the third section, we will assess the fateful year of 1982 and its consequences on the developing world, international organisations and commercial banks. The fourth and last section will conclude the chapter.

Clouds gathering: the view from the top

Old threats, new challenges, same responses

The second oil price escalation posed a new and greater threat to the world order devised in 1974. The main issue at stake was the possible reaction of the international financial community to the destabilising influences of the shock. Unlike the first increase in oil prices, where the oil surplus of around US$60 billion had been halved by 1975, the second wave of price increases in 1979 had not halved by 1980 and had actually doubled. The WP3 started to assess the impact of the second oil crisis in March 1980 in a restricted note entitled 'Financing Problems of Non-Oil Developing Countries'[13] with the intent to evaluate the size and nature of the non-oil developing countries' adjustment and financing requirements following the second oil shock and the 'potential problems' for them relating to the recycling of the OPEC surplus funds through the private banking system and in other ways.

By early 1980, it seemed justified to speak of potential problems because, since the end of 1979, the continuous progression towards easier terms and increased lending volumes which had characterised the market for medium-term bank credits over the last few years 'began to show some signs of reversing'[14] and market sentiment seemed about to change.

In particular, the political developments of 1979 such as the Iranian Revolution and the Soviet invasion of Afghanistan led to a growing uneasiness amongst bankers. US banks, in particular, were cautiously reducing their international activities, ceding place to European and Japanese banks and focusing more on the domestic market, given an increasing demand for loans and tightening monetary conditions. The IMF remarked that since 1977 the average annual increase of net international lending for all banks included in the BIS reporting system had been of the order of 25 per cent, compared to only 14 per cent for US-based banks. In the light of increasing risks, the financial community started to ask for stronger involvement from international organisations such as the Fund in the form of sound financial programmes.

Recycling through international capital markets was at the centre of two staff papers of the IMF prepared by the Exchange and Trade Relations Department[15] and of the mid-year discussion of the Executive Board in 1980.[16] The first paper recognised that:

> The present concern, which is shared by banks themselves, is much more clearly focused on the riskiness for banks of continued rapid expansion of exposure to cross-border risk . . . At the same time there is concern that *if banks do not in fact continue to increase their lending*, the recycling of the surpluses of oil exporting countries could break down, precipitating precisely the sort of crises for individual borrowers which underlie the uneasiness about expanded lending [emphasis added].[17]

The events seemed to point towards a recalibration of the lending spree of recent years. The same staff paper reported the bankers 'uneasiness' about continuing to lend to deficit-developing countries at the high rate of the previous years.

The second staff paper developed in greater detail the arguments of the first one and framed the present issues at stake in the context of the renewed 'battle' between controllers and free-marketeers which had emerged in the last years of the 1970s.

Once the effects of the first oil crisis seemed to have subsided, a renewed interest in regulation began to emerge by the late 1970s. Germany was, again, at the forefront of the battle. This time it had lost an ally, Switzerland, but gained a more powerful one, the United States.

After the successful experience of the first recycling and with the oil surpluses declining before the second oil crisis, the *Bundesbank* renewed its efforts to impose minimum reserve requirements on Eurodollar reserves on the same grounds as in the early 1970s, namely speculative pressures on the DM causing higher than optimal exchange rates and unemployment in the case of non-intervention, and increasing money supply and higher inflation in the case of intervention. In its Annual Report, the *Bundesbank* remarked that 'the accelerated expansion of both the Euro-markets and traditional foreign lending activities, together with the risks this involves, has given a *new impetus* to the discussion of the possibilities of exercising *better control* over international banking [emphasis added]'.[18] The United States argued that the worldwide demand for dollars, facilitated by the Euromarket, exerted a continuous pull on the supply of dollars.

In May 1979 the Federal Reserve prepared its proposal to control the Euromarket through the application of minimum reserve requirements akin to those existing in the home market.

Unfortunately, as the effects of the second oil crisis were starting to be felt, the American and German proposal to impose reserve requirements quickly ran

Central banks urge Euromarkets curbs

Figure 5.1 Renewed interest in regulating the Euromarket.

Source: *Financial Times*, 8 November 1979.

out of steam. As the *Financial Times* reported on 8 November 1979 (Figure 5.1) 'it would be difficult to impose US and West German style minimum reserve requirements on the banking system of other countries. Also, there is a fundamental opposition from Britain and Switzerland, which doubt whether such a far-reaching move is necessary'. Given the opposition of the most important centre of Eurofinance (the City of London), the two allies opted for the imposition of capital and liquidity ratios on banks' consolidated balance sheets. Just as in the earlier attempts to regulate the Euromarket, the timing was very unfortunate for the controllers.

The renewed interest in regulating the Euromarket and the American fervour further nuances the approach of existing narratives focusing on the hegemonic role of the US.[19] This second attempt to regulate the market, largely ignored by existing literature, seems to confirm that international finance in the 1970s was a more complex game than simply an American affair and that the attitude of the US was much more nuanced and less clear-cut than commonly assumed. Original material from American sources is needed to substantiate more thoroughly our claims, but it seems that the United States was not the hegemon able to impose its will on subservient states but a member of a complex international financial order where taking decisions was far more contentious than commonly assumed. Despite the 'downsizing' of the controllers' ambitions, the challenge of recycling represented an insurance on the Euromarket's life. As the *Financial Times* reported on 17 December 1979 'Central Banks from the main industrial countries, which have been discussing for several months the possibility of toughening controls on the Euromarket, now appear *unlikely to take any direct action* next year to curb the growth of international bank lending [emphasis added]'.[20]

Apart from the recycling challenge, the American proposal was received very coldly in Europe for practical and juridical reasons. Practical, because the mechanism would have involved a complex statistical apparatus in order to gather, on a consolidated basis, the daily accounts of branches, subsidiaries and offices of banks scattered around the world. Many developed countries would not be touched by these measures, putting participating banks at a disadvantage. Juridical problems would arise because of the lack of jurisdiction over foreign subsidiaries.

The second oil crisis was saving international finance, again. At a time when the Euromarket would continue to be called upon to recycle a large part of the increased surpluses of oil producers, a consensus was growing amongst central banks that '*undue interference* – the *Financial Times* concluded – *with the essentially free market for international loans would do more harm than good* [emphasis added]'. With the help of the second oil crisis, the Bank of England had won the second battle of Basel.

By early 1980, the balance between control of excessive risks and the smooth functioning of the Euromarket thus swung decisively in favour of the latter. The second IMF staff document recognised this 'cyclical pattern' of the attitude towards international capital flows, with a 'conservative' attitude prevailing in times of economic expansion (early 1970s and the period 1976–78) and a more 'liberal' attitude in times of economic contraction and disruption in international payments (1973–74 and 1979–80).

Ultimately, the Fund was profoundly sceptical of the usefulness of bank regulation and supervision and was in favour of a *laissez-faire* approach. The document noted that:

> [t]here is always a danger that *regulation can go too far* . . . In the long run *excessive regulation could reduce the efficiency of international banking*, causing spreads between lending and deposit rates to rise above the economically necessary levels . . . Another sort of danger is that changes in regulation and supervision . . . by their nature or the abruptness with which they are introduced could be disruptive in the short term [emphasis added].[21]

The views of the paper reflected what the Interim Committee (IC) of the Fund, the successor to the C-20, had deliberated in April that year in its fourteenth meeting in Hamburg. During the meeting, the IC 'while recognizing the need for prudential supervision, the Committee expressed concern that such *supervision should not impede recycling* [emphasis added]'.[22] On the same occasion, Sir Geoffrey Howe, the Chancellor of the Exchequer of the first Thatcher government, made this rather revealing remark:

> I have become more and more impressed by *how little governments can do directly to transform the behaviour of the economies for which they are responsible* . . . Our approach to the work of international institutions is . . . based on the reality that *it is probably the market and the influences of the marketplace which are . . . dominant and beneficent.* Of course . . . the market can sometimes go to the extremes, which cause avoidable harm, and it is our legitimate function to temper such consequences through the efforts of international collaboration for mutual benefit . . . Given prudence and care, I am convinced that the international banking system will again respond *with skill and . . . with more flexibility* than governments to the needs of the world after further oil prices increases [emphasis added].[23]

The mutual trust and the identity of interests between the financial community and politicians was strong like rarely before.

It is worth pointing out that, besides the members of the IC, Jacques de Larosière as Managing Director of the IMF, Alexandre Lamfalussy of the BIS, Emile Van Lennep of the OECD, Olivier Long of the General Agreement on Tariffs and Trade (GATT), René Ortiz of OPEC and François- Xavier Ortoli of the European Commission, as well as representatives of the United Nations Conference on Trade and Development (UNCTAD), United Nations (UN) and World Bank were present at the discussions. The IC functioned essentially as the Fund's main policy advisory body at the ministerial level from 1976 to 1999. Gradually, the Committee outgrew its merely advisory character and became the most important source of ministerial guidance, basically 'the Board of Governors . . . acquiesced in his role played by the IC'.[24]

The Governor of the Bank of England (and former Chairman of the merchant bank, Schroders), Gordon Richardson, mirrored the trust of the Chancellor of the Exchequer. In his speech at the annual banquet of the London Overseas Club on February 1980, Richardson remarked that:

> The last six years have clearly demonstrated that *international financial markets are resilient and constructive*. International banking activity has grown fourfold since the end of 1973 and with it has increased the ability of the banking system as a whole to take deposits and to lend on a large scale [emphasis added].[25]

After acknowledging the strength and efficiency of the Euromarket, he described the challenges ahead for a successful recycling: 'The greatly increased international exposure of the banks, recent political developments and the more cautious attitude on the part of monetary authorities across the world towards expansion in the Euromarkets may together temper the bank's willingness to lend'. Richardson then laid down the Bank's point of view on the appropriate recycling measures and the role of commercial banks: 'It is in the interest of all of us that the recycling operation should be carried through smoothly and efficiently; and *it is impossible to envisage a successful operation without a major contribution from international banking flows* [emphasis added]'. The long-established propensity towards 'soft' and autoregulation was reasserted. Ultimately, '*the primary responsibility for the prudent conduct of their business must lie with the banks* [emphasis added]'.[26] Commercial banks were both the players and the referees in the global financial arena.

With any proposal for the regulation of international finance crushed under the weight of around US$60 billion of surpluses in 1979 and around US$120 billion in 1980 (equivalent to around US$500 billion in current terms), the Executive Board of the IMF, convened on 6 August 1980, officialised this liberal position. Alternate Director Michael Casey of Ireland remarked that '*too much prudence* would clearly undermine the prospects for successful recycling [emphasis added]'.[27] Silvio E. Conrado of Nicaragua added that:

> [g]iven the contribution required from the private financial markets in the present recycling process, and the importance of the availability of a continuous

and smooth flow of funds he agreed that . . . in framing bank regulations, particular effort should be made to ensure that access to international bank lending by developing countries was not restricted.[28]

He insisted on the fact that all efforts had to be made to prevent a drastic reduction of funds available, or a sizable increase in their cost.[29] Mentré de Loye of France remarked that 'the Fund, through its contacts with the BIS and the financial authorities in individual countries, should do *all possible to encourage private recycling* [emphasis added]'.[30] One voice against the consensus view was, once more, that of Byanti Kharmawan of Indonesia, who 'strongly opposed' Mentré de Loye's call for closer cooperation between the Fund and commercial banks. He stressed that the Fund's activities 'should remain apart from those of commercial banks'[31]. Interestingly, international economist (and Executive Director of the IMF for 32 years) Alexandre Kafka of Brazil agreed with Kharmawan.

With the regulators not willing to regulate, the risk of controls neutralised, huge sums of petrodollars to invest and a lack of alternative plans, the Euromarket could continue untroubled to function as the main recycling instrument despite worrying signs. As the BIS remarked in 1980: 'the international banking sector continued to act as a principal outlet for the OPEC surpluses and as a major source of credit both for the industrial countries and, after some hesitancy in the earlier part of the year, for the developing world.[32]

By the end of 1980, the external claims of banks in the G-10, Switzerland, Austria, Denmark, Ireland, and the branches of US banks in the offshore centres of the Caribbean and Far East, increased by almost 20 per cent compared to 1979 to reach US$1,323 billion. International bank lending grew by 26 per cent or US$165 billion.

Not surprisingly, the most important factor behind the growth of international capital was the continued effect of the second wave of oil surpluses. A second factor was represented by the supply of funds by American banks and the weakness of the Eurobond and international bond market because of the inverted yield curve. Interest rate volatility and exchange rate uncertainties were a third important element and, finally, as the BIS noted, 'the rapid growth of lending observed last year was made possible by the continued efforts of the large commercial banks *to expand the international side of their business* [emphasis added]'.[33]

On the demand side, the need to finance import bills by developed and developing countries played the lion's share. Mexico was the biggest borrower of 1980 with US$10.4 billion, followed by Brazil with US$6.5 billion and Argentina with US$5.8 billion. The BIS recognised bluntly that it would seem very unlikely they would see the international flows of non-bank capital taking over the role played by the banks.[34] The reality was that no one was active in the quest for alternatives to the recycling of petrodollars through commercial banks.

Even though the growth of the outstanding public and publicly guaranteed medium- and long-term external debt was remarkable (according to some IMF statistics it stood at US$250 billion by the end of 1979, twice the amount of 1975 and three times the amount of 1973),[35] it is worth stressing the shifts in the composition of LDC debt since the first oil shock. By the end of the 1970s long-term debt to private creditors approached almost 50 per cent of the total outstanding, while at the end of 1973 only one-third of it was in private hands.

What is more, in the early 1970s the component held by private creditors was divided about evenly between financial institutions and other private lenders. By the end of the decade, the picture was radically different. As the end of 1979 approached, almost 80 per cent of the privately held debt was in the hands of private financial institutions, reflecting the increasingly prominent role of international commercial banks in lending to developing countries during the decade.[36]

The BIS opposed the proposed measures to control the international activities of banks on the same grounds as the Fund, namely that they would limit the smooth functioning of the recycling mechanism; nevertheless, it welcomed a bigger role for the IMF but only in order to reassure the markets and complement the action of commercial banks. For the BIS, despite some minor over-lending phenomena in the past, the role of the banks had been irreplaceable and the future looked, on the whole, bright: 'There is reason to believe that the banks can continue to play a major role in international lending *without problems* arising that would undermine the functioning of the adjustment process and the soundness of international financial markets [emphasis added]'.[37] Reality would quickly prove them wrong.

In December 1980, the picture was clear. Despite minor changes, the recycling process would remain a matter in the hands of commercial banks. The position was made explicit in a meeting between a task force on oil recycling of the IMF and a group of international bankers in Mexico in October 1980. Despite the efforts of the IMF in modifying its activities by increasing its emphasis on supply programmes and by permitting countries to draw up to 600 per cent of quota in certain circumstances, it had become evident that '*the Fund can never be a complete substitute for commercial bank financing* [emphasis added]'.[38]

The writing's on the wall

The year 1981 brought the worst recession in the US since the Great Depression, while worsening terms of trade brought the world one step closer to the edge of chaos. For the developing world, the sluggishness of economic activity in the West depressed growth and worsened their terms of trade. Deteriorating terms of trade, together with rising interest rates, aggravated their debt-servicing burden and wiped out most of the benefits coming from the decline in the price of oil. For the first time since the end of the Second World War, the industrial world was confronted with a peculiar situation. On the one hand, in the battle with inflation there had been some notable successes, while developments in the oil market had removed a powerful factor of disequilibrium in international payments; on the other, rising unemployment in the industrial countries and the alarming worsening of the position of the developing countries represented a growing source of concern.

The situation was becoming trickier than expected and the BIS Annual Report of 1982 reported that 'Between the Scylla of a renewed acceleration of inflation and the Charybdis of protracted stagnation the path looks extremely narrow'.[39]

In fact, real GNP amongst major industrial countries (except Japan) ranged between 3 per cent for Canada and −1.0 per cent for the UK, with Italy at −0.2 per cent, Germany at −0.3 per cent and France at +0.2 per cent.[40] In the developing world, growth was slowing, inflation was rising and debt/export ratios were increasing at an alarming pace as we can see from Table 5.1. Despite the worsening situation in Latin America, the first troubles in the developing world emerged in Eastern Europe, more precisely in Poland, in the second quarter of 1981 as a result of a marked slowdown in economic activity, a rise in unemployment because of the recessionary influences of their capitalist neighbours, strikes organised by the independent union organisation *Solidarnosc* ('Solidarity') formed in August 1980 by Lech Walesa, and increasingly costly industrialisation programmes by President Edward Gierek.[41]

Facing the prospect of repaying, just in 1981, US$678 million to German, US$575 million to American, US$378 million to French and US$220 million to British banks, Poland (the largest market for commercial banks in the socialist world outside the Soviet Union) had to acknowledge to the international financial community its inability to pay its annual debt charges.[42]

On 31 March, the representatives of the 23 biggest creditor banks were convened at Armourer's Hall in the City of London for a meeting with Bank Handlowy, the Polish Bank for foreign trade, to discuss refinancing the debt falling due in 1981. The meeting was followed by an official telex on 8 April, when Poland confirmed its inability to meet the repayments on its debt due between 27 March and 30 June.[43] In August 1981, another socialist country, Romania, encountered difficulties in repaying its external debt. The Romanian Bank for Foreign Trade (RBFT) was in arrears with US$590 million of repayments of interbank credits and by October, total payment delays had reached US$1.5 billion. The regionalisation syndrome also affected Hungary, which had to ask for the intervention of the BIS and became a member of the IMF in May 1982. Until the Mexican default, Poland was the biggest fish, up to that point, being caught in the net of debt. Despite that, the WP3 of the OECD, writing at the end of April 1981, seemed to ignore the writing on the wall, insisting that 'at present there is little evidence that the international financial system is in general danger of being seriously eroded through large-scale default by NODCs [Non-oil developing countries]'.[44] The confidence

Table 5.1 Economic situation in heavily indebted countries.

	Average 1969–78	1979	1980	1981	1982	1983	1984
Per capita GDP (annual change)	3.6	3.6	2.6	−1.6	−2.7	−5.5	−0.1
Inflation (annual rate)	28.5	40.8	47.4	53.2	57.7	90.8	116.4
Debt/export ratio	N/A	182.3	167.1	201.4	268.8	289.7	272.1

Source: Jeffrey D. Sachs (ed.), *Developing Country Debt and the World Economy*, University of Chicago Press, Chicago and London, 1989, 2. Data refer to 15 heavily indebted countries: Argentina, Bolivia, Brazil, Chile, Colombia, Côte d'Ivoire, Ecuador, Mexico, Morocco, Nigeria, Peru, Philippines, Uruguay, Venezuela, Yugoslavia. Data are from the IMF World Economic Outlook, April 1987. Inflation refers to the consumer prices index (CPI).

of international organisations came in part from the so-called 'Umbrella doctrine' which made creditors believe that the Soviet Union would not let a member of the Council for Mutual Economic Assistance go bankrupt.

By the middle of 1981, the full impact of the second round of oil price escalations was becoming clearer. In its 'World Economic Outlook' of August 1981, the IMF estimated the current account surpluses of oil-exporting countries to have increased from US$4.5 billion in 1978, to US$69 billion in 1979 and around US$115 billion in 1980. Over the same period, the current account balances of the industrial countries swung from a combined surplus of US$29 billion in 1979, to a deficit of US$14 billion in 1979 and US$54 billion in 1980. Non-oil developing countries experienced an even worse deterioration, with their combined deficit increasing by US$36 billion in 1978 to US$56 billion in 1979 and to US$72 billion in 1980.[45]

World economic growth was indeed faltering under the weight of restrictive measures by all major industrial countries. In the OECD countries, growth rates declined, on average, from 3.4 per cent in 1979 to 1.2 per cent in 1980 and 1.0 per cent in 1981.[46] In the developing world, inflation continued to rise throughout the year, while terms of trade continued to deteriorate, reflecting increases in US dollar import prices and decreasing export prices.

Between March and April 1981, a staff team of the Fund made another round of informal meetings with bankers, bank supervisory authorities and international organisations. The team reported that, despite several worrisome elements, bankers appeared less concerned than the previous year about the risk of lending to developing countries as they seem more inclined to focus on economic fundamentals – the potential strength of the economies of most of the major borrowers – rather than simply on the enormity of the financial magnitude involved.[47]

The second half of 1981 was characterised by high but decelerating inflation amongst industrial countries because of the restrictive demand-management policies associated with rising unemployment, escalating inflation in the developing world, a marked decrease in output growth in the industrial world reflecting the US recession started in July 1981 and deflationary policies in the UK and, finally, persisting current account imbalances across the globe. From the monetary point of view, the main characteristics of 1981 were the persistently high interest rates hampering new investments, weakening the financial structure of businesses and increasing the debt-servicing burden of developing countries. On a more positive note, by the end of the year, the OPEC surpluses had been almost completely wiped out because of the economic contraction and the introduction of energy conservation policies with the replacement of other energy sources for oil.

The apparent 'paradox of the 1970s' persisted in the early 1980s; against a backdrop of macro-economic instability, 1981 was another year of strong growth in the international financial markets and banks. The gross external assets of the BIS reporting banks grew (on an exchange-rate adjusted basis) by US$268 billion, compared to US$242 billion in 1980, and by 21.5 per cent or US$165 billion on a net basis, bringing the total stock of funds channelled through the international banking sector to about US$940 billion at the end of 1981.

The geographical pattern of the sources changed markedly. New deposits from OPEC countries declined to just US$3 billion, but this decline was compensated by new funds coming from the United States. External assets of banks in the US rose by US$76.5 billion. Yet the pattern of uses remained almost unchanged. Non-oil developed countries continued to be the biggest customers of international commercial banks.

Non-OPEC developing countries did not benefit from the decline of OPEC surpluses. The high interest rates continued to negatively affect their debt-servicing burden, and the stagnation in the industrial world continued to prove detrimental to their exports. Consequently, the current account deficits of the developing world continued to worsen. The BIS reporting banks' claims on these countries rose by US$41.6 billion to a total of US$230 billion. Latin American countries continued to account for the largest share of new borrowing, receiving around three-quarters of new credits, i.e. US$32.6 billion. The biggest individual borrowers were Mexico (US$14.2 billion), Brazil (US$6.5 billion) and Argentina (US$4 billion). Outside the Latin American region, South Korea (US$3 billion) was the largest borrower. Eastern Europe suffered from the consequences of the Polish situation and received in total only US$4.8 billion in new credits compared to US$7 billion in 1980. Almost all new credits were contracted by the Soviet Union and the German Democratic Republic.

All in all, the situation at the end of 1981 was similar to that following the first oil shock, with a large net outflow of new capital from the main industrial countries through the international banking sector to the rest of the world.[48] After several meagre years, activity on the Eurobond and foreign bond market picked up again too despite the uncertain economic context: gross new issues amounted to US$47.8 billion (US$30 billion on a net basis), up by US$10 billion on 1980.[49]

By the end of 1981, the external assets of banks in reporting European countries grew by US$136 billion to a total of US$992 billion. The main Euromarket centre in Europe remained the UK, where the external assets in foreign currencies of banks expanded by US$74.7 billion, accounting for 63 per cent of the total increase for all reporting European banks.[50] The external claims of banks in the US rose by US$76.5 billion and their liabilities by US$38 billion. The remarkable growth in gross external assets of banks in the US was partly the result of the creation by the Federal Reserve Board of the so-called International Banking Facilities (IBF) in December 1981. The purpose of IBFs was to allow banking offices to conduct a deposit and loan business with foreign residents, including foreign banks, without being subject to reserve requirements or to the interest rate ceiling then in effect.[51] The facilities were exempt from the insurance coverage and assessments imposed by the Federal Deposit Insurance Corporation (FDIC). As a result, the banking offices located in the US could conduct transactions with foreign residents in a regulatory environment very similar to the Euromarket without the need to use an offshore facility.

The situation for the global economy looked extremely shaky by the end of 1981. Global economic growth was faltering under the weight of restrictive demand-management policies in the industrial world while the developing world was more and more entangled in a debt spiral made worse by declining export prices and increasing debt-servicing ratios. It is important to analyse in the next section how the commercial banks in our story behaved after the second oil crisis and how they dealt with increasing challenges.

Further expansion and increasing risks

For European banks, the new decade continued where the 1970s had ended. Overall, the European banking sector continued its outward expansion into new countries, products and ventures before receiving a rude wake-up call in 1982. The literature on European banking history is still limited on the 1970s and almost totally non-existent for the 1980s; the general tendency has been to play down the role of European banks and focus on their American counterparts. This assumption is incorrect and must be rejected for two main reasons. First, European banks were important actors in the Euromarket and, subsequently, in the recycling business. Edwin M. Truman, Director of the International Finance Division of the Board of Governors of the Federal Reserve System from 1977 to 1998, wrote in 1986:

> It is important to remember that claims on these [developing] countries are held by banks in many countries – not just by banks in the United States. The share of U.S. banks in total bank claims on developing countries and Eastern Europe can be estimated at less than 25 percent as of the middle of 1986. *U.S. banks hold one quarter of all banks' claims on non-OPEC developing countries, less than one fifth of claims on OPEC members, and less than one tenth of claims on Eastern Europe* [emphasis added].[52]

The second reason is that, by the early 1970s, European banks had successfully pushed back the American threat and now figured amongst the biggest and most active in the world. According to the magazine *The Banker* (Table 5.2), in 1980 only two American banks figured in the global top ten, BankAmerica and Citicorp, respectively at numbers four and six. All the other banks were European. *Crédit Lyonnais* was in second place, *Société Générale* in fifth, Barclays in tenth. Looking at pre-tax earnings, the picture is not radically different. Barclays was in first place, Midland in fifth, Lloyds in seventh while BankAmerica figured in third and Citicorp in fourth. Consequently, both in terms of sheer size and in terms of involvement in the developing world, European banks were crucial actors in the game. In terms of average total international assets, BBI alone (US$ 44.2 billion) was comparable to Bank of America (US$44.3 billion) and Chase (US$38.3 billion). In terms of manpower, BBI employed 41,000 people, LBI 11,000, Citicorp 27,000, Bank of America 21,000 and Chase 13,000.[53]

The challenges and opportunities faced by continental banks that we have previously introduced, namely internationalisation, cooperation, autonomous initiatives and internal reorganisations, developed in different ways from before and a new challenge made its way into our banks' strategies: exposure.

Table 5.2 Performance of international banks 1980.

Bank	By pre-tax earnings US$m(% on assets)	Bank	By deposits US$m
1 Barclays Group	1,178 (1.95)	1 Banque Nationale de Paris	97,383
2 National Westminster	982 (1.73)	2 Crédit Lyonnais	89,820
3 BankAmerica	948 (0.97)	3 Credit Agricole	85,560
4 Citicorp	871 (0.93)	4 BankAmerica	84,985
5 Midlands Bank	703 (1.77)	5 Société Générale	76,809
6 Deutsche Bank	634 (0.72)	6 Citicorp	70,291
7 Lloyds Bank	616 (1.72)	7 Dresdner Bank	66,715
8 Chase Manhattan	550 (0.90)	8 Deutsche Bank	61,825
9 Compagnie Financière de Paris et des Pays Bas	492 (1.79)	9 National Westminster Bank	59,043
10 Banco do Brasil	485 (1.32)	10 Barclays Group	58,504

Source: *The Banker*, Top 500, June 1980.

Internationalisation continued to be the number one priority for most European banks until the crisis of 1982. Barclays pursued its expansion notably in Asia and the United States; Lloyds aggressively expanded in Latin America and the Middle East; Midland focused on Western Europe, Australasia and the US. Unfortunately, the American banking market looked like a 'market for lemons' in the 1970s and Midland bought one of the biggest of them all. Ultimately, Lloyds and Midland were badly affected by their international expansion. Midland had a 'disadvantage of backwardness' and was too eager to make up for time lost in correspondent banking by acquiring a major American bank without the necessary due diligence. The French banks continued to focus on traditional French exporting areas, with a particular emphasis on Eastern Europe, Latin America and South East Asia. Their international expansion was based on the assumption of a sustained growth in international trade and expansion of French companies able to compensate for slackening domestic activity. When the crisis erupted, this model was largely impaired, according to a study of the French Banking Commission; the net profits of the foreign branches of 24 banks between 1978 and 1984 grew from FF340.9 million to FF1,262 million to represent 19.4 per cent and 53.7 per cent of global profits. Afterwards, profits fell sharply to FF380.9 millions (18.3 per cent of global profits) as a consequence of debt provisions.[54]

After reaching its zenith in the mid-1970s, the 1980s would mark the end of cooperative banking. Clubs and consortia represented a crucial and cost-effective link between two different visions of international banking, the scattered and independent initiatives of the 1950s and 1960s and the autonomous initiatives of the 1980s onwards; and herein lies their merit.

Nevertheless, by the early 1980s, clubs and consortia saw their intrinsic limits gradually becoming liabilities, since the efforts required to keep them afloat outweighed the benefits.

While cooperative initiatives de facto ended in the early 1980s, the autonomous initiatives continued to flourish despite the clouds gathering on the horizon. This time, the bulk of the new overseas investments were independent initiatives, unlike the first part of the decade. The autonomous initiatives became gradually more and more ambitious. Gaining a foothold in the United States became the ultimate goal of many European banks, reversing the situation prevailing just a few years before when American banks were building up their presence in Europe.

The ambitious and continued activity on international markets produced increasing risks for banks, with excessive exposure became a looming threat on the banks' outlook. As anticipated, the quantity of loans to LDCs reached sky-high levels and, in a context of restrictive monetary policies and decreasing commodity prices, servicing these loans became untenable.

The crisis of 1982 would represent a transformative moment for the European banking sector. Under the weight of the large exposure to developing countries, most commercial banks put aside the 'big-at-any-cost' strategy and re-focused their activities on a more manageable number of products and markets. The most visible example of the reorganisations of the 1980s is Lloyds Bank. As we will see, under the new CEO, Sir Brian Pitman, and the Chairmanship of Sir Jeremy Morse, the Bank decided to 'domesticise' its activities by focusing primarily on the British market. The strategy would prove extremely successful and Lloyds gradually became the most profitable bank in the UK and one of the most profitable in the world.

At the opposite of the spectrum, we find Midland. As we will see further on in this chapter, the acquisition of Crocker proved to be a total failure, for the Bank was extremely exposed to the Latin American market, a factor concealed during the phase of negotiations. The French banks decided to limit their international expansion and also to focus on improving profitability. As Edward Gardener and Philip Molyneux argued:

> The 1982 debt crisis provided a further impetus for banks to focus their attentions elsewhere in order to compensate for the lengthening maturity structure of their loan books as well as the decreasing value of their assets. This led to a broad reassessment of the nature of credits risks and credit standards, and also reduced banks' previous emphasis on balance-sheet growth 'at any cost'. It was a major fillip to the securitization phenomena.[55]

Indeed, by the second half the 1980s, new challenges were looming. Disintermediation, deregulation and the creation of the European Union in 1992 represented further challenges and opportunities to European commercial banks. A new period of transformation ensued which would further transform the face of European banking.

Global overstretch

During the early 1980s, the path of internationalisation was not modified despite increasingly alarming signs coming from the periphery. Barclays remained the most conservative of the clearers and continued to focus mostly on North America and Asia while gradually limiting its presence in Latin America. Its deposits, current and other accounts in that region declined from around 7 per cent in 1980 to just 2.45 per cent by 1982.[56] Lloyds, on the other hand, continued to bet heavily on Latin America and would pay harsh for this decision. Midland focused on Asia and North America. The French banks continued to expand in socialist countries, Latin America, the Middle East and South East Asia. Ultimately, the banking sector was overstretched, with too many representations in the developing world bringing too few profits and far too many risks.

As we mentioned in Chapter 4, the change at the helm of BBI did not modify the route. Barclays continued to be more conservative in its operations than its smaller competitors such as Lloyds and Midland. Its policy would ultimately prove correct and Barclays weathered the LDC debt crisis better than most of its direct competitors

Even though certain authors have criticised the post-Tuke era,[57] BBI remained an extremely profitable company throughout the 1970s and early 1980s: between 1971 and 1977, profit growth ranged between 13 per cent in 1973 to 62 per cent in 1977, an average of 23 per cent.[58] BBI contributed £381 million towards the total Group profit of £562 million in 1982.

The 1977–81 Corporate Plan outlined BBI's strategy: developing integrated wholly owned subsidiaries and wholesale branches especially in North America (Canada and US), Western Europe (Belgium, Holland, Switzerland, France and West Germany) and South East Asia and Australasia (Australia, Japan, Singapore, New Zealand, South Korea and Hong Kong). The Middle East was a priority, but several political constraints were pending. The efforts were devoted to deriving at least 60 per cent of the Group's profits from areas other than the African continent by 1981.

The plan involved £25 million of new investments in Europe and North America, £15 million in the Middle and Far East, £7 million in the Caribbean and Latin America and £12 million in the remaining countries.[59]

In 1980 the minority interest of Nomura Securities (33 per cent) in the Hong-Kong-based merchant bank, Trident International Finance, was bought for £28 million and the Bank was renamed Barclays Asia (the other partner, Merrill Lynch, having been bought out in 1976). In the US, Barclays Bank of New York bought 31 branches from Bankers Trust Company in the State of New York, bringing the number of branches to 64. New offices were opened in Miami, Seattle and Dallas.

The Far East occupied a special place in BBI's strategy. Chairman Lambert personally visited the region in October 1980, spending one week in Japan, a few days in Seoul and Hong Kong and, finally, 11 days in China at the invitation of the Bank of China. As usual, these visits included meeting with high-ranking officials at the central banks, commercial banks, Ministry of Finance, etc. The strengths, weaknesses, opportunities and threats faced by BBI can be aptly summarised in a SWOT matrix (Figure 5.2). The strengths consisted mainly in the vast overseas network, the overall state of Barclays' financial position and the name, which was certainly one of the most recognisable in the market. Still further possibilities to

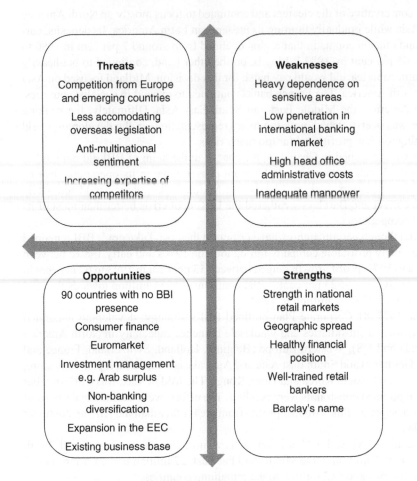

Figure 5.2 BBI's SWOT matrix as of 1978.

Source: BBA, 80/5912, 'BBI strategy: 1979–1983', 29 March 1978.

expand existed as around 90 countries had no BBI presence and the Euromarket had huge growth potential, as did the management of oil surpluses. Threats and weaknesses were represented by increasing competition, heavy dependence on some sensitive areas in the developing world and by the difficulty in finding adequate manpower in a context of sustained growth.

Lambert's trip to China proved positive. In 1981 BBI received the authorisation from the Bank of China to open a representative office in Beijing, providing 'a valuable stepping stone for the Bank and its customers to this huge but largely untapped market'.[60]

In New Zealand, BBI now held a 49.8 per cent stake in the New Zealand United Corporation, a merchant bank. In Latin America, a representative office was inaugurated in Colombia. In Europe, BBI bought an 85 per cent stake in the *Banco de Valladolid*, gaining a considerable presence in Spain, which was at that time negotiating its accession to the EEC. Representative offices were also opened in Lisbon and Stockholm.

In the US, new offices were opened in Miami, Seattle, New Orleans, Cleveland, Minneapolis and Dallas. An Edge Act corporation, Barclays International Banking Corporation, was inaugurated in Houston. An IBF was established in December in New York. Following the acquisition of Aetna Business Credit, Barclays America Corporation was renamed Barclays America/Business Credit, Inc. The expansion in the US partly reflected the views expressed in an internal note to the Chair and general managers prepared by Peter Stuart Ardron,[61] General Manager responsible for the International Division. The document saw in the changes in US banking legislation a great threat to European banks, since these changes would most probably involve a wave of mergers and acquisitions.

The result would be that by the end of the 1980s 'our main international competitors, Citibank, Bank of America and Chase, are going to be mammoth banks and become almost unbeatable on the international banking scene because of their sheer size'.[62] In order not to be dwarfed by the American competitors, European banks had to fight back and do something. In the eyes of Barclays, French banks were not good candidates to lead the pack, since they were 'bemoaning their fate under the fear of further nationalisation and having to live with Mitterrand and a Socialist regime for the next five years [in reality Mitterrand would remain president for 14 years]'.[63] Other candidates included German and British banks. In the early 1980s, German banking was in poor shape as *Dresdner*, *Hypo-Bank* and *West-Deutsche Landesbank* had all reduced their dividends, while *Commerzbank* paid no dividend at all. Share prices were at all-time lows, and legislation to require them to consolidate the activities of their subsidiaries in Luxembourg was underway at the *Bundestag*. Therefore, the document concluded that 'the onus seems to be on us'.[64] Expansion in the US was part of this effort to counteract the overseas expansion of American banks and the acquisition of a controlling interest in a major bank was being considered at that time. Another part of the counter-offensive was to strengthen the Bank's position in crucial European markets, notably Germany. The outright purchase of *Commerzbank* or the acquisition of a controlling interest in *Dresdner Bank* (thanks to the common interest in ABECOR and SFE) were both considered in 1981. Even an approach to *Deutsche Bank* was mentioned but, because of its close relations with Midland and its strategic position as the number one bank in the country, the option was quickly discarded. To finalise the counter-offensive plan and to create a 'worldwide banking empire [sic]' an association with a Japanese bank such as the Bank of Tokyo, *Dai-Ichi Kangyo* or *Sumitomo* was envisioned. The document concluded that:

[c]learly International Banking is going to change as much in the next twenty years as it has in the last two decades and these suggestions for discussion are made with a view to ensuring that we are still in the forefront of World Banking at the end of the century.[65]

In 1981 the Bankers Trust of Hudson Valley was acquired, bringing a further 26 branches to the American network. By the end of that year, BBI had more than 2,000 offices in over 80 countries and around 54,000 employees. South Africa and Namibia now accounted for only 15 per cent of deposits, current and other accounts, the Caribbean and Latin America for 8 per cent, Europe for 14 per cent, the UK, from which the Euro-business was routed, for 40 per cent and North America for 11 per cent. Asia accounted for 6 per cent while the rest of Africa accounted for less than 5 per cent. The Tuke era came to a definitive end in 1981, when Sir Anthony decided to quit the chairmanship of Barclays Limited (albeit remaining a director until 1990) and took the helm of Rio Tinto Zinc. During his chairmanship, the Group's balance sheet had tripled and new offices had been opened in 28 countries, as we can see from Figure 5.3. The Tuke years marked the apex of the international ambitions of Barclays up to that point and he made a crucial contribution to transforming the Bank into a truly global and not merely a multinational one. Timothy Bevan, heir of Francis Augustus Bevan, the first Chairman of Barclays, was nominated as the new Chairman, perpetuating the tradition of giving the chairmanship to heirs of the 'funding fathers' (the two Goodenough's remained the only chairmen recruited outside the family circles until 1987).

As we have seen, until the late 1950s, BOLSA was primarily an overseas bank with a presence in Latin America, New York and the Iberian Peninsula. With the appearance of Eurodollars, the business of BOLSA started to change by assuming a growing international financial role in the provision of medium-term Eurodollar credits out of London. Nevertheless, the activities on the unregulated Eurodollar market did not radically modify the structure and scope of Lloyds, which remained 'a relatively small bank, becoming more internationally oriented but still mainly retail in outlook, with only limited representation in the major financial capitals of continental Europe'.[66]

The international ambitions of Lloyds were reinforced by the events of 1971 and, especially, of 1973. The acquisition of 100 per cent ownership of LBI marked the desire to extend the Bank's geographic presence into all the major financial centres of the world and to develop its capability in international capital markets. Once the Strategic Review of 1979 had been implemented, a new policy guidance for the financial year 1980–81 was laid down by the Chief Executive, Eric Y. Whittle. LBI's corporate objectives, as approved by the Group board and LBI board, were four: first, to recognise growth as a measure of strength and a requirement for survival; second, to develop globally a diversified financial services organisation continuously seeking new opportunities for growth; third, to avoid excessive concentrations of capital, assets and earnings in any single country; and, fourth, to attain a profitable growth capable of putting LBI in the top 30 banks in the world.[67]

At the heart of LBI's new strategy was the concept of 'niche'. The market strategy was based on market segmentation and concentration on chosen segments/countries. LBI could rely on its existing global network, its international experience and expertise and on the size and reputation of the Lloyds Group.

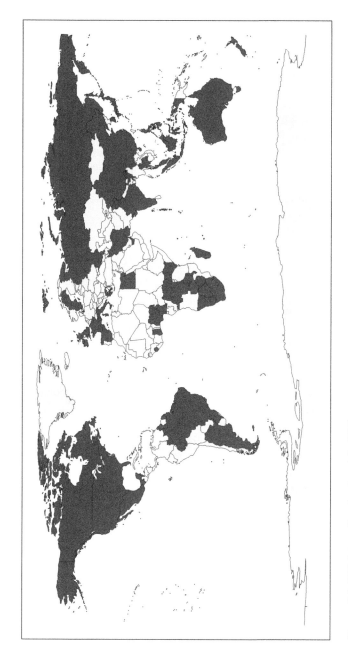

Figure 5.3 BBI International network in 1981.

Source: BBA, 'A world of banking 1981'.

The Latin American presence was seen as a 'competitive advantage' and the region continued to be the most important source of profits to LBI.

As for target markets, multinational corporations came in first place, followed by local companies with international operations and the 'big and growing' government market. Trade finance and fee-earning services were the two product priorities. Implicit in these plans was the need for continuing geographical expansion. There was still great scope for manoeuvre for LBI, since it had representations in 44 countries compared to over 90 for Citibank and over 80 for Barclays.

Specifically, the expansion in Europe involved the upgrading of the Milan representative office to a branch and further investments in Spain, Portugal, France and Germany. Focusing on merchant banking services, such as medium-term syndicated lending and Eurobond issues, was a priority. In order to do this, special attention was to be devoted to activities in Switzerland, Paris, Cannes, Monte Carlo and Guernsey.

In the Far East, substantial growth was planned. Further opportunities in Australia and South Korea were examined. New branches were to be opened in Hong Kong. Other countries of particular interest were Singapore, Taiwan, Sri Lanka, Indonesia, Malaysia, Thailand and China.

In July 1980 Lord Armstrong, Midland's Chairman since 1975 and former 'right hand' of Prime Minister Edward Heath, died and was succeeded by the 'stop-gap' Chairman, Sir David Barran.

The first year of Barran's presidency was not exceptional. Pre-tax profits amounted to £232 million, a reduction of £84 million compared to 1979, which had been a record year for the Bank. The sluggish growth was the result of increasing costs and provisions for bad debts, which increased from £12 million to £83 million.[68]

Nonetheless, the 'Own Initiative', implemented in 1974, continued its course: direct presence especially in Europe and the US remained a priority. The two major developments of the year were the preliminary agreement with Crocker National Corporation of California and the purchase of a majority shareholding in the West German private bank *Trinkhaus und Burkhardt* (T&B) from Citibank.

The acquisition of a controlling interest in T&B, provided Midland with a new tool to penetrate the German corporate market, thanks to its branches in several German cities and its presence in Switzerland and Luxembourg. The purchase complemented the French activities of Midland Bank France and BCT Midland Bank. An EEC representative office was inaugurated that same year.

The number of employees working across the globe continued to rise. In 1976 Midland had around 63,000 employees, in 1978 around 69,000 and in 1981 almost 83,000.

Together with North America and Western Europe, a growing field of expansion for Midland was the Asia Pacific region. Up to 1974, business was conducted almost exclusively through correspondent banking in each country. As we have seen previously, this policy of exclusive reliance of correspondent networks was supplemented by direct representations starting from the reorganisation of 1974. It is worth outlining the major developments in that strategic region.

In South East Asia, the most important markets were Singapore, Hong Kong, China and Japan. By the early 1980s, a branch was inaugurated in Singapore as well as a merchant bank, Midland Montagu Asia, jointly owned by Midland and its controlled merchant bank, Samuel Montagu. The location was particularly useful to cover the time zone between Bahrain and Tokyo, where Midland already had branches. In Hong Kong, an existing representative office was upgraded to a branch, and an allied deposit-taking company, Midland Finance (H. K.) was formed to complement the branch's operations and operate in foreign exchange dealing and in the syndicated Eurocurrency lending. The most important opening of 1980 was the inauguration in November of the Beijing representative office, the first bank in Europe. The first branch had been opened in 1978 in Tokyo.

In Australasia, the banking presence was assured by the participation of Samuel Montagu in the merchant bank, Capel Court, and by Midland's participation in the Euro-Pacific Finance Corporation, with branches in Melbourne, Sydney and Brisbane.

The growth of the international activities of French banks had been astonishing throughout the 1970s. As the *Banque de France* remarked, in 1970 the foreign activities of French banks accounted for just 14 per cent of the total balance sheet while they accounted for 35 per cent a decade later.[69]

The paths of international development of *Société Générale* and *Crédit Lyonnais* followed the course established in the second half of the 1970s without major shake-ups. *Société Générale* maintained its focus on the major international financial centres, on traditional French exporting areas (Francophone Africa, the European Common Market and socialist Europe), on North America and, finally, on three crucial areas which emerged after the oil crisis: OPEC countries, Latin America and South East Asia.

In Eastern Europe, *Société Générale* had an extensive network made up of representative offices in Moscow, Warsaw, Berlin East, Sofia and Prague, a subsidiary in Budapest and a branch in Bucharest. In North America, after the reopening of the New York branch in 1979, other offices were added in Houston and Los Angeles.

In the developing world, new branches were inaugurated in the Arab Emirates, Bahrain, Oman and Nigeria and representative offices were opened in Mexico and Venezuela. The existing presence in Latin America was reinforced with a new branch in Panama, devoted to offshore banking and financial operations, and the acquisition of a 24 per cent stake in *Banco Sogeral* in Brazil.

In South East Asia, *Société Générale* had a regional head office in Singapore. Subsidiaries were located in Seoul, Jakarta and Sydney while branches were located in Hong Kong, Singapore, Manila and Taipei. There were representative offices in Indonesia, Thailand and China (Beijing and Canton). The contribution of the overseas network to the consolidated results of *Société Générale* amounted to 32 per cent in 1980, compared to 27 per cent in 1979 and just 19 per cent in 1978.

Crédit Lyonnais remained particularly focused on socialist countries (USSR, East Germany and Poland), Latin America, the Middle East and Asia Pacific. The latter half of the 1970s and early 1980s would mark the low ebb of the cooperation, as it had been for other banks in our study. Between 1976 and 1981, syndicated rollover Eurocredits managed by DOFI increased from US$1.1 billion to US$2.3 billion. However, the share of DOFI in the total amount of financial operations decreased from 56.8 per cent to 38.4 per cent. This was the result of the increasing number of operations being managed by foreign branches.[70]

By the early 1980s, *Crédit Lyonnais* was active in 41 countries: in 15 countries it had branches and in 26 of them subsidiaries or associated banks. By 1980, the total balance sheet of foreign branches was FF150 billion and by 1981 it had increased to FF212 billion.[71]

Growing exposure and declining profitability

The continued international expansion brought along increasing risks to most European banks. Barclays can be considered partially an outlier given its more limited exposure to LDC debt than its peers. We attribute this result to the experience of international markets accumulated since the creation of DCO in the 1920s and the size of its existing network at the time of its international expansion in the early 1970s. Barclays entered the 1970s with a well-defined network and, probably because of the conservative ambience dominating the Bank where the founding families still exerted their influence, did not radically alter its priorities, preferring to develop its network along the same lines. Essentially, we could argue that Barclays grew *organically* from its existing outposts while other banks, like Lloyds, saw their international expansion radically altered by the acquisition of a regionally focused bank like BOLSA, which was subsequently implanted on an existing structure. Lloyds continued to expand in Latin America despite the numerous writings on the wall, with important losses in early 1980s in Argentina, considered the 'jewel in the crown' of LBI's network.

Midland is another case of a bank that expanded too quickly overseas without the necessary competences after half a century of correspondent banking. As we have already remarked, on the creation of its International Division, Midland had no foreign branches or subsidiaries and just four representative offices. The acquisition of Crocker weakened its balance sheet and inflicted important losses. The two-headed management structure did not play in Midland's favour, as the two general managers undertook separate responsibilities and held different views on the future expansion of the Bank. *Société Générale* expanded further in Latin America by opening a branch in Panama in 1981. Cooperation entered its terminal phase as *Société Générale* reopened its branch in New York. *Crédit Lyonnais* became even more aggressive in the Eurocurrency business, bought two new banks, one in Argentina and one in the Netherlands. The Europartners de facto ceased to exist as more and more branches were opened in neighbouring countries invalidating one of the purposes of banking clubs, i.e. not competing on each other's turf.

During the years up to 1982, European commercial banks overall continued to make profits, but profitability, after reaching a high in the years 1979–80, boosted by the second oil crisis, entered a decline. Profits required ever more capital and increasing leverage. As we can see from Table 5.3, British banks remained the

Table 5.3 Bank profitability (pre-tax earnings on assets %) of selected banks in different countries, 1979–82.

	1979	*1980*	*1981*	*1982*
US				
Citicorp	0.93	0.80	0.74	1.11
BankAmerica	0.97	0.97	0.59	0.44
Chase Manhattan	0.40	0.78	0.77	0.50
UK				
Barclays	1.95	1.56	1.32	0.91
National Westminster	1.73	1.29	1.27	0.89
Midland	1.77	1.02	0.70	0.56
Lloyds	1.72	1.55	1.62	1.01
Germany				
Deutsche Bank	0.72	0.72	0.68	0.67
Dresdner Bank	0.46	0.34	0.32	0.38
Commerzbank	0.35	0.14	0.14	0.26
France				
BNP	0.28	0.38	0.42	0.36
Crédit Lyonnais	0.27	0.35	0.33	0.43
Société Générale	0.37	0.40	–	0.29
Italy				
Banca Commerciale Italiana	0.33	0.49	–	0.64
Banco di Roma	–	0.25	0.26	0.23

Source: *The Banker*, Top 500, June 1983.

most profitable banks in Europe, and probably in the world, while French banks remained the laggards in profitability.

A study of banking profitability would take us too far afield, but in our opinion the most important element behind the French performance is public ownership, which 'did not require a market return on its equity investment'[72] and used the banking sector as a vehicle to foster public interests instead of shareholders. As we can see from Table 5.3, public ownership had a similar negative influence on the performance of Italian banks, which shared many common elements with French banks in terms of governance but showed some distinctive and discomforting traits, notably the promiscuity between banks, politics and organised crime as exemplified, for example, by the Michele Sindona and Roberto Calvi scandals.

The first annual review of BBI's exposure to countries took place in December 1980. Tuke expressed some concerns over the exposure towards South Korea but it was recognised that 'the fact that Barclays is an international bank necessitates exposure to many countries, and the real answer was to ensure that we are adequately compensated for the risks involved'.[73]

As Bevan remarked in its annual address: 'The recycling of OPEC surpluses has continued to occupy the attention of the international banking system'.[74] The Polish troubles did not seem to worry the Chairman; he argued instead that there were good reasons why banks should 'wish to lend to governments, private corporations and banks in other countries in the same way as they do to any other customer'. In some cases, Barclays had relationships going back over many years involving trade finance. Lending had resulted from the support of major export projects, whether from the UK or other countries in which the Bank operated. After the war, Bevan remarked, 'many of these projects were financed largely by governments or international funds, but *in the 1970s the commercial banks became increasingly involved* [emphasis added]'.[75]

As for geographical diversification, BBI was entering the new decade with around 210 offices in Europe and the Mediterranean, 510 offices in North America, more than 1,000 offices in Southern Africa (and 300 in the rest of the Continent), 106 offices in Latin America and the Caribbean, 35 offices in Australia and the Pacific and, finally, 26 offices in Asia.

As we anticipated earlier, Barclays Limited and BBI were less exposed to Latin America than its direct competitors, Lloyds and Midland. Having inherited a large network of branches in some parts of the globe, it did not need to build its operations from scratch, like some of its competitors, but could develop in waves around some strategic hubs, notably North America, Europe and the Pacific Rim. The existence already of a path to follow and develop further allowed Barclays and BBI to avoid taking decisions based on 'fads'; on the contrary, it allowed the Group to grow organically without taking excessive risks.

Despite increasing problems in Latin America, notably bad debts in Argentina, LBI planned further expansion in the region and would become the single largest creditor to Argentina.

The director of the Latin American Division (Guy Huntrods, later co-chair of the Advisory Committee for Argentina) was, surprisingly by today's standards, based in London and not on the American continent, so it proved challenging to assess the real extent of such losses. A Chief Inspector was asked to investigate and reported that 'the [Latin American] Circuit had come under some strain as a result of the expansion of business over the past few years'.[76]

The expansion in the country was achieved 'by an energetic and aggressive marketing policy which, in the competitive environment in Argentina, led to a *relaxation of lending standards* as branch managers struggled to produce the level of profits expected of them [emphasis added]'.[77]

In order to follow more closely the regional activities, a stepping up in the number of visits to branches by regional managers was put forward. Further bad debts were being reported. A special team composed of a Chief Manager and several senior inspectors was sent to Buenos Aires in October 1980 along with the Chief Inspector. Mistakes in credit assessment, errors of judgement and unprepared workforces were found; some managers were reassigned or fired. Moreover, lending guidelines were modified in order to be more stringent. Huntrods remarked that despite the excesses of the Argentinian activities 'the aggressive marketing policy of the last five years has resulted in many bad debts but it has also produced . . . the considerable profit figure of $31 million'.[78]

The management felt satisfied with the measures being taken, and expansion in Latin America could continue. Further openings were planned in the northern part of Argentina. In Brazil, the focus was on wholesale banking in the region of Sao Paulo. Other markets included Uruguay, Paraguay and Chile. On the organisational side, the responsibility for the activities in Central America (BOLAM), Venezuela, Colombia and Ecuador was transferred to the New York office, which already covered Mexico, the US and Canada. Merchant banking units, operating in project finance, export finance, syndicated lending and oil finance, were envisioned in Buenos Aires, New York and Australia.

The Middle East continued to be a minor but growing element in LBI's strategy, especially considering that until the first oil crisis 'LBI's activities were almost non-existent'.[79] LBI's network by the early 1980s was comparable to its main competitors, except those with historical presence in the region such as Standard Chartered, Barclays and Grindlays.

Overall, 1980 proved to be a very profitable year for LBI. Pre-tax profits were up 60.8 per cent at £64.5 million compared to 1979. This number was the result of risky operations, such as in Argentina, and increasing leverage ratios.[80] Between 1975 and 1980, Eurocurrency lending grew exponentially. In 1975 it represented only 39 per cent of total lending, while 61 per cent was local lending. In 1980 the picture was markedly different with Eurocurrency lending representing 51 per cent of total lending compared to 49 per cent lent in local currencies.[81] Even with the losses experienced in some Central and South American countries, the Latin America Division continued to be the jewel in the crown (Argentina remained profitable despite bad debt provisions). By the end of 1980, the division represented only 10 per cent of total assets, but 24 per cent of the profits came from that region. Amongst the other divisions, Europe was a loss-making machine representing 22 per cent of total assets, but only 12 per cent of total profits. The pre-tax return on average total assets for Latin America was the highest amongst all other profit centres standing at 2.09 per cent in 1980 compared to 0.48 per cent for Europe, 1.02 for the Far East, 1.22 for the Middle East and North America and 0.5 for the UK Division.[82]

As we can see in Figure 5.4, the year 1981 marked the apex of LBI's ambitions. The six months to March 1981 were the most successful so far, pre-tax profits were up by 122 per cent (post-tax profits up by 172 per cent) compared to the six months to March 1980. By implementing the niche strategy mentioned above, by focusing on specific markets and eliminating marginal activities, loan volume grew, wider margins were achieved, non-interest revenues (i.e. fee-earning services, notably trade finance, currency trading, and merchant banking services) were increased and productivity was improved (the percentage of income absorbed by operating costs fell from 70 per cent to 55 per cent).

Despite sluggish global economic activity, commercial loans increased by 30 per cent compared to 1980. Eurocurrency lending was growing much faster than local lending (15 per cent growth compared to 8.5 per cent) and now represented 55 per cent of total lending at £3,431 million.[83]

By the end of 1981, pre-tax profits increased from £65 million to £121 million thanks to a sharper focus on a defined number of activities and markets and the elimination of marginal activities. As a counterpart to this growth, provisions against

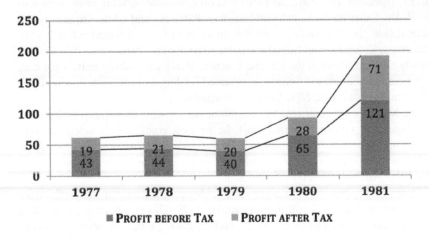

Figure 5.4 LBI profits (£m), 1977–81.

Source: LBA, LBI Report and Accounts 1981.

bad and doubtful loans increased to £44 million compared to £19 million in 1980. Throughout the year, new offices were inaugurated across the globe, notably in Brazil, Egypt, Hong Kong, Japan, Spain, Taiwan and Uruguay.

Of course, we must not think that the expansionary process was a seamless one. For example, in Australasia plans had to be scaled down because of several constraints, highlighting the challenges to internationalisation. In Australia, a shortage of suitable staff put back plans for opening in Brisbane and Perth. Negotiations in Malaysia and Sri Lanka proved unsuccessful because of local regulations and capital requirements.

The Strategic Review of 1979 took place in an unfavourable context for LBI. The growth rate in earnings per share between 1972 and 1978 stood at 10.5 per cent, half that of their leading competitors. By 1978 return on equity was down to 9.7 per cent and dropped further to 8.8 per cent in 1979. The major problems for LBI were insufficient size relative to major competitors, inadequate earnings relative to inflation and to the competition and, finally, dependence on too few countries and products.[84]

Commercial lending grew from 53 per cent to 70 per cent of total assets. Several activities were discontinued, notably money management, UK-based trust services, non-banking business in Latin America and retail banking in France. Workforces were reshaped through an ambitious programme of selective early retirements and redundancies. Further changes were implemented at the organisational, planning and technological levels.

The efforts implemented to compensate these shortcomings paid off between 1979 and 1981.

Nonetheless, the problem was that LBI was extremely exposed to a limited number of countries, especially in Latin America. Between 1978 and 1981, aggregated exposure to Brazil and Argentina grew from around £1 billion to around £1.6 billion; these two countries accounted for more than one-quarter of LBI's total income. In the same period, Eurocurrency lending grew at an average growth rate of 37.7 per cent. The objectives of 1979 were confirmed: priority was to be devoted to extending existing commercial and merchant banking activities to new customers and areas, to increase the size of LBI in its target markets, to avoid disproportionate concentration of capital, assets and earnings and to achieve a compound growth in real terms in assets of 10 per cent. Unfortunately, the risks taken were already too large and the situation quickly took a turn for the worse.

After the aborted attempt at buying Heller, Midland decided to bid for the Californian bank Crocker National Bank. The bid marked the zenith of Midland's international ambitions and the beginning of the end under the weight of loan losses and bad investment decisions. Less than a year after the Heller's attempt, and maybe not coincidentally, on 4 July 1980: 'The Board noted that a bank in North America had been identified as a suitable investment'.[85] A press release was issued on 15 July 1980 stating the terms of the negotiations.

This decision would have long-lasting consequences on Midland's fortunes and would give an important contribution to its disappearance in the early 1990s. Nonetheless, the purchase of an important American bank in one of the most interesting states seemed a profitable bet and the ultimate consecration of Wilcox's own initiative. In October 1980:

> The Board was advised of good progress in the negotiations for the acquisition of a controlling interest in Crocker; of the favourable reactions which had been received from certain Bankers [sic] who attended meetings of the International Monetary Fund and World Bank in Washington; of the satisfactory relations with other members of EBIC and with European American Bank; of the friendly attitude of senior officials in Washington who would be concerned in Midland's application to the Federal Reserve Board, and of enthusiasm of the Crocker management.[86]

The approval of the Securities and Exchange Commission arrived in November 1980 and the extraordinary general meetings of both companies were convened in December. At the extraordinary general meeting summoned on 11 December 1980, Midland's shareholders voted in favour of the investment, while Crocker's shareholders did the same at a special meeting on 22 December.

The year of 1981 was modestly better than the previous year. Midland suffered relatively minor losses in Poland; total medium-term loans amounted to US$33.8 million. At the managerial level, the double-manager structure in place since 1974 took a bow with the retirement of Wilcox, the mastermind behind Midland's international expansion and American ambitions. The organisational structure returned to one sole Chief General Manager, Stuart Graham, assisted by two Deputy Chief General Managers and three Assistant Chief General Managers in charge respectively of corporate finance, international and branch banking.

The Crocker operation was slowed by an increasing number of community groups, fearing that Midland might be 'insensitive' to the needs of Californians or might be 'prejudiced' in its lending criteria.[87] Despite the benevolence of the Federal Reserve Board, the parties were given a few days to respond to such allegations. Further meetings followed in Washington with the Federal Reserve in order to discuss the operational autonomy of Crocker. Midland ultimately decided to grant Crocker 'co-operative independence', a very risky move, as we will see later. A formal response from the Federal Reserve was received at the beginning of September 1981 granting its permission to purchase a 57 per cent interest in Crocker, at that time the 14th largest bank in the US. The total investment amounted to an astounding US$820 million. Midland had been the slowest of the clearing banks to expand overseas directly, but the acquisition of a large bank like Crocker with assets of US$19 billion (a third of Midland) seemed the perfect choice. Tom Wilcox, Crocker's Chairman, announced to the press

Financial Times Friday October 16 1981

Today Midland Bank and Crocker National create a new force in international banking.

This alliance is the result of Midland Bank making a majority investment in Crocker National Corporation.

Through this unique association of two banking organisations we are now in an even stronger position to help develop your business worldwide.

Whether your interests are in the United States of America, Europe, the Pacific Basin, or elsewhere, contact your nearest Midland office to see how this new partnership can work for you.

 **Midland Bank Limited**
Midland Bank Limited, Head Office, 27-32 Poultry, London EC2P 2BX.

In London, Midland Bank Limited, International Division, 60 Gracechurch Street, London EC3P 3BN. Telephone: 01-606 9944.

Figure 5.5 The Midland-Crocker deal.

Source: *Financial Times*, 16 October 1981.

(Figure 5.5) that the agreement marked 'the beginning of the *largest alliance in history* between two banking institutions [emphasis added]'.[88]

The combined assets of the two banks were in the region of US$80 billion making the Group one of the ten largest banks in the world. The first stage of the acquisition involved the purchase of 51 per cent of the company (6.5 million shares at US$50) while the second stage involved the purchase of 2.5 million shares at US$90 over four years, increasing its share to 57 per cent.

Overall, pre-tax profits stabilised at the same level as 1980 while profit after taxation increased from £169.7 million to £192 million. Bad debt provisions increased by £30.8 million to £113.5 million.

Apart from Crocker, Midland continued its overseas expansion in several territories. Canadian activities were granted chartered bank status under the new Canadian Banking Act and a representative office was opened in Mexico City. Presence in France was strengthened through quotation on the Paris stock exchange, the first overseas stock market listing; a new representative office was opened in Amsterdam and the Madrid office was converted into a branch. Sir David Barran retired as Chairman of Midland, being succeeded by Sir Donald Barron and, by the end of 1981, international activities represented around 40 per cent of the Group's profits before tax compared to 55 per cent in 1980.

The new Chairman remarked in the 1981 Annual Report that Midland was now a truly international banking institution amongst the top ten leading banks in the world with a diverse geographic base and capable of serving its customers' needs worldwide. Despite the optimism, Midland discovered quickly that it had invested too much money in a shaky bank, which was accumulating bad debts on property-related US loans and debt-ridden developing countries.

The growth of *Société Générale*'s exposure to Latin American countries was particularly alarming too. Latin American countries, essentially Mexico, Brazil, Panama, Venezuela and Argentina, accounted for 38 per cent of the total LDC exposure by the end of 1981 (socialist European countries excluded).[89] *Société Générale* had expanded at an astounding pace in a decade, as we can see from Table 5.4. In only ten years, the foreign network had tripled in size while the contribution of the international activities to the Group's balance sheet amounted to more than 30 per cent.

An important contribution to the expansion of *Société Générale* in Latin America was given by the Panama branch, opened in 1981. A first positive study on the feasibility of a branch in Panama had been established in August 1979 (other, inconclusive, studies had been prepared in 1974 and 1976). The main argument in favour of the opening was the tax-haven status of the country and its strategic location, suitable for serving both Central and Latin America and the Caribbean. Until the establishment of the Panama branch, all Central American activities were conducted from the representative office in Mexico. The President of Panama, Aristides Royo, its Vice-President, the Ministry of Finance and the president of the *Banco Nacional* received very favourably the team sent from Paris. Given the support of local authorities and the strategic position of the country, an offshore branch was opened in March 1981.

Table 5.4 International expansion of *Société Générale,* 1971–81.

Year	Size Foreign Network (no. of establishments)	Contribution to Group's Balance Sheet
1971	30	–
1976	–	18%
1978	63	19%
1979	72	27%
1980	83	31%
1981	92	–

Source: SGA Board Minutes, various years.

Panama became one of the most important centres for Eurofinance on the American continent, competing globally with Hong Kong, Singapore and Bahrain, and provided an important element to cover the Central and Andean part of the continent. The branch played an important role in increasing the exposure of *Société Générale* to that part of the world.

After the decision to reopen the New York branch, cooperation rapidly disintegrated and meetings took place more and more infrequently. By the early 1980s, most of the major commercial banks in the Western World had their own branches, subsidiaries, representative offices, etc. In September 1981, for example, *Société Générale* decided to cut its ties, followed by Midland, with the *Banque Européeene pour l'Amérique Latine* (BEAL), one of the many creations of the EBIC, because of the existing operations in Brazil and Argentina. The fate was similar for a gradually increasing number of joint activities, like FRAB Bank and the European-American Bank.

These banks were increasingly manifesting a wish for independence from the individual banks but, at the same time, they were interested in benefiting from the local activities of members' banks. This 'schizophrenic' attitude was pushing several members of the EBIC to open fully owned vehicles. Other problems involved the exclusivity and solidarity principles which had been at the centre of the whole EBIC idea. Several members had opened branches and subsidiaries in Latin America or in the Arab world without informing other members; branches had been opened in neighbouring countries; offices in New York had been reopened despite the presence of the EAB.

As for exposure, by 1982 the largest country risks (above US$200 million) were highly concentrated in a handful of countries: four in Latin America, one in Africa, one in Eastern Europe, one in Western Europe, three in Asia as we can see from Table 5.5. Despite the high levels of debt accumulated by socialist countries, the region remained a valuable customer, especially for French exporters.

Looking at *Crédit Lyonnais*, in May 1980, the manager of Eastern Europe remarked that the Bank had proved to be, until 1979 and with the exception of the Soviet Union, more restrictive than its peers and, consequently, its market positions both with socialist countries and with its French customers had somewhat suffered. Thus, while the Bank would continue with its policy of caution

Table 5.5 Société Générale country-risk exposure 1982 (US$m).

Country	Exposure	% Total
Mexico	1,100	25%
Brazil	830	19%
Nigeria	410	9%
URSS	380	9%
Venezuela	350	8%
Spain	340	8%
Philippines	295	7%
Argentina	275	6%
South Korea	240	5%
Indonesia	213	5%

Source: SGA, 81142, 'Liste des principaux risques pays', 4 May 1983.

and selectivity in respect of these countries, it should aim to maintain its presence or strengthen it.[90]

In order to gain market shares, especially in support of French exports, *Crédit Lyonnais* decided to become more aggressive in its marketing efforts by extending the number of collateral credits and financial credits in Eurocurrencies. DOFI decided to become more hawkish too by focusing on obtaining management or co-management positions in syndicated Euroloans. In its 1981 Plan, it clearly stated that '*greater aggressiveness* in terms of conditions and presence with potential customers is an essential requirement to manage more issues [emphasis added]'.[91]

Ultimately, the foreign currency operations expanded dramatically in the 1970s and early 1980s as we can see from Figure 5.6. Foreign currency activities represented just 25.9 per cent of total assets in 1973, while in 1981 they represented 40 per cent.

The most important foreign acquisitions of *Crédit Lyonnnais* in the early 1980s were *Banco Tornquist* in Argentina, bought entirely in 1981, and the 50 per cent stake in *N.V. Slavenburg Bank* based in Rotterdam. The timing of the first acquisition was far from perfect. *Banco Tornquist*, founded in 1830, was the 23rd largest bank in Argentina with dollar assets estimated at US$487 million in 1981. The Bank had 32 branches and employed 750 people. The initial option of creating a branch was discarded because of the associated costs. The Slavenburg Bank, founded in 1925, had 2,827 employees and 107 branches throughout the country. It had branches in Europe, notably Hamburg, Frankfurt, Dusseldorf, Zürich, Brussels, London and in New York and Curaçao. Total assets in December 1980 amounted to FL11 billion. The decision to acquire was a 'second best' since the original plan to expand in the Netherlands was through a full branch because the existing Dutch operations of the Europartners were considered unsatisfactory. Because of bureaucratic problems associated with the establishment of a branch, *Crédit Lyonnais* decided to buy Slavenburg Bank.

As the acquisition of a controlling interest in a Dutch bank would indicate, one of the original purposes of the Europartners, i.e. not competing on the partners'

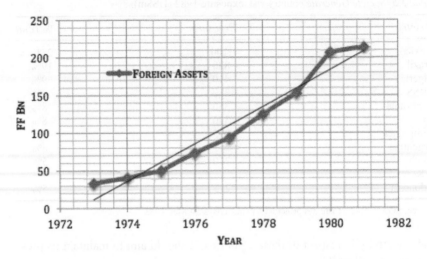

Figure 5.6 Growth of foreign assets at *Crédit Lyonnais* (FFbn) 1973–81.

Source: CLA, 110AH2, DCAIC 'Tableaux de bords', various years.

turf, was no longer valid. In the previous chapter, we had already anticipated that cooperation would take a serious blow in 1976 when *Crédit Lyonnais* opened a branch in Frankfurt (Dusseldorf followed in 1977 and Hamburg in 1979) and *Commerzbank* opened one in Paris. The meeting of the Europartners in Frankfurt in May 1976 had ratified the '*pragmatisme concerté*' of the cooperation. From that moment on, strict cooperation was maintained in domains such as manpower, exchange of information, public relations and publications, while on the more sensitive and strategic subjects such as international financial operations only a limited form of cooperation was contemplated. Other domains had to remain totally independent from the other Europartners, notably trade finance and international activities (branches, representative offices and subsidiaries).

The counterpart to international expansion was, like most of its peers, an increased level of exposure to shaky regions. By September 1982, bad debt provisions amounted to FF289 million compared to just FF120 million one year earlier.[92]

1982 and its aftermath

From the vantage point of development economics, the debt crisis announced the end of 'state capitalism'[93] or 'state-led industrialisation',[94] which had meant an increasing focus on industrialisation as a mainstay of development and a considerable expansion of the scope of the state in several developing countries, notably in Latin America. If in the years preceding the Euromarket many LDC governments had relied on foreign direct investments in import-substituting activities as a reliable source of external financing to build up a modern industrial sector, in the 1970s more and more states 'discovered a new way of becoming the principal source of capital accumulation: foreign borrowing'.[95]

Critical junctures

The debt crisis definitely marked a 'critical juncture' in contemporary financial history or, as some authors have argued 'a major turning point in the history of the world economy because it marked *the coming of age* of the international financial system [emphasis added]'.[96] The debt crisis had a crucial impact on several developing countries and, consequently, on their economic policies and on the relations between developed and developing economies.[97]

Moreover, the failure of the development strategies implemented would have a fundamental role in paving the way to 'the triumph of the doctrine of neoliberalism and the policy of structural adjustment'.[98] The shift involved the belief that the role of the state in the economy had to be curbed, that economies should be opened to the outside world and that import-substitution strategies should lead the way to an export-led growth strategy. As Jeffry Frieden has noted: 'Over five to ten years after 1982 one developing country after another liberalized trade, deregulated banks, sold off government enterprises, raised taxes and cut spending and integrated its economy into world markets'.[99]

The crisis also had a crucial impact on the role of the IMF. After a period of relegation to a niche within the financial system, the crisis provided the IMF with an opportunity to play a critical role in the global market as a global 'crisis manager'[100] by coordinating the actions of debtors and creditors and providing a mechanism to check the adherence of developing countries to the agreements over time.

A critical juncture was reached in 1982, not only for international organisations and LDCs but for all the banks in our book as well. The debt crisis sounded the death knell for the 'big-at-any-cost' phase of international expansion for the many banks which had expanded, often too energetically, overseas since the early 1970s. Thus, Barclays, Lloyds, Midland, *Crédit Lyonnais* and *Société Générale* went through a period of crisis first, and then reconfiguration of their international strategy. Some of these banks decided to restructure their activities and retreat into realism, others were too critically impaired by their overseas investments and entered a downward spiral which would ultimately bring them down and some managed to weather the storm and continued their transformation into global banks.

Despite the mixed results of this first wave of internationalisation, the role of banks in modern societies did not diminish after 1982. The Euromarket was not touched by regulations and continued its growth to become the complex financial system we live in and experience everyday. The expansion of international financial markets continued and new products continued to be developed by new actors. In the following sections we will first analyse the crisis of 1982 and then look at its impact on the reconfiguration of the British and French banking sector.

Crisis

The details of the debt crisis, which erupted in August 1982 when Mexico declared it did not have the funds to meet its interest payments and which then spread to 27 countries by October 1983, are well known.[101] The persistence of high interest rates, coupled with declining export prices put further pressure on the balance of payments of the developing world. As we can see from Table 5.6, many countries all over the world were forced to default on their debt throughout the 1980s.

These countries had become too dependent on bank lending and the amounts to be refinanced had reached intolerable levels. Mexico was the first country to fall under the weight of the debt accumulated. Between August and December 1982, it received money through arrangements with the United States, the BIS, the IMF, the World Bank and commercial banks themselves.

Table 5.6 Countries in default during the 1980s, rated issuers, foreign currency bank debt.

Country	Years in default
Chile	1983–1990
Poland	1981–1994
Mexico	1982–1990
South Africa	1985–1987, 1989
Trinidad & Tobago	1988–1989
Philippines	1983–1992
Egypt	1984
Morocco	1983, 1986–1990
Costa Rica	1981–1990
Guatemala	1986
Panama	1983–1996
Peru	1980, 1983–1997
Vietnam	1985–1998
Dominican Republic	1982–1994
Bolivia	1980–1984, 1986–1993
Brazil	1983–1994
Romania	1981–1983, 1986
Jamaica	1981–1985, 1987–1993
Senegal	1981–1985, 1990
Paraguay	1986–1992
Uruguay	1983–1985, 1987, 1990
Venezuela	1983–1988, 1990
Turkey	1982
Ecuador	1982–1995
Argentina	1982–1993

Source: Standard & Poor's *Ratings Performance 2002. Defaults, Transition, Recovery, and Spreads*, February 2003, 93.

Note: Several other unrated borrowers defaulted on their bank debt throughout the 1980s: Angola, Burkina Faso, Cameroon, Cape Verde, Central African Republic, Congo (Brazzaville), Congo (Kinshasa), Cuba, Gabon, Gambia, Ghana, Guinea, Guinea-Bissau, Guyana, Haiti, Honduras, Iraq, Côte d'Ivoire, Liberia.

A good overview of the debt phenomenon in LDCs is given in Table 5.7 below. As the BIS remarked, 'the acute debt problems which emerged in 1982 marked the end of a nine-year period during which international indebtedness, much of it originating in sovereign lending by banks, had expanded very rapidly'.[102] The rate of growth in international bank claims declined to 10 per cent in 1982, compared to 21 per cent in 1981 and an average of 23 per cent between 1976 and 1980.[103] BIS reporting banks' external assets declined from US$265 billion to US$174 billion. On a net basis, the BIS estimated the total amount of new credit channelled through institutional markets at US$145 billion compared to around US$195 billion one year earlier. The decline in international bank credits reflected a shift away from bank lending to capital markets, notably Eurobonds, because of high dollar interest rates, the strength of the American currency and hopes of capital gain. After a sluggish decade, new international bond issues increased from US$49 billion to US$72 billion.[104]

Unexpectedly, socialist countries were the worst hit by the decline in international flows once it was clear that the 'Soviet umbrella' was missing and the Soviet Union would not step in to cover the losses of its allies. Flows to non-oil LDCs remained strong until the first half of the year, amounting to US$11.8 billion in new credits, but declined rapidly (before coming to a halt by the end of the year) as soon as the first difficulties in countries such as Mexico (August), Argentina (September) and Brazil (December) – which accounted for around 90 per cent of Latin American indebtedness – emerged. In the oil-exporting world, the huge surpluses of the preceding years disappeared, leaving a deficit of US$3 billion. The picture looked grim and relevant systemic questions loomed ahead, notably on the future of international credit intermediation on which the world economy has depended so heavily since 1974.

Table 5.7 Evolution over time of key debt indicators, 1980–89.

Country group, by region	Share of 1988 total debt %	Debt/service ratio				Debt/export ratio			
		1980	1982	1985	1988	1980	1982	1985	1988
Sub-Saharan Africa	12	11.0	19.3	30.8	27.2	98.3	181.9	239.7	361.2
East Asia and the Pacific	18	13.6	18.0	25.1	19.5	89.9	114.8	139.3	108.9
South Asia	8	11.6	14.5	22.6	27.5	159.6	207.1	265.1	276.2
Europe and the Mediterranean	14	18.1	20.4	25.5	26.6	102.2	119.7	158.9	139.2
Middle East and North Africa	10	20.3	21.3	23.8	37.9	136.7	145.6	188.0	286.1
Latin America and the Caribbean	37	36.9	47.6	42.7	40.5	194.5	269.1	308.4	311.0

Source: World Bank, World Debt Tables 1989–1990, Washington, DC, 11.

Note: Debt ratios are based on total external debt, i.e. long-term debt, short-term debt, use of IMF credit and associated debt service payments

The crisis highlighted the new role of international banking and financial institutions as the centrepiece of the new market-based monetary system, which had emerged after the demise of the Bretton Woods regime. As economist, David Folkerts-Landau, pointed out in 1985: 'During the past 15 years, the provision of development finance has undergone major institutional changes. The international market for bank loans has replaced the markets for international bonds and direct investment as the major source of private capital for development'.[105]

Between 1973 and 1982, net external assets of BIS reporting banks increased from US$155 billion to US$1,020 billion, as we can see from Figure 5.7.

During the same period, gross indebtedness of non-oil LDCs to BIS reporting banks increased seven-fold from US$32 billion to US$247 billion. For Eastern Europe, gross indebtedness went up from US$10 billion in 1973 to US$61 billion by the end of 1981.

The fact that by the spring of 1983 more than two dozen countries across the globe had to reschedule their debts, and many others would follow throughout the 1980s, did not compel the BIS to reconsider the policies implemented in the previous decade. On the contrary, the BIS rejected the criticism that bank lending had been 'misdirected' and 'irresponsible' because of the numerous rescheduling operations. Instead, it remarked that critics overlooked 'the extent to which the functioning of the world economy and the international financial system has since 1974, and in particular following the successive oil shocks, *depended on the rôle of intermediary played by international banks* [emphasis added].[106]

To keep the economy going, the international financial system came to be managed increasingly by private institutions. Governments and international organisations such as the BIS, the IMF and the OECD understood this, but

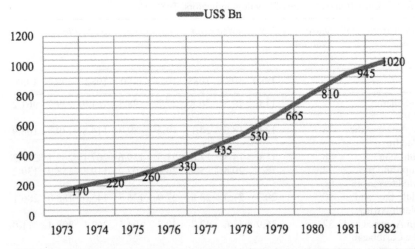

Figure 5.7 Growth of the Eurocurrency market (US$bn), 1971–82.

Source: David Lomax, *The Developing Country Debt Crisis*, Palgrave Macmillan, London, 1986, 30, based on data from the BIS'quarterly press release on international banking developments.

did not intervene against this privatisation of international capital flows, while commercial banks benefited from this situation and gradually expanded their activities to as many countries as possible. Jacques de Larosière aptly summarised this epochal shift in the balance of power in international monetary relations: 'Twenty years ago – and perhaps even as recently as ten years ago – the international monetary system was dominated by governments and official institutions. Today, the private commercial banks play a *key role* in the running of that system [emphasis added]'.[107]

A few months later, even the IMF started to recognise that:

> [m]uch of the problem . . . lay with bank lending practices. In many cases banks did not undertake the necessary analyses of countries' debt servicing prospects, and in some of these cases they lent in situations which were clearly headed for difficulty.[108]

It was a big step forward compared to the positions of its Managing Director a few months earlier when he remarked that 'on the whole the global financing and debt situation, difficult as it is, is not in my view un-manageable'.[109] Nevertheless, some of the most important regulators still did not deem it suitable to intervene in modifying banking practices. Peter Cooke, head of the banking supervision of the Bank of England and Chairman of the 'Basel Committee on Banking Supervision', i.e. the Basel Committee from 1977 to 1988, remarked in December 1982 that 'commercial banks individually are *their own masters* [emphasis added]'.[110] Prophetic words indeed.

Reorganisation

The critical year of 1982 marked a moment of profound reconsideration for the whole expansionary experience of the preceding decade. Overall, most banks decided to refocus on specific markets and reduce their international expansion.

The fact that its heritage or cultural identity was more conservative than most of its peers, did not entirely spare Barclays from the turbulences of the early 1980s. Bad debt provisions increased from £188 million in 1980 to £260 million in 1981 to £300 million in 1982.[111] The interim results of 1982 showed how hard the crisis was hitting: total BBI profits at 30 June declined to £63.7 million in 1982, compared to £129 million in 1981 and £113.5 million in 1980.[112] The disappointing results were the outcome of lower trading profits and increased provisions.

When the crisis erupted, some of the guidelines of BBI were modified. In the 1983–87 Strategic Plan, the requirement to achieve a 16.5 per cent after tax return on shareholders' funds by 1986 was omitted. The rate of annual increase in profits was reduced from 25 per cent to 20 per cent.[113]

Nevertheless, the strategy of diversification into the major financial and economic centres of the world was maintained: 'The uncertainties and risks in the current world environment will require some short term tactical response, but we must take care not thereby to jeopardise long term objectives'.[114] With regard to geographical expansion, three main priorities were singled out: first, to reinforce BBI's presence in the most promising areas; second, to buy out minority stakes where the investment was a good one in order to have 100 per cent of any investment; and third, to continue the search for major acquisitions in developed areas, notably North America and Europe. When Derek Pelly, Vice-Chairman of BBI, visited Mexico in November 1982, he came back with a grim picture:

> Visiting at a time of political vacuum between administrations, I may have seen a more lugubrious picture than will shortly emerge. Nevertheless it is clear that we have a long and complex road ahead and the bulk of our exposure of some £500 million will remain outstanding for years.[115]

Chairman, Timothy Bevan, was more optimistic and explained in its annual statement in 1982 that Barclays had not been overextended by international lending. Total Group cross-border exposure, excluding the OECD countries, represented under 10 per cent of total Group assets and in no one country was the overall exposure more than about 1 per cent of total assets.[116]

Ackrill and Hannah estimate the losses stemming from the international activities of Barclays at £507 million over the period 1985–1990. Barclays made some unfortunate decisions but their scale was decidedly smaller than the ones taken by LBI and Midland. Because of their aggressive strategy in the previous decade, these banks were the most involved in bad debts to LDCs, as we can see from Table 5.8.

After reaching 'wuthering heights' with the acquisition of Crocker, Midland entered a downward spiral which would bring the Bank into the arms of the Hong Kong and Shanghai Banking Corporation (HSBC) in 1992.

In 1983, 40 per cent of the shareholding in Samuel Montagu was sold to Aetna Life & Casualty Company. More important from a historical point of view was the sale of MAIBL to the merchant bank subsidiary of Standard Chartered Bank, marking the end of the cooperative phase of international banking for the bank. Bad debt provisions increased to £318 million in 1983 from £196.1 million in 1982 and £113.5 million in 1981. By the end of 1984, Midland had cross-border

Table 5.8 LDCs exposure of the Big Four.

	Estimate of exposure to outstanding debt of Mexico, Argentina, Brazil and Venezuela as % of capital at end 1984	1987–89 Exceptional provisions against LDC debt, £MN	Exposure to debt, after deduction of provision, as % of shareholders' funds at end of 1989
Barclays	62 %	1,733	8 %
NatWest	73 %	1,651	7 %
Midland	205 %	1,893	80%
Lloyds	165 %	2,964	50 %

Source: Margaret Ackrill and Leslie Hannah, *Barclays. The Business of Banking 1690–1996*, Cambridge University Press, Cambridge UK, 2001, 325.

Table 5.9 Midland's profits (losses) before taxation (£bn), 1981–85.

	1981	1982	1983	1984	1985
Domestic	152	186	258	281	308
International	79	65	−33	−146	43
Total	231	251	225	135	351

Source: MBA, Annual Reports, various years.

outstanding loans of £1.9 billion towards Brazil, £1.6 billion towards Mexico and £0.8 billion towards Argentina, representing respectively 2.5, 2 and 1.2 per cent of total Group assets. Midland's results for 1981–85 are shown in Table 5.9.

After initial profits of US$92 million in 1982, in 1983 Crocker reported a loss before tax of US$20 (£17 million) million because of huge amounts of non-performing loans in the real estate and agricultural sectors. The operational autonomy granted to Crocker at the time of the acquisition was revoked.

John Harris, one of Midland's executive directors, moved to San Francisco and was nominated Vice-Chairman of Crocker. Despite Midland's intervention, Crocker's situation was worsening at lightning speed and in 1984 losses sky-rocketed to £222 million. Bad debt provisions continued to increase and reached the staggering amount of £616 million in 1984 with Crocker accounting for £456 million compared to £120 million in 1983. Total provisions outstanding amounted to £848 million compared to £673 million in 1983. In December 1983, Crocker was even forced to sell its headquarters in San Francisco for US$358 million.

Despite the acquisition of 100 per cent of Crocker and its integration, the American adventure of Midland ended on 7 February 1986, when it announced the sale of Crocker to Wells Fargo for £750 million.

In May 1987, Sir Kit McMahon, former Deputy Governor of the Bank of England, took over the chairmanship of Midland. He reshaped Midland in three divisions: Investment Banking, Global Banking and UK Banking. That same year HSBC acquired a 15 per cent stake in the company. The results of the Bank continued to be disappointing and became an easy prey for its healthier competitors. On 17 March 1992, HSBC made a takeover bid for Midland and, after a battle with Lloyds, the latter gave up in June when HSBC 'sweetened' its deal. On 25 June 1992, HSBC obtained 63.58 per cent of Midland's shares for £3.6 billion. Midland's name was used until 1999 before being phased out after more than 160 years of existence.

Lloyds' situation could have mirrored Midland's but ultimately it did not happen. Conversely, Lloyds became the most profitable of the clearers up to the beginning of the new millennium under the towering leadership of CEO, Sir Brian Pitman, probably the most revered banker of his generation, and the Chairmanship of Sir Jeremy Morse.

As we have illustrated earlier in our book, Lloyds had implemented an aggressive strategy since the acquisition of BOLSA and the creation of LBI in 1973. Because of its heritage, it had a strong presence in the Latin American continent, and throughout the 1970s, it expanded further in the developing world, notably in South East Asia.

By 1982, like Midland, the Bank was suffering under the weight of its acquisitions. In September, bad debt provisions increased from £44 million in 1981 to £116 million in 1982 and pre-tax profits fell from £121 million to £71 million.[117] The situation continued to worsen: by the year end of 1982, bad debt provisions increased further to £218.9 million while pre-tax profits declined by 18 per cent to £315.9 million. Brian Pitman was nominated Chief Executive while Jeremy Morse became Chairman of Lloyds. From that moment on, a total reconsideration of Lloyds' international expansion began and a firm decision was taken to gradually reduce exposure to LDCs. In 1984 the strategy was reviewed for a first time by Pitman because, since the 1970s, the nature of the Group and its profit sources had changed considerably. At the beginning of the 1970s, Pitman argued, Lloyds was a 'domestic bank with a few foreign investments'; since then, the Bank had expanded and diversified, geographically and by product, so as to become a 'major international group engaged in banking and financial services'.[118] He further recognised that 'growth in banking accelerated following the oil shock of 1973 and 1979, largely reflecting an *explosion of debt* [emphasis added]'.[119] The strategy review of 1984 posited a 'major change' in Lloyds' strategy and a 'superior return on equity' was adopted as the central goal.

The new policy gained momentum in 1985 when £1.8 billion low-yielding assets were written down and headcount reduced by 3,000. Just as Midland had with Crocker, Lloyds sold its Californian activities (Lloyds Bank California acquired from World Airways the First Western Bank in 1974 for US$118 million) to the Japanese bank Sanwa Bank for US$263 million. As part of the deal, Lloyds retained US$250 million of bad debts mainly from Mexico (when Midland sold Crocker to Wells Fargo it kept non-performing loans of US$3.5 billion). Interests in Malaysia, New Zealand, Sri Lanka, Italy, Costa Rica, El Salvador, Nicaragua, Peru, Indonesia, Philippines, Bahrain, Nigeria and Egypt were sold too.[120] In 1986 a new radical strategy was adopted: Lloyds decided to focus on sound local business and products which could travel across boundaries.[121]

It is not a coincidence that Lloyds' emblem is a skittish dark horse, since the Bank's decisions are often difficult to justify. The £1.17 billion bid for Standard Chartered in April 1986, in the middle of a corporate restructuring, is a good example of such corporate 'schizophrenia'. The bid was a total failure and was quickly rejected by Standard Chartered. Michael McWilliam, the Group Managing Director, remarked defiantly: 'Lloyds has *a dismal record of overseas banking management* and we are particularly proud of the way in which we have run our international business [emphasis added]'.[122] The failed bid for Standard Chartered undoubtedly played a role in Lloyds' decision to focus exclusively on local opportunities. The situation of Lloyds was well summarised in an internal document of the Strategic Planning Unit:

In conclusion, the strategic direction as originally envisaged [in 1969], given the concern for the U.K. economy, was probably correct, but cross border lending to developing countries, particularly in Latin America, was allowed to grow too rapidly. In the less benign 1980s what we have is a *few pockets of strength* overseas, a *large exposure* to third world debt and *a number of weaker market positions* which hold little prospect of achieving a satisfactory return [emphasis added].[123]

In July 1987, Sir Jeremy Morse established an International Strategy Working Party, comprising four other members in total. After three months, the conclusions were decisively in favour of a definitive 'domesticisation' of Lloyds' business: 'We believe that our international business should in the first place stem from our customer-base and market-share in the U.K. This will emphasise products like correspondent banking, trade finance, export finance, private banking, investment management and treasury'.[124] From that moment, Lloyds transformed into a (mainly) domestic bank, as we can see from Table 5.10, showing the composition of Lloyds' assets.

Did this decision have negative consequences on Lloyds' performance? Absolutely not. On the contrary, and despite some problems with bad debts in the UK in the early 1990s, Lloyds recovered from its Latin American misfortunes and transformed into the most profitable of the clearing banks. The Cheltenham & Gloucester building society was acquired in 1994; in 1995 Lloyds acquired the Trustee Savings Bank (becoming briefly the largest bank in the world); and the acquisition of Scottish Widows followed in 1999. In 1998 Lloyds had a capitalisation of £42.1 billion; rightfully *The Economist* hailed Lloyds as 'the world's most valuable bank'.[125]

The story of Lloyds, the bank at the forefront of international expansion in the 1970s and the champion of domestic banking in the 1990s, is a revealing one. The Bank showed how wise strategies need not be complicated or overly ambitious but that 'boring banking' still had its merits and it was capable of delivering good results to its shareholders and to the general public at large. Maybe this could be a lesson of some help to today's bankers.

For the French banks in our study, information concerning their experience in the 1980s is still limited. Undoubtedly, this is because we are dealing with

Table 5.10 Composition of assets of Lloyds Bank (£bn), 1982–87.

Year	Group £bn	Domestic %	International %
1982	31.1	39	61
1983	37.2	40	60
1984	43.0	38	62
1985	42.8	43	57
1986	46.4	45	55
1987	48.2	51	49

Source: LBA, HO/Ch/MOR30, Strategic Planning Unit, 'The Development of Lloyds Bank's International Business', 10 September 1987.

Table 5.11 Société Générale country-risk exposure 1983 (US$m).

Country	Exposure	% Total
Mexico	1,085	32%
Brazil	948	28%
Nigeria	247	7%
Venezuela	208	6%
Yugoslavia	190	6%
Poland	164	5%
Algeria	152	4%
Argentina	151	4%
South Korea	146	4%
Spain	143	4%

Source: SGA, 81137, 'Note de Synthèse-Limites-Pays', No date.

very recent events in historical terms, but from the documents in our hands, we can sketch some broad lines, leaving the finer details for the near future. *Société Générale* was badly hit by its Latin American activities. In May 1983 it was remarked:

> Last year [1982] was characterised by the economic and financial debacle of almost all the countries in Central and Latin America. With the exception of Colombia, all the countries in which Société Générale is established have applied for external debt restructuring.[126]

Société Générale decided explicitly not to take a central role in the 'Advisory Committees' created to deal with LDCs rescheduling, since the efforts required were not compensated by the remuneration, leaving the most important role to American and British banks. The mood was definitely changing, and austerity became the new keyword:

> That is why, when the overall results of the banks may be seriously affected by adverse economic circumstances and by the necessity of important provisions because of the rise of international risks, a strict policy of fiscal discipline is needed, particularly in terms of staff, including expatriate managers.[127]

The activities in Mexico and Brazil were the first where the reduction in costs was implemented. By the year end of 1983, the main sovereign risks had changed slightly compared to 1982, as we can see from Table 5.11.

We will need to wait a little longer to get the full picture of *Société Générale*'s strategies after 1982, although we can posit that its behaviour was not much different from *Crédit Lyonnais*. The new president of *Crédit Lyonnais*, Jean Deflassieux, remarked in December 1983:

> Considering the critical state of the economic and international environment which necessitates increased scrutiny, *it is now less crucial to focus on a*

quantitative and continuous expansion of our network than to deepen and consolidate our operations and improve our performances, notably in certain priority sectors [emphasis added].[128]

In fact, between 1976 and 1986, the number of foreign vehicles (branches and subsidiaries) had dramatically increased from 106 to 272, the budget of foreign branches increased from FF500 million to FF2 billion and the capital invested in foreign subsidiaries grew from FF350 million to FF3.3 billion. Now the situation was markedly different, since new challenges were on the horizon, notably deregulation and disintermediation. These elements required 'another strategy'.[129] The main geographical targets were now in Europe, because of the creation of the European Union in 1992, and in Asia Pacific.

Both *Société Générale* and *Crédit Lyonnais* decided to refocus their efforts on a limited number of core regions, mainly in the developed world, to rationalise costs and to expand in the brave new world of innovative financial products.

End times?

The years preceding the debt crisis of 1982 were years of continued expansion for the banking and financial sector. That was the result of the continuation of the strategies implemented after the first oil crisis and of the impact of the second oil crisis. Ultimately, the decision to recycle the oil surpluses fell, again, on the shoulders of the banking sector. Despite the similar response to the first and second oil shocks, the macro-economic conditions were markedly different.

The fight against inflation became a priority for most Western governments and national policies became increasingly focused on tightening monetary aggregates. The change in monetary policy was particularly harsh in the United States, where interest rates became positive and reached sky-level heights after the 'Volcker Shock' of October 1979, which targeted monetary aggregates to limit the growth of money. A global recession ensued, commodity prices fell, capital flows to the developing world dried up and by the end of 1983, more than 25 countries had to reschedule their debt and many others soon followed.

As some authors have argued,[130] the IMF became the crucial crisis manager, implementing, for the first time on such a large scale, new adjustment policies, assuming the role of policy adviser and credit rating service:

> The conditions for debt rescheduling urged by the IMF . . . involve domestic implementation of market-oriented policies aimed at economic stabilization. The purpose of economic stabilization programs is to discipline Third World economies in which inflation, price distortions, excessive demand, industrial protection, and profligate government spending are alleged to cause the debt problem.[131]

Such austerity policies had clear distributional implications, affecting in particular the urban poor and the working class because of their impact on subsidy cuts, real wage reductions and price increases stemming from devaluations and the elimination of public services. The fiscal austerity adopted by Latin American governments in the 1980s involved 'large costs in terms of productivity, welfare and institutional losses'.[132] Popular protests (food riots, violent demonstrations, general strikes, etc.) exploded in several countries on a scale rarely seen since the European revolts of 1848. As similar measures have been implemented or supported in several European countries following the European debt crisis, we are left wondering whether these represent a viable option for a healthy and socially sustainable economic recovery.

On a more positive note, several of the countries entangled in the debt spiral moved towards democracy during the 1980s. The Argentinian *junta* fell under the weight of the Falkland's debacle and economic disaster; the Brazilian one followed suit; and the 'People Power' revolution in the Philippines was a product of the killing of Benigno Aquino Jr. but found its support in the growing economic discontent of the population. In Poland the appeal of *Solidarnosc* increased greatly in a context of economic deprivation, while the same dissatisfaction with the economic consequences of the crisis weakened the socialist regimes in Hungary and Romania. As Barry Eichengreen pointed out 'the planned economies . . . experienced a debt crisis, an inflation crisis, and a growth crisis, until the system broke down completely at the end of the 1980s'.[133]

Thanks to the support of international organisations, national governments and the failed attempt at regulating the Euromarket, the European banking sector continued its international expansion in the years immediately following the second oil shock. Not one of the banks in our analysis altered its strategy significantly until the explosion of the crisis in Mexico. On the contrary, as we have shown in the preceding sections, the exposure towards developing countries of French and British banks increased enormously after the second oil shock. At least in part this attitude indicates a belief in the fact that banks would be bailed out if necessary as hinted in the G-10 communiqué of September 1974.

What followed after the debt crisis was a 'retreat into realism'. On the one side, commercial banks in the West participated in the debt restructuring of developing countries; on the other, they reshaped their international activities in order to respond to the new challenges of the 1990s. Some of the banks in our sample managed to remain independent, while others fell prey to competitors in better economic shape. British banks were particularly hit by the debt crisis, coming in second place in terms of exposure after the US, while French banks figured amongst the most involved on the continent.

The debt crisis did not mark the end of the rise of finance: over the course of the 1980s, the banking sector continued its transformation as new actors entered the market.

The distinction between commercial and investment banks became increasingly blurred through deregulation and securitisation. Even the distinction between domestic and Euro-markets gradually disappeared with the liberalisation of capital movements, notably in Europe, during the 1980s and early 1990s. The effect of such changes is beyond the scope of this book; nevertheless the transformation of the banking and financial industry is remarkable by any standard. As some authors have correctly summarised:

> *Wall Street is now everywhere*, as gas station proprietors speculate in oil futures to hedge their business against shocks in the Middle East, American homeowners find their mortgages owned by Norwegian villagers, and Midwestern toll roads end up being owned by Australian pension funds. And traditional notions of risk and power have been wildly reshuffled thanks to the financial revolution, rendering our old maps of the financial system deceptive and our regulatory system comically mismatched to the entities it is supposed to oversee [emphasis added].[134]

As we have witnessed during the Great Recession, the transformation of the banking and financial sector has indeed radically reshaped the way the sector impacts on our lives, not always in a positive way.

Notes

1 Speech by Margaret Thatcher to the General Assembly of the Church of Scotland, Edinburgh, 21 May 1988.
2 BEA, 6A43/1, Secret document, 'Recycling of oil surpluses by the international financial markets', 31 December 1979.
3 Claudio Borio, Gianni Toniolo and Piet Clement (eds), *Past and Future of Central Bank Cooperation*, Cambridge University Press, Cambridge, UK, 2008, 60.
4 BIS Annual Report 1980, 114.
5 Ibid.
6 Both documents can be found in the Archives of the Bank of England, 3A143/1.
7 Robert Devlin and Ricardo Ffrench-Davis, 'The Great Latin America Debt Crisis: A Decade of Asymmetric Adjustment', *Revista de Economia Politica*, Vol. 15, No. 3 (59), Julho–Setembro, 95, 117.
8 Luis Bértola and José Antonio Ocampo, *The Economic Development of Latin America Since Independence*, Oxford University Press, Oxford, UK, 2012, 198.
9 Philip A. Wellons, *Passing the Buck. Banks, Governments, and Third World Debt*, Harvard Business School Press, Boston, MA, 1987, 3.
10 Dwight B. Crane and Samuel L. Hayes III, 'The New Competition in World Banking', *Harvard Business Review*, July–August 1982, 88.
11 See for example Bela Balassa, 'Structural Adjustment Policies in Developing Economies', *World Development*, Vol. 10, No. 1, 1982, 23–38.
12 Laura D'Andrea Tyson, 'The Debt Crisis and Adjustment Responses in Eastern Europe: A Comparative Perspective', *International Organization*, Vol. 40, Issue 2, March 1986, 250.
13 OECDA, WP3 Documents 1980, DES/NI(80)8, 12 March 1980.
14 IMFA, SM/80/55, 'International Capital Markets – The Current Outlook', 25 February 1980, Electronic Document.
15 IMFA, SM/80/55, 25 February 1980 and SM/80/159, 30 June 1980.
16 IMFA, EBM/80/150, 6 August 1980.
17 Idem.
18 *Bundesbank* Annual Report 1979, 49.
19 For example, Eric Helleiner, *States and the Reemergence of Global Finance*, Cornell University Press, Ithaca, NY and London, 1994 and Ethan B. Kapstein, *Governing*

the Global Economy. International Finance and the State, Harvard University Press, Cambridge, MA, and London, 1994.

20 *Financial Times*, 'Central banks unlikely to act on Euromarkets', 17 December 1979.

21 IMFA, SM/80/159, 'International Capital Markets-Recent Developments and Near-Term Prospects', 30 June 1980, Electronic Document.

22 IMFA, Press Release no. 80/34, 'Press Communiqué of the Interim Committee of the Board of Governors on the International Monetary System', 25 April 1980, Electronic Document.

23 BEA, 6A227/1, Sir Geoffrey Howe Statement at the Interim Committee meeting in Hamburg, 25 April 1980.

24 Alexander Mountford, 'The Historical Development of IMF Governance', Background Paper of the Independent Evaluation Office of the International Monetary Fund, BP/08/02, May 2008, 13.

25 BEA, Quarterly Bulletin 1980, 'Speech by the Governor of the Bank of England at the Annual Banquet of the Overseas Bankers Club', London, 4 February 1980.

26 Idem.

27 IMFA, EBM/80/121, 'Minutes of Executive Board Meeting 80/121', 6 August 1980, Electronic Document.

28 Idem.

29 Idem.

30 Idem.

31 Idem.

32 BIS Annual Report 1981, 99.

33 Idem, 101.

34 Idem, 110.

35 See, for example: IMFA, ID/80/4, Confidential Report, 'World Economic Outlook-Situation of the Non-Oil Developing Countries', 31 March 1980, Electronic Document.

36 Idem.

37 Idem, 111.

38 BEA, 6A43/2, 'Meeting of IMF Task Force in Mexico October 1980', 6 November 1980.

39 BIS Annual Report 1982, 8.

40 BIS Annual Report 1982, 11.

41 On Poland's recent economic history see, for example: Kazimierz Poznanski, 'Economic Adjustment and Political Forces: Poland since 1970', *International Organization*, Volume 40, Issue 2, March 1986, 455–488. For a comparative perspective of the debt crisis in Eastern Europe, see Laura D'Andrea Tyson, 'The Debt Crisis and Adjustment Responses in Eastern Europe: A Comparative Perspective', *International Organization*, Volume 40, Issue 2, March 1986, 239–285.

42 Data are from the *Financial Times*, 'Poland debts to leading creditors', 31 March 1981.

43 *Financial Times*, 'Poland confirms it cannot meet bank repayments', 8 April 1981.

44 OECDA, WP3 Documents 1981, CPE/WP3(81)5, 29 April 1981.

45 IMFA, ID/80/7, Confidential Paper 'World Economic Outlook-General Survey' 22 August 1980, Electronic Document.

46 BIS Annual Report 1982, 11.

47 IMFA, SM/81/133, 'International Capital Markets – Recent Developments and Short-Term Prospects', 10 June 1981, Electronic Document.

48 Idem.

49 BIS Annual Report 1982, 132.

50 Data are from the 1982 BIS Annual Report.

51 On the IBF see for example Sydney J. Key and Henry S. Terrell, 'International Banking Facilities', *International Finance Discussion Papers*, Board of Governors of the Federal Reserve System, Number 333, September 1988, 1–29.

52 Edwin M. Truman, 'The International Debt Situation', *International Finance Discussion Papers*, Board of Governors of the Federal Reserve System, Number 298, December 1986, 4–5.

53 LBA, F/1/D/Boa/3.3, LBI Review of Corporate Strategy, January 1982.

54 Joel Métais, 'International Strategies of French Banks', in Christian de Boissieu (ed.), *Banking in France*, Routledge, London and New York, 1990, 149.

55 Edward P. M. Gardener and Philip Molyneux, *Changes in Western European Banking. An International Banker's Guide*, Routledge, London, 1994, 67.

56 BBA, BBI Annual Report, various years.

57 Martin Vander Weyer, *Falling Eagle. The Decline of Barclays Bank*, Weidenfeld & Nicolson, London, 2000.

58 BBA, 80/5912, 'The Strategic Plan 1979–1983', mid-February 1978.

59 BBA, 80/5911, BBI 'Corporate Plan 1977–1981', no date.

60 BBA, Barclays Bank International Limited Report and Accounts 1981.

61 BBA, 80/1215, Note to General Managers 'Future International Expansion', 22 June 1981.

62 Idem.

63 Idem.

64 Idem.

65 Idem.

66 LBA, F/1/Ce/Off/1, Secret document 'Review of Corporate Strategy', July 1979.

67 LBA, F/Ce/Off/2.1, Confidential Document 'Policy Guidance 1980/81 from the Chief Executive', April 1980.

68 MBA, Report of the Directors and Accounts 1980.

69 BFA 1415200610-24, Direction Générale des Services Etrangers, 'Les Euro-crédits: Contrôle étatique et rôle des banques centrales', 11 August 1980.

70 CLA, 110AH12, 'Programme DOFI 1981', 4 June 1980.

71 CLA, 110AH14, Exposé de M. de Montbel 'Le Crédit Lyonnais à l'Étranger', 3 June 1981.

72 Philippe Szymczak, 'Bank Profitability in France', in Christian de Boissieu (ed.), *Banking in France*, Routledge, London and New York, 1991, 120.

73 BBA, 80/1224, 'Minutes of the Meeting of the Group Policy Committee', 17 December 1980.

74 BBA, 'Barclays Bank Plc Report and Accounts 1981'.

75 Idem.

76 LBA, F/1/D/Boa/3.1, Internal Document from the Director of the Latin American Division, Guy Huntrods, to the Chairman's Committee, 15 January 1981.

77 Idem.

78 Idem.

79 LBA, F/1/D/Boa/3.1, LBI Middle East and Africa Division Report, November 1980.

80 The leverage ratio, measured as the ratio between average assets and average equity capital, grew from 24 to 31 between 1975 and 1980. See LBA, F/1/D/Boa/3.1, Strictly Confidential Document, 'Management Briefing', December 1980.

81 Idem.

82 LBA, F/1/D/Boa/3.1, Strictly Confidential LBI 'Management Briefing', June 1981.

83 LBA, F/1/D/Boa/3.1, Strictly Confidential Document, 'Management Briefing', June 1981.

84 LBA, F/1/D/Boa/3.2, Secret document, 'Review of Corporate Strategy', January 1982.

85 MBA, Board Minutes, 4 July 1980.

86 MBA, Midland Board Minutes, 3 October 1980.

87 MBA, Midland Board Minutes, 3 July 1981.

88 *Financial Times*, 'Midland Bank takes 51% of Crocker for $595m', 16 October 1981.

89 SGA, 81145, Service des études économique, 'L'endettement de l'Amérique Latine', 16 February 1982.

90 CLA, 110AH12, Memorandum of A. Wolkenstein on Socialist countries, 12 May 1980, 'Le Crédit Lyonnais s'est montré jusqu'en 1979, plus restrictif, à l'exception de l'URSS que nos confrères et nos positions commerciales, tant auprès des banques socialistes que des clients français, en ont quelque peu souffert. Tout en poursuivant sa politique de prudence et de sélectivité à l'égard de ces pays, il doit avoir pour objectif de maintenir sa présence ou de la renforcer'.

91 CLA, 110AH12, 'Programme DOFI 1981', 4 June 1981.

92 CLA, 119AH010, 'Contrôle budgétaire au 30 juin 1982'.

93 See for example: Robert E. Wood, *From Marshall Plan to Debt Crisis*, University of California Press, Berkeley, CA and London, 1986, 250 and James M. Boughton, 'From Suez to Tequila: The IMF as Crisis Manager', *IMF Working Paper*, WP/97/90, July 1997.

94 See for example Luis Bértola and José Antonio Ocampo, *The Economic Development of Latin America Since Independence*, Oxford University Press, Oxford, UK, 2012, 138–197.

95 Ibid.

96 James M. Boughton, 'From Suez to Tequila: The IMF as Crisis Manager', *IMF Working Paper*, WP/97/90, July 1997, 16.

97 On the IMF and the Debt Crisis see Harold James, *International Monetary Cooperation since Bretton Woods*, International Monetary Fund and Oxford University Press, Washington, DC and Oxford, UK, 1996.

98 Robert Gilpin, *Global Political Economy*, Princeton University Press, Princeton, NJ and Oxford, UK, 2001, 313.

99 Jeffry Frieden, *Global Capitalism*, W. W. Norton & Company, New York, 2007, 376.

100 Joseph P. Joyce, *The IMF and Global Financial Crises*, Cambridge University Press, Cambridge, UK, 2012, 52.

101 See for example: Michael Moffitt, *The World's Money. International Banking from Bretton Woods to the Brink of Insolvency*, Simon & Schuster, New York, 1983; William R. Cline, *International Debt: Systemic Risk and Policy Response*, MIT Press, Cambridge, MA and London, 1984; David F. Lomax, *The Developing Country Debt Crisis*, Macmillan, London and Basingstoke, UK, 1986; Philip A. Wellons, *Passing the Buck. Banks, Governments, and Third World Debt*, Harvard Business School University Press, Cambridge, MA, 1987; Robert Devlin, *Debt and Crises in Latin America. The Supply Side of the Story*, Princeton University Press, Princeton, NJ, 1989; Barry Eichengreen and Peter H. Lindert (eds), *The International Debt Crisis in Historical Perspective*, MIT Press, Cambridge, MA, and London, 1989; Harold James, *International Monetary Cooperation since Bretton Woods*, International Monetary Fund and Oxford University Press, Washington, DC and Oxford, UK, 1996; James M. Boughton, *Silent Revolution. The International Monetary Fund 1979–1989*, International Monetary Fund, Washington, DC, 2001.

102 BISA, BIS Annual Report 1983. 118.

103 IMFA, SM/83/74, 'International Capital Markets-Developments and Prospects 1983', 10 May 1983, Electronic Document.

104 BIS Annual Report 1983, 109.

105 David Folkerts-Landau, 'The Changing Role of International Bank Lending in Developing Finance', *IMF Staff Papers*, 32, June 1985, 317.

106 Idem, 130.

107 IMFA, European Department-Subject Files Box 146, 'Remarks by J. de Larosière to the Meeting of the International Financial Group', Ditchley Park, 8 May 1982.

108 IMFA, EBS/82/194, Confidential Document, 'The Adequacy of Existing Arrangements to Deal with Major Strains in the International Financial System', 22 October 1982, Electronic Document.

109 IMFA, European Department-Subject Files Box 146, 'Remarks by J. de Larosière to the Meeting of the International Financial Group', Ditchley Park, 8 May 1982.

110 BEA, Quarterly Bulletins March 1983, W. P. Cooke Speech 'The international banking scene: a supervisory perspective' at the Financial Times World Banking conference, London, 9 December 1982.
111 BBA, 156/97, 'BBI Group Provision 30.06.1982', no date.
112 BBA, 156/97, Strictly Private and Confidential Note, 'Head Office International Newsletter', August 1982.
113 BBA, 156/97, 'BBI Strategic Plan 1983/1987', November 1982.
114 Idem.
115 BBA, 156/97, 'Mr Pelly's Visit to Mexico and California', November 1982.
116 BBA, Barclays Bank Limited Report and Accounts 1982, 'Address by the Chairman Timothy Bevan'.
117 LBA, F/1/D/Boa/3.3, Strictly Confidential Management Briefing, LBI 'Objectives and Performance', December 1982.
118 Idem.
119 Idem.
120 LBA, HO/Ch/Mor/30, Secret Note for the Board, 'Restructuring International Banking Division', 18 March 1986.
121 LBA, HO/Ch/Mor/30, 'Minutes of a Meeting of the International Strategy Working Party', 30 July 1987.
122 *Financial Times*, 'Standard Chartered Rejects £1.17bn. Lloyds Bank Bid', 16 April 1986.
123 LBA, HO/Ch/Mor/30, 'Lloyds Bank's Expansion of International Operations', Strategic Planning Unit, 7 September 1987.
124 LBA, HO/Ch/Mor/30, 'Report of the International Strategy Working Party', 19 October1987.
125 *The Economist*, 'The Lloyds money machine', 15 January 1998.
126 SGA, 81145, 'Compte-rendu de la réunion annuelle du Secteur Amérique Latine', 25 May1983.
127 Idem.
128 CLA, 332AH180, Letter of President Deflassieux to the DCAIC, 30 December 1983.
129 CLA, 332AH180, Internal Memo, 'La Politique', 1987?
130 Louis W. Pauly, *Who Elected the Bankers?*, Cornell University Press, Ithaca, NY, 1997, 116:

> In a sense, of course, the Fund has always been involved in financial crises; under a regime of pegged exchange rates, every major exchange-rate realignment constituted a crisis of sorts for the particular governments involved. But *only in the past fifteen years has the Fund's role as crisis manager fully developed*. In the midst of the developing country debt crisis that began in 1982 and the transitions to capitalism in the former Soviet Union and its allies later in the decade, that role came to constitute *a primary rationale for the continued existence of the Fund*. In an era when international capital markets have been expected to render superfluous its financing role, the Fund and its surveillance mandate became, not less, important [emphasis added].

131 John Walton and Charles Ragin, 'Global and National Sources of Political Protest: Third World Responses to the Debt Crisis', *American Sociological Review*, December 1990, Vol. 55, issue 6, 876.
132 Santiago Capraro and Ignacio Perrottini, 'Revisiting Latin America's Debt Crisis: Some Lessons for the Periphery of the Eurozone', *Cambridge Journal of Economics*, 2013, 37, 627.
133 Barry Eichengreen, *The European Economy since 1945*, Princeton University Press, Princeton, NJ and Oxford, UK, 2007, 295.
134 Gerald F. Davis, *Managed by the Markets. How Finance Re-Shaped America*, Oxford University Press, Oxford, UK and New York, 2009, 102.

Conclusion

Interregnum

At all events, every capitalist development of this order seems, by reaching the stage of financial expansion, to have in some sense announced its maturity: it was a sign of autumn.[1]

Accounting for the rise of international finance

The decade between 1973 and 1982 marked a new phase of radical expansion and modernisation for the global banking and financial sector and, as far as this book is concerned, for European banks after the conservative years of Bretton Woods.

European banks moved from being safe and domestic entities, relegated to the role of simply allocating credit, to complex organisations spanning the globe providing a wide range of services. We are now accustomed to a hypertrophic banking and financial sector, but what we have tried to illustrate throughout this book is that this transformation, or, at least, the pace of it, was far from inevitable.

Despite the opposition of the international financial community and the changes to the original proposals, the system developed in Bretton Woods was based on the limited role of financial capital and the subservient role of the banking sector. The ideological foundations had a severe impact on international banking and financial activities.

Gradually, European banks retrenched behind domestic borders and what remained of their colonies, limiting their activities to trade finance and retail banking activities within the local communities. Banking was ultimately made 'boring' but safe. In the early days of Bretton Woods, the conservative character of post-war finance bear its fruits in terms of economic stability, lack of large-scale financial crises and low levels of inequality.

The Bretton Woods regime was successful from an ideological point of view, but less so from the practical one as capital gradually found a way to move across borders and remain there. Dollars came to be increasingly accumulated outside American borders, mainly in the City of London, and, little by little, these funds gave birth to a parallel monetary market outside the competences of the US government.

Like many scholars before us, we recognised in the Eurodollar market the *primum movens*, or prime mover, able to usher in a new era of financial globalisation.[2] Nonetheless, after carefully looking at the histories of several banks, we quickly realised that by the mid- to late 1960s, the face of European finance was in many ways still less sophisticated than in the 1920s and that several elements were missing in order to spark the rise of international finance in Europe. Few customers, only prime borrowers, had access to the Eurodollar market; few banks, a handful of American and European banks, were participating in it and the amounts exchanged on this market were still very limited compared to domestic activities. Even the most international bank on the European continent, Barclays, was essentially a colonial bank or, as some authors have argued, an African bank still influenced in its scale and scope by its colonial heritage.

Much more than the fall of the dollar exchange standard, which 'even before the Arab-Israeli War and the OPEC oil embargo of 1973 . . . had fallen into disarray',[3] we have argued that the most important catalyst for the liberalisation of finance was the crisis of 1973 as huge flows of petrodollars were channeled to developing countries through large American, European and Japanese banks.

In our book we have posited that the crisis of 1973 and the imbalances it created represented a critical juncture in contemporary financial history, because the quadrupling of oil prices ignited a systemic growth in the financial markets. A similar dynamic in 1979 reinforced this tendency.

By focusing on some aspects neglected by existing literature, we have argued that the first oil crisis crucially accelerated the rise of international finance for three reasons. First, the crisis of 1973 put a definitive end to the German proposal of regulating the Euromarket through coordinated capital controls, because the recycling need shifted priorities in the international agenda. As the recycling priority superseded regulation, the interests of the financial community and of the international policymakers were realigned after the break with Bretton Woods. Second, the first and second recycling challenges provided huge funds, crucially lacking in the 1960s and early 1970s, which the banking sector was able to invest in international operations. Finally, the two energy crises gave powerful incentives to expand overseas given the grim economic outlook in the Western world, pushing European banks to enter new countries, to develop new products and to create new alliances.

The impact of the 1973 energy crisis is apparently paradoxical. On the one hand, the crisis is universally credited as marking the symbolic end of the postwar boom based on the Fordist system of accumulation; on the other, it had a pivotal role in re-empowering the banking and financial sector by putting commercial banks and the Euromarket at the centre of the recycling mechanism. As a consequence, the activity level in the Euromarkets skyrocketed. In this volume, we have answered this apparent paradox by establishing a causal link between industrial crisis and financial expansion, as banks became the crucial clog between surplus and deficit countries.

The 1970s, thus, appear increasingly as years of 'crisis' and 'interregnum' to the financial historian. Antonio Gramsci famously wrote that: 'La crisi consiste appunto nel fatto che il vecchio muore e il nuovo non può nascere: in questo interregno si verificano i fenomeni morbosi più svariati'.[4]

Jagged edges

The primary concern of this book has been to provide new archival-driven understandings of the rise of international finance by concretely explaining how international finance was able to rise from the ashes of the restrictive Bretton Woods regime and analysing the impact of the reopening of international capital markets on commercial banks in France and the United Kingdom, two former colonial empires with an established history of international banking presence. Despite the existence of a vast literature on the rise of finance in the last decades, we sought to limit the scope of our analysis by addressing three jagged edges in particular.

First, why was the Eurodollar market, the progenitor of modern finance, ultimately kept unregulated in the early 1970s even though several proposals were on the table, notably at the Bank for International Settlements (BIS) in Basel? Second, how did European commercial banks become one of the main actors in the recycling of petrodollars by lending directly to governments in LDCs? Finally, what impact did the reopening of finance have on the European banking and financial sector?

In order to find credible answers to these questions, it was essential to get our hands dusty and explore the archives of international organisations, central banks and commercial banks in France and the UK.

Recently disclosed documents of the BIS and central banks in France and the UK enabled us to illustrate the birth, growth and the regulatory threats pending on the Euromarket. The possibility of regulation of this offshore and unregulated market was strong because of German pressures. Ultimately, the market was saved by a stroke of good luck as the oil shock and the recycling of petrodollars superseded regulatory proposals, and the smooth flow of petrodollars became the number one priority in international financial circles in order to save the world economy and the 'open international system that had been the legacy of Bretton Woods'.[5] The lack of regulation of the Euromarket is a crucial element for understanding the subsequent rise of international finance. The success of the German proposal would have critically impaired the attractiveness of the Euromarket by reducing the regulatory distortions in its favour and possibly limiting its appeal to potential lenders and borrowers. Consequently, the reduced attractiveness would have given a stronger role to official instruments of recycling.

Ultimately, the proposal arrived on the table of the G-10 Governors in the summer of 1973. The two 'Battles of Basel' were a pivotal moment in the history of finance, a moment where two opposite visions of international finance (and society) faced each other: the free-marketeers against the controllers. According to more recent archival evidence, it seems there was much more contention about the future of the Euromarket than existing US-centric analyses presume. In the early 1970s and, again, in the late 1970s, the German and German-American initiatives were put aside because of the imperatives of recycling. Thus, in our work, the oil crisis takes a central stage in explaining the rise of international finance. Once the market was freed and commercial banks received some reassurance that they would be bailed out in case of crisis, after the G-10 Governors communiqué of September 1974, the most important transfer of wealth in history could begin, with all the consequences that we have described in the previous chapters.

A second jagged edge is represented by the negotiations at the BIS, the IMF and OECD on the Euromarket and the recycling challenge. To the best of our knowledge, these negotiations have received limited attention by historians. We have been able to show the inner workings on how the re-equilibrating task was ultimately delegated to commercial banks, highlighting the interactions between international organisations and commercial banks and the impact of such interactions. The oil crisis led to the international financial community gathering around the IMF, the BIS and the OECD in a critical situation. The usual tools of monetary policy could not be used in order to avoid a recessionary spiral, the conservative position of Germany was weakened by the need to facilitate the inflows of funds and the need to create new outlets for European exports contributed to the decision to delegate the process of re-balancing international disequilibria to the Euromarket and consequently to the banking sector.

The oil crisis and the subsequent need to recycle oil money changed the 'ballgame', as we have seen in Chapter 3, as international priorities shifted and the need to re-equilibrate international imbalances quickly became the number one priority in international financial circles. In order to keep the economy going and avoid an economic depression in the West, a consensus was reached not to fight the oil-induced deficits but to accommodate them and to re-equilibrate the imbalances through a recycling of dollars from surplus to deficit countries. Western governments now needed banks to act as intermediaries between developed and developing countries and help domestic industries export their products, and the Euroloans they provided to LDCs became crucial for the creation of new markets. The interests of the international and financial community were finally realigned.

The process of recycling the oil wealth accumulated by oil-exporting countries was the result of a consensus reached by Western central bankers and finance ministers on the fact that the international economy had to keep going and that the worst enemy for the health of the global economy was a depression like the one experienced in the 1930s, when the world economy collapsed under the weight of nationalisms. Official channels, like the IMF Oil Facilities, soon proved inadequate because of the mistrust, for opposite reasons, of the Americans and the oil producers. The chosen mechanism for re-equilibrating global imbalances was found in the Euromarket because of the flexibility and anonymity offered to the lenders.

The European banking sector could embark upon a process of financial intermediation on a global scale. To be adequate to the challenge, European commercial banks had to readapt and reshape their international activities.

Thus, the third and final jagged edge resided in the analysis of the transformation of the European banking sector. How was the European banking sector transformed? How did established institutions react to the rapidly changing economic context? In order to expand existing literature, we have focused on five of the most important banks in the UK and France. The first timid changes in the European banking sector took place in the late 1960s under the influence of domestic measures and the growth of the Eurodollar market. Internal structures and overseas strategies were gradually reshaped, but, until the oil crisis, even the largest British and French banks looked very similar to their pre-war ancestors. The transformation of the European banking sector accelerated dramatically with the new funds deposited by oil producing countries, and a new phase of expansion was inaugurated. Relying on a comparative account, we identified several recurring and interrelated challenges faced by European banks in the period studied, namely, internationalisation, cooperation, autonomous initiatives, internal reorganisations and, from the late 1970s, exposure.

Under the influence of the Euromarket, European banks were forced to sever their ties to the old practices of colonial and correspondent banking and to open up to a new world of potential customers. One of the favourite ways to respond to the internationalisation challenge was to cooperate with other continental banks through clubs and consortia. The recycling challenge greatly reinforced the tendency to expand overseas and gave a whole new dimension to the process, as almost all the major continental banks entered into a cooperative phase. As the 1970s progressed, European banks gradually became more confident to devise autonomous initiatives to enter new markets through representative offices, but especially branches and subsidiaries around the globe. Not surprisingly, such changes put internal structures under strain and new structures had to be devised to tackle the challenges. International departments were created or readapted and new international subsidiaries were created. By the end of the decade, the result of the international spree were increasingly high levels of exposure to LDC debt, which forced European banks to reconsider their overseas expansion and to focus on selected markets. The second half of the 1970s and the early 1980s were hectic years, with the imperative of getting bigger at any cost supplanting once and for all the conservative banking practices of the post-war era. Some of the banks studied took very poor strategic decisions. Probably the clearest example is Midland and its acquisition of Crocker. The Californian bank was burdened by bad debts made in the United States and, particularly, in LDCs estimated at around US$ 200 million.[6]

The European banks in our study expanded their international business in a remarkable way. Even though some initiatives predate the oil crisis and the recycling of petrodollars, the petrodollar *bonanza* radically transformed the scale and scope of their activities by providing much needed fuel to the engine of international growth. Throughout the decade, commercial banks in the UK and France gradually moved from being 'multi-domestic' at best to becoming much more global institutions, with a new mix of clients and products. Commercial banks extended loans to governments and companies in the developing world, and new offices were opened from Argentina to the Philippines, from Mexico to South Korea.

It should be clear by now that throughout our research we have not tried to argue that the rise of finance in Europe witnessed in the 1980s, 1990s and 2000s would not have taken place without the events of the 1970s. What we have argued instead is that the 1970s gave a fundamental contribution to the rise of international finance in Europe and that that process was greatly accelerated during the decade by the recycling challenge and by the lack of regulation on the Euromarket. Overall, we can give an affirmative reply to Mexican historian, Carlos Marichal's, question and say that yes, these flows of capital represented without any doubt the progenitors of the financial globalisation to come.[7]

Change and opportunity

Our historical account ends in the early 1980s with the crisis of LDCs and the advent of a 'lost decade' for many of them, notably in Latin America but also on the African continent.

What is most intriguing is the fact that the response to the worst crisis since the Great Depression has not been a return to the practices and ideals of Bretton Woods but, instead, a continuation of neo-liberal policies and even an acceleration in the process of financial globalisation as measured by the sum of foreign assets and foreign liabilities known as the International Financial Integration (IFI) ratio and other measures of financial openness. Along with the continued growth of finance, inequalities have exploded in the last decades. According to a study on American wealth by economists Emmanuel Saez and Gabriel Zucman, the share of wealth owned by the top 0.01 per cent of the population in 2012 (fortunes of more than US$110 million, around 16,000 families in the US) represented 11.2 per cent of total wealth, as much as in 1916 and more than in 1929. This is in striking contrast to the Bretton Woods era when the losses experienced by the wealthiest families from the late 1920s to the late 1970s were so large that in 1980, the average real wealth of the top 0.01 per cent families (US$44 million in constant 2010 prices) was half its 1929 value (US$87 million).[8] Intriguingly, the rise in inequality roughly coincides with the financial liberalisation ushered in by the Euromarket and the renaissance of Western banking. This could simply be a coincidence or a more revealing phenomenon worth further investigation.

The 1980s were a decade of tremendous transformations, even though most of the neo-liberal reforms implemented during the Thatcher and Reagan years were a ratification of the state of things in place already in the 1970s.[9]

The crisis of 1982 erupted because of the *largesse* in borrowing, but if some authors quickly put the blame on the banking sector for reckless lending[10] (and this is more than justified), we have highlighted how the decision not to regulate the Euromarket and delegate the recycling task to the private sector was a political one, taken, essentially, by the same people in Basel, Washington and Paris. As historians, we have a duty to add a further layer of complexity to existing histories on financial globalisation, because too often the prevailing view is similar to Hollywood's representation of finance portrayed by popular films such as Oliver Stone's 'Wall Street' or Martin Scorsese's 'The Wolf of Wall Street'. Despite the many qualities of these films, the representation of the financial world is overly simplistic as finance executives seem to operate in a world where politics, in the form of government, central banks, etc. is almost totally absent.

The rise of international finance we have witnessed in the last 40 years is not (solely) the product of unstoppable 'market and technological developments'.[11] Accommodating national and international institutions have fostered these epochal changes. Once the existence of the Euromarket securing a competitive deregulatory dynamic was ignited, the banking community used the 'competitive pressures of the Euromarket to force domestic deregulation'.[12] In France the decision of the Mitterrand government to give up its expansionary fiscal policy under the pressure of international financial speculation had important consequences both at home and abroad as 'the embedded liberal framework of thought that the Mitterrand government had endorsed . . . was rejected overnight in favour of a neoliberal focus on monetary discipline and market liberalization'.[13]

At the industry level, the crisis of 1982 forced commercial banks to reassess the nature of credit risks and credit standards, and also reduced the banks' previous emphasis on balance-sheet growth at any cost. The period following the debt crisis saw the rapid move away from asset growth to asset and liability management through securitisation. Since the 1980s, the institution-based intermediation centred around banks gradually came to be replaced by market-based intermediation based on financial markets. Non-marketable bank assets such as Euroloans were replaced by marketable ones such as Note Issuance Facilities (NIF), i.e. bank loans immediately sold on the market, allowing the bank to earn income fees and other compensation. A second type of securitisation involved the transformation of illiquid assets on the balance sheets of financial institutions into marketable ones.

The growth of securitisation was a symptom of a broader shift towards off-balance-sheet activities (OBS), such as derivatives and over-the-counter transactions. The growth in OBS activities was fostered by the lack of extra regulatory costs to the banks, partly allowing banks to limit the decline of profitability caused by increasing competition in financial markets. These activities did not require banks to put aside reserves or capital and provided a source both of profit and also of potential losses. As Chicago-based, financial economist Luigi Zingales has pointed out, there is no evidence at present showing that 'the creation of the junk bond market, the option and future markets, or over-the-counter derivatives are positively correlated with economic growth'.[14]

As a decade ended and a new one began, banks continued to move into fee- based services and, when regulations allowed, investment banking and other financial activities.

Following a wave of deregulation and convergence, culminating in the creation of the European Single Market, the lines between Euro and domestic markets became increasingly blurred as well as the distinction between an investment bank, a commercial bank and an insurance company.

The 1990s saw a continuation and acceleration in the process of financial globalisation. New capital flows to developing regions, which greatly decreased after 1982, had picked up again by the early-1990s. By 1996, borrowings from banks, portfolio equity flows and net bond issues amounted to US$244 billion compared to just US$36 billion in 1989.[15] Most of these funds went to the 'Asian Tigers' (Hong Kong, Singapore, South Korea and Taiwan) and to a lesser extent to Latin America. The Mexican crisis of 1994 and the Asian crisis of 1997 did not stop the globalisation of finance, and the 2000s continued to expand the role of finance in our everyday lives. In the United States, the regulations of the 1930s were repealed in 1999 under the 'Financial Services Modernization Act' of 1999, which allowed the creation of financial conglomerates.

First, the subprime crisis, then the European debt crisis and several scandals like the LIBOR rigging scandal, pushed many people from different backgrounds to publicly criticise the role of banks and bankers. Public investigations into the origins of the financial crisis have been conducted in the US[16] and the UK,[17] with embarrassing results. The former Governor of the Bank of England, Sir Mervyn King, and the former Chairman of the Financial Stability Authority (FSA), Lord Turner, called for a change in bank culture after the explosion of the LIBOR scandal, talking about 'excessive levels of compensation' and 'a degree of cynicism which is quite shocking'.[18] Zingales has argued that 'at the current state of knowledge there is no theoretical reason or empirical evidence to support the notion that all growth in the financial sector over the last 40 years has been beneficial to society'.[19] Other economists have started to reconsider the dogma of a positive monotonic relationship between finance and economic growth, arguing that there can be 'too much finance' especially when credit to the private sector reaches 100 per cent of GDP.[20]

Unfortunately, in our opinion, as times goes by and the memories of the damages of financial turbulences fade away, the hopes of a new 'Bretton Woods moment'[21] seem to evaporate into thin air. Talking at the 125th anniversary of the *Financial Times*, the Governor of the Bank of England, Mark Carney, argued that 'a vibrant financial sector brings substantial benefits'.[22] Carney's quote captures one of the most important lessons coming out of our research. If modern finance has become a large casino,[23] it is because politics has allowed it to do so.

Indeed, the international forums of discussion did not do much to stop the deregulating and liberalising wave in the last decades: the opposite was the case as these institutions have fallen prey to regulatory capture and have gradually become tools to protect and consolidate the power of sectarian interests. As we have shown, the UK regulator, the Treasury and the banking sector were entangled in a promiscuous relationship as part of the famous 'Bank of England-Treasury-City' nexus.[24] Even though the US is not part of our study, deregulatory pressures were strong there too; we mentioned the International Banking Facility under the pressure of Wall Street bankers as one example. These two countries were not alone in their efforts to liberalise and deregulate. What is now called the Basel Committee on Banking Supervision first met in February 1975, and its first two Chairmen were Sir George Blunden and Peter Cooke from the Bank of England, two people not exactly in favour of tougher regulations. More generally, there has been a systematic tendency from other states to:

> [d]efer to US and UK representatives on regulatory questions, because they were home country regulators for institutions in the City of London and Wall Street and therefore had most exposure to the latest practices and technologies of the biggest banks and the best grasp of the issues at stake.[25]

We saw a vivid example of this tendency when the BIS relied on the material and data of the Bank of England during the debate on the Euromarket.

The lobbying of interest groups in international financial matters has been already analysed by a large literature.[26] As a consequence, financial institutions have been left in charge of making 'their own rules'.[27] The Institute of International Finance (IIF), the world's only association of financial institutions created after the LDC debt crisis, played a fundamental role in the writing of the final policy script of the Basel II agreement. After the financial meltdown of the late 2000s, there has been strong lobbying by the banking and financial sector against the new rules of the Basel III agreements. As a consequence of banks' lobbying, the *New York Times* reported that 'the new international capital requirements for banks known as Basel III . . . were significantly relaxed by regulators'.[28] As a result of pressures from the financial community, the full implementation of the agreement has been postponed to 2019 from 2015. The fact that financial lobbies are the largest contributors both in the US and in Europe might have played a role.

Revolving doors have facilitated the flow of people between the public and private sector and vice versa. Many of the characters we presented in our research came from the civil sector: Marc Viénot, Sir Jeremy Morse, Lord Armstrong of Sanderstead, Sir Kit McMahon just to mention a few, and moved from national and/ or international institutions to the banking sector. In the US there have been studies on the 'Wall Street-Washington corridor' to describe the permeability between public offices and appointments at financial firms.[29]

An important difference to current practices is that most of the bank managers remained at the helm for several years if not decades in the banks they managed, similarly to the rest of the employees. Now, the career span of financial executives and employees within the same institution is much shorter.

The damages produced by the financial debacle of 2008–2010 have been immense and have shown that the banking and financial sector is able to prostrate entire countries for many years. In their 'World Economic Situation and Prospects' for 2016, the United Nations pointed out that 'More than seven years after the global financial crisis, policymakers around the world still face enormous challenges in stimulating investment and reviving global growth'.[30]

If we wish, at least, to limit the severity of financial crises and their impact on society in the future, the banking and financial sector must radically change. The link between financial firms and political power must be severed. If freeing the markets was a political decision, then the process has to be reversed politically. If a political unity to take this decision cannot be attained, measures to limit the negative externalities of the financial sector have to be found. Proposals of 'ring-fencing' retail banking from wholesale/investment banking are a meaningful starting point which deserves to be implemented to limit the size of financial conglomerates and, consequently, their weight on the shoulders of taxpayers when things get nasty. If the casino cannot be closed, at least individuals should be allowed to decide whether to opt in.

If we want to create a safer but also 'a liquid, highly innovative financial system', bold actions have to be taken before time flies over us, leaving its shadow behind.

Notes

1 Fernand Braudel, *Civilization and Capitalism, 15th–18th Century: The Perspective of the World*, University of California Press, Berkeley, CA, 246.
2 Edwin Dickens, 'The Eurodollar Market and the New Era of Global Financialization', in Gerald E. Epstein (ed.), *Financialization and the World Economy*, Edward Elgar, Cheltenham, UK and Northampton, MA, 2005.
3 David Harvey, *A Brief History of Neoliberalism*, Oxford University Press, Oxford, UK and New York, 2005, 12.
4 Antonio Gramsci, *Quaderni del Carcere*, Vol. 1, Quaderni 1–5 (1929–1932), Einaudi, Torino, 2007, 311. The quote in English is as follows: 'The crisis consists precisely in the fact that the old is dying and the new cannot be born; in this interregnum a great variety of morbid symptoms appear'.
5 Harold James, *International Monetary Cooperation since Bretton Woods*, International Monetary Fund and Oxford University Press, Washington, DC and New York-Oxford, 1996, 316.
6 William R. Cline, *International Debt: Systemic Risk and Policy Response*, MIT Press, Cambridge, MA and London, 1983, 24.
7 Carlos Marichal, *Nueva historia de la grandes crisis financieras. Una perspectiva global, 1873–2008*, Editorial Debate, Madrid, Mexico City and Buenos Aires, 2010, 181. Carlos Marichal asked himself: 'Es por esto que una pregunta que hacemos en las paginas siguientes consiste en saber si es posible afirmar que los verdaderos antecedentes de la globalización financiera moderna se encuentran en estos poderosos flujos internacionales de capital de los años 1970 a 1982'.
8 Emmanuel Saez and Gabriel Zucman, 'Wealth Inequality in the United States since 1913: Evidence from Capitalized Income Data Tax', *Quarterly Journal of Economics*, Vol.131, Issue 2, 519–578.
9 On the transformation of the financial sector in the 1980s and 1990s see, for example, Robert Solomon, *Money on the Move. The Revolution in International Finance Since 1980*, Princeton University Press, Princeton, NJ, 1999.
10 Robert Devlin, *Debt and Crisis in Latin America. The Supply Side of the Story*, Princeton University Press, Princeton, NJ, 1989.
11 Eric Helleiner, 'Explaining the Globalization of Financial Markets: Bringing States Back In', *Review of International Political Economy*, Vol. 2, No. 2, Spring 1995, 334.
12 Eric Helleiner, *States and the Reemergence of Global Finance*, Cornell University Press, Ithaca, NY and London, 1994, 138.
13 Idem, 143.
14 Luigi Zingales, 'Presidential Address: Does Finance Benefit Society ?', *The Journal of Finance*, Vol. LXX, No. 4, August 2015, 1342.
15 Robert Solomon, *Money on the Move. The Revolution in International Finance since 1980*, Princeton University Press, Princeton, NJ, 1999, 113.
16 The Financial Crisis Inquiry Report submitted by the Financial Crisis Inquiry Commission, January 2011.
17 Final Report of the Independent Commission on Banking chaired by Sir John Vickers, September 2011. A Parliamentary Commission on Banking Standards was established in July 2012 and published its Final Report in June 2013.
18 *Financial Times*, 'Regulators Call for Change in Bank Culture', 29 June 2012.
19 Luigi Zingales, 'Presidential Address: Does Finance Benefit Society ?', *The Journal of Finance*, Vol. LXX, No. 4, August 2015, 1328.
20 Jean-Louis Arcand, Enrico Berkes and Ugo Panizza, 'Too Much Finance?', *Journal of Economic Growth*, June 2015, Vol. 20, No. 2, 105–148.
21 See, for example Eric Helleiner, 'A Bretton Woods Moment? The 2007–2008 Crisis and the Future of Global Finance', *International Affairs*, Vol. 86, No. 3, 2010, 619–636.

22 Speech given by Mark Carney, Governor of the Bank of England, at the 125th anniversary of the *Financial Times*, London, 24 October 2013.

23 Susan Strange, *Casino Capitalism*, Manchester University Press, Manchester, UK, 1986.

24 Geoffrey Ingham, *Capitalism Divided: The City and Industry in British Social Development*, Macmillan, London, 1984.

25 Andrew Baker, 'Retaining Regulatory Capture? Anglo-America, Crisis Politics and Trajectories of Change in Global Financial Governance', *International Affairs*, Vol. 86, No. 3, 2010, 651.

26 See, for example, Jean Cristophe Graz and Andreas Nole (eds), *Transnational Private Governance and Its Limits*, Routledge, London, 2008.

27 Eleni Tsingou, 'Transnational Private Governance and the Basel Process: Banking Regulation and Supervision, Private Interests and Basel II', in Jean Cristophe Graz and Andreas Nole (eds), *Transnational Private Governance and Its Limits*, Routledge, London, 2008.

28 *The New York Times*, 'Easing of Rules for Banks Acknowledges Reality', 7 January 2013.

29 These include Robert Rubin, who served as Chairman of Citigroup, Henry Paulson, who served as Chairman and CEO of Goldman Sachs, William C. Dudley, Partner and Managing Director at Goldman Sachs, and Timothy Geithner, who left the post of US Secretary of the Treasury to become President of the private equity firm, Warburg Pincus.

30 United Nations, 'World Economic Situation and Prospects 2016', New York, 2016, vi.

References

Archives

Bank of England (BEA)
Quarterly Bulletins various years
3A143/1
4106/1
6A43/1, 2
6A123/1, 4, 5, 6, 7, 8, 9, 10
6A227/1
8A406/5, 6
Bank of International Settlements (BISA)
Annual Reports: 1964, 1974, 1976, 1977, 1978, 1979, 1980, 1981, 1982, 1983
7.15 (1) G10 D22
13 (a) 3 Vol. 9–11
7.18 (23) GILB
7.18 (16) HAL.4
Banque de France (BFA)
1415200610-24
1489200304-15
1495200501-577
Barclays Bank (BBA)
Barclays DCO/BBI Report and Accounts 1967, 1971, 1972, 1981, 1982
50/5116
80/1215
80/1224
80/2521
80/3173, 3175
80/5369
80/5850, 5859
80/5894
80/5902, 5904, 5906, 5907, 5908, 5911, 5912
80/6148
80/6172
80/6284
156/97
Bundesbank

Annual Reports: 1969, 1971, 1974, 1979
Crédit Lyonnais (CLA)
Board Minutes 1971, 1975
Annual Reports, various years
110AH2
110AH10, 11, 12, 14
111AH11
119AH010
143AH7, 8, 9, 10, 12, 13
332AH180
International Monetary Fund (IMFA)
European Department Division Files-EUR Division Subject Files Box 11
European Department-EURAI Subject Files Box 30
European Department-EURAI Subject Files Box 70
European Department-EURAI Subject Files Box 145 European Department-EURAI
    Subject Files Box 146
Western Hemisphere Department, WHDAI-Economic Subject Files Box 25
Exchange and Trade Relations Department, ETRAI-Director Ernest Sturc Subject Files, Box 3
Exchange and Trade Relations Department-ETRAI Subject Files Box 4
Office of the Managing Director-Jacques de Larosière Papers Box 14
DM 69/82
DM/80/48
SM/76/138
SM/77/111
SM/78/160
SM/80/55
SM/80/159
SM/81/133
SM/83/74
ID/80/1
ID/80/4, 7
ID/81/6
EBM/80/121
EBM/80/150
EBS/82/194
Press Release no. 80/34
Lloyds Bank (LBA)
LBI Report and Accounts 1978, 1980, 1981
F/1/Bd/Far/1.6
F/1/Bd/Far/2.4
F/1/Ce/Off/1, 2.1
F/1/D/Boa/3.1, 3.2, 3.3
F/1/D/Com/2.4
HO/D/Int/1
HO/Ch/Fau/11–24 H
O/Ch/Fau/34
HO/Ch/Mor/ 11–24
HO/Ch/Mor/30
Midland Bank (MBA)

Report of the Directors and Accounts 1964, 1977, 1980
Board Minutes 1974, 1975, 1976, 1979, 1980, 1981
0141/0033
0200/0749b
0200/0759 a, b
0200/0760d
0528/0008
Organisation for Cooperation and Development (OECDA)
WP3 Documents 1971, CPE/WP3/71(5)
WP3 Documents 1974, CPE/WP3(74)1, CPE/WP3(74)10
WP3 Documents 1978, CPE/WP3(78)12
WP3 Documents 1979
WP3 Documents 1980, DES/NI(80)8
WP3 Documents 1981, CPE/WP3(81)5, CPE/WP3(81)
Société Générale (SGA)
Annual Report 1974
Board Minutes 1972
81093
81119
81120
81121
81137
81142
81145
81146
81147
81156
81161
81183
81283
81466

Books

Abdelal, R., *Capital Rules. The Construction of Global Finance*, Harvard University Press, Cambridge, MA and London.

Acheson, A. L. K., Chant, J. F. and Prachowny, M. F. J., *Bretton Woods Revisited*, Macmillan Press, London and Basingstoke, UK, 1972.

Ackrill M. and Hannah L., *Barclays, The Business of Banking 1690–1996*, Cambridge University Press, Cambridge, UK, 2001.

Aglietta, M. and Rebérioux, A., *Dérives du Capitalisme Financier*, Albin Michel, Paris, 2004.

Alhadeff, D. A., *Competition and Controls in Banking. A Study of the Regulation of Bank Competition in Italy, France, and England*, University of California Press, Berkeley, CA, 1968.

Aliber, R. Z., *The New International Money Game* (6th edition), The University of Chicago Press, Chicago, IL, 2000.

Arrighi, G., *The Long Twentieth Century. Money, Power, and the Origins of Our Times*, Verso, London and New York, 1994.

Badel, L., *Diplomatie et Grands Contrats: l'Etat Français et les Marchés Extérieurs au XXe Siècle*, Publications de la Sorbonne, Paris, 2010.

Basosi, D., *Finanza e Petrolio. Gli Stati Uniti, l'oro nero e l'economia politica internazionale*, Studio LT2 Edizioni, Venice, 2012.

Battilossi, S. and Cassis, Y. (eds), *European Banks and the American Challenge. Competition and Cooperation in International Banking under Bretton Woods*, Oxford University Press, Oxford, UK and New York, 2002.

Bauman, Z., *Liquid Modernity*, Polity Press, Cambridge, UK, 2000.

Becker, W. H. and McClenahan, W. M., *The Market, the State, and the Export-Import Bank of the United States*, Cambridge University Press, Cambridge, UK and New York, 2003.

Beckhart, B. H. (ed.), *Banking Systems*, Columbia University Press, New York, 1954.

Bell, D., *The Coming of the Post-Industrial Society*, Basic Books, New York, 1973.

Bell, G., *The Euro-Dollar Market and The International Financial System*, Macmillan, London and Basingstoke, UK, 1974.

Bernanke, B. S., *Essays on the Great Depression*, Princeton University Press, Princeton, NJ, 2000.

Bértola, L. and Ocampo, J. A., *The Economic Development of Latin America Since Independence*, Oxford University Press, Oxford, UK, 2012.

Block, F., *The Origins of International Economic Disorder*, UCLA Press, Berkeley, CA and London, 1977.

Bonin, H., *Suez. Du Canal à la Finance (1858–1987)*, Economica, Paris, 1987.

Bonin, H., *Histoire de la Société Générale (I) 1864–1890*, Droz, Genève, 2006.

Bordo, M. D. and Eichengreen, B. (eds), *A Retrospective on the Bretton Woods System: Lessons for International Monetary Reform*, University of Chicago Press, Chicago, IL and London, 1993.

Bordo, M. D., Goldin, C. and White, E. N. (eds), *The Defining Moment. The Great Depression and the American Economy in the Twentieth Century*, The University of Chicago Press, Chicago, IL and London, 1998.

Bordo, M. D., Taylor, A. M. and Williamson, J. G., *Globalization in Historical Perspective*, The University of Chicago Press, Chicago, IL and London, 2003.

Borio, C., Toniolo, G. and Clement, P. (eds), *The Past and Future of Central Bank Cooperation*, Cambridge University Press, Cambridge, UK, 2008.

Boughton, J. M., *Silent Revolution. The International Monetary Fund 1979–1989*, International Monetary Fund, Washington, DC, 2001.

Bouvier, J., *Le Crédit Lyonnais de 1863 à 1882. Les Années de Formation d'une Grande Banque de Depôt*, 2 vols, SEVPEN, Paris, 1961.

Brambilla, C., Ciampi, C. A., Manzella, A. and Prodi, R., *La Sfida Internazionale della Comit*, Il Mulino, Bologna, 2013.

Braudel, F., *Civilization and Capitalism, 15th–18th Century* (3 vols), University of California Press, Berkeley, CA, 1992.

Bremner, R. P., *Chairman of the Fed. William McChesney Martin Jr. and the Creation of the Modern American Financial System*, Yale University Press, New Haven, CT and London, 2004.

Brenner, R., *The Economics of Global Turbulence*, Verso, London, 2006.

Burn, G., *The Re-Emergence of Global Finance*, Palgrave Macmillan, Basingstoke, UK and New York, 2006.

Bussière, E., *Paribas, l'Europe et le Monde. 1872–1992*, Fonds Mercator, Anvers, Paris, 1992.

Capie, F., *The Bank of England, 1950s to 1979*, Cambridge University Press, Cambridge, UK and New York, 2010.

Cassis, Y., *Capitals of Capital. The Rise and Fall of International Financial Centres 1780–2009*, Cambridge University Press, Cambridge, UK and New York, 2010.

Cassis, Y., *Crises and Opportunities 1890–2010: The Shaping of Modern Finance*, Oxford University Press, Oxford, UK and New York, 2011.

Channon, D. E., *Global Banking Strategy*, John Wiley & Sons, Chichester, UK and New York, 1988.

Chapman, S., *The Rise of Merchant Banking*, Routledge, London and New York, 1984.

Chwieroth, J. M., *Capital Ideas. The IMF and the Rise of Financial Liberalization*, Princeton University Press, Princeton, NJ and Oxford, UK, 2010.

Clarke, W. R., *Petrodollar Warfare. Oil, Irak and the Future of the Dollar*, New Society Publishers, Gabriola Island, Canada, 2005.

Clendenning, W. E., *The Euro-Dollar Market*, Clarendon Press, Oxford, UK, 1970.

Cline, W. R., *International Debt: Systemic Risk and Policy Response*, MIT Press, Cambridge, MA and London, 1984.

Crossley, J. and Blandford, J., *The DCO Story. A History of Banking in Many Countries*, Barclays Bank International Limited, London, 1975.

Danaher, K. (ed.), *50 Years is Enough. The Case Against the World Bank and the International Monetary Fund*, South End Press, Boston, MA, 1994.

Davis, G., *Managed by the Markets. How Finance Re-Shaped America*, Oxford University Press, Oxford, UK, 2009.

De Boissieu, C. (ed.), *Banking in France*, Routledge, London and New York, 1990, 137.

Desjardins, B., Lescure, M., Nougaret, R., Plessis, A. and Straus, A. (eds), *Le Crédit Lyonnais, 1863–1986*, Droz, Geneva, 2003.

Devlin, R., *Debt and Crisis in Latin America. The Supply Side of the Story*, Princeton University Press, Princeton, NJ, 1989.

Dowd, K. and Timberlake, R. H. (eds), *Money and the Nation State*, Transaction Publishers, New Brunswick, NJ and London, 1998.

Drucker, P. F., *The Practice of Management*, Harper and Row, New York, 1954.

Dufey, G. and Giddy, I. H., *The International Money Market*, Prentice-Hall, Englewood Cliffs, NJ, 1978.

Dufloux, C. and Margulici, L., *Les Euro-Crédits, Pourquoi? Comment? Aspects Techniques Micro et Macro-économiques*, La Revue Banque éditeur, Paris, 1984.

Duménil, G. and Lévy, D., *Capital Resurgent. The Roots of the Neoliberal Revolution*, Harvard University Press, Cambridge, MA and London, 2004.

Eatwell, J. and Taylor, L., *Global Finance at Risk. The Case for International Regulation*, Polity Press, Cambridge, UK, 2000.

Eichengreen, B., *The European Economy since 1945*, Princeton University Press, Princeton, NJ and Oxford, UK, 2007, 295.

Eichengreen, B., *Globalizing Capital: A History of the International Monetary System*, Princeton University Press, Princeton, NJ, 2008.

Eichengreen, B. and Lindert, P. H. (eds), *The International Debt Crisis in Historical Perspective*, MIT Press, Cambridge, MA and London, 1989.

Einzig, P., *The Euro-Dollar System. Practice and Theory of International Interest Rates*, Macmillan, London, 1967.

Epstein, G. A. (ed.), *Financialization and the World Economy*, Edward Elgar, Cheltenham, UK and Northampton, MA, 2005.

Ezrow, N. M. and Frantz, E., *Dictators and Dictatorships. Understanding Authoritarian Regimes and Their Leaders*, Continuum, New York and London, 2011.

Feinstein, C. H., Temin, P. and Toniolo, G., *The World Economy between the World Wars*, Oxford University Press, Oxford, UK and New York, 2008.

Ferguson, N., *High Financier: The Lives and Times of Sigmund Warburg*, Penguin, New York, 2010.

Ferguson, N., Maier, C. S., Manela, E. and Sargent, D. J. (eds), *The Shock of the Global. The 1970s in Perspective*, Harvard University Press, Cambridge, MA, and London, 2010.

Forsyth, D. G. and Notermans, T. (eds), *Regime Changes: Macroeconomic Policy and Financial Regulation in Europe from the 1930s to the 1990s*, Berghahn Books, Providence, RI and Oxford, UK, 1997.

Frantz, E. and Ezrow, N. M., *The Politics of Dictatorship. Institutions and Outcomes in Authoritarian Regimes*, Lynne Rienner Publishers, Boulder, CO and London, 2011.

Frieden, J., *Banking on the World: The Politics of American International Finance*, Harper & Row, New York, 1987.

Frieden, J., *Global Capitalism*, Norton, New York, 2006.

Friedman, M. and Schwartz, A. J., *A Monetary History of the United States, 1867–1960*, Princeton University Press, Princeton, NJ, 1963

Fulford, R., *Glyn's 1753–1953. Six Generations in Lombard Street*, Macmillan, London, 1953.

Galbraith, J. K., *The Great Crash of 1929*, Mariner Books, Boston, MA and New York, 1954.

Gall, L., Feldman, G. R., James, H., Holtfrerich, C.-L. and Bueschgen, H. E., *Die Deutsche Bank 1870–1995*, Beck, Munich, Germany, 1995. English translation: *The Deutsche Bank 1870–1995*, Weidenfeld & Nicolson, London, 1995.

Gardener, E. P. M. and Molyneux, P., *Changes in Western European Banking. An International Banker's Guide*, Routledge, London, 1994.

Gardner, R. N., *Sterling-Dollar Diplomacy in Current Perspective* (new, expanded edition), Columbia University Press, New York, 1980.

Garritsen de Vries, M., *International Monetary Fund 1972–1978*, Vol. III, International Monetary Fund, Washington, DC, 1985.

Ghai, D. (ed.), *The IMF and the South*, Zed Books on behalf of the United Nations Research Institute for Social Development (UNRISD) and the Institute of Social and Economic Research (ISER), London, 1991.

Gilpin, R., *Global Political Economy*, Princeton University Press, Princeton, NJ and Oxford, 2001.

Goodhart, C. A. E., *The Basel Committee on Banking Supervision. A History of the Early Years 1974–1997*, Cambridge University Press, Cambridge, UK, 2011.

Gramsci, A., *Quaderni del Carcere* (4 Vols.), Einaudi, Torino, Italy, 2007.

Graz, J. C. and Nole, A. (eds), *Transnational Private Governance and Its Limits*, Routledge, London, 2008.

Harvey, D., *A Brief History of Neoliberalism*, Oxford University Press, Oxford, UK, 2005.

Hautcoeur, P.-C. (ed.), *Le Marché Financier Français au XIXe Siècle* (Vol. 1), Publications de la Sorbonne, Paris, 2007.

Helleiner, E., *States and the Reemergence of Global Finance*, Cornell University Press, Ithaca, NY and London, 1994.

Helleiner, E., *Forgotten Foundations of Bretton Woods. International Development and the Making of the Postwar Order*, Cornell University Press, Ithaca, NY and London, 2014.

Hellema, D., Wiebes, C. and Witte, T., *The Netherlands and the Oil Crisis. Business as Usual*, Amsterdam University Press, Amsterdam, Netherlands, 2004.

Hirsch, F., *Social Limits to Growth*, Routledge, London, 1977.

Holmes, A. R. and Green, E., *Midland: 150 Years of Banking Business*, Batsford, London, 1986.

James, H., *International Monetary Cooperation since Bretton Woods*, International Monetary Fund and Oxford University Press, Washington DC and New York, 1996.

James, H., *Making the European Monetary Union*, Harvard University Press, Cambridge, MA and London, 2012.

Johnston, R. B., *The Economics of the Euro-Market. History, Theory and Policy*, Macmillan, London and Basingstoke, UK, 1983.

Jones, G. (ed.), *Banks as Multinationals*, Routledge, London and New York, 1990.

Jones, G., *British Multinational banking 1830–1990*, Oxford University Press, Oxford, UK, 1993.

Joyce, J. P., *The IMF and Global Financial Crises*, Cambridge University Press, Cambridge, UK and New York, 2013.

Judt, T., *Postwar. A History of Europe since 1945*, Penguin Press, New York, 2005.

Kane, D. L., *The Eurodollar Market and the Years of Crisis*, Croom Helm, London, 1983.

Kapstein, E. B., *Governing the Global Economy. International Finance and the State*, Harvard University Press, Cambridge, MA and London, 1994.

Kindleberger, C. P., *The World in Depression 1929–1939*, University of California Press, Berkeley, CA and London, 1973

Kobrak, C., *Banking on Global Markets. Deutsche Bank and the United States, 1870 to the Present*, Cambridge University Press, Cambridge, UK, 2008.

Krasner, S. D. (ed.), *International Regimes*, Cornell University Press, Ithaca, NY, 1983.

Krippner, G. R., *Capitalizing on Crisis. The Political Origins of the Rise of Finance*, Harvard University Press, Cambridge, MA and London, 2011.

Landis, R. C. and Klass, M. W., *OPEC. Policy Implications for the United States*, Praeger Publishers, New York, 1980.

Lomax, D. F., *The Developing Country Debt Crisis*, Palgrave Macmillan, London, 1986.

Loriaux, M., *France after Hegemony. International Change and Financial Reform*, Cornell University Press, Ithaca, NY and London, 1991.

Magdoff, H. and Sweezy, P. M., *Stagnation and the Financial Explosion*, Monthly Review Press, New York, 1987.

Marichal, C., *Nueva historia de la grandes crisis financieras. Una perspectiva global, 1873–2008*, Debate, Barcelona, Spain, 2010.

McKinnon, R., *Money and Capital in Economic Development*, Brookings Institutions Press, Washington, DC, 1973.

Michie, R. and Williamson, P. (eds), *The British Government and the City of London in the Twentieth Century*, Cambridge University Press, Cambridge, UK and New York, 2004.

Ministère de l'Economie, des Finances et de l'Industrie, *Michel Debré, un Réformateur aux Finances 1966–1968*, Comité pour l'Histoire Economique et Financière de la Frances, Paris 2005.

Moffitt, M., *The World's Money: International Banking from Bretton Woods to the Brink of Insolvency*, Touchstone, New York, 1983.

Mourlon-Druol, E., *A Europe Made of Money. The Emergence of the European Monetary System*, Cornell University Press, Ithaca, NY and London, 2012.

Obstfeld, M. and Taylor, A. M., *Global Capital Markets. Integration, Crisis, and Growth*, Cambridge University Press, Cambridge, UK, 2004.

OECD, *Fifteen Years of International Economic Co-operation. Selected Speeches of Emile van Lennep Secretary-General 1969–1984*, Paris, 1984.

Pauly, L. W., *Who Elected the Bankers?*, Cornell University Press, Ithaca, NY, 1998.

Pecchioli, R. M., *The Internationalisation of Banking*, OECD, Paris, 1983.

Pepper, G. T. and Oliver, M. J., *Monetarism under Thatcher. Lessons for the Future*, Edward Elgar, Cheltenham, UK, 2001.

Perlinge, A. and Sjögren, H., *Biographies of the Financial World*, Gidlunds Förlag, Stockholm, Sweden, 2012.

Polanyi, K., *The Great Transformation*, Beacon Press, Boston, MA, 1957.

Prasad, M., *The Politics of Free Markets. The Rise of Neoliberal Economic Policies in Britain, France, Germany, & the United States*, The University of Chicago Press, Chicago, IL and London, 2006.

Quinn, B. S., *The New Euromarkets*, Macmillan, London and Basingstoke, UK, 1975.

Rivoire, J., *Le Crédit Lyonnais*, Le Cherche Midi Editeur, Paris, 1989.

Roberts, R. and Kynaston, D. (eds), *The Bank of England. Money, Power and Influence 1694–1994*, Clarendon Press, Oxford, UK, 1995.

Roberts, R. (with Arnander, C.), *Take Your Partners: Orion, The Consortium Banks and the Transformation of the Euromarkets*, Palgrave Macmillian, London, 2001.

Roberts, R. and Kynaston, D., *The Lion Wakes. A Modern History of HSBC*, Profile Books, London, 2015.

Rogers, D., *The Big Four British Banks*, Palgrave Macmillan, London, 1999.

Rybczynski, T. M. (ed.), *The Economics of the Oil Crisis*, Macmillan Press, London and Basingstoke, UK, 1976.

Sachs, J. (ed.), *Developing Country Debt and the World Economy*, University of Chicago Press, Chicago, IL and London, 1989.

Sampson, A., *The Seven Sisters. The Great Oil Companies and the World They Made*, Hodder and Stoughton, London, 1975.

Sampson, A., *The Money Lenders. Bankers in a Dangerous World*, Viking Press, New York, 1981.

Savona, P. and Sutija, G., *Eurodollars and International Banking*, Macmillan Press, Basingstoke, UK, 1985.

Sayers, R. S. (ed.), *Banking in Western Europe*, Oxford University Press, London, 1962.

Sayers, R. S., *Lloyds Bank in the History and Banking in England*, Oxford University Press, Oxford, UK, 1957.

Scanlon, C. J. and Prochnow, H. V., *L'Eurodollar*, Calmann-Lévy, Paris, 1971.

Schenk, C., *Britain and the Sterling Area. From Devaluation to Convertibility in the 1950s*, Routledge, London and New York, 1994.

Shaw, E., *Financial Deepening in Economic Development*, Oxford University Press, New York, 1973.

Silber, W. L., *Volcker. The Triumph of Persistence*, Bloomsbury Press, New York and London, 2012.

Skeet, I., *OPEC: Twenty-Five Years of Prices and Politics*, Cambridge University Press, Cambridge, UK, 1988.

Skidelsky, R., *John Maynard Keynes: Hopes Betrayed, 1883–1920*, Penguin Books, New York and London, 1983.

Skidelsky, R., *John Maynard Keynes: The Economist as Saviour*, Penguin Books, New York and London, 1992.

Skidelsky, R., *John Maynard Keynes. Fighting for Britain, 1937–1946*, Penguin Books, New York and London, 2000.

Solomon, R., *Money on the Move. The Revolution in International Finance since 1980*, Princeton University Press, Princeton, NJ, 1999.

Spero, J. E., *The Failure of the Franklin National Bank: Challenge to the International Banking System*, Columbia University Press, New York, 1980.

Spiro, D. E., *The Hidden Hand of American Hegemony. Petrodollar Recycling and International Markets*, Cornell University Press, Ithaca, NY, 1999.

Stallings, B., *Banker to the Third World U. S. Portfolio Investment in Latin America, 1900– 1986*, University of California Press, Berkeley, CA and London, 1987.

Stedman Jones, D., *Masters of the Universe. Hayek, Friedman, and the Birth of Neo-liberal Politics*, Princeton University Press, Princeton, NJ and Oxford, UK, 2012.

Steil, B., *The Battle of Bretton Woods: John Maynard Keynes, Harry Dexter White, and the Making of a New World Order*, Princeton University Press, Princeton, NJ and Oxford, UK, 2013.

Stein, J., *Pivotal Decade. How the United States Traded Factories for Finance in the Seventies*, Yale University Press, New Haven and London, 2010.

Stein, K. W., *Heroic Diplomacy. Sadat, Kissinger, Carter, Begin, and the Quest for Arab-Israeli Peace*, Routledge, New York and London, 1999.

Stiglitz, J. E., *Globalization and its Discontents*, Penguin Books, London, 2002.

Strange, S., *Casino Capitalism*, Manchester University Press, Manchester, UK, 1986.

Strange, S., *The Retreat of the State. The Diffusion of Power in the World Economy*, Cambridge University Press, Cambridge, UK, 1996.

Strange, S., *Mad Money. When Markets Outgrow Governments*, The University of Michigan Press, Ann Arbor, MI, 1998.

Styan, D., *France & Iraq: Oil, Arms and French Policy Making in the Middle East*, I. B. Tauris, London and New York, 2006.

Toniolo, G., *Cent'anni 1894–1994. La Banca Commerciale e l'Economia Italiana*, Banca Commerciale Italiana, BCI, Milan, Italy, 1994.

Toniolo, G., *Central Bank Cooperation at the Bank for International Settlements, 1930–1973*, Cambridge University Press, Cambridge, UK and New York, 2005.

Treaster, J. B., *Paul Volcker: the Making of a Financial Legend*, Wiley, Hoboken, NJ, 2004.

VA, *Michel Debré, un Réformateur aux Finances 1966–1968*, Comité pour l'histoire économique et financière de la France, Paris, 2005.

Van B. Cleveland, H. and Huertas, T. F., *Citibank 1812–1970*, Harvard University Press, Cambridge, MA and London, 1985.

Van Dormael, A., *The Power of Money*, Macmillan, Basingstoke, UK and London, 1997.

Vander Weyer, M., *Falling Eagle. The Decline of Barclays Bank*, Weidenfeld & Nicolson, London, 2000.

Verdier, D., *Moving Money. Banking and Finance in the Industrialized World*, Cambridge University Press, Cambridge, UK and New York, 2003.

Vernon, R. (ed.), *The Oil Crisis*, W. W. Norton & Company, New York, 1976.

Wachtel, H. M., *The Money Mandarins. The Making of a Supranational Economic Order*, M. E. Sharpe, Armonk, NY, 1990.

Wellons, P. A., *Passing the Buck. Banks, Governments, and Third World Debt*, Harvard Business School Press, Boston, MA, 1987.

Winton, R. S., *Lloyds Bank*, Oxford University Press, Oxford, UK, 1982.

Wood, R. E., *From Marshall Plan to Debt Crisis. Foreign Aid and Development Choices in the World Economy*, UCLA Press, Berkeley, CA and London, 1986.

Woods, N., *The Globalizers. The IMF, the World Bank and Their Borrowers*, Cornell University Press, Ithaca, NY and London, 2006.

Yago, K., *The Financial History of the Bank for International Settlements*, Routledge, London and New York, 2013.
Zweig, P. L., *Wriston*, Crown Publishers, New York, 1995.

Articles

Arcand, J-L., Berkes, E. and Panizza, U., 'Too Much Finance ?', *Journal of Economic Growth*, June 2015, Vol. 20, No. 2, 105–148.
Baker, A., 'Restraining Regulatory Capture? Anglo-America, Crisis Politics and Trajectories of Change in Global Finance Governance', *International Affairs* 86: 3, 2010, 647–663.
Balassa, B., 'Structural Adjustment Policies in Developing Economies', *World Development*, Vol. 10, No. 1, 1982, 23–38.
Battilossi, S., 'Financial Innovation and the Golden Ages of International Banking: 1890–1931 and 1958–1981', *Financial History Review*, No. 7, 2000, 141–175.
Bernal, R., 'Transnational Banks, the International Monetary Fund and External Debt of Developing Countries', *Social and Economic Studies*, Vol. 31, No. 4, Regional Monetary Studies (December 1982), 71–101.
Bishara, G., 'The Political Repercussions of the Israeli Raid on the Iraqi Nuclear Reactor', *Journal of Palestine Studies*, Vol. 11, No. 3, Spring 1982, 58–76.
Bloomfield, A. I., 'Postwar Control of International Capital Movements', *The American Economic Review*, Vol. 36, No. 2, Papers and Proceedings of the Fifty-Eighth Annual Meeting of the American Economic Association (May 1946), 687–709.
Bordo, M. D., Eichengreen, B. and Kim, J., 'Was There Really An Earlier period of International Financial Integration Comparable to Today?', NBER, Working Paper 6738, September 1998, 1–68.
Boudreau, D. G., 'The Bombing of the Osirak Reactor', *International Journal on World Peace*, Vol. 10, No. 2, June 1993, 21–37.
Boughton, J. M., 'From Suez to Tequila: The IMF as Crisis Manager', *IMF Working Paper*, WP/97/90, July 1997.
Burk, K., 'Witness Seminar on the Origins and Early Development of the Eurobond Market', *Contemporary European History*, Vol. 1, No. 1, March 1992, 65–87.
Burn, G., 'The State, the City and the Euromarkets', *Review of International Political Economy*, 6: 2, Summer 1999, 225–261.
Capraro, S. and Perrottini, I., 'Revisiting Latin America's Debt Crisis: Some Lessons for the Periphery of the Eurozone', *Cambridge Journal of Economics*, 2013, 37, 627–651.
Cerny, P. G., 'The Dynamics of Financial Globalization: Technology, Market Structure, and Policy Response, *Policy Sciences*, 1994, Vol. 27, No. 4, 319–342.
Crane, D. B. and Hayes, S. L. III, 'The New Competition in World Banking', *Harvard Business Review*, July–August 1982, 88–94.
D'Andrea Tyson, L., 'The debt crisis and adjustment responses in Eastern Europe: a comparative perspective', *International Organization*, Vol. 40, No. 2, March 1986, 239–285.
De Cecco, M., 'International Financial Markets and US Domestic Policy Since 1945', *International Affairs*, Vol. 52, No. 3, July 1976, 381–399.
Devlin, R. and Ffrench-Davis, R., 'The Great Latin America Debt Crisis: A Decade of Asymmetric Adjustment', *Revista de Economia Politica*, Vol. 15, No. 3 (59), Julho–Setembro 1995, 117–142.
Feldman, S., 'The Bombing of Osiraq-Revisited', *International Security*, Vol. 7, No. 2, Autumn 1982, 114–142.

Ferguson, N., 'Siegmund Warburg, the City of London and the Financial Roots of European Integration', *Business History*, Vol. 51, No. 3, 2009, 364–382.

Fishlow, A., 'Lessons from the Past: Capital Markets During the 19th Century and the Interwar Period', *International Organization*, Vol. 39, No. 3, Summer 1985, 383–439.

Folkerts-Landau, D., 'The Changing Role of International Bank Lending in Developing Finance', *IMF Staff Papers*, 32, June 1985, 317–363.

Frieden, J., 'Third World Indebted Industrialization: International Finance and State Capitalism in Mexico, Brazil, Algeria, and South Korea', *International Organization*, Vol. 35, No. 3, Summer 1981, 407–431.

Ganoe, C., 'Banking Consortia: Are They Here to Stay?', *Columbia Journal of World Business*, Vol. 7, August 1972, 51–57.

Genillard, R. L., 'The Eurobond Market', *Financial Analysts Journal*, Vol. 23, No. 2, March–April 1967, 144–151.

Goodhart, C. A. E., 'Competition and Credit Control: Some Personal Reflections', *Financial History Review*, Vol. 22, No. 2, August 2015, 235–246.

Haldane, A., Brennan, S. and Madouros, V., 'What is the Contribution of the Financial Sector: Miracle Or Mirage?', in Adair Turner *et al.*, *The Future of Finance: The LSE Report*, London School of Economics and Political Science, London, 2010.

Helleiner, E., 'Explaining the Globalization of Financial Markets: Bringing States Back In', *Review of International Political Economy*, Vol. 2, No. 2, Spring 1995, 315–341.

Helleiner, E., 'A Bretton Woods Moment? The 2007–2008 Crisis and the Future of Global Finance', *International Affairs*, Vol. 86, No. 3, 2010, 619–636.

Hewson, J. and Sakakibara, E., 'The Impact of U. S. Controls on Capital Outflows on the U. S. Balance of Payments: An Exploratory Study', *IMF Staff Papers* (1975) 22, 37–60.

Ikenberry, G. J., 'A World Economy Restored: Expert Consensus and the Anglo-American Postwar Settlement', *International Organization*, Vol. 46, No. 1, Winter 1992, 289–321.

Johanson, J. and Wiedersheim, F., 'The Internationalization of the Firm – Four Swedish Cases', *Journal of Management Studies*, Vol. 12, No. 3, October 1975, 305–323.

Key, S. J. and Terrell, H. S., 'International Banking Facilities', *International Finance Discussion Papers*, Board of Governors of the Federal Reserve System, Number 333, September 1988.

Kirshner, J., 'Keynes, Capital Mobility and the Crisis of Embedded Liberalism', *Review of International Political Economy* 6: 3, Autumn 1999, 313–337.

Knopping, O. A., 'Why an Interest Equalization Tax?, *William & Mary Law Review*, Vol. 5, No. 2, 1964, 230–279.

Krause, L., 'Private International Finance', *International Organization*, Vol. 25, No. 3, June 1971, 523–540.

Lazonick, W. and O'Sullivan, M., 'Maximizing Shareholder Value: A New Ideology for Corporate Governance', *Economy and Society*, Vol. 29, No. 1, February 2000, 13–35.

Madsen, P. H., 'Changing Role of International Capital Flows', *The Journal of Finance*, Vol. 18, No. 2, May 1963, 187–210.

Major, A., 'The Fall and Rise of Financial Capital', *Review of International Political Economy*, 15: 5, December 2008, 800–825.

Métais, J., 'Le processus de multinationalisation des grandes banques commerciales', *Revue Économique*, Vol. 30, No. 3, 1979, 487–517.

Mountford, A., 'The Historical Development of IMF Governance', Background Paper of the Independent Evaluation Office of the International Monetary Fund, BP/08/02, May 2008.

Poznanski, K., 'Economic Adjustment and Political Forces: Poland since 1970', *International Organization*, Vol. 40, No. 2, March 1986, 455–488.

Quennouelle-Corre, L., 'The State, Banks and Financing of Investments in France from World War II to the 1970s', *Financial History Review*, Vol. 12, Part 1, April 2005, 63–86.

Reinhart, C. M. and Sbrancia, M. B., 'The Liquidation of Government Debt', *NBER Working Paper Series*, WP 16893, March 2011, 1–64.

Ross, D. M., 'European Banking Clubs in the 1960s: A Flawed Strategy', *Business and Economic History*, Vol. 27, No. 2, Winter 1998, 353–366.

Ruggie, J. G., 'International Regimes, Transactions, and Change: Embedded Liberalism in the Postwar Economic Order', *International Organization*, Vol. 36, No. 2, Spring 1982, 379–415.

Saez, E. and Zucman, G., 'Wealth Inequality in the United States Since 1913: Evidence from Capitalized Income Data Tax', *Quarterly Journal of Economics*, forthcoming 2016.

Schenk, C., 'The Origins of the Eurodollar Market in London: 1955–1963', *Explorations in Economic History*, Vol. 35, No. 2, April 1998, 221–238.

Schenk, C., 'Summer in the City: Banking Failures of 1974 and the Development of International Banking Supervision', *English Historical Review*, Vol. CXXXIX, No. 540, October 2014, 1129–1156.

Snyder, J. C., 'The Road to Osiraq: Baghdad's Quest for the Bomb', *Middle East Journal*, Vol. 37, No. 4, Autumn 1983, 565–593.

Sore, J. M., 'L'évolution des institutions financières internationales: Entre redéploiement et fragilité, une restructuration systémique en chantier', *Annuaire française de droit international*, Vol. 52, 2006, 481–504.

Standard & Poor's, *Ratings Performance 2002. Defaults, Transition, Recovery, and Spreads*, February 2003.

Sweezy, P. M., 'The Triumph of Financial Capital', *Monthly Review*, Vol. 46, No. 2, June 1994.

Truman, E. T., 'The International Debt Situation', *International Finance Discussion Papers*, Board of Governors of the Federal Reserve System, Number 298, December 1986.

Uche, C., 'Lonrho in Africa: The Unacceptable Face of Capitalism or the Ugly Face of Neo-Colonialism', *Enterprise & Society*, Vol. 16, No. 2, April 2015, 1–27.

Underhill, G. R. D., 'State, Market, and Global Political Economy: Genealogy of an (Inter-?) Discipline', *International Affairs*, Vol. 76, No. 4, 2000, 805–824.

Underhill, G. R. D., 'The Changing State-Market Condominium in East-Asia: Re-thinking the Political Underpinnings of Development', *New Political Economy*, Vol. 10, No. 1, March 2005, 1–24.

Von Clemm, M., 'The Rise of Consortium Banking', *Harvard Business Review*, Vol. 49, May–June 1971, 125–141.

Walton, J. and Ragin, C., 'Global and National Sources of Political Protest: Third World Responses to the Debt Crisis', *American Sociological Review*, December 1990, Vol. 55, No. 6, 876–890.

World Bank, 'World Debt Tables 1989–90', World Bank, Washington, DC, 1990.

Wriston, W. B., 'Technology and Sovereignty', *International Affairs*, Vol. 67, No. 2, Winter 1988, 63–75.

Zingales, L., 'Presidential Address: Does Finance Benefit Society?', *The Journal of Finance*, Vol. LXX, No. 4, August 2015, 1342.

Index

Taylor & Francis eBooks

Helping you to choose the right eBooks for your Library

Add Routledge titles to your library's digital collection today. Taylor and Francis ebooks contains over 50,000 titles in the Humanities, Social Sciences, Behavioural Sciences, Built Environment and Law.

Choose from a range of subject packages or create your own!

Benefits for you

» Free MARC records
» COUNTER-compliant usage statistics
» Flexible purchase and pricing options
» All titles DRM-free.

Benefits for your user

» Off-site, anytime access via Athens or referring URL
» Print or copy pages or chapters
» Full content search
» Bookmark, highlight and annotate text
» Access to thousands of pages of quality research at the click of a button.

REQUEST YOUR **FREE** INSTITUTIONAL TRIAL TODAY

Free Trials Available
We offer free trials to qualifying academic, corporate and government customers.

eCollections – Choose from over 30 subject eCollections, including:

Archaeology	Language Learning
Architecture	Law
Asian Studies	Literature
Business & Management	Media & Communication
Classical Studies	Middle East Studies
Construction	Music
Creative & Media Arts	Philosophy
Criminology & Criminal Justice	Planning
Economics	Politics
Education	Psychology & Mental Health
Energy	Religion
Engineering	Security
English Language & Linguistics	Social Work
Environment & Sustainability	Sociology
Geography	Sport
Health Studies	Theatre & Performance
History	Tourism, Hospitality & Events

For more information, pricing enquiries or to order a free trial, please contact your local sales team:
www.tandfebooks.com/page/sales

 Routledge
Taylor & Francis Group

The home of Routledge books

www.tandfebooks.com

For Product Safety Concerns and Information please contact our EU
representative GPSR@taylorandfrancis.com Taylor & Francis Verlag GmbH,
Kaufingerstraße 24, 80331 München, Germany

Printed and bound by CPI Group (UK) Ltd, Croydon, CR0 4YY
01/05/2025
01858420-0003